The Presidency and Economic Policy

The Presidency and Economic Policy

Chris J. Dolan, John Frendreis,
and Raymond Tatalovich

ROWMAN & LITTLEFIELD PUBLISHERS, INC.
Lanham • Boulder • New York • Toronto • Plymouth, UK

ROWMAN & LITTLEFIELD PUBLISHERS, INC.

Published in the United States of America
by Rowman & Littlefield Publishers, Inc.
A wholly owned subsidiary of The Rowman & Littlefield Publishing Group, Inc.
4501 Forbes Boulevard, Suite 200, Lanham, Maryland 20706
www.rowmanlittlefield.com

Estover Road, Plymouth PL6 7PY, United Kingdom

British Library Cataloguing in Publication Information Available

Library of Congress Cataloging-in-Publication Data

Dolan, Chris J.
  The Presidency and economic policy / Chris J. Dolan, John Frendreis, and
Raymond Tatalovich.
     p. cm.
  Includes bibliographical references and index.
  ISBN-13: 978-0-7425-4728-5 (cloth : alk. paper)
  ISBN-10: 0-7425-4728-0 (cloth : alk. paper)
  ISBN-13: 978-0-7425-4729-2 (pbk. : alk. paper)
  ISBN-10: 0-7425-4729-9 (pbk. : alk. paper)
  1. United States—Economic policy. 2. Executive power—United States. 3.
Presidents—United States. I. Frendreis, John P. II. Tatalovich, Raymond. III. Title.
  HC103.D65 2008
  339.50973—dc22

                                                                  2007006606

Printed in the United States of America

♾™ The paper used in this publication meets the minimum requirements of
American National Standard for Information Sciences—Permanence of Paper
for Printed Library Materials, ANSI/NISO Z39.48-1992.

To Holly and Braiden Dolan;

To Laura Vertz;

To Anne Tatalovich

Contents

Figures and Tables

FIGURES

TABLES

Preface

The economy, it is sometimes said, is like the weather: people talk a lot about it, but nobody does anything about it. A corollary to this might be: people talk a lot about the economy, but they do not actually know much about it. A major reason for this paradox is that the study of the economy falls mainly to economists, and modern economics can be a daunting subject, filled with mathematical formulae, complicated graphs, and specialized jargon. Moreover, most people are less concerned with the functioning of the economy as it pertains to economic theory than they are to the functioning of the economy as it pertains to their lives. Thus, they are only partially concerned with how the economy works and more interested in how the economy might be made to work better.

Concern for making the economy work better is a central element of political debate and a subject that thus far attracts the attention of many political scientists. Yet, despite the fact that managing economic policy is a standard topic in introductory American government classes, there are almost no books on the subject that are written in such a way as to be accessible to a general audience. As teachers and researchers, we have felt a need for such a book. *The Presidency and Economic Policy* is the result. It has roots in *The Modern Presidency and Economic Policy*, written by John Frendreis and Raymond Tatalovich and published in 1994. That volume was arguably the first attempt to provide an overview of the president as the "manager of prosperity" but, to bring a fresh perspective to this topic as well as updated and expanded coverage, we asked Chris J. Dolan to join us as the lead author on this revision.

As before, the focus of our analysis is the management of the American economy. This has been a particular objective of the national government—and particularly of U.S. presidents—since World War II, and we cover in detail the experiences of postwar presidents from Harry S. Truman through George W. Bush. The book is written for several audiences. Its primary audience, we hope, will be students enrolled in classes studying the presidency, U.S. public policy, and American economic policy. In teaching the first two types of classes, we have found that the treatments of economic policy making in presidency and public policy texts are much too brief to give students an adequate understanding of this vital and complex subject. We also hope the book will be read by others—students and nonstudents—who wish to learn more about economic policy making. Finally, the book contains much information (including tables and figures) that represents original research of interest to scholars, particularly those whose previous research has dealt only indirectly with presidential economic policy making.

We wish to thank a number of people. Foremost is Niels Aaboe, Executive Editor at Rowman & Littlefield, who saw the pedagogical benefits of revising the 1994 volume and who urged us to move expeditiously on this project. Asa Johnson deserves special thanks, for his diligent stewardship of this volume during the production process. Finally, Holly Dolan, Laura L. Vertz, and Anne Tatalovich provided much encouragement and assistance throughout the writing of this book, beginning with data collection and continuing through final copyediting. We hope these simple words can convey the real gratitude we feel to all these people, our professional colleagues and our beloved family.

1

The Origins of
Economic Policy Making

On March 1, 1991, President George H. W. Bush's approval rating stood at 91%, the highest level recorded in the more than half century of systematic public opinion polling. One year later, his approval had dropped to 39%.[1] In the process, President Bush's image had gone from victor of the Persian Gulf War, viewed as virtually unbeatable for reelection to a second presidential term, to beleaguered president, whose reelection was very much in doubt, facing powerful challenges first from within his own party and later from a formidable Democratic opponent.

What happened during this time that produced such a dramatic change in presidential fortunes? A number of factors contributed to the decline in President Bush's popularity (e.g., the unclear aftermath of the Gulf War and the onset of the presidential election), but the overwhelming cause of this decline was the poor performance of the U.S. economy. A lengthy downturn in the economy had begun during the summer of 1990. Although this downturn had been underway for over six months before the peak of the president's popularity in March 1991, the approaching hostilities in the Persian Gulf had limited the degree to which the public had translated their concern over the economy into negative evaluations of presidential leadership. The public euphoria following the swift victory of allied ground forces in the spring of 1991 led, however, to public expectations that the economy would shortly begin to improve. Although some improvements were seen during the summer, by the fall the performance of the economy was again faltering. As unemployment continued to rise, public discontent with the president's performance increased. Although George Bush was able to withstand the opposition within his own party to his renomination, he eventually was defeated in his bid for reelection in the general election in

1

November 1992, in what was widely viewed as a referendum on the performance of the economy during his term in office. In effect, George Bush's political fate became inextricably linked to the public's perception of his performance as the "manager of prosperity."

PUBLIC EXPECTATIONS CONCERNING THE ECONOMY

This brief account of the changing popular fortunes of the first Bush presidency illustrates three important facts concerning the performance of the U.S. economy and U.S. politics. First, how well the economy performs is of great—sometimes paramount—interest to the U.S. public. It is easy to see why this is the case. Behind the mass of economic statistics which are collected and disseminated to the public are the basic realities of a person's everyday life: Do you have a job? Is your rent going up? Do groceries, children's clothes, and textbooks cost more than they did last year? Are interest rates low enough that you can afford to buy a new car or finance a home mortgage?

This is not to say that economic questions are the only ones which engage people's attention. During times of national emergency, such as during a war, Americans have traditionally viewed economic issues as being of less importance than questions of war and peace. At other times, other issues—crime, drugs, political scandals—may also compete for the public's attention. However, in normal times, the performance of the economy, particularly the performance of a few key indicators such as unemployment and inflation rates, is regarded by the public as the single most important issue in the political arena.

Second, the American public expects the government—and especially the president—to take actions that will improve the performance of the U.S. economy. Put somewhat differently, the American public sees the U.S. economy as something that can be manipulated by governmental policy, and it expects governmental leaders to enact public policies that lead to the achievement of beneficial economic goals, in effect, to *manage the economy*. As we shall see later in this chapter, this is a fairly recent expectation in historical terms. Although presidents and political parties have always been looked to for leadership during times of economic difficulty, it is only in the twentieth century that a generalized expectation has taken hold that the government, particularly the president, should continually monitor the economy and take steps to influence its performance.

Third, there is a clear linkage between economic performance and the political fortunes of our governmental leaders. Once again, this is particularly true for the president, whose popularity often waxes and wanes with major changes in politically significant statistics such as the inflation rate and the number of unemployed persons. Indeed, the president has become so uniquely associated in the public mind with economic management, that downturns in the economy are associated with losses in congressional elections by the president's party rather than with losses by the party which actually controls Congress (when Congress is controlled by the president's opposition).[2] In some ways, national elections—even for offices other than the president—are at least partially referenda on the performance of the economy.

MANAGING THE U.S. ECONOMY

Policy Goals in Managing the Economy

As one author notes, "economic policy has a number of goals, all of which are socially desirable, but some of which are not always compatible."[3] The same author notes that the four traditional goals of economic policy, sometimes labeled the **golden quadrangle**, are "economic growth, full employment, stable prices, and a positive balance of payments from international trade."[4] Each of these goals deserves some elaboration.

Economic growth essentially means an increase in the amount of goods and services produced by the economy. The value of all of the goods and services produced in a country is known as the **gross national product (GNP)**, and an increase in the GNP may come about three ways: (1) when more of the productive capabilities of the society are employed to produce goods and services (e.g., when more people are hired), (2) when the productive capacity of the society is increased (e.g., when new factories are constructed), or (3) when the productivity of the existing resources is increased (e.g., workers' productivity rises due to new training or changes in production techniques). Although undesirable costs may be incurred to achieve this economic growth, the economic growth itself is essentially beneficial, since it means that more goods and services are available to be distributed among the population. Since in most societies population generally increases, a rising GNP (economic growth) is essential if the average person's position is going to be improved over time. If economic growth does not keep pace with population increases, economic gains for some *must* come at the expense of others, a situation which generally leads to social conflict.[5] On the other hand, if the rate of economic growth exceeds the rate of population increase, it is at least *possible* that some may gain without anyone losing, although this is not necessarily the only distribution of the additional goods and services that might result.

Besides GNP, another commonly reported measure of the size of the economy is GDP, or **gross domestic product**. The two measures are closely related, differing only in how they treat the goods and services produced in the United States by labor and property supplied by non-U.S. residents and the goods and services produced outside of the United States by labor and property supplied by U.S. residents. GNP includes the latter but not the former, while GDP includes the former but not the latter. While the distinction between GDP and GNP is important for national income calculations for some nations, in the United States they are very close (less than 1% apart in 1990). Because the U.S. government reports some data series in terms of GNP and others in terms of GDP, we utilize both of these measures throughout the book.[6]

Achievement of the second broad goal of economic policy, **full employment**, means that all those willing and able to work are employed. Put somewhat differently, all of the productive human resources of a society are being employed in the production of goods and services. Note that this does not mean that all people are employed. A society may decide that some people should not or may not be employed, for example, children. Alternatively, some people may not wish to be employed in the economy, for example, students or adults caring for children or other dependents. Full employment also does not mean that the unemployment rate is zero. In the United States, the **unemployment rate** is calculated as the number of persons who are not employed but wish to be employed divided by this number plus the total number of employed persons, that is, the unemployment rate = [number of unemployed / (number of unemployed + number of employed)] × 100.

Experts on the labor market generally believe that it is not possible to reduce the number of unemployed persons to zero, for two reasons. First, at any given time, a certain number of people will be between jobs, if only temporarily. Far from being unfortunate, this is in fact desirable, since for the labor market to function efficiently, employment should be constantly in a process of adjustment across geographic labor markets and different firms in order to meet new demands and to incorporate technological innovations. Second, a certain number of people may not possess the necessary skills to be productively employed within the economy. For example, there is a limit to the number of jobs that can be filled by people who are illiterate. If the number of people wishing to work who possess this limitation exceeds the number of available jobs, unemployment must result. Note that this source of unemployment is a function of two things: the skill level of the workers (what is sometimes called their human capital) and the demands of the labor market. Changes in either can cause the degree of this sort of unemployment to rise or fall.[7] This latter source of unemployment is not considered desirable, although it may result from otherwise desirable events such as productivity enhancing technological innovations. An obvious response to this problem, however, is to alter the workers' human capital (skill level) so that they may be productively employed, and demands are often directed toward the government to promote this sort of worker retraining.

Collectively, these two sources of unemployment produce the rate of **structural unemployment**, the level of unemployment that exists when the country is actually at the full employment level. What is this level in the United States? A traditional answer has been 3% unemployment, although some economists (and political leaders) would claim that the actual level is higher, perhaps as high as 5% or 6%. Whatever answer is given is clearly a mixture of both technical and political considerations, since it rests in part upon an assessment of how many people our society feels can or should be left in the category of unemployed workers with inadequate human capital to be productively employed by our economy.

The third broad goal of economic policy is stable prices. Over time, the prices for various goods and services fluctuate. When prices are generally rising for goods and services, this is described as a period of **inflation**; the opposite condition, generally falling prices, is referred to as **deflation**.[8] In the United States, price stability is measured by the government with a number of statistics, the best known of which is the **consumer price index (CPI)**, which calculates the current prices of a predetermined (and fixed over time) set of goods and services. The current value of the CPI is simply the ratio of the current price to the price of the same set of goods in the base period of 1982–1984, multiplied by 100. Thus, the CPI had an average value of 100 during the period 1982–1984; periods with higher prices have a CPI over 100, while periods with lower prices have a CPI below 100. In August 1992, the value of the CPI was 140.9, which means that the same set of goods which cost $100.20 in August 1983 cost $140.90 in August 1992.[9] The CPI is calculated monthly, and a rising value indicates price inflation, while a falling value indicates price deflation.

Although in recent years the periods of inflation have far exceeded those of deflation, historically both of these patterns have been seen with regularity, and when severe, both are highly disruptive. In general, changes in prices in either direction will produce both winners and losers. Since during inflationary periods, both wages and prices tend to rise, the losers tend be those for whom price increases exceed increases in wages, or more precisely, income.[10] Thus, people on fixed incomes, such as retired people and people relying on income from long-term, fixed-interest investments, will suffer. Similarly, individuals and corporations that have made long-term loans (e.g., thirty-year, fixed-rate mortgages) will see these assets decline in value, as the future value of the principal (loan amount) and interest will be less than the current value of the principal. (This was one major problem faced by the savings and loan industry during the period of high inflation in the United States during the 1970s.) On the other side of the coin, those who have borrowed money at lower interest rates will generally gain from inflation, since their rising wages will make it easier to repay these loans. During deflationary periods, the winners and losers are reversed: people with fixed incomes and lenders are winners, while borrowers are losers. In fact, though, prolonged or severe inflation or deflation is bad for the economy, since they make it difficult to confidently make long-term economic decisions.

The final element of the "golden quadrangle" is a positive **balance of payments** from international trade. The balance of international payments is actually made up of three components: the current account (essentially trade in goods and services), the capital account (long- and short-term movement of capital), and movement of gold-and-reserve assets.[11] The most visible of these components is the current account, which is largely made up of the trade in merchandise and the so-called invisibles, such as travel, shipping fees, and insurance fees. The current account is sometimes called the balance of trade, and when the total value of all exports exceeds the total value of all imports, this is referred to as a positive or "favorable" balance of trade. The reverse is a negative or "unfavorable" balance of trade. Actually, the terms "favorable" and "unfavorable"—in fact the overall goal of a "positive balance of international payments"—are unfortunate, since there are periods in a nation's development when a negative balance is more beneficial than a positive balance. Although in the public mind (and in the public statements of many political leaders) a negative balance of trade or international payments appears to represent a situation where the United States is becoming poorer at the expense of our trading partners, this is not necessarily the case. As we discuss more fully in chapter 7, the merits of positive or negative international payments balances depend more on the reasons the surpluses or deficits are run rather than on the simple fact that there is a positive or negative balance. Although the public often focuses its attention on a few summary statistics such as the balance of trade, the actual goal of economic policy in the area of international economics is that the nation's economy interacts with the international economy in such a way that other economic goals—stable prices, full employment, productive capital investment—are achieved. Over a very long period of time (e.g., a century) this will probably be manifested in small or moderate (but not excessively large) positive balances in international payments, although during particular periods, more benefit may come from negative balances than from positive ones.

In addition to the four components of the "golden quadrangle," economic policy is also directed toward the achievement of other goals. Two are particularly worthy of mention: structural change and the distribution of wealth. The first of these has both a domestic and an international dimension.[12] On the domestic side, the U.S. economy is always in a process of change, wherein some industries are expanding while others are declining, the nature of production is being altered, and the regional (in fact, global) concentration of production is changing. A general goal of economic policy is to promote structural changes that will support the other goals, like economic growth or price stability. Historically, the major activities of the U.S. government in this regard have been one step removed from actual decisions on where and how to produce goods and services. Two examples of this less direct form of promoting structural change are government support for infrastructure development (e.g., canals, railroads, roads) and support for education, particularly in such areas as agricultural and scientific research. A developing debate in the United States, however, is whether the government should take an even more active role in promoting structural change through the creation of a **national industrial policy**. The clearest model for such a policy is Japan, where the national government organizes and subsidizes the activities of private corporations directed at developing new industries that have significant prospects for growth, often through expanded global exports. According to some proponents of such a policy in the United States, the U.S. government should play a similar role in targeting key areas for research and new product development. Opponents respond that such a policy is not necessary, since private actors will themselves identify such opportunities; in this view, government intervention simply acts to distort what they see as the more efficient decision-making processes of private corporations. Whether indirect or direct, intrusive or reactive, a portion of economic policy is directed toward the management of domestic structural change—even if only to leave it largely to the decisions of private actors.

The international dimension of the management of structural change relates to efforts to bring about structural changes in the economies of other nations or in features of the international economic system. Examples of policies directed toward this goal are actions directed toward stimulating consumer spending in certain U.S. trade partners (e.g., Japan) and toward reducing government deficits in debtor nations. The domestic and international dimensions of structural change may even converge: much of the U.S. policy debate over a national industrial policy is double-edged, dealing not only with the extent to which the U.S. government should promote such a policy domestically, but also to what extent the U.S. will be comfortable with the use of such policies by its economic competitors.

A final goal of economic policy concerns the distribution of wealth. To some in the United States, the distribution of wealth is not a question addressed by economic policy, it is a given: wealth accrues to those who acquire it within the normal operation of the free market, capitalist system. Indeed, there are few people in the United States who would not broadly support some version of this statement. At the same time, there are few significant decisions the U.S. government makes in connection with taxing and spending that do not raise distributional questions. For example, because the portion of earnings saved (known as the marginal propensity to save) increases as your income rises, a government interested in cutting taxes in order to increase private savings would get the greatest result by targeting the tax cut only to the wealthiest people. Because such a policy would have the added effect of literally "making the rich richer," it would in all likelihood not be adopted—not because it would not promote economic growth or stabilize prices or promote the balance of payments, but because it would alter the distribution of wealth in a way society does not wish to see it altered. Unlike the first three goals discussed (but similar to the last one), there is no clear, consensual goal for U.S. economic policy regarding the distribution of wealth. At the same time, influencing this distribution (or not influencing it, for some) remains one of the ends against which various economic actions are measured.

The Philosophical Foundation of U.S. Economic Policy

How wealth will be generated and distributed is not only a basic issue in economics. It is also one of the fundamental issues of politics. Indeed, among the most basic questions answered in each society is the one that addresses how the goods and services produced by that society will be allocated. Over the last 150 years, a fundamental debate has occurred between two theories of how this should be done: **capitalism** and **socialism**. For a number of reasons capitalism has been the dominant economic ideology within the United States. Much of the basic debate over how to structure and manage the U.S. economy has dealt with different views of how to improve a capitalist economy rather than whether a capitalist system is itself desirable.

In very simple terms, a capitalist economic system is one in which ownership and control over the basic means of economic production—land, labor, and capital (e.g., machinery)—rests with individuals. The types, quantities, and prices of the goods and services produced by the economy are determined by a myriad of individual transactions occurring in free markets. In addition to leading to the most efficient use of available resources, such a system of production and distribution maximizes individual choice and the individual pursuit of self-interest, two attributes also highly prized by the American political culture.[13]

Rather than arguing over whether individuals or the state should own the factors of production, a basic debate within the U.S. economic context has focused on how well the U.S. capitalist system operates and whether there are circumstances in which government intervention in private markets is desirable. As we show later in this chapter, this debate commenced in earnest during the Great Depression of the 1930s, leading to fundamental changes in public expectations concerning what the government can and should do to secure economic prosperity—in effect, to the view that government action should be directed toward the achievement of the economic goals detailed above.

Policy Tools for Managing the Economy

To achieve the diverse, and sometimes conflicting, goals of economic policy, the government has three basic tools: fiscal policy, monetary policy, and regulatory policy. Since these are discussed in much greater detail in later chapters, we discuss them only briefly at this point.

Fiscal policy refers to the taxing and spending policies of the government. Since the 1930s, this has been the chief weapon in the government's economic arsenal. Fiscal policy is important in a number of ways. First, the overall level of taxation and governmental spending has a powerful effect on the aggregate demand for goods and services in the country, which in turn exerts a strong influence on such things as inflation and unemployment. Since the end of World War II, and particularly during the 1960s and 1970s, the federal government has attempted to influence the economy by adjusting taxing and spending levels (and thus, the federal budget surpluses or deficits), often following an economic doctrine known as Keynesian economics, which is described in more detail later. In addition to the overall effect of fiscal policy on aggregate demand, specific elements of taxing and spending policy may also be directed at achieving the various goals of economic policy. For example, changes to the tax code may be written in such a way as to alter the distribution of income or stimulate particular kinds of economic activity. Similarly, spending decisions may be taken with an eye toward creating structural changes in the U.S. economy. A significant example of this is represented by postwar decisions on the locations of major federal facilities and defense contractors, which are thought to have been influential in the transformation of the South from a relatively underdeveloped, poor region to an area of strong economic growth in the last decades of the twentieth century.[14]

Monetary policy involves the regulation of the money supply. Unlike fiscal policy, which is under the control of elected officials like the Congress and the president, control of monetary policy rests with the Federal Reserve Board, an independent body relatively insulated from the public. Through the variety of mechanisms described in chapter 5, the Federal Reserve Board regulates the amount of money in circulation. Since money includes bank deposits and other financial instruments as well as currency, much of the Federal Reserve Board's activity is directed at financial institutions, which it also plays a role in regulating. Monetary policy is considered of great importance regarding price stability, and, according to an economic theory known as monetarism (an alternative to Keynesian theory), may even be a more effective vehicle than fiscal policy for influencing overall economic performance.

The final major tool of economic policy, **regulatory policy**, is really a variety of devices, all involving government attempts to control or influence the behavior of individuals and corporations, in effect, altering the existing operation of the marketplace.[15] Important forms of economic regulation include the supervision of securities markets, regulation of financial institutions, requirements concerning labeling and the disclosure of information necessary for informed behavior by consumers, establishment of procedures affecting labor relations, and the prohibition of activities regarded as anticompetitive (e.g., price-fixing). In general, regulatory policy has two basic purposes, which are not always complementary. The first is the promotion of conditions deemed necessary for the efficient functioning of the marketplace. The second is the prevention of socially undesirable outcomes, even though they may be the normal product of market interactions. While regulatory policy is, like all political questions, the subject of much debate, it is those aspects of regulation related to the latter purpose which are the subjects of the most intense political conflict. During the Reagan and Bush presidencies, there was very serious conflict over the costs and benefits of regulation, particularly over regulations—such as environmental and health and safety regulations—that are not directly concerned with the production of goods and services but that are viewed by some as having important (negative) economic effects.

Control of Economic Policy

Control over the various tools of economic policy is not concentrated in the hands of any one political authority but rather is dispersed among many actors, a common feature of much of U.S. governmental policy, particularly domestic policies. Despite this dispersion of power, from a political perspective much of the credit or blame concerning the performance of the U.S. economy goes to the president. There are at least three reasons for this. First, the president is the most visible of all governmental officials, and, particularly during the twentieth century, has come to be viewed by the public as the **manager of prosperity**.[16] Second, the president has more direct and indirect influence over economic policy than any other actor. Through such things as the preparation of the annual budget, the exercise of influence within the legislative process, appointment of heads of regulatory bodies and executive agencies, and the statutory presidential responsibility for collecting economic statistics and describing the nation's economic health, the president plays some role in virtually every action relating to management of the economy. Third, the quadrennial presidential election process firmly connects the performance of the economy to the political fortunes of the president in a way that is not true for any other governmental official. Whether the voters use the election as a referendum of past performance or a chance to choose among alternative futures, a significant issue in all recent presidential elections has been the performance of the economy. As a result, from a political perspective—the perspective from which this book is written—it is useful to consider the historical record of economic performance as being divided into periods defined by the terms of the various presidents. This produces, in effect, a "presidential economic scorecard."

RATING PRESIDENTS ON ECONOMIC PERFORMANCE

In 1980 Ronald Reagan asked the electorate a rhetorical question: "Are you better off today than you were four years ago?" In effect, he asked Americans to think about the performance of the economy under President Carter, and a large part of the reason for Ronald Reagan's decisive electoral victory over President Carter that year was that most voters felt that they could not answer "yes" to his question.

To better understand the performance of the U.S. economy and assess the efforts of postwar presidents to manage it, in the last chapter of this book we will present and discuss a presidential economic scorecard. This economic scorecard is based on five macroeconomic indicators: GNP, unemployment, inflation, balance on the current account (which includes the balance of trade), and productivity. The first four are components of the "golden quadrangle" and the fifth—productivity—is very important for improving the standard of living in the United States. Productivity generally means the average output per hour by each worker. If each worker becomes more efficient (because of improved training or better equipment), then the economy produces more goods and services without generating higher costs or inflation.

The scorecard reports figures for all postwar presidential terms, beginning with the second Truman term, the first full term after the end of World War II. We begin at this point because it marks in a genuine sense the onset of the period in which the U.S. public has had the expectation that the government, especially the president, should—and can—*manage* the economy. Since the postwar period includes presidents from both political parties, our scorecard begs some important questions. Which president had the best economic performance? The worst? Does political party have any relationship to the stewardship of our economy? In some ways, the scorecard is as much an indication of the economic challenges faced by each president as a report on a president's performance.

Economic policy management is now a day-to-day executive responsibility constrained by high public expectations. How did we arrive at this point? Our purpose in describing the presidential economic scorecard here is to set the stage for the discussion in the following chapters. To fully understand what these economic indicators suggest about presidential performance in managing the economy, you need to have a complete understanding of the mechanics and politics of economic policy making. We now turn to the historical origins of modern American economic policy by chronicling the evolution of the political economy: laissez-faire capitalism, the Great Depression, Franklin D. Roosevelt and policy experimentation, John Maynard Keynes and economic activism, and the Employment Act of 1946. Passage of the Employment Act of 1946 marks the point at which economic stewardship—previously viewed as being best left outside of the realm of government activity—was formally declared to be a primary responsibility of the federal government.

LAISSEZ-FAIRE ECONOMICS

Throughout American history, an underlying value consensus premised on capitalism and the free market has provided a measure of direction to economic policy.[17] This free market ethos is widely held among policy makers. Former assistant treasury secretary Gerald Parsky once explained that "the market mechanism is on the whole the most efficient method of assuring that supply and demand of commodities are kept in balance in a dynamic world. Although markets do not always operate efficiently, the appropriate remedy is to strengthen their functioning, not intervene, or further impede market operations."[18] The free market ethos is based on the capacity of the private sector to promote economic prosperity and stability. However, capitalism has not discounted a role by the president and the bureaucracy, which take actions to ensure a relatively effective economic policy.

After the Civil War, the role of the federal government in the economy was quite limited. The chief policies were tariffs to promote industrialization, land grant colleges to agricultural research and development, and subsidies to encourage Western development. Later, rural interests pressured Congress to regulate the railroads, and the Interstate Commerce Commission (ICC) was established in 1887. But macroeconomic policy making was largely an alien concept, because the *business cycle*—the fluctuations between economic expansion (periods of prosperity) and contraction (recessionary periods)—was accepted by most Americans. As President Warren G. Harding proclaimed in 1921: "There has been vast unemployment before and there will be again. There will be depression and inflation just as surely as the tides ebb and flow."[19]

This sentiment reflected the influence of **laissez-faire economics**, which was popularized in 1776 by Adam Smith in his *Inquiry into the Nature and Causes of the Wealth of Nations*. That treatise argued that labor, capital, and land are the vital resources that generate the national wealth, which are distributed as wages, profits, and rent. To increase national wealth and the collective well-being, therefore, Smith believed that private enterprise must be free from government control so entrepreneurs can pursue their own economic self-interest in a competitive environment. Government would have few duties to perform: provide for the common defense, administer justice, subsidize public works, safeguard foreign commerce, support elementary schools, and maintain "the Sovereign or Commonwealth."

Over the next 150 years, the primary concern of economists schooled in the laissez-faire tradition was **microeconomics**. It sought to understand how prices fluctuate within competing markets, while concerns about unemployment were left unanswered.[20] The microeconomic framework simply assumed that, as each individual market reaches "equilibrium," the sum of all markets would reduce the unemployment rate.[21]

Laissez-faire economics held sway until 1936, when British economist John Maynard Keynes introduced a revolutionary understanding of economic processes premised on government involvement. Keynes's theories gained acceptance because the political underpinnings of laissez-faire orthodoxy were shattered by the Great Depression of the 1930s. As author Walter Lippman observed, the "acceptance by the government of responsibility for recovery . . . mark great changes in a political system which until 1929 was committed to the general doctrine of laissez-faire."[22]

THE GREAT DEPRESSION

On October 28, 1929 (a day that became known as "Black Monday"), over 9 million shares of stock were sold at a net loss of $14 million. Although stocks had been falling since the summer, this massive collapse of investor confidence in late October came to represent in the public mind the onset of the massive economic downturn that followed. While the stock market collapse did not cause the Great Depression, it undermined business confidence and discouraged capital investment. Employment, production, and prices fell from 1929 through March 1933. During this period, GNP dropped by one-third, reflecting a massive loss of industrial production and staggering numbers of unemployed Americans.[23] Roughly 3% of the workforce was unemployed in 1929, as compared to roughly 25% in 1933.[24]

While prices fell, the decrease was less than the drop in incomes. Therefore per capita disposable (after taxes) personal income fell from $1,236 in 1929 to $893 in 1933. Corporate profits plummeted so much that, by

1932–1933, the cost of production exceeded business revenue. The collapse of America's economy lasted until 1941, when America entered World War II and full employment was reestablished.[25]

FRANKLIN D. ROOSEVELT AND POLICY EXPERIMENTATION

Although federal spending almost tripled as a percentage of GNP during the period from 1929 to 1933, the infusion of public funds was inadequate to reverse the downward spiral. Spending increases were not a deliberate federal strategy to counteract the depression, because President Herbert Hoover believed that a balanced budget was essential to economic recovery. Presidential candidate Franklin D. Roosevelt agreed with Hoover and referred to the deficit of $1.6 billion as "so great that it makes us catch our breath."[26] One week after his inauguration, President Roosevelt reiterated that fact: "Too often in recent history liberal governments have been wrecked on the roots of loose fiscal policy. We must avoid this danger."[27] At his urging, Congress adopted the Economy Act on March 20, 1933, which reduced the salaries of federal employees and veterans benefits to save $450 million.

But FDR's retrenchment was only temporary, because he came to appreciate that government could not provide work relief to the unemployed and balance the budget at the same time. He chose to confront the economic crisis by using a three-pronged strategy known as the **New Deal**: temporary relief for the jobless, recovery from the economic contraction, and reform of capitalism. Although federal relief for the unemployed was first enacted with the Federal Emergency Relief Act of 1933, rising unemployment and the slowness of direct relief efforts led FDR to promote temporary public works projects as more effective methods. The Public Works Administration (PWA) funded and administered the construction of airports, dams, aircraft carriers, bridges, schools, and hospitals; the Works Progress Administration (WPA) employed workers on construction projects and funded artists and writers; the Civilian Conservation Corps (CCC) supplied jobs to unemployed urban youth in the nation's forests and parks; and the National Youth Administration (NYA) provided work to high school and college students to help them earn income to pay their expenses. By 1934, roughly 28 million Americans obtained some form of federal relief.[28]

For New Dealers the main assault on the Great Depression called for economic recovery. As FDR told Congress, "the machinery necessary for a great cooperative movement throughout all industry in order to obtain wide reemployment, to shorten the working week, to pay a decent wage for the shorter week, and to prevent unfair competition and disastrous overproduction."[29] On June 16, 1933, the National Industrial Recovery Act (NIRA) was enacted, creating the National Recovery Administration (NRA). Each industry was urged to formulate a "code of fair competition" to establish fair practices regarding wages, hours, and working conditions, as well as collective bargaining agreements. The NRA codes were binding on all companies. By May 1935, there were 557 basic and 189 supplemental codes affecting about 95% of all industrial workers.[30]

The counterpart for the agriculture sector was the Agricultural Adjustment Act (AAA) of May 12, 1933. As commodity prices fell, farmers tried increasing output in order to maintain their income, which only further depressed farm prices. The purpose of the AAA was to guarantee that farm producers would obtain the same purchasing power relative to the value of nonfarm goods that existed between 1910 and 1914, a time of general farm prosperity. Farmers who agreed to production quotas would receive federal revenue, which was funded by a tax on food processors.

The NRA and AAA were public cartels aimed at restricting the operation of the free market so that desirable outcomes could be achieved through regulations. But they were short-lived experiments. The NIRA was nullified by the Supreme Court in 1935 in *Schecter Poultry Corp. v. United States* and the AAA was declared unconstitutional one year later in *United States v. Butler*. In each case the high court found that executive power exceeded the authority of the federal government. Then FDR responded with his Second New Deal, which emphasized using fiscal policy to stimulate economic growth. This development was compatible with the principles of activist government being advocated by British economist John Maynard Keynes.

Finally, other New Deal regulatory programs that survive to this day were enacted to reform key business practices, labor-management relations, and social welfare measures. The Federal Deposit Insurance Corporation (FDIC) guarantees bank deposits; the Fair Labor Standards Act of 1938 requires minimum wages and maximum hours for workers engaged in interstate commerce; the Securities and Exchange Commission (SEC) regulates stock and bond markets; and the National Labor Relations Board (NLRB) monitors the efforts of workers who wish to organize unions. Most significant was the 1935 Social Security Act, which created the modern retirement system, benefits for the disabled and needy, and a federal-state unemployment compensation system.

KEYNES AND THE DAWN OF ECONOMIC ACTIVISM

Keynesianism is premised on the argument that government could be an agent for increasing aggregate demand, either directly through increased federal spending or indirectly through reduced taxes to stimulate private consumption and investment.[31] In a depression, government must act to increase aggregate demand, because high unemployment will cause a decline in consumer spending as well as in business investment. Keynes argued that fiscal policy—cutting taxes and increasing spending—is a much more effective strategy to generate economic recovery than monetary policy (cutting interest rates to increase the supply of money and credit).[32]

On the one hand, Keynes concluded that an activist fiscal policy could be effective when interest rates were low relative to historic levels. Either an increase in government spending or a reduction in taxes (or both) was needed to increase aggregate demand and shift the equilibrium toward the full employment level. In other words, the federal government should increase the budget deficit in order to reduce unemployment.

On the other hand, in an economy operating at full employment, Keynes's prescriptions could be applied to combating inflation.[33] The thinking was that inflation was caused by excessive demand, to mean a level of demand for goods and services that exceeded what the economy could produce. The Keynesian remedy is to increase taxes or reduce federal spending, either of which should lead to a governmental budgetary surplus.

In both the laissez-faire and Keynesian schools of thought, the quantity of goods and services produced and the prices of these goods and services are determined by the aggregate demand for goods and services and the aggregate supply of goods and services by society. Equilibrium is the intersection of aggregate demand and aggregate supply.[34]

In response to a deep recession during 1937–1938 that stalled the economic recovery, FDR employed Keynesian principles. This new downturn prompted New Dealers to reconsider their views of budgets and fiscal policy. Some of FDR's advisers had long argued against efforts to balance the budget. As early as 1933, Rexford G. Tugwell stated: "We cheerfully and without criticism raised some 20 billions of dollars in two years to fight a war in 1917–1918, and no one ever questioned its repayment."[35] Prior to Keynes some economists had promoted a so-called pump-priming theory.[36] According to economist Alvin H. Hansen, pump priming meant that "a certain volume of public spending, varying under different conditions, will have the effect of setting the economy going on the way toward full utilization of resources on its own power, without further aid from government spending."[37] This view argues that federal deficit spending is a temporary economic stimulation that would lead to the establishment of long-term full employment. But Keynes extended this reasoning by arguing that government intervention in the economy must be permanent to assure full employment. This view of **countercyclical policy** holds that government must act to stimulate the economy through job training, work relief, and unemployment programs whenever employment falls. In June 1934 Keynes advised the Roosevelt administration to engage in federal deficit spending to reach the $400 million per month threshold that was required to bring about full economic recovery. However, the philosophical rationale for government stimulation of the economy was not widely understood in the 1930s. With the exception of Marriner Eccles, who chaired the Federal Reserve Board, and Lauchlin Currie, an Eccles aide who became the first economic specialist in the White House, no leading economic policy maker in the Roosevelt administration understood how to use fiscal policy to bring about economic recovery.[38] Indeed, Keynes informed Labor Secretary Frances Perkins that he had "supposed the President was more literate, economically speaking." He even remarked to Alvin H. Hansen: "I don't think your President Roosevelt knows anything about economics."[39]

The Roosevelt administration did not reach Keynes's target of deficit spending until 1941 when the nation mobilized for World War II. It is noteworthy that the sharp decline in deficit spending between 1936 and 1938 coincided with a new recession. Therefore, from a technical perspective, the New Deal was not successful. As E. Cary Brown observes, fiscal policy "seems to have been an unsuccessful recovery device in the thirties—not because it did not work, but because it was not tried."[40] Brown determined that federal spending was never sufficient to reach full-employment level. By 1940 Keynes was distressed by the failure of FDR's countercyclical policy. "It seems politically impossible," he wrote, "for a capitalistic democracy to organize expenditures on the scale necessary to make the grand experiment which would prove my case—except in war conditions."[41]

In the end, World War II ended the Great Depression, thanks to a massive dose of deficit spending in support of civilian and military mobilization. In 1941 the federal government spent $13.2 billion and ran a $6.1 billion deficit. But during 1942–1945, total spending was nearly $307 billion and the federal deficit exceeded $184 billion, since revenues accounted for only 40% of expenditures. By the end of war, the federal debt stood at more than $250 billion, six times the figure of 1940. These huge expenditures coupled with the war's manpower requirements (12 million soldiers) caused the economy to achieve full employment. As late as 1941, unemployment was 9.9% (almost three times the 1929 level), but during the next four years unemployment fell to 1.2% by 1944.[42]

EMPLOYMENT ACT OF 1946

On January 5, 1942, FDR stated: "I am confident that by prompt action we shall control the price development now and that we shall prevent the recurrence of a deep depression in the post-war period."[43] Three years later he pondered the adverse impact of much-reduced federal spending in his 1945 budget message, stating that "full employment in peacetime can be assured only when the reduction in war demand is approximately off-set by additional peacetime demand from millions of consumers, businesses, and farmers, and by Federal, State, and local governments."[44]

With the influence of Keynesian economics, the experience of World War II, and the vivid memories of the Great Depression in the minds of most policy makers and citizens, President Harry S. Truman signed the **Employment Act of 1946** (PL 79-304). It made the federal government responsible for the health of America's economy. This measure represents a turning point toward the dominance of Keynesianism and countercyclical policy in postwar economic policy making. The Employment Act sets economic goals for the national government but does not supply the president with a mandate to implement formal Keynesian policies:

> The Congress hereby declares that it is the continuing policy and responsibility of the Federal Government to use all practicable means consistent with its needs and obligations and other essential considerations of national policy with the assistance and cooperation of industry, agriculture, labor, and State and local governments, to coordinate and utilize all its plans, functions, and resources for the purpose of creating and maintaining, in a manner calculated to foster and promote free competitive enterprise and the general welfare, conditions under which there will be afforded useful employment, for those able, willing, and seeking to work, and to promote maximum employment, production, and purchasing power.

It is noteworthy that this language does not mandate "full" employment. Rather the goal is for government to create economic conditions under which "maximum" employment would occur alongside maximum production and purchasing power within an environment of "free competitive enterprise."

The Employment Act established several important economic policy measures. First, the act provided for countercyclical or **compensatory fiscal policy** to "moderate" the severity of the ups and downs of the business cycle. During recessionary periods, the federal government would intervene in the economy by increasing spending or cutting income taxes to stimulate demand. Second, the 1946 Act transferred responsibility for managing the economy to the president. Specifically, it directs the president to present an official report, called the *Economic Report of the President*, outlining national economic performance, including unemployment, production, and inflation, to Congress in every legislative session. Third, the act created the president's Council of Economic Advisers (CEA) within the Executive Office of the President (EOP). It is a formal group of three professional economists, nominated by the president with Senate approval, who advise the president on economic performance. Fourth, the law created a Joint Economic Committee (JEC) in Congress, which was authorized to make its own recommendations and report them to Congress.

Despite its limitations, the 1946 Act is a watershed in the development of the American economy. It signaled that intellectual opinion had changed since "hundreds of economists and government policy planners had come by the end of the thirties to accept the Keynesian analysis as the new orthodoxy."[45] Economists began disparaging the assumption that balanced budgets are an imperative, and they accepted deficits as necessary during economic recessions. The issue was no longer laissez-faire versus intervention. Instead, the debate focused on the extent to which the president could manage the economy and what policy tools were most effective.

Twenty-two years later, under President Carter, Congress passed the Full Employment and Balanced Growth Act (PL 95-523), commonly known as the **Humphrey-Hawkins Act**. The original version of that legislation proposed that the federal government be the "employer of last resort" in order to achieve a 3% unemployment rate, but like the battle over the 1946 Act, the legislative process yielded a final bill which does little more than raise public expectations. The purpose of the Humphrey-Hawkins Act is "the fulfillment of the right to full opportunities for useful paid employment at fair rates of compensation of all individuals able, willing, and seeking to work."[46]

THE ECONOMIC PROBLEM: BUSINESS CYCLES

While presidents possess a number of fiscal instruments, the actual operation of the economy is largely beyond their direct control. Often presidents and their political fortunes are at the mercy of the business cycle. During the 1930s, the National Bureau of Economic Research (NBER) formalized the concept of the **business cycle**, which has been described by *Business Conditions Digest* as "sequences of expansion and contraction in various economic processes that show up as major fluctuations in aggregate economic activity."[47] The high point of each cycle—the point at which economic activity ceases to rise and begins to decline—is the **business peak**. The low point, when conditions begin to improve, is the **business trough**. However "while recurrent and pervasive, business cycles of historical experience have been definitely non-periodic and have varied greatly in duration and intensity, reflecting changes in economic systems, conditions, policies, and outside disturbances."[48]

Especially important are periods of contraction and expansion. According to the NBER, a contraction is a significant decline in economic activity, spread across the economy, and lasting more than a few months. A recession begins just after the economy reaches a peak of economic activity and ends as the economy reaches its trough. Between trough and peak, the economy is in an expansion, which is the normal state of the economy. Overall, from June 1857 to 2006, the United States experienced 558 months (31.7%) of contraction and 1,205 months (68.3%) of expansion. Since 1945 most recessions have been rare and relatively short-lived. From 1945 to 2006, there have been 112 months of contraction (15.3%) compared to 620 months of expansion (84.7%).

Table 1.1.   Business Cycle Contractions and Expansions, 1857–2006

| Business Cycle Dates | | Duration in Months | | | |
| | | Contraction | Expansion | Cycle | |
Peak	Trough	Trough from Previous Peak	Trough to Next Peak	Trough from Previous Trough	Peak from Previous Peak
	December 1854	—	—	—	—
June 1857	December 1858	18	30	48	—
October 1860	June 1861	8	22	30	40
April 1865	December 1867	32	46	78	54
June 1869	December 1870	18	18	36	50
October 1873	March 1879	65	34	99	52
March 1882	May 1885	38	36	74	101
March 1887	April 1888	13	22	35	60
July 1890	May 1891	10	27	37	40
January 1893	June 1894	17	20	37	30
December 1895	June 1897	18	18	36	35
June 1899	December 1900	18	24	42	42
September 1902	August 1904	23	21	44	39
May 1907	June 1908	13	33	46	56
January 1910	January 1912	24	19	43	32
January 1913	December 1914	23	12	35	36
August 1918	March 1919	7	44	51	67
January 1920	July 1921	18	10	28	17
May 1923	July 1924	14	22	36	40
October 1926	November 1927	13	27	40	41
August 1929	March 1933	43	21	64	64
May 1937	June 1938	13	50	63	93
February 1945	October 1945	8	80	88	93
November 1948	October 1949	11	37	48	45
July 1953	May 1954	10	45	55	56
August 1957	April 1958	8	39	47	49
April 1960	February 1961	10	24	34	32
December 1969	November 1970	11	106	117	116
November 1973	March 1975	16	36	52	47
January 1980	July 1980	6	58	64	74
July 1981	November 1982	16	12	28	18
July 1990	March 1991	8	92	100	108
March 2001	November 2001	8	120	128	128
Total		558 (31.7%)	1,205 (68.3%)	1,763	1,755

Source: National Bureau of Economic Research, "Business Cycle Expansions and Contractions," November 26, 2001, http://www.nber.org/cycles.html#announcements.

These data indicate that the U.S. economy has shifted markedly toward expansion since World War II. In fact, the three longest periods of economic expansion since 1854 have occurred after 1960: (1) February 1961 to February 1969; (2) November 1982 to July 1990; and (3) March 1991 to March 2001. While there are no policy solutions to prevent business cycles, the use of fiscal policy measures by modern presidents has reduced the frequency and severity of recessions. Although the performance of the economy has improved, the cyclical pattern of economic activity has not ended, which translates into political difficulties for presidents.

THE POLITICS OF PRESIDENTIAL
ECONOMIC POLICY MAKING

With the Employment Act the president was expected to guarantee a prosperous economy through strong economic policy leadership. However, presidents do not formulate economic policy in a vacuum. Economic decisions are conducted within a highly political environment as policy considerations are impacted by public expectations, organized interests, bureaucratic constraints, and economic globalization.

Public Expectations

A service-providing government has transformed the presidency into an office that must build and sustain direct ties with the citizenry. Since the New Deal, presidents have made far-reaching promises in order to get elected. Though resources are limited, presidents can try to manipulate the economy with certain fiscal policy tools in an attempt to improve economic conditions in the short run, thereby enhancing their party's public image. Yet, public expectations are unrealistically high, because the public believes that presidents can issue policy solutions to pressing economic problems. Too often the public becomes impatient and pressures the president to find quick fixes for economic problems.

Public opinion forces presidents to tackle the most significant economic problem that threatens to disrupt prosperity or to destabilize the economy.[49] In 1974 President Gerald Ford, in confronting the rising prices that resulted from the Arab OPEC oil embargo and the Vietnam War, decided to cut federal spending. The economy responded, however, by slipping into a recession, which led to his electoral defeat in 1976. Frustrated with Keynesian fiscal solutions to stagflation (stagnant economic growth with rising prices), President Carter deregulated key industries (for example, the airlines), cut taxes, and increased spending to unleash business investment. Nonetheless interest rates on consumer loans and inflation soared and the advent of double-digit inflation contributed to Carter's defeat in 1980.

Organized Interests

Presidents must also contend with coalitions from many and sometimes conflicting groups that may limit their ability to attain economic objectives.[50] Key groups in organized labor, business, agriculture, and on Wall Street subject the president to a number of pressures that influence the capacity of presidential administrations to formulate economic policy. Groups that advocate certain interests are very attentive to economic issues impacting their members and constituents. For example, the National Grange and the American Farm Bureau seek to obtain government subsidies to support agriculture interests and favor lower interest rates to make credit more available. Presidents have recognized the political value of making targeted economic appeals to organized interests and to mobilize those groups in support of their economic policy program.

Among the most important business groups are the United States Chamber of Commerce and the Business Roundtable. Major unions, like the United Auto Workers (UAW), American Federation of Labor–Congress of Industrial Organizations (AFL-CIO), and the Civil Service Employees Association (CSEA), donate money and support candidates in both congressional and presidential elections. Business groups concentrate lobbying efforts to obtain tax breaks and corporate investment incentives, whereas unions seek to improve occupational and safety standards, obtain higher salaries and better benefits, and receive job security guarantees from employers.

In 1981 President Reagan proposed defense spending increases and tax cuts that appealed to constituencies within the Republican Party even though it meant producing record-high peacetime budget deficits. Reagan's strategy also targeted marginalized groups within the Democratic Party who were displeased with Carter, namely Catholics, southerners, and blue-collar workers.[51] Reagan's strategy worked insofar as blue-collar workers and southerners strongly supported Reagan, who soundly defeated Walter Mondale in the 1984 presidential election.[52]

Bureaucratic Constraints

Since the 1950s, small departmental advisory staffs with international responsibilities have turned into full-fledged bureaus and agencies within the Executive Office of the President and have become more active in economic matters. Furthermore, the jurisdictional lines between those agencies with responsibility for domestic economic policy and those involved with foreign economic policy have become blurred because domestic and international ("intermestic") issues have become much more intertwined. Decentralized authority within the bureaucracy has made it difficult for presidents to manage the economy. Agencies and departments compete against each other to secure budgets, turf, and clientele. Presidents, therefore, have had to try a variety of administrative strategies to coordinate the economic policy making process.

The relative independence of the Federal Reserve Board (the Fed) also presents certain institutional challenges to the president's management of economic policy. In 1994, for example, Fed chairman Alan Greenspan opposed a Clinton administration proposal to create a Federal Banking Commission that would have consolidated monetary regulation into one agency. And although Alan Greenspan had endorsed President Bush's original proposal for tax cuts, he later resisted Bush's call for another round of tax cuts in 2003. By 2003, the Fed preferred a balanced budget rather than more tax cuts.

Economic Globalization

Presidents are also limited by the economic actions of foreign governments and international organizations as well as the forces of global interdependence. International economic transactions, foreign trade, and monetary issues directly influence the ability of presidential administrations to promote domestic economic policies. On the one hand, the United States has benefited from the global economy. Globalization has increased America's standard of living by roughly $1 trillion per year. Since 1945 the average household is $9,000 per year wealthier, and since 1991 annual U.S. income has increased by $500 billion.[53] On the other hand, since 1990 the United States has run persistent and sizable trade deficits, which has resulted in a net trade debt of 25% of GDP in 2004. A defining feature of the postwar international economic system has been sustained growth of global trade. Global trade's share of world GDP rose from 13% in 1970 to 21% in 1995.[54]

Presidents have to contend with an array of economic forces both within and outside the borders of the United States. Macroeconomic conditions such as unemployment, the GDP, interest rates, and inflation are impacted by economic fluctuations of international markets, foreign currencies, and capital flows. Two current domestic economic problems that are directly related to globalization are the rising U.S. dependence on imported oil and the decline of the American manufacturing sector.

OVERVIEW OF THE BOOK

Our grand objective in this book is to assess whether or not presidents can govern economic policy in an intensely political environment. In chapter 2, we explore why the responsibility for delivering economic prosperity lies with the president and how the president faces unrealistic public expectations. Too high public expectations undermine presidential leadership.

Presidential leadership is also limited by the kind of economic policy advice he receives. Chapter 3 examines the policy making roles of the most important decision makers and agencies with jurisdiction over economic policy. Fiscal policy and budgets are essential for economic management, and in chapter 4 we explore how presidential power and congressional authority interact in the budgetary process. The extent to which monetary policy serves macroeconomic goals is discussed in chapter 5, where we examine the Federal Reserve System.

An assessment of both fiscal and monetary policy provides the context for evaluating the economic policy making styles of each president since Truman and the politics of countercyclical policy. Chapter 6 assesses the economic objectives of each presidential administration and explains why economic policy is an expression of the president's partisan and ideological values.

Economic policy depends on the international economy, and presidents are constrained by the global economic and financial system. Chapter 7 deals with the increasingly important global economy and its impact on presidential economic policy making.

Chapter 8 draws conclusions about the effectiveness of presidential management of economic policy based on a presidential economic scorecard that includes the five primary indicators of macroeconomic performance: unemployment, inflation, economic growth, production, and the global current account balance.

KEY TERMS

balance of payments
business cycle
business peak
business trough
capitalism
compensatory fiscal policy
consumer price index (CPI)
countercyclical policy
deflation
Employment Act of 1946
fiscal policy
full employment
golden quadrangle
gross domestic product (GDP)

gross national product (GNP)
Humphrey-Hawkins Act
inflation
Keynesianism
laissez-faire economics
manager of prosperity
microeconomics
monetary policy
national industrial policy
New Deal
regulatory policy
socialism
structural unemployment
unemployment rate

ADDITIONAL READINGS

Bailey, Stephen K. *Congress Makes a Law*. New York: Columbia University Press, 1950. An interesting case study by a political scientist of the enactment of the Employment Act of 1946.

Chandler, Lester V. *America's Greatest Depression, 1929–1941*. New York: Harper & Row, 1970. A thorough examination of the causes and impact of the economic collapse of the 1930s and the effects of New Deal programs in aiding economic recovery.

Galbraith, John Kenneth. *The Great Crash: 1929*. Boston: Houghton Mifflin, 1954. A very readable account by a prominent economist of the conditions underlying the 1929 stock market crash.

Harrod, Roy F. *The Life of John Maynard Keynes*. London: Macmillan, 1951. A biography of the founder of modern macroeconomic theory, his upbringing, and professional career.

Keynes, John Maynard. *The End of Laissez-Faire: The Economic Consequences of the Peace*. London: Prometheus Books, 1926; reprinted 2004. John Maynard Keynes (1883–1946) was one of the most influential economists of the first half of the twentieth century. In this volume Keynes presents a brief historical review of laissez-faire economic policy.

Samuelson, Paul A. and William D. Nordhaus. *Economics*, 18th ed. New York: McGraw-Hill, 2004. *Economics*, the largest-selling economics textbook, provides understandable coverage of both microeconomics and macroeconomics.

Schlesinger, Arthur M. Jr. *The Coming of the New Deal*. Boston: Houghton Mifflin, 1958. Volume II in the Age of Roosevelt series focuses on anti-Depression policy during 1933 and 1934, including the National Industrial Recovery Act.

Schlesinger, Arthur M. Jr. *The Crisis of the Old Order, 1919–1933*. Boston: Houghton Mifflin, 1957. Volume I in the Age of Roosevelt series discusses the failed political leadership of the 1920s and the causes of the Great Depression.

Terkel, Studs. *Hard Times: An Oral History of the Great Depression*. New York: Avon, 1971. Interviews by arguably America's best-known oral historian of ordinary people who recall their economic hardships during the 1930s.

NOTES

1. The March 1, 1991, *USA Today* poll reported a 91% approval rating; the March 6, 1991, *Washington Post* poll reported a 90% approval rating; and the February 28–March 3, 1991, Gallup Poll reported an 89% approval rating, the highest in Gallup's fifty-year measurement of presidential approval. The February 19–20, 1992, CNN/*USA Today* poll measured President Bush's approval at 39%.

2. A large amount of work has been written on this and related questions, beginning with Edward R. Tufte, "Determinants of the Outcomes of Midterm Congressional Elections," *American Political Science Review* 69 (September 1975): 812–826. This is discussed in more detail in chapter 9.

3. B. Guy Peters, *American Public Policy: Promise and Performance*, 2nd ed. (Chatham, NJ: Chatham House, 1986), 156.

4. Peters, *American Public Policy*, 157.

5. Lester Thurow, *Zero Sum Society* (New York: Basic, 1980).

6. A clear discussion of GNP and GDP is in "Gross Domestic Product as a Measure of U.S. Production," *Survey of Current Business* 71 (August 1991): 8.

7. For example, in 1900, a large percentage of the U.S. population resided in rural areas and was employed in the agricultural sector, where skills such as literacy are less relevant. As agricultural productivity increased during the twentieth century due to the mechanization of agriculture, the demand for unskilled agricultural workers decreased. If no other changes had occurred in the U.S. labor market (e.g., if the demand for urban industrial workers had not risen during the same period), this would have lead to an increase in unemployment.

8. These definitions and the following discussion of price stability are taken from the discussion in Paul A. Samuelson and William D. Nordhaus, *Economics*, 14th ed. (New York: McGraw-Hill, 1992), 587–594.

9. CPI figures are for CPI-U, the consumer price index for all urban consumers, which covers approximately 80% of the population. Although the average CPI-U over the entire base period of 1982–1984 was 100, the closest monthly figures to 100 were 99.9 in July 1983 and 100.2 in August 1983. The CPI is calculated for particular components of goods and services, such as energy, food, and housing costs, and overall, that is, for all of the goods and services considered together. The overall index is the most commonly cited statistic. A new series was begun in 1987 with a 1987 base equal to 100; monthly CPI statistics continue to be reported using the 1982–1984 base, although some statistics are also reported with the 1987 and 1967 bases.

10. Increases in prices and wages are obviously interrelated, since wages are an element in the cost of producing goods and services, and hence in the prices charged for these goods and services.

11. This discussion of the balance of international payments is based on Samuelson and Nordhaus, *Economics*, 671–674.

12. This is identified as a fifth basic goal, along with the four elements of the "golden quadrangle," in Peters, *American Public Policy*.

13. It should be noted that in economic terms, efficiency means that the factors of production are employed in such a way as to obtain the greatest return, regardless of what is actually being produced. It may be more efficient, in these terms, for a society to produce luxury speedboats for the wealthy than enough food for the poor—if these goods compete for the same factors of production and the wealthy are willing to pay more for speedboats than the poor are willing (or able) to pay for food.

14. See Kirkpatrick Sale, *Power Shift* (New York: Random House, 1975) and David C. Perry and Alfred J. Watkins, eds., *The Rise of the Sunbelt Cities* (Beverly Hills: Sage, 1977).

15. Kenneth J. Meier, *Regulation: Politics, Bureaucracy, and Economics* (New York: St. Martin's, 1985), 1.

16. Clinton Rossiter, *The American Presidency* (New York: Harcourt Brace, 1960).

17. Herbert McClosky and John Zaller, *The American Ethos: Public Attitudes Toward Capitalism and Democracy* (Cambridge: Harvard University Press, 1984).

18. Parsky quoted in Karen Mingst, "Process and Policy in U.S. Commodities: The Impact of the Liberal Economic Paradigm," in *America in a Changing World Political Economy*, ed. William P. Avery and David Rapkin (New York: Longman, 1982), 193.

19. Quoted in Stephen K. Bailey, *Congress Makes a Law* (New York: Columbia University Press, 1950), 6.

20. Price stability is measured by the federal government's consumer price index (CPI), which calculates the current prices of a predetermined (and fixed over time) set of goods and services. The current value of the CPI is simply the weighted average of prices of goods and services purchased by wage earners.

21. The unemployment rate is calculated as the number of persons who are not employed but wish to be employed divided by this number plus the total number of employed persons: number of unemployed / number of unemployed + number of employed. Full employment does not mean that the unemployment rate is zero. Economist William Beveridge observed that 3% unemployment represented full employment. It could also be suggested that a range of 2%–7% unemployment represent full employment, but such estimates may reflect particular political biases. In 1999, the Organization for Economic Cooperation and Development (OECD) put forth a "full-employment unemployment rate" between 4% and 6.4%. This was estimated as the "structural" unemployment rate or the level of unemployment that exists when a country is really at full employment. In the United States, full employment has been 3% unemployment, although some economists (and political leaders) would claim that the actual level is perhaps as high as 5% or 6%.

22. Walter Lippman, "The Permanent New Deal," *Yale Review* 24 (1935): 661.

23. GNP is the total dollar value of all final goods and services produced for consumption in society during a particular time period. Its rise or fall measures economic activity based on the labor and production output. In December 1991, the Bureau of Economic Analysis in the U.S. Department of Commerce began using the gross domestic product (GDP) rather than the GNP as the primary measure of U.S. economic production. GDP measures output generated through production by

28 Chapter 1

labor and property within the United States. Unlike GNP, GDP excludes income earned by Americans overseas. GDP is calculated as personal consumption + private investment + government expenditures + exports – imports.

24. See Lester V. Chandler, *America's Greatest Depression, 1929–1941* (New York: Harper & Row, 1970).

25. Chandler, *America's Greatest Depression.*

26. Quoted in Lewis H. Kimmel, *Federal Budget and Fiscal Policy, 1789–1958* (Washington, DC: Brookings, 1959), 166.

27. Quoted in Kimmel, *Federal Budget and Fiscal Policy,* 176.

28. Chandler, *America's Greatest Depression,* 194.

29. Chandler, *America's Greatest Depression,* 223.

30. Chandler, *America's Greatest Depression,* 229–230.

31. See John Maynard Keynes, *General Theory of Employment, Interest, and Money* (New York: Harcourt, 1965) and John Maynard Keynes, *The End of Laissez-Faire: The Economic Consequences of the Peace* (London: Prometheus, 1926; reprinted 2004).

32. According to Keynes, during an economic contraction a "liquidity trap" occurs. Under this condition, the interest rate would be so low that it could not be driven down further by policy makers. However much the money supply is increased, dollars would be held idle because people have no financial incentive to purchase bonds. Altering the money supply would thus have no significant effect on aggregate demand.

33. Inflation is defined as an increase in the general level of prices representing a decline in the purchasing power of dollars in the economy. The CPI provides a measure of inflation by tracking prices of consumer goods and services. The CPI is a fixed-quantity price index and a sort of cost-of-living index. A rising value indicates price inflation, while a falling value indicates price deflation, which is a rise in the purchasing power of dollars in the economy. Disinflation involves slowing the rate of inflation over time; that is, prices rise at a slower rate.

34. See Paul A. Samuelson and William D. Nordhaus, *Economics,* 14th ed. (New York: McGraw-Hill, 1992), chap. 4, 26, for a fuller discussion of the role of aggregate supply and aggregate demand in the macroeconomy.

35. Rexford G. Tugwell, "How Shall We Pay for All This," *American Magazine* 116 (1933): 87.

36. In the UK, "The Minority Report of the Poor Law Commission" (1905–1909) had recommended that public works expenditures be undertaken when unemployment reached 4% of the labor force. For an extensive discussion of the minority report see Sidney and Beatrice Webb, *English Local Government: English Poor Law History, Part II, The Last Hundred Years* (London and New York: Longmans, Green, 1929), chap. 7, 631–715.

37. Alvin H. Hansen, *Fiscal Policy and Business Cycles* (New York: Norton, 1941), 262.

38. See, for example, the discussion of Eccles in Arthur M. Schlesinger Jr., *The Politics of Upheaval* (Boston: Houghton Mifflin, 1960), 407.

39. Schlesinger, *The Politics of Upheaval,* 406.

40. E. Cary Brown, "Fiscal Policy in the Thirties: A Reappraisal," *American Economic Review* 46 (December 1956): 857–879.

41. John Maynard Keynes, "The United States and the Keynes Plan," *New Republic* 103 (1940): 158.

42. For data on specific economic conditions during the Great Depression and World War II, see Geoffrey H. Moore, *Business Cycles, Inflation, and Forecasting* (Cambridge, MA: Ballinger, 1980) and Paul Krugman, *Peddling Prosperity* (New York: Norton, 1994).

43. Quoted in Kimmel, *Federal Budget and Fiscal Policy*, 233.

44. Quoted in Kimmel, *Federal Budget and Fiscal Policy*, 234.

45. Bailey, *Congress Makes a Law*, 20.

46. The balance of international payments is comprised of three elements: the current account (trade in goods and services), the capital account (long- and short-term transfer of capital), and fluctuations in gold-and-reserve assets. The most visible of these is the current account, which is made up of the trade in merchandise and the so-called invisibles, such as travel, shipping fees, and insurance fees. The current account is sometimes called the balance of trade, and when the total value of all exports exceeds the total value of all imports, it is referred to as a positive or "favorable" balance of trade.

47. "Cyclical Indicators," *Business Conditions Digest* 29 (December 1989): 1. The NBER is a private, nonpartisan institute that collects, interprets, and increases knowledge of economic statistics and economic theory. It has achieved semiofficial status because many of its analyses have been incorporated into U.S. government publications, such as *Business Conditions Digest* and the *Survey of Current Business* both published by the U.S. Department of Commerce.

48. "Cyclical Indicators," 1.

49. Samuel Kernell, *Going Public: New Strategies of Presidential Leadership* (Washington, DC: CQ Press, 1997), 230–237.

50. Kernell, *Going Public*, 237–241.

51. Dick Kirschten, "The 'Revolution' at the White House: Have the People Caught up with the Man?" *National Journal* (August 29, 1981): 1532.

52. Rich Jaroslovsky, "Economic Upturn Aids President's Popularity, but It Is Not a Panacea," *Wall Street Journal*, April 28, 1983; Everett Carll Ladd, "On Mandates, Realignments, and the 1984 Presidential Election," *Political Science Quarterly* 100 (Spring 1985): 1–25; and William Schneider, "The New Shape of American Politics," *Atlantic* (January 1987).

53. C. Fred Bergsten, *The United States and the World Economy* (Washington, DC: Institute of International Economics, 2004).

54. U.S. Department of Commerce, Bureau of Economic Analysis, "U.S. Net International Investment Position, 2005," news release, http://www.bea.gov/bea/newsrel/intinvnewsrelease.htm.

2

The President, the Public, and Economic Policy

The values that Americans hold toward politics and economics shape the fundamental character of the U.S. political economy. This is not to say that people have a well-defined ideology about the political economy or that they are knowledgeable about macroeconomic policy. Most citizens lack the motivation and time to become fully informed about such matters, although this does not stop them from expressing opinions. What people believe may carry more political significance than economic reality. Public perceptions of the economy may constrain how the president defines his economic goals and what policy instruments he uses to address important economic problems.

At the turn of the twentieth century a new conception of the president as opinion leader took hold. Under Theodore Roosevelt, Woodrow Wilson, and Franklin D. Roosevelt, the presidency became an institutional fulcrum for publicizing economic policy for the American people. Modern presidents have to operate from a power base of personalized leadership, not simply partisan attachments, as they are expected to mobilize popular influence and bring it to bear on the policy process. Presidents shifted from relying on a bargaining strategy with Congress to a **"going public" strategy** whereby they mobilize constituents to pressure Congress to support presidential initiatives.[1]

According to author Theodore J. Lowi, a new public philosophy has accompanied modernity. It accepts the necessity of pervasive government regulation but also lauds it as the result of free competition among political coalitions in the policy process.[2] Government has been transformed into a service provider for which the presidency is responsible for delivering domestic prosperity. In this chapter we discuss the parameters of public opinion regarding the political economy and assess their impact on presidential conduct of economic policy making.

PUBLIC OPINION AND THE ECONOMY

Within broad parameters public opinion constrains economic policy makers. Broad support for capitalism and limited government means that most debates over economic policy take place within a fairly narrow range of options. For example, the debate in the mass media and in Congress over the Clinton administration's proposed national health care plan did not go so far as to endorse a government-managed health care system, as found in Canada and Great Britain. Although such programs exist across Europe and in Japan as well, the option of "socialized" medicine is deemed illegitimate given the deep-seated commitment to free markets in the American political culture.

In addition to these broadly defined parameters of public opinion, policy makers are also guided by public attitudes toward specific economic problems and solutions. That is, the public plays an important role in elevating issues to prominence by defining and setting the economic policy agenda. For example, President George H. W. Bush's decision to raise taxes in 1990 as part of a deficit reduction measure led many voters to perceive Bush as having reneged on his "read my lips, no new taxes" pledge during the 1988 campaign. After Bush was defeated by Clinton, the public debate throughout the 1990s over how to deal with the budget deficits was constrained by the assumption that the electorate would punish officials who tried to raise taxes on the working- and middle-class.

Setting the Economic Policy Agenda

Samuel Kernell, a professor of political science, has counseled presidents to "go public" and promote "policies in Washington by appealing to the American public for support."[3] Presidents have used this strategy in recent decades when faced with policy gridlock on Capitol Hill. But in order to successfully solicit the aid of the public, the president must first attract the attention of the mass media. One negative implication from this "going public" strategy is that the president is tempted to promise the American people much more than he is able to deliver. To assure national economic well-being, in fact, is no easy task and many components of economic policy are largely beyond the president's direct control.

The going public governing strategy seems to entail a **"general problem-solving" approach** to managing the economy. That is, Kernell argues, that Democrats, Republicans, and independents would share a common understanding of the economy, and for that reason the president is virtually required to address the most important economic problem facing the country at any point in time.[4] By implication, moreover, a general problem-solving approach to economic policy means that the president will *not* promote the economic preferences of any specific constituencies within his own party, nor will he too closely align the White House with any particular electoral coalition in order to maximize short-term political gains. Instead, he will publicly tackle whatever economic problem is widely perceived as a threat to the stability and growth of the economy.

Opposite the general problem-solving approach is a situation where presidents pursue a "**marginals**" **strategy** by appealing to specific groups and political coalitions.[5] Under this scenario, partisanship becomes a key factor that influences how economic policy is formulated and, as important, how the public evaluates the president's handling of the economy. The partisan approach means that the policy preferences of key constituency groups significantly influence economic policy insofar as policy makers internalize those constituency demands.[6]

A plausible argument could be made that macroeconomic policies, at least to some degree, are guided by political considerations. The Republican Party seems more concerned about rising prices because small businesses, corporations, and Wall Street financiers believe that the erosion of real income from inflation is a greater threat to economic stability than cyclical periods of higher unemployment. On the other hand, because blue-collar workers, minorities, and the poor (who generally vote Democratic) are more vulnerable during economic recessions, Democratic administrations would want to design policies to maximize employment. Paul Samuelson was one well-known economist who concluded that partisanship does matter, and thirty years ago he observed that "the difference between the Democrats and the Republicans is the difference in their constituencies" and because Democrats "are around the median incomes or below . . . these are the ones whom the Republicans want to pay the price and burden of fighting inflation. The Democrats [are] willing to run with some inflation [to increase employment]; the Republicans are not."[7] A more recent advocate of this partisanship thesis is Douglas Hibbs. He argues that "the relative priority given inflation as opposed to unemployment is markedly lower among Democratic partisans than among others [Republicans and independents] helps explain the tendency of presidents—particularly Republican presidents—to pursue policies aimed at trading extra unemployment for reduced inflation."[8]

The economy, like national security, is one issue that easily captures the attention of the electorate, because severe economic fluctuations such as rapid changes in the inflation or unemployment rates are given significant media exposure. And such economic fluctuations invariably are exploited by the opposition party to attack White House policy. The cumulative effect of these interactions between the media, political leaders, and the public is that a consensus emerges about the key economic problem that America faces. Opinion polls are an important source of information about what troubles Americans, and since 1935 the Gallup Poll has asked: "What do you think is the most important problem in this country today?" The trend from 1935 to 2006 indicates that public perceptions of the "most important problem" generally reflect current events.

In table 2.1, the state of the economy, but especially the issues of unemployment and the high cost of living, tend to dominate the list, although at times they are supplanted or supplemented by international tensions, wars, and more recently, terrorism. During the Great Depression unemployment was the primary concern. Joblessness was less important with the coming of World War II, after which Americans again worried about a postwar recession. Foreign affairs dominated the political agenda until the early 1960s, after which the Vietnam War preoccupied the public's attention. During the mid to late 1970s, the high cost of living predominated and, in the 1980s, the high cost of living, unemployment, and international tensions were considered among the most important problems.

As would be expected, Gallup polls show that public concern about the economy increases during periods of recession: 1953–1954, 1957–1958, 1960–1961, 1969–1970, 1973–1975, 1980, 1981–1982, 1990, and 2001–2002. After Vietnam, however, the high cost of living was named most frequently from 1973 until 1981 (during a relatively sustained bout of high inflation), with unemployment being ranked second most years. One analysis of these trends from 1946 through 1976 revealed that inflation is cited most often as the primary economic concern, almost twice as often as unemployment.[9] One reason may be that inflation affects nearly everyone, whereas unemployment affects only a fraction of the population. Also, according to researcher Tom W. Smith, inflation correlates with stages in the business cycle:

> Low points [in our concern for inflation] occurred in 1949, 1954, 1958, and 1961, during postwar recessions, and similar drops appeared during the 1970–1971 slowdown and the 1975 recession. Peaks appeared in 1966 and 1974. The 1966 point in part reflects the beginning of the 1966–1975 inflationary spiral, but in part appears to reflect the relative absence of unemployment. . . . The 1974 crest, on the other hand, probably reflects the double-digit inflation that crested that year.[10]

Joblessness again surfaced as the key economic concern in 1982, when the nation experienced its highest unemployment rate since the 1930s. Unemployment surfaced again as the most important problem in 1992, in the aftermath of recession, but then slipped back to second place during the rest of the 1990s as prosperity took hold.

Table 2.1.   Gallup Trends on "Most Important Problem"

Year	Most Important Problem
1936	unemployment
1938	keeping out of war
1940	keeping out of war
1942	winning war
1944	winning war
1946	high cost of living
1948	keeping peace
1950	labor unrest
1952	Korean War
1954	keeping peace
1956	keeping peace
1958	unemployment
1960	keeping peace
1962	keeping peace
1964	Vietnam War
1966	Vietnam War
1968	Vietnam War
1970	Vietnam War
1972	Vietnam War
1974	high cost of living
1976	high cost of living
1978	high cost of living
1980	high cost of living
1982	unemployment
1984	unemployment
1986	international tensions
1988	(no data)
1990	federal deficit
1992	unemployment
1994	crime and violence
1996	crime and violence
1998	crime and violence
2000	education
2002	terrorism
2004	terrorism
2006	Iraq War

Source: Sourcebook of Criminal Justice Statistics Online, http://www
.albany.edu/sourcebook/pdf/t212006.pdf.

In both 1994 and 1996 crime and violence were cited as the most important problems. In 1998, amid a strong economy, crime and violence were seen as most important and in the presidential election year of 2000, education was seen as the most important issue. Two years later, during a period of peace and prosperity, education and moral decline were mentioned as most important whereas the problem of inflation was third in importance.[11] In 2002 the public believed terrorism and international tensions were the most important problems.[12] Regarding economic performance, however, public opinion was deeply split along partisan lines since 57% of Republicans believed that the economy was in excellent or good condition as compared to only 37% of independents and even fewer (24%) Democrats.[13]

In 2004 the most important problems confronting the electorate were (1) terrorism, (2) the war in Iraq, and (3) the state of the economy. On the economy, U.S. senator John Kerry and the Democrats enjoyed an average twelve-point lead throughout the election year (46% to 34%).[14] And again public perceptions about the economy were filtered through partisan lenses, because 63% of Republicans but only 20% of Democrats judged the economy as thriving. That assessment also was held by no more than 31% of independents.[15]

In contrast, when asked about protecting the United States from terrorist attacks and the Bush administration response to the 9/11 attacks, 68% of the public, including the majority of Republicans, Democrats, and independents, supported President Bush. Fully 64% of those Americans polled considered him to be a strong leader during international crises.[16] As the 2004 election approached, Republicans increasingly stressed national security issues and Bush's success in protecting the country from additional terrorist attacks, but Democrats emphasized the direction of the economy and the war in Iraq. For the most part independents agreed with the Democratic position early in the election season but later became more concerned with terrorism and national security. By the time of election day the Bush campaign successfully convinced most voters to focus on national security issues rather than the state of the economy. In January 2004, 35% of respondents identified the economy as the most important national problem, but by September this number had declined to 26%.[17]

A mixed economic performance during the first two years of Bush's second term contributed to negative public perceptions about his handling of the economy. On the one hand, economic growth averaged a robust 3.5% and the unemployment rate stayed relatively low, around 4.8%.[18] On the other hand, soaring crude oil prices pushed the inflation rate up and, even worse, wages and salaries comprised the lowest share of gross domestic product (GDP) since 1947.[19] Perhaps public perceptions of the economy were clouded by the public's anxiety over such high-profile issues as the prolonged wars in Iraq and Afghanistan, government corruption, the ineffectual emergency response to Gulf Coast hurricane Katrina, and rising health care costs. Whatever the cause, the partisan gap between Republicans and Democrats on the state of the economy was a full 33%, and between Republicans and independents, it was 28%.[20] This economic polarization stands in stark contrast to the Clinton administration when positive views

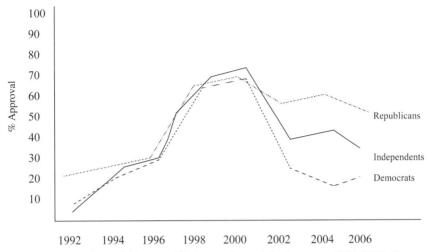

Figure 2.1.   Partisan Divide on Public Perceptions of the Economy, 1992–2006. *Source:* Pew Center for the People and the Press, "Economy Now Seen through Partisan Prism," (January 24, 2006), http://people-press.org/reports/display.php3?ReportID=268.

of the economy rose gradually at roughly the same rates among Democrats and Republicans.[21]

Perhaps the implications of "candidate-centered" presidential campaigns may help to explain the Democratic-Republican divide on perceptions of the economy. Since it is assumed that candidate-centeredness revolves around the personality of the candidates, not the political parties, then presumably party identification and party loyalties will erode in importance. But author James Campbell argues that presidential campaigns succeed in pulling disaffected partisans back into the partisan fold. And since the trailing candidate's party would have more disaffected partisans (which explains why that candidate was behind in the first place), this resurgence of party loyalty by previously disaffected partisans would have the effect of reducing the front-runner's lead.[22] Although other research suggests that partisanship is not a significant factor in voter choice, nonetheless, authors Geoffrey Evans and Robert Andersen still conclude that political party affiliation does influence public perceptions of the candidates.[23]

ECONOMIC CRISIS AND SUPPORT FOR THE SYSTEM

The support Americans display for the existing economic system is not only widespread but relatively deep. Although business contractions might undermine public support for capitalism—disillusionment causes people to consider economic alternatives—this scenario has not proven to be the case in the United States. Our most severe economic crisis was the Great Depression, when roughly one-fourth of the workforce was unemployed. Even in the face of this severe economic downturn, however, relatively few people rejected the basic structure and promise of the American political economy. A 1938 Roper Poll asked whether "the great age of economic opportunity and expansion in the U.S. is over or that American industry can create a comparable expansion and opportunity in the future." Only 13% chose the pessimistic response, whereas 72% saw hope in America's future. Even more significantly, only 5% of those polled believed that "the systems of private capitalism and democracy are breaking down, and we might as well accept the fact that sooner or later we shall have to have a new form of government."[24]

Since the 1930s, the country has enjoyed relative prosperity despite periodic downturns in the business cycle, but the nation's resolve was tested again during the 1970s when stagflation (slow growth with high inflation) was experienced. In 1975 the United States suffered its worst recession (up to that time) since the 1930s, but one study "showed an overwhelming majority of Americans still remain faithful to our economic system: 64 percent said they felt free enterprise was the best economic system . . . [and] only 10 percent thought socialism was a better economic system."[25]

An even more severe recession occurred during 1981–1982, and its effect on support for the system was evaluated by an ABC News/*Washington Post* survey that asked several times during the contraction if survey participants agreed or disagreed with the statement: "It is true in this country that if you work hard, eventually you will get ahead." The results showed a slight relationship between short-term economic conditions and support for the existing economic system, but the changes in opinion were not very large: 63% agreed with that statement in 1981, before the economic downturn hit, declining to 58% by the end of 1982 (when unemployment was at record levels), then rising to 66% in November 1983, after the long period of economic expansion had begun.[26] Today, 71% of Americans have expressed strong public support for the American free market system.[27]

PUBLIC OPINION AND ECONOMIC ISSUES

Attitudes toward Government

During the period when the Constitution was established, government was decried as an oppressive force, and the American colonists rebelled against "taxation without representation." This strain of antigovernment thinking has not dissipated, as politicians continue to run for office by running against big government. In his 1971 State of the Union address, President Nixon departed from his prepared text to add: "Let's face it. Most Americans today are simply fed up with government at all levels."[28] Ten years later attacks on government spending, federal waste, and high taxes were the mainstay of President Reagan's first inaugural address, as he declared, "Government is not the solution to our problem; government is the problem."[29]

The Gallup Poll has regularly asked: "Which of the following do you think will be a bigger threat to the country in the future—big business, big labor or big government?" For over two decades, through both Republican and Democratic presidencies, most Americans usually picked government as the biggest threat. The popular image of government is one staffed by overpaid and underworked bureaucrats who spend too much money and create too much red tape. A 1977 Gallup Poll found that most Americans believed that compared to private sector employees, federal employees are paid more and get more fringe benefits but do not work as hard. In addition, 67% thought there were too many federal employees.[30]

How much tax revenue do people think is wasted by government? A University of Michigan survey found that the percentage saying that "a lot" of money is wasted grew from 47% in 1964 to 78% in 1980 before dropping to 66% in 1982.[31] Similarly, Gallup asked, "Of every tax dollar that goes to the federal government in Washington, D.C., how many cents of each dollar would you say are wasted?" In 1978, 1979, and 1981 the estimate was that forty-eight cents of each federal dollar was wasted, a much higher figure than the estimates given for waste by state or local government.[32] In 1990 this assessment remained the same, according to Gallup, since the public again estimated waste at forty-eight cents for each federal dollar, compared to forty cents and thirty-five cents for states and localities, respectively.[33]

After 9/11, public attitudes toward the federal government temporarily improved. According to the National Election Study, 60% believed that the federal government "just about always" or "most of the time" can be trusted to do what is right for the country, the highest level in thirty years. Responses were different, however, about specific issues. While 68% said they trusted government "when it comes to handling national security and the war on terrorism," only 38% indicated the same level of trust "when it comes to handling the economy, health care, Social Security, and education."[34] By 2005 Americans were again expressing negative views of government, as favorable ratings for the federal government dropped from 59% in 2004 to 45% in 2005.[35]

Spending

Interestingly, there is a paradox in public attitudes toward government spending. When the public is asked about their feelings in the abstract,

Americans express antigovernment sentiments, but a very different picture emerges when the public is asked to evaluate specific federal programs. This paradox is characterized by authors Lloyd A. Free and Hadley Cantril as meaning that Americans are **"ideological conservatives"** but **"operational liberals."**[36] With few exceptions, the public wants spending for most domestic programs continued at the same rate or increased. The General Social Surveys taken between 1972 and 1994 showed that a majority believed the federal government spends "too little" money on the environment, health, crime, drug addiction, and education. Only three areas—space exploration, welfare, and foreign aid—found substantial numbers of Americans saying that "too much" money is spent.[37]

The most dramatic shift in priorities affected defense spending. Between 1973 and 1978 support for military spending increased, but by 1983 this trend was reversed. By 1990 support for higher defense spending had completely evaporated, returning to the low levels of the early 1970s. On the other hand, sharp fluctuations seem not to affect domestic programs, so perhaps most Americans do not want major cuts in those programs that support the quality of our everyday lives. If anything, the data show that most people want more spending. Between 1986 and 1990 there were noticeable increases in support for increased spending across an array of domestic policy areas—the environment, health, urban problems, crime, and drugs—despite the fact that the federal budget was registering historically high deficits.[38]

At the start of his second term, President Reagan proposed cuts in the middle-class entitlement programs, prompting several news organizations to poll the American people on that retrenchment in federal spending priorities.[39] They found that the majority of respondents backed retrenchment in two specific programs but refused to support cutbacks in eight others, including veterans' care, food stamps, and aid to families with dependent children. The public even voiced opposition to cuts in farm subsidies (71% opposed) and in the Small Business Administration (81% opposed) even though the vast majority of Americans do not benefit directly from those programs. This finding would imply tremendous resistance to cuts in middle-class programs.

According to the General Social Surveys taken between 1994 and 2000, federal spending on health care topped the list, with support for spending on education a strong second. Social Security also has gained a great deal of support, moving from tenth place in 1993 to third in 2000. Spending money to halt crime dropped consistently, but spending on space and foreign aid continued to be the least popular federal expenditures. As would be expected in the wake of 9/11, surveys taken in 2002 and 2004 showed that increased spending on defense along with health care and education were highly ranked by the public as important federal programs deserving of more funds.[40]

This cognitive paradox whereby people voice one opinion about an abstract value but then express another opinion when asked about specific examples is also reflected in public attitudes toward government performance. In the abstract, Americans give the federal government dismal performance ratings. When asked about specific popular programs, however, public support for the federal government improves. Thus, 74% in a 1998 survey believed that the government does a fair or poor job managing its programs, and 64% agreed that government programs are inefficient and wasteful. Yet 52% believed that the government does a good job providing Social Security and Medicare for the elderly as compared to only 20% who described those efforts as poor.[41]

If government performance failures undermine public trust, it is probably because Americans have high expectations with respect to the role that government should play in public life. In 1998, 72% believed that government should make sure that nobody goes without food, clothing, or shelter—the same percentage as in the 1960s. Many Americans also say that it is the federal government's responsibility to ensure economic prosperity (68%), conserve natural resources (52%), and provide health care for the elderly and the poor (46%).[42]

Looking at welfare, the level of public support varies across social groups and according to the specific program. It is well documented that Americans are hostile to "welfare" programs but that generalized hostility may hide more than it reveals about public attitudes.[43] Despite that sentiment, Americans express support for maintaining and expanding most social and economic programs. Most people believe that government must shield individuals from poverty and take actions to enlarge the scope of economic opportunity.[44] Nonetheless, arrayed against these positive sentiments is a powerful and widely held belief that affirms the widespread existence of economic opportunity in America and the primacy of individual achievement.[45] This disconnect between abstract values and programmatic specifics is undoubtedly related to the fact that most Americans are not well-informed about social policy.[46]

If the public is ill informed about public policy, then their judgments can be influenced by the specifics of each program, the beneficiaries of those programs, and the way the mass media portrays those programs and beneficiaries. The media coverage frames and directs public attention to groups, dimensions of poverty, and aspects of economic policy.[47] In doing so, they shape the beliefs that people hold about poverty and the welfare state. Thus, Americans are more likely to support federal programs that they believe assist "deserving" beneficiaries, that preserve personal responsibility, and that promote or reward work. Therefore large majorities favor maintaining or increased spending for social insurance programs—Social Security and Medicare—and for education.[48] There is less public support for public assistance programs, such as public housing, or for policies aimed at income redistribution.[49] Public assistance programs such as Medicaid will elicit majority support if they are viewed as temporary programs designed to promote job opportunities and reward hard work. The commitment to improve employment opportunities, for example, has resulted in widespread preference among liberals and conservatives for making health care, child care, transportation, and job training the cornerstone of economic and social reforms.[50] The greatest degree of public support, however, is reserved for programs that offer universal benefits.

Taxes

In 1947 Gallup began asking Americans if they considered the amount of federal income tax they pay as too high, about right, or too low. The question has since become a standard barometer of tax satisfaction. However, the United States faces a policy dilemma on taxes because, despite these antitax feelings, revenues are necessary in order to fund all the programs that the public apparently wants. Surveys consistently indicate that people feel that taxes are too high, and they are particularly unhappy about federal income taxes. This sentiment was reflected in Harris surveys taken between 1969 and 1980 showing that the number of people who believed they "reached the breaking point on the amount of taxes" ranged from 57% to 72%.[51] Polls commissioned by the Advisory Commission on Intergovernmental Relations (the ACIR has since been terminated) allowed respondents to evaluate the federal income tax relative to other kinds of taxes, and into the 1980s most people called the federal income tax "the worst tax, that is the least fair."[52]

Despite public discontent, no sustained outcry has mobilized the electorate on the tax issue. One analysis of election issues from 1960 to 1980 found that no more than 3.1% (in 1964) cited taxes as "the most important problem facing the country." Polls from 1991 and 1992 showed comparable figures of 3% and 6% respectively.[53] However, the number of people indicating that they would vote against a party or a candidate based upon the tax issue rose appreciably from 7.0% in 1976 to 14.8% in 1980.[54] The increased political salience of this issue reached a climax at that time because, as author Jack Citrin observed, "by late 1978 the confluence of anxiety over future economic conditions, anger about high taxes, and skepticism about the performance of government had created a climate of opinion that strongly favors cuts in public expenditures."[55]

Concern over taxes undoubtedly encouraged Ronald Reagan in his 1980 presidential campaign to formally pledge that, as president, he would work to cut federal income taxes by 30%. Once elected, Reagan proceeded to vigorously (and successfully) push through Congress a bill to cut marginal federal income tax rates by 25%. Although this was a very popular move, this enactment dramatically reduced projected revenues, which produced large deficits for the next seventeen years. During the 1984 presidential election, Reagan's Democratic opponent, Walter Mondale, declared that he would raise taxes to close the budget deficit, but Reagan reiterated his opposition to tax increases. Mondale's declaration is believed to have contributed to his overwhelming defeat, and Democratic leaders have avoided taking similar stands ever since.

During the 1988 presidential campaign, Vice President George H. W. Bush reiterated the Reagan position in a dramatic way, by declaring: **"Read my lips. No new taxes."** But in 1990 President Bush broke this pledge by agreeing to a bipartisan budget compromise that involved both tax increases and spending cuts. Although it is not clear what effect this action had on Bush's overall popularity, his reversal on taxes caused him severe difficulties with conservative Republicans and fueled a 1992 primary challenge from conservative Pat Buchanan.[56] By 1992 the public had begun to name the Democratic Party as more trustworthy in holding down taxes, a historic reversal brought on by pledges by several Democratic candidates to cut taxes.[57]

Regardless of which party or candidate reaps a temporary political advantage from the tax issue, the public's attitude toward taxes clearly complicates efforts to address budget deficits. The public favors balanced budgets, more spending in a variety of areas, and also lower taxes.[58] Since 1981 the lowest priority for elected officials is the policy option that is least transparent to the voters—a balanced federal budget. In 1993 President Clinton proposed a deficit reduction program that combined increased taxes with spending cuts, a measure that did not garner one Republican vote in either the Senate or the House. The 1993 program, along with another deficit reduction measure in 1997, helped to produce budget surpluses between 1998 and 2001.

Even after three tax cuts, huge budget deficits, and the mounting costs of warfare in Afghanistan and Iraq under President George W. Bush, most Americans still believe they are paying too much in taxes. In 2005, 55% claimed the amount of federal taxes they pay is too high compared to 33% who believed the amount is about right. This represents a five-point increase since 2004, though below the average response since 1947 (58%). Also 77% believed that the tax code "needs major changes" or "needs to be completely overhauled," and another 54% said that they were willing to forego some deductions and credits to simplify the tax system.[59]

Taxes are paid in return for government services, so how does the public assess this trade-off? In 2005 two-thirds rated the value they personally received from the federal government for their taxes as poor or fair, with only 3% saying excellent. Though it falls short of an endorsement of federal services, this represents an improvement from 1993 when 80% of the public said the value received for their taxes was fair or poor. Moreover, 34% favored cutting both taxes and services, while just 13% favored expanding services and boosting taxes; 30% favored no change.[60]

Budgetary Politics

Americans traditionally express the belief that the federal budget should be balanced. In 1936, in the midst of the Great Depression, a Gallup Poll asked whether it was "necessary at this time to balance the budget and start reducing the national debt?" Despite the economic collapse, 70% agreed.[61] A heightened awareness of government spending during the 1970s led Gallup to ask: "How important do you think it is to balance the Federal budget—very important, fairly important, or not so important?" Even though Keynesian deficit financing was the dominant paradigm in macroeconomic policy making, 60% of the public said "very important" in 1973.[62] By 1990 this grew to 70%.[63] Public opinion even hardened to the point that there was overwhelming support for a constitutional amendment to achieve a balanced budget.[64]

However, federal budgets routinely show expenditures exceeding revenues. Even President Reagan, a rhetorical advocate of government frugality, oversaw deficits in excess of $100 billion almost every year he served. This sorry fiscal record might lead one to conclude that America's historic devotion to balanced budgets is either dead or empty rhetoric. And that is precisely the argument made by economists James Buchanan and Richard Wagner, who argue that the Keynesian new economics undermined the "fiscal constitution" which once existed in the United States: "Once democratically elected politicians, and behind them their constituents in the voting public, were finally convinced that budget balance carried little or no weight, what was there left to restrain the ever-present spending pressures."[65]

During Clinton's second term, the public debate shifted to how excess revenues resulting from three consecutive years of budget surpluses would be allocated. A broad consensus emerged to (1) not commit the surplus to any single use, (2) devote more resources to protecting Social Security and Medicare, (3) reduce the national debt, (4) increase spending on education, and (5) cut taxes. The public generally wanted the surplus devoted to multiple goals, especially to strengthen Social Security and Medicare, and less than 5% of respondents favored allocating the surplus to one objective. Republicans favored tax cuts while Democrats and independents supported additional funding for Social Security and Medicare. During the 2000 campaign, Vice President Albert Gore proposed modest tax cuts along with new initiatives to shore up Social Security, Medicare, and education, whereas George W. Bush proposed tax cuts that he claimed would not endanger his other priorities.[66]

Even today, while most Americans regard deficit reduction as a worthwhile goal, the budget deficit simply does not have the same resonance that it did during much of the 1990s. Currently the deficit is barely an asterisk on the public's list of most important problems. In January 2006 the Iraq War was cited as the biggest problem facing the nation (23%), followed by the economy (11%). Just 2% of Americans pointed to the budget deficit, a number that has remained stable throughout Bush's presidency. Although the public disapproves of deficits, research shows that voters do not express significant support for any measure designed to reduce the red ink and, in addition, have little understanding of how deficits and debt impact the economy and fiscal policy.[67] Several factors probably contribute to the contemporary lack of concern about deficits. Key events, notably the 9/11 terrorist attacks, a long and costly War on Terrorism, and devastating natural disasters cause the public to support new government spending with little concern for its impact on the debt. Also during the mid-1990s, the Republican Party campaigned on reducing the budget deficit, but Democrats approached that issue somewhat defensively. Independent presidential candidate H. Ross Perot attacked the budget deficit in his 1992 campaign, and the Republican Party tried to mobilize public support behind a balanced budget during the 1994 midterm congressional elections. Those assaults on federal authority had an impact. In July 1994 two-thirds of Americans agreed that "the Government is almost always wasteful and inefficient" and 47% agreed with that sentiment in 2000.[68]

Now the tables have turned, as 62% of Democrats and 56% of independents mention reducing the budget deficit as a top priority for the president and Congress compared to just 45% of Republicans.[69] Even when the deficit was viewed as a major national crisis, the public showed little appetite for budget austerity. One option for increasing revenues, which 63% supported, was to roll back the Bush tax cuts for people with incomes over $200,000. But support for this policy also varied along partisan lines, with 81% of Democrats and 64% of independents but only 48% of Republicans in favor.[70]

International Trade

Since the end of the Cold War, a political culture has emerged in the United States that might be termed "**pragmatic internationalism**." Americans seem generally supportive of free trade and strong U.S. global leadership. Opinion polls indicate that Americans tend to view economic rather than military power as the most significant measure of global strength. In 1998, 63% of Americans expressed that view in one survey.[71] However, the public is also acutely aware that free trade has both positive and negative implications for their everyday lives. As pragmatic internationalists, the public tends to largely conceptualize U.S. foreign policy as an instrument for achieving personal economic security. Overall public interest in foreign relations and knowledge about other countries declined from 36% in 1990 to 29% in 1998. In 1999, 39% of Americans believed that they were somewhat knowledgeable about trade policy as compared to 44% reporting little or no knowledge. A 1998 survey found that competition from low wage countries was considered a critical threat by 42% of respondents. And among the most serious public concerns was "protecting American jobs," with 80% of Americans mentioning it as a high priority presidential policy goal.[72]

Over the last decades American economic dependence on the global economy has gained saliency in the public mind. During this period, the United States has experienced persistent and sizable trade deficits, cumulating in a trade debt for 2005 that represents 26% of gross domestic product. From 1998 to 2004 imports rose by 63% while exports increased only 24%. As a consequence, the U.S. trade deficit increased from $209.6 billion in 1998 to roughly $636 billion in 2004. This expansion represents more than a doubling of the trade debt as a share of GDP—from 2.4% to 5.4%.[73]

It is commonly assumed that international economic issues have limited visibility for most Americans, although highly publicized policies will surface on the public agenda. In a 1994 poll, only 5% could identify the North American Free Trade Agreement (NAFTA), which was enacted in 1993, as compared to 44% who identified a crime bill. Moreover, public attitudes toward NAFTA have changed erratically. In 1991, 70% of Americans believed that NAFTA would benefit the United States but support sharply dropped in late 1992 to 46%.[74] That shift likely can be attributed to the strident attacks against NAFTA by independent presidential candidate H. Ross Perot during his 1992 presidential campaign. The impact of NAFTA and free trade engendered even more uncertainty during 1992 and 1993. In addition to the anti-NAFTA bashing of H. Ross Perot and public worries over competition with low-wage workers in Mexico, public anxiety may have been fueled by the "jobless recovery" following the 1990 recession. By November 1993 only 41% supported NAFTA and 40% were opposed. During the years 1994–1997, most Americans expressed the belief that NAFTA hurt domestic U.S. interests. A plurality, ranging from 35% to 48%, felt that NAFTA had "more of a negative impact" on the United States than not.[75]

Being supportive of NAFTA is analogous to being generally supportive of free trade. In 1999, for example, 69% of Americans believed that imports help poorer families reduce their cost of living. There also has been broad public support for reducing tariffs. In 1997, 79% believed that reducing trade barriers was an important way to increase U.S. economic strength.[76] As a consequence, NAFTA has been seen in a slightly more positive light in recent years. A 2004 poll found that 44% believed that NAFTA benefited "consumers like me" and 51% thought it was good for our "standard of living."[77] It is probably the case that rising public support for NAFTA affected public attitudes toward the Central American Free Trade Agreement (CAFTA). CAFTA was supported by 50% of respondents in June 2005, with only 39% opposed.[78]

ECONOMICS AND PRESIDENTIAL POPULARITY

The public approval rating of presidential performance is one of the most anxiously watched political barometers. For Washingtonians a president's approval rating is a bellwether of popular support, because the president is the only political leader whom the entire electorate can hold responsible for the performance of government and the national well-being.[79] Also the presumption is that presidents with higher public standing are better able to exert their influence over the policy agenda and to gain congressional support for their legislative initiatives. Over the course of their four-year term, however, most presidents suffer a gradual decline in their public approval, thereby forcing presidents to contend with the eventual loss of public support.[80] One explanation for this temporal decline in presidential popularity is due to what John Mueller calls a "coalition of minorities" dynamic, which means that a president is not elected with majority support for specific policies but rather builds a majority coalition from a multitude of minority interests. As the president makes controversial policy decisions during his term, those decisions will invariably alienate certain groups within his electoral coalition.[81]

Politicians have always assumed that bad economic times hurt incumbent presidents and their parties, and recently this relationship has been given systematic attention by scholars. To measure presidential popularity, researchers use a Gallup Poll question asked at least once each month since the late 1930s: "Do you approve or disapprove of the way _____ is handling his job as president?" The percentage approving is the presidential **approval rating**. Survey respondents are forced to choose between "approve" or "disapprove" (unless they answer "don't know"). Its regular use through nearly seven decades is testimony that Gallup views this question as a valid and reliable "thermostatic" measure of public opinion toward the president.[82] It is assumed that whatever variables shift presidential approval upward or downward will affect all individuals or perhaps groups the same way over time.[83] The scholarly research has sought to answer two basic questions: (1) Do economic conditions have a positive or negative impact on presidential popularity? and (2) Which economic conditions are the most important?

Presidential approval can be an important political resource with respect to economic issues. The odds of enacting the presidential economic policy agenda are stronger under conditions of high public approval.[84] And presidents who enjoy high levels of public approval are more likely to be reelected.[85] For President Reagan, much of his popular support was based on his likeable personality and leadership qualities rather than on policy as such. Known as the "teflon president," Reagan weathered high inflation, rising unemployment, and a recession before he was able to preside over a strong economy that further increased his approval ratings in his second term. The steep descent in presidential approval during George H. W. Bush's administration shows how fragile presidential popularity can be when the public attention shifts from national security (the Persian Gulf War) to focus on difficult economic times.[86] President Clinton's popularity derived from positive assessments of economic prosperity despite widespread discontent with his personal failings. President George W. Bush has been much less popular than President Clinton, largely because Bush's popularity has been shaped more by national security issues than the strength of the economy. And unlike his immediate predecessors, Bush and his economic stewardship have been evaluated by a partisan lens, with Republicans generally approving but Democrats disapproving.[87]

Inflation versus Unemployment

That the economy has an impact on presidential approval has been accepted wisdom for some time.[88] As political scientist V. O. Key argued many years ago, a "rational" public would punish incumbents for poor economic performance.[89] But the story is not quite as simple as Key suggested, since we need to know if Americans are judging the economy from the standpoint of their own situation or from the perspective of the entire country.[90] Thus, it is entirely rational for an individual to care about his or her own finances while, at the same time, believing that the overall economy is a better indicator of presidential economic competence. However people choose to evaluate the economy, to do so requires information. If citizens assess their own economic self-interest, they may look at the economic condition of people in their own economic class, or compare their current income against previous years, or consider the impact of price increases on their cost of living. Even though personal income may grow slowly, as witnessed during the second Bush administration, still Americans might take solace in knowing that the booming real estate market meant that they had more equity in their own homes. To make personal assessments of economic conditions is a very complex calculation.

To judge overall economic performance is even more complicated. But the task is made easier because the federal government periodically publishes well-publicized indicators of economic performance. Two closely watched indicators are inflation rates and unemployment rates, both of which can influence presidential approval. Increases in inflation or unemployment are expected to lower presidential approval ratings, while decreases in either rate are likely to boost a president's popularity.[91] But inflation and unemployment may have differing impacts on a white-collar versus a blue-collar household. As Douglas Hibbs et al. explain, changes in the unemployment rate matter most for lower income groups who are most sensitive to economic downturns and recessions.[92] For those in the middle-class, concerns about prices and the cost of living may be more important. Of the two indicators, inflation is most likely a stronger influence on presidential popularity than unemployment. While increases in the jobless rate would have a severe impact on certain segments of the population (blue-collar workers), rising prices adversely affect virtually all people.

Not all the research on this point is conclusive, however. Samuel Kernell found that unemployment rates were not a strong determinant of presidential approval.[93] Research by Kristen Monroe did find that prolonged inflation hurts presidential approval ratings. "While there is some immediate response to inflation, the major response is a cumulative one. This suggests that the public does not blame the president for brief periods of inflation but will hold him responsible for sustained inflation. The public is not easily distracted by sudden declines in inflation which immediately precede an election."[94] Monroe agrees with Kernell insofar as she found no relationship between unemployment and presidential popularity, and another study by Michael B. MacKuen offers added confirmation that inflation was the more important influence on presidential approval.[95]

In sum, unemployment likely undermines presidential popularity among blue-collar workers, because they are more sensitive to the downturns in the business cycle, whereas white-collar employees and retirees are more alert to the inflation rate. Douglas Hibbs et al. emphasize this partisan difference in economic outlooks: "The political approval indices for Democrats and Independents were far more responsive to movements in unemployment and the real income growth rate, and less responsive to movements in the inflation rate, than is the approval index of Republican partisans."[96] Figure 2.2 shows the ebb and flow of presidential popularity along with unemployment and inflation.

Public Expectations

Bad economic conditions hurt the president much more than a good economy helps him. This finding implies that public opinion expects prosperity, or at least the absence of recession, to be the norm. The debate over this question was begun by Gerald H. Kramer's 1971 analysis of congressional elections from 1896 to 1964, which showed that "a 10% decrease in per capita real personal income would cost the incumbent administration

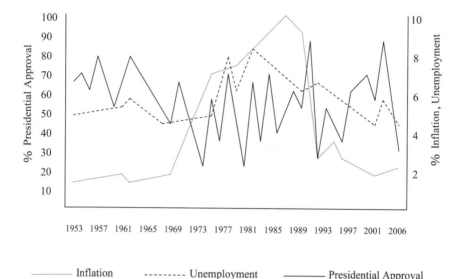

.... Inflation   -------- Unemployment   ———— Presidential Approval

Figure 2.2. Inflation, Unemployment, and Presidential Popularity, 1953–2006. *Sources:* Data for public approval of the president is adapted from the Gallup Poll and compiled by Gerhard Peters of the American Presidency Project, http://www.presidency.ucsb .edu/data/popularity.php; U.S. Department of Labor, Bureau of Labor Statistics, "Employment Status of the Civilian Non-institutional Population, 1940 to 2006"; U.S. Department of Labor, Bureau of Labor Statistics, "Consumer Price Index," ftp://ftp.bls.gov/pub/special .requests/cpi/cpiai.txt.

4 to 5 per cent of the congressional vote, other things being equal."[97] A later study by Edward R. Tufte found comparable results, although other researchers have doubted the validity of Kramer's findings.[98] One of the best studies to date, by Howard S. Bloom and H. Douglas Price, distinguishes between economic downturns and upturns by examining the congressional vote during the period 1896–1970. They wished to determine the likely impact of changes in real per capita income on partisan voting, and their model verifies an asymmetrical version of Kramer's "throw the rascals out" thesis. That is, "economic downturns reduce the vote for the party of the incumbent President, but economic upturns have no corresponding effect."[99] Both Republicans and Democrats were affected by this phenomenon. Later research by Robert S. Erikson and Gregory B. Markus also found a connection between economic conditions—especially changes in personal income—and success of the incumbent party's presidential candidate.[100]

The previous research assumes that voters are reacting to existing or previous economic conditions. When voters evaluate an incumbent seeking reelection according to his or her performance in office, that approach is called **retrospective voting**. But a very different assumption guided the research of Professors MacKuen, Erikson, and James A. Stimson, who argue that it is the expectations of *future* economic conditions, rather than existing conditions, that lead to changes in presidential approval. Of course actual economic conditions are not irrelevant, because they are the factual developments from which individuals make assessments about future economic conditions. However, the most significant conclusion from the MacKuen, Erikson, and Stimson analysis is that the public is forward-looking—or prospective—in its evaluations rather than being retrospective or backward-looking.[101]

ELECTIONS AND THE ECONOMY

The state of the American economy and public perceptions of how presidential leadership has managed the economy are important factors that help determine how citizens vote. Voters are influenced to a large extent by the overall performance of the economy. Voters do not solicit official economic reports to gauge economic performance but rather gauge the economy through news reports and their own personal experiences. Retrospective evaluations of the economy are an important influence on how citizens vote for president. Tough economic times, indicated by recession or poor economic growth, may cause the electorate to lose confidence in the incumbent president or his political party.

The Political Business Cycle

A research question that has received a great deal of scholarly attention is whether the president is motivated by reelection to manipulate the economy in order to bolster the odds of his winning office. Initially this question was raised by economist William Nordhaus in 1975 based on an econometric model he developed for nine Western democracies.[102] Economic fluctuations in the United States gave strong support for his hypothesis that unemployment falls prior to a presidential election but rises thereafter. This relationship was further tested by Edward Tufte, who documented that U.S. policy makers tend to increase benefits to constituents before elections and delay tax increases until afterward. These decisions are precisely the kind of behavior that would be expected if presidents had sought to manipulate the economy for electoral gain.[103] This thesis is known as the **political business cycle**, and its powerful implication is that the economy can be manipulated by policy makers in such a way as to peak right before regularly scheduled elections.

The historical record seems to point to a connection between economic performance and presidential victories, but the fundamental question is "what causes what?"[104] Many scholars who have given this research question systematic analysis in the years since have failed to uncover empirical support for the Nordhaus-Tufte political business cycle hypothesis.[105] A summary review of the research on the political business cycle thesis led James Alt and Alec Chrystal to argue that the weight of scholarly evidence is strongly against that interpretation:

> No one could read the political business cycle literature without being struck by the lack of supporting evidence. There must be cases where politicians have undertaken electorally motivated interventions. It is difficult to imagine politicians not exploiting some extra information or other resources. But while this clearly happens, and happens particularly clearly in some cases, such cycles may be trivial in comparison with other economic fluctuations.[106]

Their point is that political manipulations probably will only have a marginal impact on the business cycle. It would take a massive infusion of federal spending to really impact the economy in ways that would guarantee a president's reelection.

The Election-Year Economy

A strong election-year economy will likely provide an incumbent president or an incumbent party's presidential candidate with the opportunity to make a strong appeal to voters for continuity in government. Incumbent presidents enjoy several advantages. One involves general risk avoidance, meaning that voters may prefer continuity to change and therefore may prefer an experienced president rather than an untested challenger. Politically capable and effective incumbents are able to wage a so-called **Rose Garden strategy**, whereby presidents blur the distinction between the incumbent and the office by appearing to be above the "political fray." Incumbents can direct debates to issues on which they have an electoral edge.[107] Therefore incumbent presidents are usually reelected.

Since Truman, ten presidential elections (1948, 1956, 1964, 1972, 1976, 1980, 1984, 1992, 1996, and 2004) have pitted an incumbent against a challenger. Incumbents won reelection seven times, whereas challengers won only three elections (1976, 1980, and 1992). However, candidates representing a party seeking more than two consecutive terms seem to have no better prospects than opposition party candidates, and their margins of victory tend to be extremely close. John Kennedy defeated Richard Nixon 49.8% to 49.6% in 1960; Nixon defeated Hubert Humphrey 43.4% to 42.7% in 1968, and George W. Bush defeated Al Gore in the Electoral College 271–266 in 2000, though he lost the popular vote 47.9% to 48.4%.[108]

The state of the economy in presidential election years is a strong indicator of the magnitude of electoral success. Political scientist James Campbell argues that a useful indicator is economic growth, as measured by the percentage increase in the GDP in the election year, and especially in the second quarter (April to June). Campbell says that election-year economies fall into "strong" (more than 4% growth), "moderate" (2.5% to 4% growth), and "poor" (less than 2.5% growth) categories of performance.[109]

It has been rare for an incumbent president or the incumbent party's presidential candidate to lose when election-year economies grow in excess of 4%. In 1968, after President Johnson opted not to seek reelection, Vice President Hubert Humphrey became the Democratic presidential candidate but was edged out by Republican candidate Richard Nixon by only 0.7%, even though economic growth was a strong 4.8%. Also in 1976 President Gerald Ford campaigned at a time when the economy exhibited a strong growth rate of 5.3%. But Ford was also running for reelection while carrying the weight of the Watergate scandal and his controversial pardon of Nixon. Nonetheless, Ford was defeated by Jimmy Carter by only 2.1%.[110]

During weak election-year economies, voters will most likely reject the incumbent president. Negative economic growth of -0.2% in 1980 contributed to President Jimmy Carter's devastating loss to Ronald Reagan. Although economic growth expanded by a solid 3.3% under President George H. W. Bush, most of that growth occurred toward the end of the year, so the public did not perceive economic improvement until a year later. As a result, President Bush was unable to translate this positive economic growth into sufficient political capital on election day, and he was defeated by Arkansas governor Bill Clinton. Clearly, the voters blamed Bush for the recession, which produced a paltry 1.9% growth rate in 1990 and negative growth rate of -0.2% in 1991. The only candidate to win reelection during a weak election-year economy was President Eisenhower in 1956. Economic growth was barely 1.9%, but a rebound in the second quarter helped Eisenhower offset that dismal first quarter.[111]

In election years when there is moderate economic growth, the incumbent party candidate or the incumbent president is about as likely to win as to lose. An interesting case is the 2000 presidential election in which incumbent party candidate Vice President Al Gore was defeated in the Electoral College by Texas governor George W. Bush. This was an odd outcome, however, since Gore won the popular vote by over six hundred thousand votes. While the 2000 election-year economy posted moderately high economic growth (3.8%) buttressed by low unemployment (4.0%), low inflation (2.5%), rising budget surpluses ($69 billion), and President Clinton's relatively high popularity (60%), Gore still lost the contested election.[112] What happened? The accepted wisdom is that popular approval of an administration mainly reflects its management of the economy, and the 2000 campaign was waged during a time of peace and prosperity. Throughout 2000, Clinton told Democrats to be optimistic and take credit for the economy, but Gore failed to champion the message of Democratic prosperity. Put simply, the economy did not add to Gore's prospects, because Gore was apprehensive about associating himself too closely with Clinton given Clinton's personal scandal and impeachment charges.

The 2000 election demonstrated that the state of the economy does not necessarily determine electoral outcomes. Rather the economy is one important issue that shapes the campaign strategies utilized by presidential candidates to make appeals consistent with the general perceptions of the electorate.[113] While President Clinton was widely regarded by the voters as an effective chief executive, his political and moral character was questionable. Thus, Gore's ability to embrace Clinton-era prosperity was politically undercut.[114] Gore had calculated that a tie to Clinton the man would diminish his prospects more than a tie to the Clinton economy would enhance them. Gore denied himself access to the strong economy as a political issue and, in doing so, allowed Governor Bush to shape voter perceptions of the state of the economy.

Although voters would not have accorded Al Gore full credit for the strong growth, as Clinton's successor he was well positioned to receive a substantial amount of political credit. The decision by Al Gore not to conduct a retrospective campaign that emphasized the Clinton administration's accomplishments but, instead, a prospective campaign with an antibusiness emphasis was a totally unanticipated development in the 2000 campaign. It may have been a mistake given the historical record. During the elections of 1980–1996, among voters who approved of the incumbent president's management of the economy, 88% voted for the incumbent or the incumbent party candidate. But in 2000, only 67% of those who approved of Clinton's handling of the economy voted for Gore.[115]

In early 2001 waning economic optimism was one of the first problems confronting President Bush. At that time there was a marked increase in the number of Americans who expected to be worse off financially; 27% expressed that view in January 2001 compared to about 10% in January 1999. Not surprisingly, therefore, the state of the economy gained importance in the eyes of the public, with 81% saying that keeping the economy strong should be the top priority for Bush and the Congress.[116]

The 2004 reelection campaign by President George W. Bush was waged with an economy that showed moderately strong growth. During the first six months of 2004, growth was 3.8%, which was slightly weaker than eight presidential elections since 1952 but stronger than six others. Bush's economic numbers in the first six months of 2004 were not much worse than the economic growth rate under Clinton during the first six months of 1996 (4.6%), the year he faced reelection. Nonetheless, the 2004 election was much closer, with Bush defeating Kerry by 2.5% as compared to Clinton's 1996 defeat of Bob Dole by 8.5%. Major economic drags in Bush's first term were the 1.3% increase in the unemployment rate coupled with a 1.5% decline in wages and salaries. Yet, overall the annual growth rate for 1996 (3.8%) and 2004 (3.1%) was not so dissimilar from the 3.3% growth rate recorded in 1992, when President George H. W. Bush was defeated by Clinton. The key difference, unfortunately for the senior Bush, was that economic recovery came too late in the year.[117]

The difference was that perceptions of the economy were filtered through more of a partisan lens in 2004 than in 1996. In 1996 Dole was forced to run a character-focused campaign since he could not challenge Clinton on the economy. As a result, Republicans and Democrats converged in their opinions of how well the economy was performing in 1996. Exit polls revealed that 55% thought the economy was good or excellent, including 42% of Dole voters and 70% of Clinton voters, whereas only 10% of Dole voters and 4% of Clinton voters thought the economy was in poor shape.[118]

Polling during the 2004 presidential election showed that 59% of the voters disapproved of President Bush's management of the economy. Voters also had a negative picture of the economy, with 45% perceiving that economic performance had worsened over the year and only 24% thinking that it improved. Overall voter perceptions of the economy were overwhelmingly negative by November 2004—52% to 39%.[119] Still, of the people who thought the economy was in good shape, 87% voted for Bush in 2004.[120] In total, 47% of Americans expected the economy to improve, but that figure masked a deep partisan divide between Bush and Kerry supporters. Exit polls showed that only 13% of Kerry voters expected the economy to improve as compared with 80% of Bush voters, and 33% of Kerry voters thought the economy was in poor shape, compared to only 2% of Bush voters.[121]

The economy in 2004, however, was overshadowed by other considerations. Bush's response to the 9/11 attacks and his counterterrorism measures generated high presidential approval ratings on national security that dominated voter perceptions of the economy. By the time the election was held, the most pressing concern among voters was terrorism and, to Bush's advantage, the Republican Party had framed the election as a referendum on Bush's counterterrorism policies. Eighty-five percent of voters were worried there could be another major terrorist attack inside the United States, but 54% of Bush voters believed that the United States was safer because of the president.[122] Furthermore, Bush used military force to promote regime change in both Afghanistan and Iraq, which sparked a measure of patriotism that enabled the president to strengthen his national security credentials long enough to secure reelection. When asked about the most important problem facing America, 45% of the voters cited terrorism and another 28% referred to the War in Iraq, but only 18% mentioned the economy.[123]

Midterm Elections and the Economy

According to pollster Andrew Kohut, history suggests that "presidents whose approval ratings tumble end up costing their party seats in the midterm elections."[124] In some of the recent midterm elections, if not all, adverse economic conditions contributed to the decline in presidential popularity. During 1954, amid a recession with -0.4% GDP and a surge in unemployment to 5.5% from 2.9% the previous year, President Eisenhower's approval rating fell from 73% to 57% and Republicans lost control of both houses of Congress in the 1954 midterm elections.[125] The Watergate scandal was a primary cause for Democratic victories in the 1974 midterm elections, but they also coincided with the Arab oil embargo and a period of unusually high inflation. In contrast, positive economic conditions may bolster presidential popularity and allow the political party in office to do better than expected in the midterms. The best example was 1998 when, despite the impeachment charges, President Clinton enjoyed widespread public approval at 65% due entirely to the booming economy, and the Democrats beat the historical odds by gaining five seats in the House of Representatives. In 2006, political scientists predicted that Republicans would lose seats in the House and Senate based on multiple-variable statistical models, which included President Bush's depressed approval rating.[126]

Those models were accurate. The Democrats took control of the House for the first time since the 1994 Republican revolution and of the Senate for the first time since 2002. Throughout 2006 it seemed that a majority of voters were willing to support a candidate in the congressional elections who opposed President Bush's economic program. A Gallup Poll in early 2006 found a 46% to 34% plurality, saying the country would be better off if Democrats rather than Republicans controlled Congress. That same poll found that 67% disapproved of the way the Republican Congress was handling the economy, compared with 48% in January 2005.[127] Such discontent has not been this high since 1993–1994. The 2006 data points to a desire for change almost as strong as the one that began building in 1993, one year before the historic 1994 election that gave Republicans control of Congress.

Although GDP was very strong in the first quarter of 2006 (5.6%), economic growth slowed significantly in the second quarter to 2.5%.[128] Indications of a slowing economy have come amid high budget deficits, rising energy and gasoline prices, and stagnating wages and salaries, although unemployment has remained relatively low. Even more problematic has been that retail sales have dropped considerably and the housing market has been cooling. However, President Bush's low approval of 39% in August 2006 spelled trouble for Republican control of Congress as only 29% of the public rated the economy as good or excellent and 61% believed that the economy was getting worse. Moreover, public perceptions of the economy remained deeply split along partisan lines, with Republicans most positive at 60%, Democrats most negative at 20%, and independents at 28% being more negative than positive.[129] The rating by independents in March was thirteen points lower than in January.

Most troubling for President Bush was the decreased level of support that he got from conservative voters upset with the rapid increase in government spending. According to the Office of Management and Budget, spending increased from 18.4% of GDP in 2000 to 20.3% in 2005 before slightly dropping to roughly 20% in 2006. Although much of the spending increase has been devoted to national security and the new Medicare drug benefit, domestic discretionary spending and spending on pork-barrel projects also have risen.[130] In May 2006 Gallup reported a 13% drop in Republican support for Bush, because they saw out-of-control spending as an abandonment of conservative principles. Moreover, the Pew Research Center for the People and the Press found that Bush suffered a 24% drop in his approval among voters who backed him in 2004, from 92% in January 2005 to 68% in May 2006.[131]

Exit polls from the 2006 midterm congressional elections showed that 42% of voters cited corruption as a very important issue that affected their choices at the polls, followed by terrorism at 40%, the economy at 39%, and the Iraq War at 37%. On the economy, 72% of voters perceived the economy as either extremely important or very important compared to the 16% who believed the economy was somewhat important or not important. Although exit polling revealed that 49% contended that the economy was in excellent or good condition, 50% believed the economy was in fair or poor condition. This divide was reflected in partisan perception. Seventy percent of Republicans, but only 28% of Democrats believed that the economy was in excellent or good shape, while 77% of Democrats and 21% of Republicans saw the economy in poor shape.[132]

Overall, however, rising opposition to the Iraq War appears to have been the driving force behind the Democratic successes in the 2006 midterm elections, and the shifting allegiance of independent voters was a key factor in that electoral outcome. Voters who said national issues were most important tended to support the Democratic candidate by a 52% to 44% margin, even though economic conditions were not among the most important national issues. On the other hand, there was a strong correlation between voter attitudes toward the Iraq War and their party preference in the congressional races. In fact, 81% of voters who believed that the Iraq War was a mistake voted Democratic, whereas 83% of those who believed the war was not a mistake voted Republican.[133]

KEY TERMS

approval rating
general problem-solving approach
going public strategy
ideological conservatives
marginals strategy
operational liberals
political business cycle
pragmatic internationalism
"Read my lips. No new taxes."
retrospective voting
Rose Garden strategy

ADDITIONAL READINGS

Alesina, Alberto and Howard Rosenthal. *Partisan Politics, Divided Government, and the Economy*. Cambridge MA: Cambridge University Press, 1996. Because Democrats and Republicans have polarized preferences on policy, middle-of-the-road voters seek to balance the president by reinforcing in Congress the party not holding the White House, thus leading to relatively moderate policies.

Beard, Charles A. *An Economic Interpretation of the Constitution*. New York: Macmillan, 1913. A classic work that argues that the Founding Fathers wrote the Constitution to protect their economic interests.

Hibbs, Douglas A. Jr. *The American Political Economy: Macroeconomics and Electoral Politics*. Cambridge, MA: Harvard University Press, 1987. A comprehensive analysis of the relationship between partisan politics and macroeconomic policy in the postwar era.

Keech, William R. *Economic Politics: The Costs of Democracy*. Cambridge, UK: Cambridge University Press, 1995. Looks at the effects of democratic institutions for economic performance and concludes that the "costs" of democracy are bearable and do not produce inferior economic policies.

Kiewiet, D. Roderick. *Macroeconomics and Micropolitics: The Electoral Effects of Economic Issues*. Chicago: University of Chicago Press, 1983. Concludes that voters evaluate political incumbents based on their perceptions of national (not personal) economic conditions.

McClosky, Herbert and John Zaller. *The American Ethos: Public Attitudes toward Capitalism and Democracy*. Cambridge, MA: Harvard University Press, 1985. A definitive empirical study of how the general public and political elites assess economic and democratic values.

McDonald, Forrest. *We the People: The Economic Origins of the Constitution*. Chicago: University of Chicago Press, 1958. This study refutes the Charles Beard thesis by arguing that the Founding Fathers did not profit economically from the Constitution.

Tufte, Edward R. *Political Control of the Economy*. Princeton, NJ: Princeton University Press, 1978. This book provoked much scholarly debate by arguing that a political business cycle affects macroeconomic policy making in the United States.

NOTES

1. Samuel Kernell, *Going Public: New Strategies of Presidential Leadership* (Washington, DC: Congressional Quarterly, 1997).

2. Theodore J. Lowi, *End of Liberalism: The Second Republic of the United States* (New York: Norton, 1979).

3. Kernell, *Going Public*, 2.

4. Kernell, *Going Public*, 230–237.

5. Kernell, *Going Public*, 237–241.

6. Alberto Alesina and Howard Rosenthal, *Partisan Politics, Divided Government, and the Economy* (Cambridge: Cambridge University Press, 1995); Douglas A. Hibbs Jr., R. Douglas Rivers, and Nicholas Vasilatos, "The Dynamics of Political Support for American Presidents among Occupational and Partisan Groups," *American Journal of Political Science* 26 (1982): 312–332; John Frendreis and Raymond Tatalovich, "Accuracy and Bias in Macroeconomic Forecasting by the Administration, the CBO, and the Federal Reserve Board," *Polity* 32 (2000): 623–632; Douglas A. Hibbs Jr., "Political Parties and Macroeconomic Policy," *American Political Science Review* 71 (1977):1467–1497; and Edward Tuft, *Political Control of the Economy* (New Jersey: Princeton University Press, 1978).

7. Paul Samuelson, "Some Dilemmas of Economic Policy," *Challenge* 20 (1977): 30–31.

8. Douglas A. Hibbs Jr., *The American Political Economy: Macroeconomics and Electoral Politics* (Cambridge, MA: Harvard University Press, 1987), 183–184.

9. Tom W. Smith, "America's Most Important Problem—A Trend Analysis, 1946–1976," *Public Opinion Quarterly* 44 (Summer 1980): 164–180.

10. Smith, "America's Most Important Problem," 169–170.

11. For a compilation of this Gallup data, see: http://www.albany.edu/sourcebook/pdf/t212006.pdf. Also see George H. Gallup, *Gallup Report*, Report No. 226, 17; Report No. 235, 20, 21; Report No. 252, 28, 29; Report No. 260, 6, 7; Report No. 277, 6, 7; Report No. 285, 4, 5; Report No. 290, 6 (Princeton, NJ: Gallup Poll); George Gallup Jr., *The Gallup Poll*, March 14, 1991, 2, 3; April 3, 1992, 1, 2; January 30, 1997, 2 (Princeton, NJ: Gallup Poll); George Gallup Jr., *Gallup Poll Monthly*, No. 298, 14; No. 340, 43; No. 352, 7; No. 396, 34 (Princeton, NJ: Gallup Poll); and *The Gallup Poll* [Online]: http://www.gallup.com/poll/releases/pr990528.asp [July 20,1999]; http://www.gallup.com/poll/releases/pr000331.asp [March 31, 2000]; and http://www.gallup.com/poll/releases/pr010205.asp [February 5, 2001].

12. See http://www.albany.edu/sourcebook/pdf/t212006.pdf; http://www.gallup.com/poll/releases/pr020320.asp [March 27, 2002]; and http://www.gallup.com/poll/releases/pr030213.asp [February 19, 2003].

13. Pew Research Center for the People and the Press, "Americans Thinking about Iraq, but Focused on the Economy," (October 10, 2002). Also see Pew, "Bush Confronts State of Economic Unease," (January 23, 2003).

14. CBS News/*New York Times*, "Poll: Bush's Approval Sinking," (January 17, 2004); Pew, "Economy Now Seen through Partisan Prism," (January 24, 2006), http://people-press.org/reports/display.php3?ReportID=268; and Pew, "Public Faults Bush on Economy," (August 12, 2004).

15. Pew, "Economy Now Seen."

16. Pew, "Economy Now Seen."

17. See http://www.albany.edu/sourcebook/pdf/t212006.pdf; http://www.gallup.com/poll [June 28, 2004]; and Pew, "Bush Margin Widens Again, Despite Vulnerabilities," (September 28, 2004).

18. U.S. Department of Commerce, Bureau of Economic Analysis, "GDP and Other Major NIPA Series, 1929–2006"; U.S. Department of Labor, Bureau of Labor Statistics, "Employment Status of the Civilian Non-institutional Population, 1940 to 2006."

19. Steven Greenhouse and David Leonhardt, "Real Wages Fail to Match a Rise in Productivity," *New York Times*, August 28, 2006; U.S. Department of Commerce, Bureau of Economic Analysis, "GDP and Other Major NIPA Series, 1929–2006"; U.S. Department of Labor, Bureau of Labor Statistics, "Consumer Price Index," ftp://ftp.bls.gov/pub/special.requests/cpi/cpiai.txt; U.S. Department of Labor, Bureau of Labor Statistics, "Employment Status of the Civilian Non-institutional Population, 1940 to 2006"; Sue Kirchhoff, "Energy Costs Help Elevate Inflation Rate," *USA Today*, May 26, 2006; and Edmund Andrews, "Bernanke Talks Tough on Inflation," *New York Times*, June 6, 2006.

20. Pew, "Economy Now Seen"; Pew, "Economic Pessimism Grows, Gas Prices Pinch: Independents Back Democrats on Most Issues, Congressional Midterms," (September 15, 2005).

See also Andrew Kohut, "Midterm Match-up: Partisan Tide vs. Safe Seats," Pew Research Center for the People and the Press (February 13, 2006), http://people/press.org/commentary/display.php3?AnalysisID=127.

21. William Schneider, "Bush's New Low: For Presidents, a 40 Percent Approval Rating Means Trouble," *Atlantic Monthly* (September 6, 2005): 22; Seymour Martin Lipset, "Public Opinion and the Clinton Legacy," *AEI Studies in Public Opinion*, American Enterprise Institute (January 2000), http://www.aeipoliticalcorner.org/KB%20Articles/psbowman3.pdf.

22. James E. Campbell, "Nomination Politics, Party Unity, and Presidential Elections," in *Understanding the Presidency*, ed. James Pfiffner and Roger H. Davidson (New York: Longman, 2004).

23. In Michael S. Lewis-Beck, "Does Economics Still Matter? Econometrics and the Vote," *Journal of Politics* 68 (2006): 208–212 and Geoffrey Evans and Robert Andersen, "The Political Conditioning of Economic Perceptions," *Journal of Politics* 68 (2006): 194–207.

24. Reported in *Public Opinion* 7 (February–March 1984): 28.

25. David Caplovitz, "Making Ends Meet: How Families Cope with Inflation and Recession," *Public Opinion* 1 (May–June 1978): 53.

26. National Opinion Research Center, "General Social Surveys," (July 1984), 87–92.

27. Program on International Policy Attitudes, "20 Nation Poll Finds Strong Global Consensus: Support for Free Market System, But also More Regulation of

Large Companies," (January 11, 2006), http://www.worldpublicopinion.org/pipa/articles/btglobalizationtradera/154.php?nid=&id=&pnt=154&lb=btgl.

28. Richard Nixon, State of the Union address (January 22, 1971).

29. Ronald Reagan, inaugural address (January 20, 1981).

30. American Institute of Public Opinion, *Public Opinion 1972–1977*, vol. 2 (Wilmington, DE: Scholarly Resources, 1978): 1111–1114.

31. Arthur Miller, "Is Confidence Rebounding?" *Public Opinion* 6 (June–July 1983): 20.

32. *Gallup Report*, No. 185 (February 1981), 44–45.

33. ABC News/*Washington Post* survey (September 7–11, 1990).

34. Brian J. Gaines, "Where's the Rally? Approval and Trust of the President, Cabinet, Congress, and Government after 9/11," *PS: Political Science and Politics* 35, no. 3 (September 2002): 531–536; Tom G. Palmer and John Samples, "Limited Government after 9-11," *CATO Policy Report* (March–April 2002): 12–14; and Timothy Cook and Brian Gronke, "Trust, Distrust, Lack of Confidence: New Evidence of Public Opinion Toward Government and Institutions from 2002" (paper presented at the annual meeting of the Southern Political Science Association, Savannah, GA, 2002.)

35. Pew, "Public Sours on Government and Business," (October 25, 2005).

36. Lloyd A. Free and Hadley Cantril, *The Political Beliefs of Americans* (New York: Simon & Schuster, l968), chap. 3.

37. See "1972–1994 General Social Survey Cumulative File" at http://ist-socrates .berkeley.edu:7502/GSS/HTMLBOOK/gssf01.html.

38. See "1972–1994 General Social Survey Cumulative File."

39. These various surveys are reported in *Public Opinion* (February–March, 1985): 19–20.

40. James A. Davis, Tom W. Smith, and Peter V. Marsden, *General Social Survey, 1972–2004*, release 2 (Chicago, IL: National Opinion Research Center, 2005 [producer]; Storrs, CT: Roper Center for Public Opinion Research, 2006).

41. Pew, "Deconstructing Distrust: How Americans View Government," (March 10, 1998).

42. Pew, "Deconstructing Distrust."

43. Martin Gilens, *Why Americans Hate Welfare: Race, Media, and the Politics of Anti-Poverty Policy* (Chicago: University of Chicago Press, 2000).

44. Lawrence Bobo and Ryan A. Smith, "Anti-Poverty Policy, Affirmative Action, and Racial Attitudes," in *Confronting Poverty: Prescriptions for Change*, ed. S. Danziger, G. Sandefur, and D. Weinberg (Cambridge: Harvard University Press and the Russell Sage Foundation, 1994).

45. James R. Kluegel and Eliot R. Smith, *Beliefs about Inequality: Americans' Views of What Is and What Ought to Be* (New York: Aldine de Gruyter, 1986).

46. R. Kent Weaver, *Ending Welfare as We Know It.* (Washington, DC: Brookings, 2000).

47. Shanto Iyengar, "Framing Responsibility for Political Issues: The Case of Poverty." *Political Behavior* 12 (1990): 19–40.

48. Gilens, *Why Americans Hate Welfare.*

49. Yeheskel Hasenfeld and Jane Rafferty, "The Determinants of Public Attitudes Toward the Welfare State," *Social Forces* 67 (1989): 1027–1048.

50. Fay Lomax Cook and Edith J. Barrett, *Support for the American Welfare State: The Views of Congress and the Public* (New York: Columbia University Press, 1992); Stanley Feldman and Marco R. Steenbergen, "The Humanitarian Foundation for Public Support for Social Welfare," *American Journal of Political Science* 45, no. 3 (2001): 658–677; and Gilens, *Why Americans Hate Welfare*.

51. Reported in Everett Carll Ladd Jr., "The Polls: Taxing and Spending," *Public Opinion Quarterly* 43 (Spring 1979): 127.

52. The 1979 results are discussed in Ladd, "The Polls: Taxing and Spending," 23. Similar results for 1988 are reported in "Opinion Roundup," *Public Opinion* (March–April 1989): 23.

53. *Gallup Monthly* (April 1992), 30.

54. Susan B. Hansen, *The Politics of Taxation* (New York: Praeger Special Studies, 1983), 176–177.

55. Jack Citrin, "Do People Want Something for Nothing: Public Opinion on Taxes and Government Spending," *National Tax Journal* 32, no. 2 (June 1979): 116.

56. See Stuart Rothenberg, "Politics '92: Taxes Are No Longer Just a GOP Issue," *The Public Perspective: A Roper Center Review of Public Opinion and Polling* 3 (March–April 1992): 25–27.

57. Rothenberg, "Politics '92."

58. To further complicate the picture, survey majorities also indicate that they would favor tax increases for specific purposes, such as antidrug policies or programs to extend health benefits to those who cannot afford them. See "What Americans Are Saying about Taxes," *Public Opinion* (March–April 1989): 21.

59. Tax Foundation, "2006 Annual Survey of U.S. Attitudes of Taxes and Wealth," no. 141 (April 2006), http://www.taxfoundation.org/files/sr141.pdf.

60. Tax Foundation, "2006 Annual Survey of U.S. Attitudes of Taxes and Wealth."

61. George H. Gallup, *Gallup Poll: Public Opinion 1935–1971*, vol. 1 (New York: Random House, 1972), 12.

62. *Gallup Report*, no. 188 (May 1981), 31. Various polls on this question are reported in Paul E. Peterson, "The New Politics of Deficits," in John E. Chubb and Paul E. Peterson, eds., *The New Direction in American Politics* (Washington, DC: Brookings, 1985), 387.

63. *Gallup Poll Monthly*, no. 296 (May 1990), 27.

64. *Gallup Report*, no. 281 (1979–1989), 3.

65. James Buchanan and Richard Wagner, *Democracy in Deficit* (New York: Academic, 1977), 50.

66. Harris Poll, "On the Federal Budget Surplus, Voters Sound Balanced Note While Pundits and Politicians Are Sharply Divided," (March 2, 2000), http://www.harrisinteractive.com/news/allnewsbydate.asp?NewsID=67.

67. Guido Tabellini and Alberto Alesina, "Voting on the Budget Deficit," *American Economic Review* 80 (March 1990): 37–49.

68. Tabellini and Alesina, "Voting on the Budget Deficit."

69. Pew, "Do Deficits Matter Anymore? Apparently Not to the Public," (March 14, 2006), http://pewresearch.org/obdeck/?ObDeckID=10.

70. Harris Poll, "On the Federal Budget Surplus."

71. John E. Rielly, ed., *American Public Opinion and U.S. Foreign Policy 1999* (Chicago Council on Foreign Relations, 1999), http://www.ccfr.org.

72. Rielly, *American Public Opinion and U.S. Foreign Policy 1999* and John E. Rielly, ed., *American Public Opinion and U.S. Foreign Policy 1995* (Chicago Council on Foreign Relations, 1995), http://www.ccfr.org.

73. U.S. Department of Commerce, Bureau of Economic Analysis, "U.S. Net International Investment Position, 2005," news release, http://www.bea.gov/bea/newsrel/intinvnewsrelease.htm; TradeStats Express website, http://tse.export .gov/NTDMap.aspx?UniqueURL=ybvlr155rnbz5eihiuyfesqo-2005-12-8-15-50-36.

74. Gallup, "NAFTA and the Public," (October 11, 1992).

75. NBC News/*Wall Street Journal*, "NAFTA," (July 26, 1994 to July 28, 1997).

76. Ipsos-Reid, "Thinking about NAFTA," Ipsos-Reid/Cook Political Report (November 2002).

77. Program on International Policy Attitudes (PIPA), "NAFTA: Good or Bad," (January 2004).

78. PIPA, "Thinking about CAFTA," (June 2005).

79. Theodore Lowi, *The Personal President* (Ithaca, NY: Cornell University Press, 1985).

80. Lowi, *The Personal President.*

81. Robert K. Goidel, Todd G. Shields, and Mark Peffley, "Priming Theory and RAS Models: Toward an Integrated Perspective of Media Influence," *American Politics Quarterly* 35 (1997): 287–318; Mark J. Hetherington, "The Media's Role in Forming Voters' National Economic Evaluations in 1992," *American Journal of Political Science* 41 (1996): 372–395; and Richard Nadeau, Richard G. Niemi, David P. Fan, and Timothy Amato, "Elite Economic Forecasts, Economic News, Mass Economic Judgements, and Presidential Approval," *Journal of Politics* 61 (1999): 109–135.

82. James A. Stimson, Michael B. MacKuen, and Robert S. Erikson, "Dynamic Representation," *American Political Science Review* 89 (1995): 543–565.

83. Hibbs et al., "The Dynamics of Political Support for American Presidents," 312–332; Hibbs, *The American Political Economy*; and Kent Tedin, "Change and Stability in Presidential Popularity at the Individual Level," *Public Opinion Quarterly* 40 (1986): 1–21.

84. Paul Brace and Barbara Hinckley, *Follow the Leader: Opinion Polls and the Modern Presidents* (New York: Basic, 1992); Richard A. Brody and Simon Jackman, "The Lewinsky Affair and Popular Support for President Clinton" (paper presented at the annual meeting of the Midwest Political Science Association, Chicago, IL, April 17, 1999); Kernell, *Going Public*; and Gary King and Lyn Ragsdale, *The Elusive Executive* (Washington, DC: Congressional Quarterly Press, 1988).

85. George C. Edwards, *The Public Presidency* (New York: St. Martin's, 1983) and John Mueller, "Presidential Popularity from Truman to Johnson," *American Political Science Review* 64, no. 1 (March 1970): 18–34.

86. Brace and Hinckley, *Follow the Leader*, chap. 7.

87. Paul Gronke, "Policies, Prototypes, and Presidential Approval" (paper presented at the annual meeting of the American Political Science Association, Atlanta, GA, 1999).

88. Gerald H. Kramer, "Short-Term Fluctuations in U.S. Voter Behavior, 1896–1964," *American Political Science Review* 65 (1971): 131–143 and Edward R. Tufte, *Political Control of the Economy* (New Jersey: Princeton University Press, 1978).

89. V. O. Key, *The Responsible Electorate: Rationality in Presidential Voting* (Cambridge, MA: Belknap, 1966).

90. Alesina and Rosenthal, *Partisan Politics*; Alberto Alesina and Howard Rosenthal, "Partisan Cycles in Congressional Elections and the Macroeconomy," *American Political Science Review* 83 (1989): 373–398; and Hibbs, *The American Political Economy*.

91. Nathaniel Beck, "Comparing Dynamic Specifications: The Case of Presidential Approval," *Political Analysis* (1991): 51–87 and Michael B. MacKuen, Robert S. Erickson, and James A. Stimson, "Peasants or Bankers? The American Electorate and the U.S. Economy," *American Political Science Review* 86 (1992): 597–611.

92. Hibbs et al., "The Dynamics of Political Support for American Presidents," 312–332.

93. See Henry C. Kenski, "The Impact of Economic Conditions on Presidential Popularity," *Journal of Politics* 39 (August 1977): 764–773; "The Impact of Unemployment on Presidential Popularity from Eisenhower to Nixon," *Presidential Studies Quarterly* 7 (Spring–Summer, 1977): 114–126; "Inflation and Presidential Popularity," *Public Opinion Quarterly* 41 (Spring 1977): 86–90; Samuel Kernell, "Explaining Presidential Popularity: How Ad Hoc Theorizing, Misplaced Emphasis, and Insufficient Care in Measuring One's Variables Refuted Common Sense and Led Conventional Wisdom Down the Path of Anomalies," *American Political Science Review* 72 (June 1978): 506–522.

94. Kristen R. Monroe, "Inflation and Presidential Popularity," *Presidential Studies Quarterly* 9 (Summer 1979): 339. A critique of this methodology which assumes a "lag" structure in public opinion is found in Helmut Norpoth and Thom Yantek, "Macroeconomic Conditions and Fluctuations of Presidential Popularity: The Question of Lagged Effects," *American Journal of Political Science* 27 (November 1983): 785–807.

95. Kristen R. Monroe, "Economic Influences on Presidential Popularity," *Public Opinion Quarterly* 42 (Fall 1978): 360–369 and Michael B. MacKuen, "Political Drama, Economic Conditions, and the Dynamics of Presidential Popularity," *American Journal of Political Science* 27 (May 1983): 191.

96. Hibbs et al., "The Dynamics of Political Support for American Presidents," 328.

97. Gerald H. Kramer, "Short-Term Fluctuations in U.S. Voting Behavior, 1896–1964," *American Political Science Review* 65 (March 1971): 141.

98. Edward R. Tufte, "Determinants of the Outcomes of Midterm Congressional Elections," *American Political Science Review* 69 (September 1975): 812–826 and George Stigler, "Micropolitics and Macroeconomics: General Economic Conditions and National Elections," *American Economic Review* 63 (May 1973): 160–167. Also see Francisco Arcelus and Allan H. Meltzer, "The Effect of Aggregate Economic Variables on Congressional Elections," *American Political Science Review* 69 (December 1975): 1232–1239.

99. Howard S. Bloom and H. Douglas Price, "Voter Response to Short-Run Economic Conditions: The Asymmetric Effect of Prosperity and Recession," *American Political Science Review* 69 (December 1975): 1240–1254.

100. Robert S. Erikson, "Economic Conditions and the Presidential Vote," *American Political Science Review* 83 (1989): 567–573 and Gregory B. Markus, "The Im-

pact of Personal and National Economic Conditions on Presidential Voting, 1956–1988," *American Journal of Political Science* 36 (1992): 829–834.

101. MacKuen et al., "Peasants or Bankers?" 597–611.

102. William H. Nordhaus, "The Political Business Cycle," *Review of Economic Studies* 42 (April 1975): 169–189.

103. Edward R. Tufte, *Political Control of the Economy* (Princeton: Princeton University Press, 1978), chap. 2.

104. This point is also discussed in a recent paper by William R. Keech and G. Patrick Lynch, "Business Cycles and Presidential Elections in the United States: Another Look at Key and Downs on Retrospective Voting" (paper presented at the annual meeting of the American Political Science Association, Chicago, IL, September 3–6, 1992).

105. See, for example, John T. Woolley, "Partisan Manipulation of the Economy: Another Look at Monetary Policy with Moving Regression," *Journal of Politics* 50 (May 1988) 336:n2.

106. James Alt and Alec Chrystal, *Political Economics* (Berkeley: University of California Press, 1983), 125.

107. See James E. Campbell, *The American Campaign: U.S. Presidential Elections and the National Vote* (College Station: Texas A&M University Press, 2000) and Lee Sigelman, "Presidential Popularity and Presidential Elections," *Public Opinion* 43 (1979): 532–534.

108. Alice McGillivray, Richard Scammon, and Rhodes Cook, *America at the Polls 1920–2004* (Washington, DC: CQ Press, 2005).

109. Campbell, *The American Campaign* and James C. Campbell, "Forecasting the Presidential Vote in 2004: Placing Preference Polls in Context," *PS: Political Science & Politics* (2004): 763–767.

110. McGillivray et al., *America at the Polls.*

111. U.S. Department of Commerce, Bureau of Economic Analysis, "GDP and Other Major NIPA Series, 1929–2006," tables 1–4.

112. McGillivray et al., *America at the Polls;* U.S. Department of Commerce, Bureau of Economic Analysis, "GDP and Other Major NIPA Series, 1929–2006"; U.S. Department of Labor, Bureau of Labor Statistics, "Consumer Price Index," ftp://ftp.bls.gov/pub/special.requests/cpi/cpiai.txt; U.S. Department of Labor, Bureau of Labor Statistics, "Employment Status of the Civilian Non-institutional Population, 1940 to 2006."

113. Andrew Gelman and Gary King, "Why Are American Presidential Election Campaign Polls So Variable When Votes Are So Predictable?" *British Journal of Political Science* 23 (1993): 409–452.

114. David Remnick, "The Wilderness Campaign," *New Yorker* (September 14, 2004).

115. Campbell, *The American Campaign.*

116. Pew, "Clinton Nostalgia Sets in, Bush Reaction Mixed," (January 11, 2001).

117. All statistics in this paragraph are cited in the following sources: McGillivray et al., *America at the Polls;* U.S. Department of Commerce, Bureau of Economic Analysis, "GDP and Other Major NIPA Series, 1929–2006"; U.S. Department of Labor, Bureau of Labor Statistics, "Consumer Price Index," ftp://ftp.bls.gov/pub/special.requests/cpi/cpiai.txt; U.S. Department of Labor, Bureau of Labor Statistics, "Employment Status of the Civilian Non-institutional Population, 1940 to 2006."

118. For a compilation of exit polling data from the 1996 presidential election, see http://www.cnn.com/ALLPOLITICS/1996/elections/natl.exit.poll/index1.html.

119. American National Election Studies, *2004 National Election Study* [dataset] (Ann Arbor, MI: American National Election Studies, Center for Political Studies, 2004), http://www.electionstudies.org. For a compilation of exit polling data from the 2004 presidential election, see http://www.cnn.com/ELECTION/2004/pages/results/states/US/P/00/epolls.0.html; NBC News/*Wall Street Journal*, "Pessimism Not Sticking to President" (May 6, 2004), http://www.msnbc.msn.com/id/4907503; John Harwood, "Despite Recovery, Bush Is Facing Doubts on the Economy, Poll Finds," *Wall Street Journal*, May 6, 2004; and Gallup Poll, "Bush Approval on Iraq, Economy and Terrorism at Low Points," (May 6, 2004).

120. Kevin Drum, "Political Animal: Bush and the Economy," *Washington Monthly* (November 8, 2004), http://www.washingtonmonthly.com/archives/individual/2004_11/005123.php.

121. American National Election Studies, *2004 National Election Study*; NBC News/*Wall Street Journal*, "Pessimism Not Sticking to President" (May 6, 2004), http://www.msnbc.msn.com/id/4907503; and Harwood, "Despite Recovery."

122. Paul Abramson, John Aldrich, Jill Rickershauser, and David Rohde, "Fear in the Voting Booth: The 2004 Presidential Election" (paper presented at the meeting "Wartime Election of 2004" at Ohio State University, Columbus, OH, January 12–15, 2006).

123. Paul Abramson, John H. Aldrich, and David W. Rohde, *Change and Continuity in the 2004 Elections* (Washington, DC: Congressional Quarterly Press, 2006); NBC News/*Wall Street Journal*, "Pessimism Not Sticking to President" (May 6, 2004), http://www.msnbc.msn.com/id/4907503; and ABC News/*Washington Post*, "Pessimism on Iraq Grows" (May 8, 2004).

124. Kohut, "Midterm Match-up."

125. Kohut, "Midterm Match-up"; U.S. Department of Commerce, Bureau of Economic Analysis, "GDP and Other Major NIPA Series, 1929–2006"; U.S. Department of Labor, "Employment Status."

126. American Political Science Association, "October 17, 2006: Political Scientists' Models Predict Democratic Takeover of House of Representatives," press release, http://www.apsanet.org/content_35328.cfm.

127. Kohut, "Midterm Match-up."

128. U.S. Department of Commerce, Bureau of Economic Analysis, "Gross Domestic Product," news release, BEA-06-33, July 28, 2006.

129. Gallup, "Republicans Alone in Viewing the Economy as in Good Shape: Independents and Democrats most Negative," (March 21, 2006).

130. Bruce Bartlett, "He Spends Too Much to be One of Us," *Los Angeles Times*, March 12, 2006.

131. Polling data is referenced in Jim VandeHei and Peter Baker, "Bush, GOP Congress Losing Core Supporters," *Washington Post*, May 11, 2006.

132. See http://www.cnn.com/ELECTION/2006/pages/results/states/US/H/00/epolls.0.html.

133. Gallup, "Democrats' Election Strength Evident Across Voter Segments," *Gallup Poll*, November 9, 2006, http://www.galluppoll.com/content/?ci=25399.

3

Economic Policy Making in the Executive Branch

Our discussion thus far may seem to imply that there is a single, coherent economic policy that is shaped according to a clear underlying theory, such as classical or Keynesian economics. In reality there is no single economic policy but rather a myriad of separate policy decisions which individually and collectively influence the economy. There is no single institutional actor with either the authority or the policy tools to develop and implement one coherent economic policy.

Although authority is fragmented and the policy vision is multifaceted, most economic policy is formulated and implemented by the president, his advisers, key agencies and departments, and Congress. The organizational capacity to formulate a coherent economic policy, therefore, is contingent on many factors, not the least being the president's goals and policy making style. This chapter examines how the president formulates macroeconomic policy. We begin with a discussion of the presidential economic advisory system. We then describe the presidential economic policy making role and examine the major decision makers who assist the chief executive. Further removed from direct presidential control are the independent regulatory bodies, notably the Federal Reserve Board. We close the chapter by asking this: Who—if anyone—controls and coordinates economic policy making within the executive branch?

THE ECONOMIC ADVISORY SYSTEM

Since presidents confront public expectations and legislative demands that the economy remain prosperous, they must formulate increasingly complex policies that depend upon expertise and learned advice. Policy advice is supplied by a myriad of executive branch actors who have become known as the **economic subpresidency**. It, explains Professor James Anderson "assist[s] the president, at his level, by providing him with assistance in defining problems and alternatives, in making and communicating decisions, and in securing acceptance and compliance with them."[1] Each president structures an advisory system according to his personal needs and style of governance. In no arrangement do all advisers enjoy equal access to the White House or carry equal influence. Presidents usually recruit staff members and agency heads who share his priorities and philosophy, but personal rivalries and jurisdictional squabbles seem endemic to bureaucratic politics.

President Franklin D. Roosevelt relied upon a personalized, informal, and ad hoc advisory system to cope with the Great Depression and to formulate his New Deal. He recruited experts in public administration, finance and economics, and corporate law from universities and big business, a group that became known as his "Brain Trust." At that time, the chief executive was not given a full-time professional staff, so most of these aides were "loaned" to FDR by various agencies where they were formally employed. The use of academic thinkers was an innovation unique to FDR, and it began a new tradition within the executive branch. As author Hugh S. Norton observes: "No present-day candidate would dream of entering the [presidential] race on a serious basis or preparing to take office without position papers on various topics. Both prior to the nomination and in the interregnum after an election, his advisers remain active, drawing up programs and proposals designed to solve 'the economic problem.'"[2]

Franklin Roosevelt was a transitional figure. His impromptu advisory network could not survive the growing and more complex demands of the contemporary federal government. Once the New Deal was established, FDR understood how much government had grown, and he appointed a Committee on Administrative Management to give him advice. Its 1937 report concluded that "The President needs help. His immediate staff assistance is entirely inadequate. He should be given a small number of executive assistants who would be his direct aides in dealing with the managerial agencies and administrative departments."[3] With this recommendation in hand, Roosevelt created the **Executive Office of the President (EOP)** in 1939 to house the administrative staff agencies for the White House. The White House Office was the first agency in the EOP; it was joined by the Bureau of the Budget (BOB), which President Roosevelt transferred from the Treasury Department.

Economic policy advisers currently serve the president in several units within the EOP, namely the Council of Economic Advisers (CEA), the Office of Management and Budget (OMB), and the Office of the U.S. Trade Representative (USTR). The secretary of the treasury and the Treasury Department also oversee domestic and international finances. The Federal Reserve Board (the Fed) is an independent agency that regulates the banking system and manipulates the money supply through monetary policy. It will be discussed in chapter 5.

Council of Economic Advisers

The **Council of Economic Advisers (CEA)**, established by the Employment Act of 1946, was mandated to provide the president with professional analysis and advice on the development and implementation of domestic and international economic policies. Subject to Senate confirmation, three members of the CEA, one being the chairman, are appointed by the president. The CEA has a support staff of roughly twenty-five to thirty economists (mostly senior university economists, statisticians, and graduate students) who are appointed for their expertise and experience. Since 1946, the CEA has given priority to policies that stimulate economic growth and promote competition and free markets. In recent decades the CEA has been a consistent advocate of global economic policies that foster free and open trade. Former CEA members took note that much of their energy and staff time focused on issues of microeconomics, often providing arguments against ill-conceived proposals from the bureaucracy or members of Congress. According to a report by Clinton's CEA: "The Council's mission within the Executive Office of the President is unique: it serves as a tenacious advocate for policies that facilitate the workings of the market and that emphasize the importance of incentives, efficiency, productivity, and long-term growth. The Council has also been important in helping to weed out proposals that are ill-advised or unworkable, proposals that cannot be supported by the existing economic data, and proposals that could have damaging consequences for the economy."[4]

The CEA has little operational responsibility and no statutory authority to conduct policy. Although CEAs in both Democratic and Republican administrations generally agree on microeconomics (the value of free markets, for example) as well as the benefits of international trade, they have different perspectives on fiscal policy. Republican presidents, especially Ronald Reagan and George W. Bush, staffed the CEA with monetarist economists who generally favored lower tax rates in order to encourage private consumption and investment. Democratic presidents prefer to staff the CEA with Keynesian economists, who generally believe that such tax effects are small. Thus, Clinton's CEA vigorously defended the increased marginal tax rates imposed by the 1993 deficit reduction measure. It argued, as did previous Democratic CEAs, that an increase in marginal tax rates would not adversely affect economic growth, because tax hikes on upper-income groups would not reduce aggregate demand (spending) by the middle class and workers.

The CEA has been the preserve of academic economists, as illustrated by the recruitment of CEA chairmen. Since 1946, all CEA chairs have been economists and most have had previous experience at universities or research institutes. There is high turnover among the CEA membership as well as its professional staff, and wholesale personnel changes almost always accompany a new incumbent in the White House. A disadvantage of this "in-and-out" recruitment pattern is that, unlike other federal agencies with permanent staff, the CEA lacks an "institutional memory." Its members lack experience in dealing with other federal agencies or the time needed to develop personal networks with key decision makers. This deficiency is ameliorated somewhat when the CEA chair has some previous experience on the council.

Table 3.1. Chairs of the Council of Economic Advisers, 1946–2006

President	Chair	Tenure	From
Truman	Edwin Nourse	1946–1950	Brookings Institution
	Leon Keyserling	1950–1953	CEA vice-chair
Eisenhower	Arthur F. Burns	1953–1956	Columbia University
	Raymond T. Saulnier	1956–1961	Barnard College
Kennedy	Walter Heller	1961–1963	University of Minnesota
Johnson	Walter Heller	1963–1964	University of Minnesota
	Gardner Ackley	1964–1968	University of Michigan
	Arthur M. Okun	1968–1969	Yale University
Nixon	Paul W. McCracken	1969–1971	University of Michigan
	Herbert Stein	1972–1974	University of Virginia
Ford	Herbert Stein	1974	University of Virginia
	Alan Greenspan	1974–1977	Townsend–Greenspan and Co.
Carter	Charles Schultze	1977–1981	Brookings Institution
Reagan	Murray Weidenbaum	1981–1982	Washington University
	Martin Feldstein	1982–1984	Harvard University
	Beryl Sprinkel	1985–1989	Harris Bank/Chicago
G. H. W. Bush	Michael J. Boskin	1989–1993	Stanford University
Clinton	Laura D. Tyson	1993–1994	UC Berkeley
	Joseph E. Stiglitz	1994–1997	Columbia University
	Janet E. Yellen	1997–1999	UC Berkeley
	Martin Baily	1999–2001	University of Maryland
G. W. Bush	Glenn Hubbard	2001–2003	Columbia University
	N. Gregory Mankiw	2003–2005	Harvard University
	Harvey Rosen	2005	Princeton University
	Ben Bernanke	2005–2006	Princeton University
	Edward Lazear	2006–	Stanford University

The CEA serves the president in four capacities, according to Walter Heller, who chaired the CEA under President Kennedy.[5] First, the CEA is supposed to provide the best data, analysis, and forecasts which state-of-the-art economics will allow. There is a daily stream of memoranda to the president and meetings, when needed, to keep him abreast of the latest economic developments. Second, the CEA advises the president on how best to achieve his macroeconomic goals. There is no assurance that the president will heed that advice, but CEA efforts at persuasion are better than not trying at all. As Gardner Ackley, CEA chair under Lyndon Johnson, noted: "If his economic adviser refrains from advice on the gut questions of policy, the President should and will get another one."[6] Third, the council also tries to "educate" the president about macroeconomic theory. On this score, both Heller and Ackley had modest success. Heller finally convinced JFK that tax cuts were needed to avoid recession, and Ackley prevailed upon LBJ to seek an income tax surcharge to curb inflationary pressures. Finally, the CEA must translate the jargon of economics into a language the president understands and can use. There is no place on the CEA for an abstract thinker. CEA influence depends entirely upon the technical expertise possessed by its professionals. Its advice can be forthright, because the CEA is beholden to nobody except the chief executive. As Walter Heller put it: "The President knows that the Council's expertise is fully at his command, undiluted by the commitments to particular programs and particular interest groups that . . . tend to build up in the various line agencies of government."[7]

However, tensions have developed between the president and the CEA chairman since its inception. President Truman hamstrung the CEA by appointing three people (Edwin Nourse as chair; Leon Keyserling as vice-chair; and John D. Clark) who held disparate views concerning the CEA's purpose. Nourse wanted the CEA to provide impartial economic advice and, therefore, he thought it inappropriate for CEA members to testify before congressional hearings. Nourse saw his role as giving Truman all sides to an economic problem and their consequences.[8] On the other hand, Keyserling was a liberal New Dealer who preferred to be an advocate for Truman's policies. During the first months of the Eisenhower administration, there was serious discussion over whether the three-member CEA should even continue. It was decided to retain the three-member CEA, because Eisenhower appreciated receiving expert advice from his staff. But the vice-chair position was eliminated so that CEA chairman Arthur Burns would dominate its operations. Ever since that reorganization under Burns, the chairman appoints the staff, hires consultants, and advises the president. The zenith of CEA political influence came during the Kennedy administration, however, because the Council of Economic Advisers reflected the philosophy of Keynesian economics that dominated the economics profession in the 1960s. Its espousal of an activist countercyclical policy also was compatible with the liberal domestic agenda of President Kennedy and the Democratic Party.

Occasionally, the CEA has clashed with the White House. CEA chair Gardner Ackley struggled to reconcile President Johnson's "guns and butter" approach to economic policy. In 1966 Johnson rejected, on political grounds, Ackley's recommendation that taxes be raised in order to fund the Vietnam War as well as the ambitious domestic programs envisioned in LBJ's Great Society and War on Poverty. Although the economy of the late 1960s was booming, massive federal spending for "guns and butter" fueled the inflation problem of the 1970s. It was President Nixon who had to cope with that inflation problem. Two of Nixon's CEA chairmen, Paul Mc-Cracken and Herb Stein, were opposed to imposing wage and price controls, but that policy was supported by Nixon's domestic policy adviser, John Erlichman, and later by Treasury Secretary John Connally. In the end Nixon agreed with Erlichman and Connally against the judgment of his CEA.

Many observers believe that the CEA's reputation declined substantially during the Reagan administration. Reagan's first two CEA chairmen, Murray Weidenbaum and Martin Feldstein, soon resigned their positions. Weidenbaum left early in 1982 over his frustration with Reagan's insistence on increasing defense spending and cutting taxes. Feldstein lost influence when he publicly called for tax increases, in response to the rising budget deficits caused by Reagan's supply-side policies. Feldstein lost repeated battles over the deficits to Treasury Secretary Donald Regan. President Reagan, now anxious to avoid any further criticism from academic economists, named business economist Beryl Sprinkel as CEA chairman, and Sprinkel proceeded to staff the CEA with supply-side economists and monetarists.

President George H. W. Bush returned to the pre-Reagan pattern of academic appointments by choosing Michael Boskin of Stanford University as his CEA chair. While there was no major shift in macroeconomic policy, Boskin's reputation and operating style improved the CEA's image. Nonetheless Boskin's influence declined as OMB director Richard Darman and Treasury Secretary Nicholas Brady gained more power.[9] In 1990, for example, Boskin tried without success to warn the president about the weakening economy, contrary to the optimistic themes being written into the president's speeches. In retrospect Boskin was prophetic because, as unemployment increased, the Bush White House was perceived as being aloof and that image hurt President Bush as he campaigned for reelection in 1992.

Clinton's appointment of Laura D'Andrea Tyson indicated that the pattern of emphasizing policy compatibility over professional reputation would continue.[10] Tyson was an outspoken advocate of new federal spending programs, and she argued the United States should pursue "a relatively cautious approach to industrial policy."[11] Tyson also supported "selective reciprocity" on global trade, a view that would deny access to U.S. markets to those nations who resisted opening their markets to American products.[12] Tyson's approach was resisted by Clinton's more fiscally conservative advisers, namely OMB director Leon Panetta, Treasury Secretary Lloyd Bentsen, and National Economic Adviser Robert Rubin.

President George W. Bush's first CEA chairman, Glenn Hubbard, wanted to be an active player in formulating policy proposals. At the time of his nomination Hubbard stated: "You have to see how these things evolve, but my hope for the Council of Economic Advisers is that it plays a very strong participatory role in developing economic policy."[13] Hubbard's advocacy of tax cuts made him increasingly willing to adopt the administration's political justifications for its proposals. Bush's second CEA chairman was N. Gregory Mankiw, a controversial economist who emphasized the economic gains from free trade. He asserted that the outsourcing of American jobs is "probably a plus for the economy in the long run."[14] While his views reflected mainstream economic thinking, he was still criticized by politicians who saw a connection between outsourcing and the slowed recovery of the U.S. labor market in early 2004. Less controversial were President George W. Bush's other CEA chairmen: Ben Bernanke (later appointed Fed chairman), Harvey Rosen, and Edward Lazear. All were outspoken in their defense of White House proposals to extend the president's tax cuts.

Even good rapport with the president does not guarantee that the CEA chairman will not lose a policy battle, but clearly the CEA is most influential when its chairman can develop a working relationship with the president. Truman preferred the liberal Keyserling to the more conservative Nourse. President Eisenhower was comfortable with Arthur Burns's cautious approach to countercyclical policy. Alan Greenspan reinforced Gerald Ford's orthodox views on economics, as author John Sloan notes: "Greenspan attained a prominent role in economic policy making because much of what he was advocating was compatible with Ford's beliefs. Ford was a moderately conservative Republican who, as a member of the House Appropriations Committee, had warned his fellow legislators for many years that the federal government had become too active and expensive."[15] A notable exception involved Martin Feldstein, who publicly feuded with Reagan's White House staff over deficits in 1983 and 1984. Not only was CEA influence reduced, but the Reagan White House staff even considered abolishing the Council of Economic Advisers. When disagreements are serious enough, CEA chairmen have chosen to quietly resign rather than stay in office and fight.

Over time more departments and agencies have hired professional economists, thereby eroding the "monopoly" of economic expertise once held by the CEA. One organizational innovation that directly challenged the CEA was the National Economic Council. President Clinton established a **National Economic Council (NEC)** to coordinate economic policies within his administration. When CEA chairwoman Laura D'Andrea Tyson resigned to become director of the NEC, her move was interpreted as a sign that the NEC would be a more influential economic decision maker in the Clinton administration than the CEA (see discussion of NEC below).

Office of Management and Budget

The **Bureau of the Budget (BOB)** was established by the Budget and Accounting Act of 1921. It became part of the EOP in 1939. Its successor agency, the **Office of Management and Budget (OMB)**, was created by President Nixon in 1970. The OMB is important due to its ongoing budgetary responsibilities and extensive institutional memory. By virtue of its expertise, accumulated experience, and contacts throughout the federal government, the OMB has a storehouse of practical knowledge going back years. The professionalism of the OMB staff, therefore, adds a dimension to the economic advisory system which newcomers like the CEA chairman and the treasury secretary cannot provide. Legislation enacted by Congress in 1974 requires the OMB director and deputy director to be appointed by the president with the approval of the Senate.

The basic function of the OMB is to prepare and execute the federal budget. The federal budget covers spending for a **fiscal year**, which runs from October 1 until September 30.[16] At any one point in time the OMB is at work on three successive budgets. First, the OMB is involved in preparing the budget for the next fiscal year. Second, the OMB monitors the execution of the budget for the current fiscal year. This means that the OMB monitors spending from numerous accounts by all executive branch agencies reporting to the president, making certain that disbursements do not proceed at a pace that will exhaust the accounts before the close of the fiscal year. Third, along with the Congressional Budget Office, the OMB audits the budget from the previous fiscal year to determine whether or not funds were properly spent.

The importance of the OMB within the economic subpresidency is mainly due to its preparation of the annual budget. The budgetary cycle begins with the OMB developing assumptions regarding the future course of the economy and predicting expenditures and revenues over the next fiscal year. These guesstimates result in a targeted deficit or surplus figure, from which the basic budgetary guidelines are derived following consultation with the president. The OMB then prepares instructions for executive branch agencies concerning how they should prepare their own budget requests. These agency requests are reviewed through several iterations by the

Table 3.2.   Directors of the Bureau of the Budget/Office of Management and Budget, 1921–2006

President	Director	Tenure
Harding	Charles E. Dawes	1921–1922
	Herbert Lard	1922–1929
Hoover	J. Clawson Roop	1929–1933
Roosevelt	Lewis W. Douglas	1933–1934
	Daniel W. Bell	1934–1939
	Harold D. Smith	1939–1946
Truman	Harold D. Smith	1946
	James E. Webb	1946–1949
	Frank Pace	1949–1950
	Frederick J. Lawton	1950–1953
Eisenhower	Joseph M. Dodge	1953–1954
	Rowland R. Hughes	1954–1956
	Percival F. Brundage	1956–1958
	Maurice H. Stans	1958–1961
Kennedy	David E. Bell	1961–1962
	Kermit Gordon	1962–1963
Johnson	Kermit Gordon	1963–1965
	Charles L. Schultze	1965–1968
	Charles J. Zwick	1968–1969
Nixon	Robert P. Mayo	1969–1970
	George P. Schultz	1970–1972
	Caspar Weinberger	1972–1973
	Roy L. Ash	1973–1974
Ford	Roy L. Ash	1974–1975
	James T. Lynn	1975–1977
Carter	Bert Lance	1977
	James T. McIntyre	1977–1981
Reagan	David A. Stockman	1981–1985
	Joseph R. Wright	1985
	James C. Miller	1985–1988
	Joseph R. Wright	1988–1989
G. H. W. Bush	Richard G. Darman	1989–1993
Clinton	Leon Panetta	1993–1994
	Alice Rivlin	1994–1996
	Franklin Raines	1996–1998
	Jacob J. Lew	1998–2001
G. W. Bush	Mitchell E. Daniels	2001–2003
	Joshua B. Bolten	2003–2006
	Rob Portman	2006–

OMB, and only at the last stage can agencies appeal OMB decisions directly to the president. The resulting "executive budget" is then submitted to Congress. During subsequent budgetary hearings in Congress held before the budget committees, the OMB director acts as the chief spokesperson for the administration.

During the Truman and Eisenhower presidencies, budgeting was largely routine and the BOB (Bureau of the Budget) monopolized the process. With Kennedy, however, its role in screening legislative requests by agencies (the "central clearance" function) was limited to routine matters. All programs showcased under President Kennedy's New Frontier legislative agenda were initiated by the White House, not the BOB, and White House control over high priority programs was continued by President Johnson when he promoted his Great Society. Nonetheless, according to Kennedy's BOB director, Kermit Gordon, White House control over budgeting does not penetrate the federal bureaucracy:

> As one moves down through the officials in the executive hierarchy, the Presidential perspective fades rapidly, and parochial conceptions take its place. Consider the official who directs the day-to-day operations of even a broadly defined program. . . . He directs the work of large numbers of people, he disposes of large sums of money, he deals every day with weighty, intricate, and delicate problems. He has probably spent most of his adult years in the highly specialized activity over which he now presides. He lives at the center of a special world inhabited by persons and groups in the private sector who stand to gain or lose by what he does, certain members of Congress who have a special interest in his actions, and a specialized press to which he is a figure of central importance. . . . The rest of the federal government may seem vague and remote, and the President will loom as a distant and shadowy figure who will, in any event, be succeeded by someone else in a few years.[17]

For this reason budget directors are skeptical about agency estimates and generally question whether all funds requested by agencies are necessary. Each budget request must be viewed in terms of presidential priorities and spending targets. The BOB gained the reputation of being a budget cutter, even during the growth years of the 1960s when economic prosperity generated more revenues for government. When Republicans assumed the presidency, at a time when the economy grew less robustly and there was more federal indebtedness, the long-standing skepticism of the BOB hardened into strenuous opposition to more federal spending.

President Nixon politicized OMB operations. The OMB became involved in controversial and illegal actions, like Nixon's **impoundments** (refusal to spend funds appropriated by Congress), and Nixon replaced OMB professionals with political operatives. In 1960 the BOB had only five appointed officials, but the 1970 reorganization that created the OMB added a new layer of "program associate directors" who were White House political appointees. Three of Nixon's four OMB directors—George Shultz, Caspar Weinberger, and Roy Ash—became public advocates for administration policies. As a consequence, the OMB became identified "more as a member of the president's own political family and less a broker supplying an independent analytic service to every President."[18] Critics of the OMB under President Nixon prefered a "neutral competent" agency like the BOB under Truman and Eisenhower. But a contrary view is that modern presidents must politicize the upper administration in order to penetrate the bureaucracy and exert meaningful control over policy making.[19]

Under President Reagan, the OMB was at the forefront of the political battle over domestic spending cuts. David Stockman is considered one of the most politically astute OMB directors. During his tenure, Stockman centralized the budgetary process within the White House and proceeded to punish some agencies with budget cuts and to reward others with spending increases. He also dominated the congressional hearings with detailed statistical trends, economic projections, and budgetary estimates. Eventually his public criticism of supply-side economics damaged his credibility within the Reagan administration. Stockman was forced to resign because the White House objected to his view that taxes had to be increased substantially to reduce the soaring deficits.

When Richard Darman took over the directorship of the OMB under President George H. W. Bush, the driving force in budget policy was the Gramm-Rudman-Hollings (GRH) deficit reduction measure. GRH imposed limits on projected budget deficits.[20] But Darman was a strong proponent of new legislation, notably the Americans with Disabilities Act, amendments to the Clean Air Act, the Civil Rights Act of 1990, and minimum wage increases, designed to showcase the difference between President Bush's "gentler, kinder" America campaign theme and Reagan's ultraconservatism. Yet Darman refused to pay for those new programs with spending cuts elsewhere in the budget. Instead, to meet deficit reduction targets, Darman influenced Bush to support new tax increases, a decision that repudiated Bush's "read my lips, no new taxes" pledge during the 1980 presidential campaign and deeply alienated Republican fiscal conservatives.[21]

For the first time in years the budget deficit became an electoral issue in a presidential campaign, mainly due to the 1992 independent candidacy of Ross Perot, who focused his entire campaign on the problem of deficit spending. Also Democratic candidate Bill Clinton promised, if elected, to balance the budget. To bring the budget into balance and impose fiscal restraint, mostly by cutting defense programs, President Clinton appointed Congressman Leon Panetta (D-CA) as his first OMB director and Alice Rivlin, a former director of the Congressional Budget Office, as the deputy budget director.[22] Both persuaded Clinton that he should drastically reduce the budget deficit and complement such efforts with free trade initiatives agreeable to Wall Street.[23] As strong advocates of fiscal discipline, Panetta and Rivlin had considerable skill in dealing with Congress and decades of budget experience. They were key players in shaping Clinton's 1993 deficit reduction initiative. When Panetta stepped down to become Clinton's White House chief of staff in 1994, Rivlin assumed control of the OMB. Her successor, Franklin Raines, was instrumental in shepherding the 1997 deficit reduction measure through the Republican-controlled Congress, which when coupled with previous tax hikes, produced budget surpluses between 1998 and 2001.

President George W. Bush's first OMB director was Mitchell Daniels, who served until 2003 when he left the White House to successfully run for governor of Indiana. Daniels instituted a new accountability system, the Program Assessment Rating Tool, that forced all agencies to issue efficiency reports to the OMB, on which Daniels derived a "traffic-light-style" management scorecard. Daniels's tenure was better remembered, however, for the transformation of a $236 billion surplus in 2001 to a $400 billion deficit in 2003.

Deputy White House chief of staff Joshua Bolten, a former investment banker and corporate lawyer, succeeded Daniels in May 2003. Bolten faced considerable political obstacles from the start, since he inherited the mammoth deficits produced under Daniel's tenure. Bolten was instrumental in integrating the budgetary and managerial functions of the OMB in ways that enhanced Bush's ability to reshape budget allocations. As a close member of President Bush's inner circle, Bolten was able to strengthen OMB control over the bureaucracy. However, the deficit has remained extraordinarily high under Bolten, due largely to his use of "supplemental" appropriations (for military operations) outside the regular budget process that were not included in the original budgetary calculations. In March 2006 Bush named Bolten as his second White House chief of staff following the resignation of Andrew Card.

U.S. Trade Representative

Since 1974 the **Office of the U.S. Trade Representative** has been responsible for establishing trade policy and representing American trade interests at multilateral organizations. Currently located within the Executive Office of the President, the U.S. trade representative (USTR) is a cabinet-level ambassador who functions as the president's principal adviser, negotiator, and spokesperson on trade issues. The USTR also serves as vice chairman of the Overseas Private Investment Corporation (OPIC) and is a nonvoting member of the Export-Import Bank.

In the policy making process, the Office of the USTR operates as an interagency organization that coordinates trade policy, resolves bureaucratic disagreements, and frames decision making. Also, through an advisory committee system, private corporations can influence negotiations and multilateral trade agreements. The USTR maintains constant contacts with five members of the House and Senate who serve as legislative advisers on trade policy.

The trade representative position was first created in 1962 by President Kennedy, who petitioned Congress for authority to discuss reciprocal tariff concessions with Europe. The Trade Expansion Act of 1962 granted the president that authority and created the Office of the Special Trade Representative to serve as the presidential representative in trade negotiations. Under the 1962 Act, the president established an interagency trade policy mechanism to assist with the implementation of these responsibilities. This organization, as it has evolved, consists of three tiers of committees: the Trade Policy Staff Committee (TPSC), the Trade Policy Review Group (TPRG), and the National Security Council/National Economic Council

Table 3.3. Special Trade Representatives (STRs) and U.S. Trade Representatives (USTRs), 1963–2006

President	Representative	Tenure
Kennedy	Christian Herder, STR	1961–1963
Johnson	Christian Herder, STR	1963–1967
	William Roth, STR	1967–1969
Nixon	Carl J. Gilbert, STR	1969–1971
	William D. Eberle, STR	1971–1974
Ford	William D. Eberle, STR	1974–1975
	Frederick B. Dent, STR	1975–1977
Carter	Robert B. Strauss, STR	1977–1979
	Reubin O'D. Askew, USTR	1979–1981
Reagan	William E. Brock, USTR	1981–1985
	Clayton Yeutter, USTR	1985–1989
G. H. W. Bush	Carla A. Hills, USTR	1989–1993
Clinton	Michael "Mickey" Kantor, USTR	1993–1997
	Charlene Barshefsky, USTR	1997–2001
G. W. Bush	Robert B. Zoellick, USTR	2001–2005
	Rob Portman, USTR	2005–2006
	Susan C. Schwab, USTR	2006–

(NSC/NEC). Together these committees constitute the principal mechanism for developing and coordinating policies on trade and trade-related investment issues.

The first special trade representative (STR), Christian A. Herder, initiated tariff-reduction talks held by the **General Agreement on Tariffs and Trade (GATT)**. However, Herder and his successor, William Roth, largely used the Office of the STR and GATT to keep communist nations in check. At that time, free trade initiatives were a bulwark for prosperous capitalist nations against nonaligned countries with command economies. Within this environment the STR assumed control over trade negotiations from the State Department, giving U.S. commercial interests one official representative.

Nixon's second STR, William D. Eberle, served during one of the most consequential periods in U.S. trade history. Eberle was instrumental in implementing Nixon's decision to withdraw the United States from the Bretton Woods System by removing the U.S. dollar from the gold standard (an ounce of gold was fixed at $35) in response to increased trade competition from Western Europe and Japan. Although protectionist sentiment was strong in Congress in the 1970s, President Nixon obtained passage of the Trade Act of 1974, which set the United States on a course toward more activist American participation in tariff reduction talks. The act increased the STR's powers and placed the office within the EOP.

Several organizational changes were made during the Ford and Carter administrations. With the issuance of Executive Order 11846, President Ford elevated the STR to a cabinet-level position. In 1979 Carter's Reorganization Plan No. 3 and Executive Order 12188 in 1980 renamed the Office of the STR to the Office of the United States Trade Representative, thereby centralizing policy making and negotiating functions for international trade, and expanded the staff to roughly two hundred analysts. The U.S. Trade Representative (USTR) position was also transformed into an official U.S. ambassador.

The Office of the USTR was further enhanced with the passage of the 1988 Trade and Competitiveness Act, which codified the status and responsibilities of the USTR previously established through Reorganization Plan No. 3 and Executive Order 12188. Specifically, the USTR was given the lead responsibility for coordinating trade policy with other agencies, serving as the president's principal trade policy spokesperson, directing all congressional testimony on trade policy, negotiating tariff reductions and international commodity agreements, and managing the Trade Policy Committee.

The end of the Cold War and the demise of the Soviet bloc transformed the world of international trade, making it a truly global enterprise. Carla Hills, who served President George H. W. Bush, was the first USTR to conduct trade negotiations in this new environment. She received considerable public attention during the Uruguay round of the GATT and in discussions surrounding the North American Free Trade Agreement. President Clinton's first USTR, Mickey Kantor, assumed the lead in negotiating labor and environmental supplemental agreements regarding U.S. membership in NAFTA, directed U.S. participation in the World Trade Organization (WTO), and managed America's response to the Mexican peso crisis in 1995 in cooperation with Treasury Secretary Robert Rubin. Clinton's second USTR, Charlene Barshefsky, was faced with the monumental task of responding to the 1997–1998 global financial contagion, negotiating China's elevation to the WTO in 1999, and steering permanent normal trade relations (PNTR) trade status toward China through Congress in 2000.

President George W. Bush's first USTR, Robert Zoellick, was one of the most accomplished and politically effective trade representatives. Under the banner of "competitive liberalization," Zoellick launched new multilateral negotiations at a Quebec trade summit and the WTO meeting in Doha, Qatar, in 2001 to further reduce tariff barriers and to bring Taiwan into the WTO. Zoellick also led the White House's legislative effort to pass the free trade agreements with Jordan and Vietnam (both of which were first negotiated by USTR Barshefsky during the Clinton administration) and to obtain passage of trade promotion authority in 2002, after a five-year absence.[24] Trade promotion authority grants the president "fast-track" authority to enter into and conclude trade negotiations with other countries. It also limits the role of Congress to either approving or rejecting such treaties within ninety days of signature without the possibility of amending them. Zoellick also managed free trade measures with the Bahrain, Morocco, the United Arab Emirates, and Oman, individual pieces of a long-range Bush strategy to pursue a greater Middle East free trade agreement. Zoellick used trade as a national security issue when he denied granting free trade meetings with New Zealand in 2003 because it opposed the U.S. war in Iraq. Similarly, he briefly delayed final ratification of the U.S.-Chile free trade agreement because of its opposition to a second UN resolution on Iraq.

On the whole, Zoellick's "competitive liberalization" set the United States on a long-term track to promote negotiations with individual nations, groups of nations, and whole regions (as a complement to its multilateral negotiations). The thinking was that providing other nations with access to U.S. markets would fuel a competitive process toward global free trade. In February 2005 Zoellick left the Office of the USTR to become deputy secretary of state. He was replaced by Rob Portman.

Secretary of the Treasury

The Department of the Treasury dates back to the Washington administration. President Washington relied heavily on Treasury Secretary Alexander

Hamilton, who acted decisively to regularize the nation's finances and credit structure. Ever since, the **secretary of the treasury** has been among the most influential economic advisers to the president. The majority have been business executives, bankers, or Wall Street financiers, and several have been recruited directly from private business. The exceptions are James A. Baker III, an attorney; John Connally, who was governor of Texas; and Lloyd Bentsen (D-TX), who left the chairmanship of the Senate Finance Committee to become Clinton's treasury secretary.

Not infrequently treasury secretaries struggle with other key advisers for influence over economic policy. During the Eisenhower administration, Treasury Secretary George M. Humphrey frequently clashed with CEA chairman Arthur Burns. Humphrey was a fiscal conservative who ardently pre-

Table 3.4. Secretaries of the Treasury, 1945–2006

President	Secretary	Tenure
Truman	Fred Vinson	1945–1946
	John W. Snyder	1946–1953
Eisenhower	George M. Humphrey	1953–1957
	Robert B. Anderson	1957–1961
Kennedy	C. Douglas Dillon	1961–1963
Johnson	C. Douglas Dillon	1963–1965
	Henry H. Fowler	1965–1968
	Joseph W. Barr	1968–1969
Nixon	David M. Kennedy	1969–1971
	John B. Connally	1971–1972
	George P. Shultz	1972–1974
	William E. Seidman	1974
Ford	William E. Seidman	1974–1977
Carter	W. Michael Blumenthal	1977–1979
	G. William Miller	1979–1981
Reagan	Donald T. Regan	1981–1985
	James A. Baker III	1985–1988
	Nicholas S. Brady	1988–1989
G. H. W. Bush	Nicholas S. Brady	1989–1993
Clinton	Lloyd Bentsen	1993–1995
	Robert Rubin	1995–1999
	Lawrence Summers	1999–2001
G. W. Bush	Paul O'Neill	2001–2003
	John W. Snow	2003–2006
	Henry Paulson	2006–

ferred balanced budgets. In a much publicized incident, Humphrey disavowed the 1958 budget on the very day that it went to Congress, warning of a "depression that will curl your hair" if cuts were not made in the amounts proposed by the president.

President Kennedy's treasury secretary was Douglas Dillon, a Republican. Dillon's view that budget deficits would hurt JFK's popularity and undermine business confidence held sway as late as January 1963. When Kennedy finally acceded to demands by the CEA that a tax cut be recommended, the final shape of that tax package reflected Dillon's view against one large tax cut. When President Nixon appointed former Texas governor John Connally as secretary of the treasury in 1972, he became the administration's spokesman for economic policy. It was Connally who persuaded Nixon, despite opposition from the CEA, to impose wage and price controls.

On the other hand, during the presidencies of Gerald Ford, Jimmy Carter, and George H. W. Bush the treasury secretaries were eclipsed by especially strong CEA chairmen. Consider President Ford's CEA chairman, Alan Greenspan, who enjoyed Ford's complete confidence, whereas Treasury Secretary William E. Seidman acted more as a cheerleader for the free enterprise system. Ford's deep concern about "uncontrollable" federal spending reflected Greenspan's influence. It is especially true that a determined, skillful, and dynamic CEA chairman can hold extraordinary influence with the president whenever the treasury secretary assumes a passive role. President George H. W. Bush's treasury secretary, Nicholas Brady, was pretty much marginalized given the dominant policy making roles played by Chief of Staff John Sununu and OMD director Richard Darman.

At a "symbolic" level the treasury secretary represents American capitalism, which explains why well-known individuals from business and finance are usually chosen. Presidents appoint treasury secretaries who will reassure Wall Street and corporate America that a responsible individual is the guardian of the nation's finances. This political requirement is undoubtedly more important for Democrats, since corporate leaders presume that Republicans are probusiness but may fear that liberal Democrats harbor antibusiness attitudes. President Kennedy appointed Douglas Dillon, a Republican, partly to reassure the business community. And President Clinton's two appointments of Lloyd Bentsen, a fiscally conservative Democrat with business experience, and then former Goldman Sachs executive Robert Rubin were both concessions to Wall Street interests.[25]

Although the Treasury Department exerts a financially conservative influence over economic policy, this bias results more from its institutional responsibilities than from how individual secretaries are recruited. Whereas the CEA provides economic forecasts and the OMB manages budgetary allocations, the Treasury Department (which includes the Internal Revenue

Service) collects revenues from taxpayers and funds the national debt. Efforts to tamper with the internal revenue code arouse concern within the Department of the Treasury because "reform" might cost the federal government money and reduced revenues, which in the face of growing expenditures means larger deficits.

Selling government securities to private individuals, banks, and foreign governments to borrow money to service budget deficit virtually every year brings the Treasury Department into direct contact with influential members of the financial community. The borrowing requirements of government can be substantial. As of 2006, interest paid on the national debt (budget deficits accumulated over time) is one of the largest expenses in the federal budget. It is also the fastest growing portion of all federal expenditures, approximating 8% of the budget.[26] When the national debt is as high as it is today—*$8.5 trillion*—debt management becomes complicated. High yearly deficits exert upward pressure on interest rates, which act to "crowd out" private borrowing for investment. Of greater concern to the federal government, high interest raises the cost to the Treasury of funding the national debt. Two ways of alleviating the costs of debt management are to keep the deficit small by maximizing revenue and stabilizing interest rates. Such concerns make Treasury a counterweight to other advisers, mainly the CEA, who might encourage tax cuts to stimulate the economy.

Treasury Secretary Robert Rubin (1995 to 1999) promoted an economic policy, known later as "Rubinomics," that centered on deficit reduction, global free trade, and public investments in education, training, and the environment. During Rubin's tenure, the United States experienced one of the longest economic expansions in its history, transforming the federal government's budgetary position from deficit to surplus.

Paul O'Neill, ex-CEO of Alcoa Aluminum with ten years experience at the OMB, was appointed treasury secretary by President George W. Bush in 2001. O'Neill was somewhat outspoken, often taking public positions against the Bush administration. O'Neill was highly critical of Bush's supply-side policies and at times would publicly lash out against Bush's tax cut proposals as being fiscally irresponsible and devastating to financial markets. A report commissioned in 2002 by O'Neill suggests the United States faced future budget deficits of more than $500 billion. That report also suggests that tax increases, massive spending cuts, or both would be unavoidable if the Bush administration was really going to meet its goals. Not only did the Bush White House omit those conclusions from the 2003 annual budget report but, soon thereafter, O'Neill became a real political liability after he failed to calm the public and corporate America following the rash of corporate scandals at Enron, MCI/WorldCom, and Adelphia.[27] O'Neill's feuds with Bush's tax-cut policies as well as his push to investigate Al-Qaeda funding via the United Arab Emirates led to his resignation in 2002. O'Neill was replaced with former CSX rail executive and Business Roundtable president John W. Snow.

Between 2003 and 2006 Snow presided over an economy that experienced relatively strong economic growth and a low unemployment rate despite expanding budget deficits, rising inflation, and poor wage and salary growth. Public anxiety over economic conditions, however, resulted in mediocre approval ratings for President Bush's handling of the economy. Although Snow was an energetic policy maker whose stewardship saw improvements in the economy, he was unable to boost Bush's public approval despite the onset of positive economic news. And despite Snow's strong advocacy for two initiatives that were the centerpiece of Bush's domestic program in his second term—Social Security reform and an overhaul of the tax code—both failed to gain enactment.

In June 2006 Snow resigned and was replaced by Goldman Sachs executive Henry Paulson, who was recruited not only to serve as a key economic policy adviser but also to help Bush garner some credit for the economy. Paulson, who was confirmed by the Senate on June 29, 2006, has been a loyal spokesman for the Bush administration insofar as he opposed tax increases, proposed reforms to Social Security and Medicare, and encouraged China to change its monetary policy. Despite the enormous deficits, Paulson promoted supply-side policies, arguing that the federal deficit is "manageable . . . and we can attack it best with a strong and growing economy" and raising taxes "would be counterproductive."[28]

The advisory role of the treasury secretary is bolstered by the Treasury Department's involvement in international monetary policy. In some areas of international finance, the Treasury Department has substantial control over the policy making apparatus.[29] Financial assets are transferred by Treasury between the United States and foreign countries in order to satisfy the balance on the current account. Technically, this task is performed by the Federal Reserve Bank of New York, which acts as an arm of the Treasury Department. An obvious consideration is the exchange rate of the U.S. dollar on world markets. Asset flows are facilitated when the rate of exchange is fixed (as it was prior to 1971 at $35 per ounce of gold) or when the floating value of the U.S. dollar (as determined by world financial markets) is relatively stable.

Although many factors can influence the rate of exchange between the U.S. dollar and foreign currencies, such as Europe's euro or Japan's yen, lower rates of inflation in the domestic U.S. economy rates help stabilize the value of the U.S. dollar abroad. These concerns encourage Treasury to adopt a cautious outlook on economic policy, especially when the threat of higher inflation resulting from international financial transactions exists. When the threat of serious financial instability does occur, the treasury secretary often asserts activist leadership. For example, in 1989 after a period of years in which a number of developing nations, especially Mexico, defaulted on their international finances, Nicholas Brady developed the Brady Plan to help third world countries sell dollar-denominated bonds.[30] A more significant example occurred in 1995 when Treasury Secretary Robert Rubin and Undersecretary of the Treasury Lawrence Summers transferred $20 billion from the Treasury Department's Exchange Stabilization Fund (ESF) and extended it as loan guarantees to the Bank of Mexico.[31]

COORDINATING ECONOMIC POLICY

Given their differing responsibilities, the major executive branch economic actors—the CEA, OMB, USTR, and Treasury—are likely to hold different perspectives about economic policy. This lack of policy consensus is magnified by often-conflicting economic goals: low inflation, low unemployment, economic growth, high productivity, global financial stability, and free trade. To achieve an optimal mix of these macroeconomic goals, policy makers must utilize fiscal and monetary policies that will impact both the domestic economy and global economies.

The responsibility of coordinating these economic decision makers rests with the president, but this task is Herculean in its scope. Until 1993 no apparatus existed within the federal government to assure this kind of coordination over economic policy making. There had been no counterpart to the National Security Council, whose purpose is to advise "the President with respect to the integration of domestic, foreign and military policies relating to the national security." As a consequence, the organization of economic policy making has been ad hoc and informal, shaped according to each president's governing style, and influenced by whatever economic problem got priority at a given time. One organizational response to this situation of policy making confusion was for presidents to attempt to centralize the economic policy making process within the White House through various mechanisms that aim to coordinate the policy units in the economic subpresidency.

White House Economic Advisory Organizations

Modern presidents have experimented with various methods of organizing their economic advisory teams. One of the most important constraints is size. The simplest advisory system exists whenever the president relies on only a few economic advisers such as the OMB director, treasury secretary, and CEA chair—known as the **"Troika"**—and possibly also the USTR. But when other economic advisers are added, the president must formalize those more complex relationships through some kind of institutional arrangement.

President Truman began with an informal arrangement revolving around a Troika that included Treasury Secretary John Snyder, CEA chair Edwin G. Nourse, and budget director James E. Webb.[32] This decentralized arrangement allowed each adviser direct access to the president but Truman eventually relied more on Webb, because Webb shared Truman's policy objectives. According to author Stephen Hess: "As relations between Truman and his budget director became more intimate, Webb emerged as a principal adviser to the president, as distinct from adviser to the presidency, the prime role assumed by past directors."[33] In his second term, Truman replaced CEA chairman Edwin Nourse with Leon Keyserling, who was ideologically more compatible with the administration.[34] But responsibility for foreign economic policy was delegated to the National Security Council and the undersecretary of state for international economic policy.

A first effort at policy coordination emerged under President Dwight Eisenhower when he created the Council on Foreign Economic Policy in 1954 with the goal of integrating international economic issues. Unlike Eisenhower, President Kennedy preferred an ad hoc organizational style, creating separate interagency committees for specific domestic economic issues while delegating foreign economic policy coordination to an interdepartmental committee of undersecretaries, Deputy National Security Advisor Carl Kaysen, and the State Department. Under President Johnson, the National Security Council coordinated foreign economic policy through Deputy Assistant Francis M. Bator; the Trade Expansion Advisory Committee handled trade issues; and Joseph Califano dominated domestic economic policy.[35]

In his first term President Nixon delegated responsibility for domestic economic policy to Treasury Secretary John Connally, who filtered most decisions through domestic policy adviser John Ehrlichman. To coordinate foreign economic policy making, Nixon created the Council on International Economic Policy (CIEP) on the advice of the Advisory Council on Executive Organization (the Ash Council), which served as a small support staff for Henry Kissinger's National Security Council.[36] But in his second term Nixon made far-reaching structural changes. In seeking to achieve more effective integration of economic issues following the collapse of the Bretton Woods System (discussed in chapter 7), Nixon created the **Council on Economic Policy (CEP)** with jurisdiction over both domestic and foreign economic policy. The CEP was the *first* attempt by a president to coordinate economic issues at the intersection of both domestic and foreign policy. Treasury Secretary George Shultz chaired the CEP, relying on a small staff headed by Kenneth W. Dam. The CEP facilitated coordination between the Treasury Department and the USTR and, except for some trade matters, assumed the lead over most economic issue areas.[37]

President Ford continued Nixon's practice of coordinating domestic and international economic issues with the **Economic Policy Board (EPB)**.[38] The EPB was directed by Treasury Secretary William Seidman, and Roger Porter served as EPB executive secretary. The EPB shared economic advisory responsibilities with the NSC, the OMB, the Domestic Council, and the Energy Resources Council. President Carter attempted to replicate Ford's EPB with the **Economic Policy Group (EPG)**, a mixture of centralized, multiple-advocacy, and ad hoc mechanisms to coordinate economic policy. In practice, however, the EPG only handled domestic issues because National Security Advisor Zbigniew Brzezinski skillfully usurped most international economic issues. In day-to-day operations the coordination of foreign economic policy was funneled through NSC staffer Henry Owen.[39]

Departing from his predecessors, President Reagan created a "cabinet council" system under White House Counsel Edwin Meese, which was organized around specific economic issues. An **Economic Policy Council (EPC)**, headed by Treasury Secretary Donald Regan, coordinated the councils and proposed specific policies, which could be reworked by Chief of Staff James Baker's Legislative Strategy Group (LSG). In Reagan's second term, the EPC integrated foreign and domestic economic issues under James Baker, who was now treasury secretary. In George H. W. Bush's administration, OMB director Richard Darman dominated most economic issues, though often in competition with Chief of Staff John Sununu and Treasury Secretary Nicholas Brady. Bush did utilize the EPC on some trade issues in cooperation with the USTR, the National Security Council, as well as the Treasury and State departments. In some cases "customized" groups were formed to handle specific issues, such as NAFTA, economic sanctions on Iraq, and foreign aid to Central and Eastern Europe. Toward the end of his tenure President Bush merged the EPC into the Domestic Policy Council, creating the Policy Coordinating Group.[40]

A significant change in the coordination of economic policy came when President Clinton created his National Economic Council (NEC) in 1993. In the NEC President Clinton attempted to coordinate and integrate both domestic and foreign economic policy. While there was no doubt that President Clinton was a relative novice in national security affairs, unlike previous presidents he was deeply interested and knowledgeable about economics. According to Clinton: "The currency of strength in this era will be denominated not only in ships, tanks and planes, but also in diplomats, patents and paychecks."[41] As one of his advisers observed, "Unlike his predecessors, he [Clinton] doesn't see the distinction between economics and politics or between the domestic economy and the international economy."[42]

Despite the previous history of presidential efforts and failures at policy coordination, Clinton was determined to try again. As Isabel Sawhill of the Urban Institute put it: "You cannot run a campaign whose slogan is 'It's the economy, stupid!' and then not have a focal point in the White House for keeping track of what's happening to the economy and coordinating policy."[43] Clinton hoped to create a mechanism for economic policy making that worked in much the same way as the National Security Council operated in foreign policy. With the advent of the post–Cold War era, seemingly the NEC was an idea whose time had come.[44]

The concept of an "economic council" bounced around Congress, universities, and think tanks years before Clinton adopted it as his own.[45] The idea also germinated in New York governor Mario Cuomo's Commission on Trade and Competitiveness.[46] In fact, there is an extensive Cuomo connection with the NEC. Clinton's first two NEC directors, Robert Rubin and Laura D'Andrea Tyson were members of that commission and Clinton's third NEC director, Gene Sperling, was a Cuomo aide who only joined the Clinton presidential campaign after it became clear that Cuomo was not running. The commission's recommendation for an "Economic Security Council" was designed to emphasize international economic policy. And no doubt, given Clinton's focus on the economy, the name must have had some cache with Clinton when commission members discussed it with him during the 1992 campaign.[47]

At the same time, the Commission on Government Renewal, sponsored by the Carnegie Endowment for International Peace and the Institute for International Economics, issued a report titled *Memorandum to the President-Elect*. Members of the commission included I. M. Destler, a prominent scholar in foreign economic policy, as well as a number of distinguished national security veterans, including Admiral William Crowe, Frank Carlucci, Morton Halperin, and General Bobby Ray Inman. According to the report: "The combination of Cold War victory and deep economic difficulties allows—and indeed, demands—a shift of priority and resources away from national security as traditionally defined, toward the broader problems of making America competitive in a fiercely competitive world." And "the Economic Council and its staff would be your instrument for assuring that economic policy gets attention equal to traditional national security, working extremely closely with the NSC and its staff when international economic issues are under consideration, and with the domestic policy Council and its staff on domestic policy matters."[48]

In the end it was Clinton's thoughts on economic policy making that translated the idea for the NEC into policy. Clinton felt that President George H. W. Bush's national security team had worked well but that his economic team was a disaster.[49] Clinton identified the idea of an economic council to be not only an effective strategy for governing, but also an attractive campaign issue. The notion first appeared in the Clinton-Gore campaign book, *Putting People First*, which states: "Economic Security Council, similar in status to the National Security Council, with responsibility for coordinating America's international economic policy."[50]

Clinton's proposed NEC was criticized, however. Zbigniew Brzezinski suggested that "an NEC-led policy making process would amplify 'turf struggles'" among competing advisers and councils in the executive office.[51] It was also alleged that Clinton's policy making system would make security and domestic issues inferior to economic issues.[52] Herbert Stein, Nixon's CEA chairman, said, "it is dumb to put the focus of economic policy on security."[53] The term "security" implied a protectionist stance toward imports, which could alarm America's trading partners. In reaction, Harvard professor Robert Reich, who directed Clinton's economic program during the transition, advised Clinton to change its name to National Economic Council (NEC).[54]

Beryl Sprinkel, Reagan's CEA chairman, argued that giving the NEC equal status with the NSC had troubling implications for the treasury secretary, who traditionally had been the president's chief spokesman for economic policy. Under Reagan and Bush the treasury secretary chaired the EPC. Asked Sprinkel: "Are you going to clip the wings of the Secretary of the Treasury? I can't believe that would work."[55] David Newsome of the *Christian Science Monitor* agreed, saying that "such a plan would establish a bureaucratic unit interposed between major cabinet officers, such as the secretaries of treasury and commerce, and the president. The president would risk being isolated from officials whom foreign representatives regard as responsible for major policy advice."[56]

Clinton's original intention was for Robert Reich to head the NEC. However, Reich expressed his preference to be labor secretary, a cabinet position that would allow him to be a more public advocate of policy. Then Clinton turned to Goldman Sachs executive Robert Rubin, who accepted, but only after Clinton assured him that the NEC's role would be taken seriously.[57] Clinton believed that Rubin's Wall Street experience and knowledge of finances would enable him to be an effective organizational broker on important issues like the budget deficit and NAFTA.[58] According to journalist Bob Woodward: "Clinton wanted someone who knew Wall Street and the bond market close to him in the White House."[59] Rubin's appointment reflected "both Clinton's stated policy priorities—his promise to focus like a laser beam on the economy—and a historical reality—that with the end of the cold war, America's difficult challenges lie in the economic realm."[60]

Rubin's key ally on the NEC was Treasury Secretary Lloyd Bentsen, since both men favored reducing the deficit over new spending and supported free trade with Mexico.[61] Bentsen was one cabinet member who supplied Clinton with "economic, political, and congressional advice" and was able to "look him in the eye as a political peer and say, 'I know what this means politically.'"[62] Bentsen could also stand up to unruly groups within the Democratic Party.[63] Rubin also found allies in OMB director Leon Panetta and Deputy Budget Director Alice Rivlin.[64]

The most difficult challenge for the NEC was to coordinate the economic policy making process and, specifically, the economic decision makers within the Executive Office of the President. Similar to the NSC, the NEC was supposed to function as an "honest broker" in coordinating the formulation and implementation of economic policies, managing the economic bureaucracy, and integrating economic issues into a coherent package consistent with President Clinton's policy objectives.[65] The director of the NEC was termed the **national economic adviser** (NEA, technically, the assistant to the president for economic affairs), who would supervise two deputies and a professional staff. It was anticipated that the national economic adviser would serve the president as his top political and policy adviser on foreign and domestic economic issues.

The NEC, also like the National Security Council, would have three structural levels: principals committee, deputies committee, and the staff. The NEC Principals Committee (NEC/PC) coordinates and integrates domestic and international economic issues. It serves as a senior interagency forum for cabinet-level officials to discuss and resolve issues not requiring a presidential decision. In addition to the president as chair and the national economic adviser as executive director, the statutory membership on the NEC/PC includes the vice president, the domestic policy adviser, the national security adviser, the science and technology adviser, the USTR, the OMB director, the CEA chair, administrator of the Environmental Protection Agency (EPA), and the secretaries of Treasury, State, Commerce, Labor, Transportation, Agriculture, Energy, and Housing and Urban Development. The treasury secretary would remain the chief economic spokesman for the administration; the OMB director would continue to manage the budget; and the CEA chair would continue as the primary source of economic expertise.

The sublevel NEC Deputies Committee (NEC/DC) is charged with monitoring the NEC interagency process and securing economic policy implementation. Members of the NEC/DC include two deputy assistants to the president, who serve as cochairs of the NEC/DC, as well as appropriate senior officials of deputy-secretary or undersecretary rank from the cabinet departments and other executive branch agencies. Interagency working groups

Table 3.5. National Economic Advisers, 1993–2006

President	Adviser	Tenure
Clinton	Robert Rubin	1993–1995
	Laura D'Andrea Tyson	1995–1997
	Gene Sperling	1997–2001
G. W. Bush	Lawrence Lindsey	2001–2002
	Stephen Friedman	2002–2005
	Alan B. Hubbard	2005–

that deal with regulatory policy, technology, infrastructure and transportation, community development, and banking policy were convened daily and were chaired by the deputies. The largest working group, in foreign policy, included members from the National Security Council staff.

Three national economic advisers served the eight years of President Clinton's tenure: Robert Rubin, Laura D'Andrea Tyson, and Gene Sperling. Rubin saw the opportunity to assert NEC's leadership as a serious policy group when two key issues emerged—the budget deficit and NAFTA, both of which caused divisions in Clinton's economic team.[66] Rubin was able to strengthen the position of the NEC by developing and cultivating ties with seasoned free traders and deficit hawks. After Rubin strengthened the NEC's role in the policy making process, it emerged as an influential adviser to President Clinton. Under Laura D'Andrea Tyson, the NEC dealt mainly with advancing a "corporate responsibility" measure and promoting U.S. trade with Japan and China. Given the pressures on the NEC to "fight fires" and solve more immediate problems, however, it was often difficult for Tyson's NEC to effectively coordinate the process. During Sperling's reign at the NEC, the most significant issues involved passing the 1997 deficit reduction measure; climate change negotiations in Kyoto, Japan; Social Security reform; and elevating China to the WTO. These policy issues were so politically sensitive—Social Security reform had long been viewed as the "third rail" of politics—that the topic of the internal meetings was officially listed as "Special Issues" so that the daily calendars of the participants would not reveal the subject matter.

President George W. Bush continued the NEC, because he believed that the NEC was able to coordinate and manage the economic subpresidency under Clinton. There was some brief speculation that the newly elected president would discard the NEC, in order to cut the White House staff, but ultimately Bush's advisers concluded the NEC could be utilized to ensure that the bureaucracy followed through on Bush's policy initiatives. During the 2000 transition, President Bush selected his campaign adviser on the economy, Lawrence Lindsey, to be his first NEA director. Lindsey brought years of political experience to the NEC, having served on the Board of Governors of the Federal Reserve System, at Harvard as an economics professor, and as a staff member on President Reagan's Council of Economic Advisers. Not only were Bush and Lindsey in agreement on the need for deep tax cuts, for de-linking environmental and labor issues from free trade agreements, and for achieving domestic spending cuts, but Lindsey also satisfied Bush's desire that a Washington insider be at the helm of the NEC. Bush and his top political advisers, namely Karl Rove and Karen Hughes, believed that Lindsey could also counterbalance Treasury Secretary O'Neill, who was judged to be an industrialist with little Wall Street experience.[67]

Lindsey transformed the advisory role of the national economic adviser. In January 2001 Lindsey moved to expand his role from being a coordinator and manager of the policy making process to acting as a policy advocate and formulator of policy. Over the objections of the Treasury Department and many in the OMB, Lindsey and the NEC staff were largely responsible for writing and shepherding the president's $1.6 billion tax cut through Congress, though the package was scaled down when finally enacted by Congress in May 2001.[68] Lindsey urged President Bush to remove federal barriers on nuclear power and drilling in the Arctic National Wildlife Refuge and, in addition, advised Bush to ignore the recommendation from EPA administrator Christie Todd Whitman that the United States remain committed to the Kyoto Treaty on the Global Environment. Furthermore, it was Lindsey who counseled President Bush to ignore the recommendations from the Treasury and State departments that the United States ought to intervene in the Argentine financial crisis in order to rescue failed business ventures and restore confidence in its battered currency. Lindsey even bypassed USTR Robert Zoellick and Commerce Secretary Donald Evans regarding U.S. trade policy with Japan.[69]

To foster cooperation between the NEC and NSC, Bush enlarged the joint NSC/NEC international economics staff by adding more international economics experts while cutting the number of security officials. According to National Security Advisor Condoleezza Rice, although the joint staff would be "physically located within the NSC structure" it would report to her and Lindsey through a newly created deputy assistant international economic policy adviser.[70] Rice and Lindsey were to be equally responsible for dealing with two issue clusters: free trade and tariff reductions as well as global financial calamities akin to the Mexican peso and Asian financial crises. Bush also ordered Lindsey and Rice to "share a foreign policy desk" in order to integrate economics with security issues and keep an eye on the bureaucracy. For Bush, the move was designed "to make sure the economic people don't run off with foreign policy and vice versa."[71]

To achieve his goal of fully integrating Treasury into the National Security Council, Bush proceeded to add the treasury secretary to the NSC Principals Committee and directed that the treasury secretary would also be the national economic adviser. A Treasury official was also designated to act as the chair of the international finance policy coordinating committee, one of seventeen such standing committees established by the new administration. Bush justified his moves by referring to the major roles played by Clinton's Treasury and State departments in formulating foreign policy toward Asia and Latin America. As Bush explained: "Globalization has altered the dynamics in the White House, as well as between the White House and the Treasury. We have to respond to that."[72]

Bush's structural reforms demonstrated that he had no intention of re-segregating the domestic and foreign components of economic policy making or of resisting the merger of economics and security issues. Rice noted that "international economic issues are still not as integrated as they should be in the policymaking process. . . . So we are going to try to do this in as seamless a way as possible."[73] Bush's insistence on structural cooperation is also an acknowledgment that economics and security are complex issues and that the trend toward centralization of the process in the White House will likely continue into the future.

In December 2002 Bush dismissed most of his economic team, including Lindsey and O'Neill, mainly for making public statements critical of the tax cuts and the huge costs associated with the U.S. invasion of Iraq. To replace Lindsey, Bush named former Goldman Sachs cochair Stephen Friedman. Friedman, who had worked with Robert Rubin between 1990 and 1992, was appointed partly to garner support from Wall Street. On the whole, Friedman served as a behind-the-scenes NEC director who allowed the new treasury secretary, John Snow, to act as the Bush administration's chief spokesman on economic issues. Friedman's choice for the NEC, however, virtually sparked a revolt among supply-side advocates. They questioned his commitment to further tax cuts because Friedman was a member of the Concord Coalition, an antideficit group. In the end Friedman became an enthusiastic supporter of the 2003 tax cuts.

After Friedman resigned in 2005, former Indiana-based E&A Industries president Alan B. Hubbard became the NEC director, and Hubbard moved to improve its public image. His appointment continued the pattern of consolidating policy making within the White House staff and populating the Bush administration with the most loyal advisers. According to former representative David McIntosh: "Al is one of those guys who understands the theory and the substance of economic policy, but he also understands the politics and how to get something done. He'll bring a lot of energy, and politely but effectively rally everyone behind the president's proposals and keep everyone on point."[74] Hubbard's primary responsibility has been to push an ambitious set of economic policy proposals, including Social Security restructuring, tax system overhaul, tort reform, and free trade. However, virtually all of Bush's domestic economic proposals were abandoned in 2006.

Hubbard's major source of frustration is the inability of the NEC to publicize positive economic performance since Bush's 2004 reelection. In light of the largely negative and sour public mood, Hubbard's efforts to have Bush highlight the good economic news did not have appreciable impact on public opinion. Perhaps the sound fundamentals of the economy were simply overwhelmed by the media coverage of the Iraq War, corruption and lobbying scandals, pension woes, bankruptcies, high-profile layoffs, budget and trade deficits, and illegal immigration. As Hubbard concluded: "We have not done a very good job of getting our message out. We have to keep reminding people that this is a remarkable economy."[75]

Hubbard's NEC was in a politically tenuous position insofar as he was supposed to promote ambitious economic agenda amid widespread public worries. But NEC limitations may have been due largely to President Bush, since Bush clearly prefers businessmen and loyalists rather than Washington politicians, academics, and Wall Street financiers. Hubbard was a loyal Bush family friend and an Indiana businessman, not a Washington politico or an economic policy expert. For his part, Treasury Secretary John Snow lacked political clout within the Bush administration and, therefore, largely acted as a traveling economic salesmen.

In the Clinton administration, particularly under NEC director Robert Rubin and Treasury Secretary Lawrence Summers, the NEC had encouraged the Treasury Department to assume the lead on economic policy. Paul O'Neill, Bush's first treasury secretary, understood economic policy but was too much of a maverick to be an influential spokesman. Snow was a more predictable treasury secretary than O'Neill, though Snow still had little input in policy making. Also, Snow was hampered by the fact that one-third of the positions within the Treasury Department were either empty or filled by "acting" officials. In sum, the NEC under Bush essentially believed that economic policy runs itself and, in fact, strong economic growth did characterize the first years of Bush's second term. The problem is that the NEC was unable to translate that economic performance into political capital for President Bush.[76]

In the final analysis the degree of coordination over economic policy making within the executive branch depends upon the president's personal skills in using the NEC to his political advantage. Clearly, the experiences of recent presidents suggest that total coordination is not really possible; there are simply too many units with diverse missions and outlooks for policy development to be either smooth or single-minded. The structural mechanisms employed to coordinate economic policy have alternated between two approaches: either centralizing control in a single powerful figure or constructing interagency organizations. Successful coordination occurs, apparently, whenever the president has had a strong interest in economic policy and is able to recruit a group of economic policy makers with a similar perspective on economic problems and policies. Thus, economic policy imposes heavy presidential responsibilities since public expectations are so high, but the scope of presidential leadership over economic policy making has real limits given the complex process of economic policy making.

KEY TERMS

Bureau of the Budget (BOB)
Council of Economic Advisers (CEA)
Council on Economic Policy (CEP)
Economic Policy Board (EPB)
Economic Policy Council (EPC)
Economic Policy Group (EPG)
economic subpresidency
Executive Office of the President (EOP)
fiscal year
General Agreement on Tariffs and Trade (GATT)
impoundments
national economic adviser
National Economic Council (NEC)
Office of Management and Budget (OMB)
secretary of the treasury
Troika
U.S. Trade Representative (USTR)

ADDITIONAL READINGS

Anderson, James E. and Jared E. Hazleton. *Managing Macroeconomic Policy: The John-son Presidency*. Austin: University of Texas Press, 1986. An in-depth examination of economic policy making during the Johnson administration, with special attention to the development of the economic subpresidency.

Hargrove, Erwin C. and Samuel A. Morley, eds. *The President and the Council of Economic Advisers*. Boulder, CO: Westview, 1984. Oral history of CEA chairmen who served from 1949 to 1980.

Juster, Kenneth I. and Simon Lazarus. *Making Economic Policy: An Assessment of the National Economic Council*. Washington, DC: Brookings, 1997. Although the NEC served Clinton well, it needs further institutionalization and the authors make several recommendations for improvement.

McDonald, Forrest. *Alexander Hamilton: A Biography*. New York: Norton, 1979. An excellent study of the first secretary of the treasury and architect of the nation's financial system.

Porter, Roger B. *Presidential Decision Making: The Economic Policy Board*. Cambridge, UK: Cambridge University Press, 1980. Superb analysis of the advisory group organized by President Ford to integrate both domestic and international economic policy.

Stein, Herbert. *Presidential Economics: The Making of Economic Policy from Roosevelt to Reagan and Beyond*. New York: Simon & Schuster, 1984. The author, CEA chairman under President Nixon, chronicles the development of fiscal policy making into the early years of the Reagan administration.

Suskind, Ron. *The Price of Loyalty: George W. Bush, the White House, and the Education of Paul O'Neill.* New York: Simon & Schuster, 2004. Suskind recounts why Alcoa CEO O'Neill was recruited to be treasury secretary and how twenty-three months later he was summarily fired for his tell-it-like-it-is brand of leadership.

Warshaw, Shirley Anne. *Powersharing: White House-Cabinet Relations in the Modern Presidency* (Albany, NY: State University of New York Press, 1996). The most challenging organizational goal for modern presidents is to structure a "powersharing" relationship between the White House staff and the cabinet so that both are involved in policy making.

Woodward, Bob. *The Agenda.* New York: Simon & Schuster, 1994. Provides a day-by-day, often minute-by-minute, account of economic policy in Bill Clinton's White House based on hundreds of interviews, confidential internal memos, diaries, and meeting notes.

NOTES

1. James E. Anderson, "The President and Economic Policy: A Comparative View of Advisory Arrangements" (paper presented at the annual meeting of the American Political Science Association, 1991), 2. See also James E. Anderson and Jared E. Hazleton, *Managing Macroeconomic Policy: The Johnson Presidency* (Austin: University of Texas Press, 1986), chap. 2.

2. Hugh S. Norton, *The Employment Act and the Council of Economic Advisers, 1946–1976* (Columbia: University of South Carolina Press, 1977), 65.

3. Quoted in Raymond Tatalovich and Byron W. Daynes, *Presidential Power in the United States* (Monterey, CA: Brooks/Cole, 1984), 217.

4. Council of Economic Advisers, *Economic Report of the President 1996* (Washington, DC: U.S. Government Printing Office, 1996), 11.

5. See Walter W. Heller, *New Dimensions of Political Economy* (Cambridge: Harvard University Press, 1966), 14–18.

6. Gardner Ackley, "The Contribution of Economics to Policy Formation," *Journal of Finance* 21 (May 1966), 176.

7. Heller, *New Dimensions*, 52.

8. Reported in Craufurd D. Goodwin and R. Stanley Herren, "The Truman Administration: Problems and Policies Unfold," in *Exhortation and Controls: The Search for a Wage-Price Policy 1945–1971*, ed. Craufurd D. Goodwin (Washington, DC: Brookings, 1975), 37.

9. Steven Greenhouse, "Bush's Economic Aides Defending Reputations," *New York Times*, November 14, 1992.

10. This is not meant to imply that recent CEA members lack significant professional reputations, but only that presidents choose economists with significant reputations from within the macroeconomic "camp" that they favor. For example, each of Clinton's CEA nominees are considered to have solid academic credentials. While CEA chair Tyson's recent reputation is based on work on international trade, Clinton's second CEA nominee, Alan Blinder of Princeton University, has a significant reputation as a macroeconomist.

11. Michael Lewis, "Econoclast: Laura Tyson's Professional Honesty," *New Republic* (February 1, 1993): 18.

12. John Judis, "Old Master: Rubin's Artful Role," *New Republic* (December 13, 1993): 21; Lewis, "Econoclast," 18–21; and Bruce Stokes, "CEA Tyson's Challenge," *National Journal* (January 30, 1993): 286.

13. Chris Suellentrop, "Glenn Hubbard: First-rate Economist. Tax-cut Champion. Presidential Yes Man," *Slate* (January 22, 2003), http://www.slate.com/id/2077330.

14. Quoted in Paul Blustein, "Survey Finds Little 'Off-shoring' Impact," *Washington Post*, June 11, 2004 and N. Gregory Mankiw and Phillip Swagel, "The Politics and Economics of Offshore Outsourcing," (July 2006), *NBER* Working Paper No. W12398.

15. John W. Sloan, "Economic Policymaking in the Johnson and Ford Administrations," *Presidential Studies Quarterly* 20 (Winter 1990): 116.

16. The fiscal year takes its number from the year in which it ends. Thus, FY 1993 covers the period 10/1/92–9/30/93.

17. Kermit Gordon, "Reflections on Spending," in *Public Policy*, vol 15, eds. J. D. Montgomery and A. Smithies (Cambridge, MA: Harvard University Press, 1966): 11–22. Reprinted in Thomas E. Cronin and Sanford D. Greenberg, eds., *The Presidential Advisory System* (New York: Harper & Row, 1969), 60.

18. Hugh Heclo, "OMB and the Presidency: The Problem of 'Neutral Competence,'" *Public Interest* 38 (Winter 1975): 87.

19. See Richard P. Nathan, *The Administrative Presidency* (New York: Wiley, 1983).

20. Gerald M. Boyd, "Reagan Aids Prod Congress on Debt," *New York Times*, October 31, 1985; Jonathan Fuerbringer, "Like It or Not, Deficit Plan Will Pass, Lawmakers Say," *New York Times*, November 21, 1985; and Peter T. Kilborn, "Future for Deficit-Reducing Law: A Political Balancing Act Is Required," *New York Times*, December 13, 1985.

21. Daniel J. Mitchell, "Bush's Rasputin: Office of Management and Budget Director Richard Darman's Failed Economic Policies," *National Review* (December 28, 1992).

22. From 1977 to 1993, Panetta was a U.S. representative from California serving from 1989 to 1993 as chair of the House Budget Committee. Panetta was a popular moderate Democrat, a deficit hawk, and a free trader. On the whole, Panetta would add to Clinton's image as a bold new Democrat who could experiment with new, even risky, economic policies. Even more, he was popular with Republicans and Democrats in the House. Clinton needed to develop a working political relationship with that institution for his economic policies to be successful. Alice Rivlin was director of the Congressional Budget Office from 1976 to 1983.

23. Elizabeth Drew, *On the Edge: The Clinton Presidency* (New York: Simon & Schuster, 1995); Bob Woodward, *The Agenda*. (New York: Simon & Schuster, 1994), 26–27; and George Stephanopoulos, *All Too Human: A Political Education* (Boston: Little, Brown, 1999), 346.

24. C. Fred Bergsten, *The United States and the World Economy* (Washington, DC: Institute of International Economics, 2005) and C. Fred Bergsten, "Foreign Economic Policy for the Next President," *Foreign Affairs* 83, no. 2 (2004): 88–101.

25. See, for example, "Reports of Clinton Nominees Ease Fears of Bond Traders," *New York Times*, December 8, 1992.

26. U.S. Office of Management and Budget (OMB), *Historical Tables: Budget of the United States Government, 2006* (Washington, DC: Government Printing Office, 2005), 7–9, and 54, http://www.whitehouse.gov/omb/budget/fy2007/pdf/hist.pdf.

27. Ron Suskind, *The Price of Loyalty: George W. Bush, the White House, and the Education of Paul O'Neill* (New York: Simon & Schuster, 2004), chap. 8.

28. Paul Blustein, "Paulson Sticks to the Script," *Washington Post*, June 28, 2006.

29. Control is actually shared to a significant degree with the Fed, acting as the United States' central bank. The treasury secretary plays a very public role in periodic formal meetings among finance ministers, while central bankers consult and coordinate with each other on a relatively continuous basis.

30. Jorge G. Castaneda, "Mexico: The Price of Denial," *Atlantic Monthly* (July 1995): 21–25; Susan Dentzer, Linda Robinson, Steven D. Kaye, and Jack Egan, "The Rescue of Mexico," *U.S. News & World Report* (January 23, 1995): 48–49; and Bradford De Long, Christopher De Long, and Sherman Robinson, "The Case for Mexico's Rescue," *Foreign Affairs* 75, no. 3 (May–June 1996): 8–14. A swap, put simply, is an arrangement, in which U.S. dollars are exchanged for a foreign currency. With respect to the Mexican peso crisis, the Treasury Department signed swap arrangements, in which dollars were swapped for pesos. At the end of the arrangement, the Treasury Department pledged to return the pesos and the Bank of Mexico would return the dollars.

31. The ESF was first established by the Gold Reserve Act of 1934, and was funded by the sale of gold. The fund provides the Treasury Department with resources to stabilize exchange rates and maintain orderly exchange market conditions. The ESF statute gives the president and the treasury secretary authority to utilize a broad range of loans and credits, including swaps of dollars for foreign currencies, and guarantees securities, gold, and foreign exchange. Most important here is that the president and treasury secretary do not need congressional approval for authorized operations utilizing ESF resources. The United States has entered into over fifty swap arrangements and bridge loans with foreign governments since 1934—most in the past fifteen years. We have provided dollars to Mexico through short-term swap arrangements five times since 1982 alone, and in 1982 we provided Mexico with support through a medium-term, one-year swap arrangement. Mexico fully repaid its obligations under all of these facilities except the existing one, which is not yet due for repayment. In response to the peso crisis, under these agreements, the United States pledged to provide three forms of support to Mexico: short-term swaps through which Mexico borrows dollars for ninety days and that can be rolled over for up to one year; medium-term swaps through which Mexico can borrow dollars for up to five years; and securities having maturities of up to ten years. For more see De Long et al., "The Case for Mexico's Rescue."

32. Stephen Hess, *Organizing the Presidency* (Washington, DC: Brookings, 1988), 44, 48 and Harry S. Truman, *Memoirs: Years of Decision*, vols. 1 & 2 (New York: Doubleday), 34–36.

33. Hess, *Organizing the Presidency*, 48.

34. Hess, *Organizing the Presidency*, 51.

35. Harold Malmgren, "Managing Foreign Economic Policy," *Foreign Policy* (1972): 22–24.

36. Joan Hoff, *Nixon Reconsidered* (New York: Basic, 1994).

37. Hoff, *Nixon Reconsidered* and Kenneth I. Juster and Simon Lazarus, *Making Economic Policy: An Assessment of the National Economic Council* (Washington, DC: Brookings, 1997).

38. Roger Porter, *Presidential Decision-Making: The Economic Policy Board* (Cambridge: Cambridge University Press, 1980).

39. Chris J. Dolan, "Presidential Coordination of Economic Policy: A Historical Analysis," *White House Studies* 3, no. 2 (2003): 157–182.

40. David B. Cohen, Chris J. Dolan, and Jerel A. Rosati, "A Place at the Table: The Emerging Foreign Policy Roles of the White House Chief of Staff," *Congress and the Presidency* 29, no. 2 (2002): 119–149.

41. David Wessel, "Economic Security Council Stirs Debate," *Wall Street Journal*, November 10, 1992.

42. Bruce Stokes, "Elevating Economics," *National Journal* (March 13, 1993): 615–619.

43. Beth Belton, "Wall Streeter with a Heart Defies Stereotype," *USA Today*, March 3, 1993.

44. Chris J. Dolan, "Economic Policy and Decision-Making at the Intersection of Domestic and International Politics: The Advocacy Coalition Framework and the National Economic Council," *Policy Studies Journal* 31, no. 1 (2003): 209–236.

45. Henry Butterfield Ryan, "US Needs a Trade Czar," *Christian Science Monitor* (September 30, 1992), http://www.csmonitor.com.

46. John B. Judis, "Old Master: Rubin's Artful Role," *New Republic* (December 13, 1993): 21–25.

47. Juster and Lazarus, *Making Economic Policy*, 8.

48. Juster and Lazarus, *Making Economic Policy*, 8.

49. Drew, *On the Edge* and Woodward, *The Agenda*.

50. William Jefferson Clinton and Al Gore, *Putting People First: How We Can All Change America* (New York: Random House, 1992), 131–132.

51. Quoted in Wessel, "Economic Security Council Stirs Debate."

52. Vincent Auger, "The National Security System after the Cold War," in *U.S. Foreign Policy After the Cold War*, eds. Randall B. Ripley and James M. Lindsay (Pittsburgh: University of Pittsburgh Press), 51.

53. David R. Francis, "Views on Clinton's Economic Council," *Christian Science Monitor* (November 13, 1992), http://www.csmonitor.com.

54. Juster and Lazarus, *Making Economic Policy*.

55. Francis, "Views on Clinton's Economic Council."

56. David D. Newsom, "Economic Council Needs More Study," *Christian Science Monitor* (November 25, 1992), http://www.csmonitor.com.

57. Paul Starobin, "The Broker," *National Journal* (April 16, 1994): 878–883.

58. Paul Starobin, James A. Barnes, Julie Kosterlitz, Margaret Kriz, and Kirk Victor, "Clinton's A-Team," *National Journal* (December 19, 1992): 2893–2897.

59. Woodward, *The Agenda*, 62.

60. Starobin et al., "Clinton's A-Team," 2893.

61. See Drew, *On the Edge*, 2 and Woodward, *The Agenda*, 60–63. Bentsen was also known for his sharp political skills and quick wit. His comment that Dan

Quayle was "no Jack Kennedy" during the 1988 vice presidential debates earned him top accolades and catapulted him to the fore of Democratic Party politics.

62. Drew, *On the Edge*, 63.

63. Stokes, "Elevating Economics," 618. At first, it was thought that the national economic adviser and treasury secretary would clash over the direction of Clinton's economic policy agenda. This was not the case between Rubin and Bentsen who shared a collegial working history. Prior to serving in the Clinton administration, Rubin once managed a blind trust for Bentsen and his family while at Goldman Sachs. On the NEC, Clinton clearly defined their political roles. Rubin would be the inside, low-profile political broker of competing bureaucratic and policy interests and Bentsen would assume the lead as the administration's public spokesman on issues.

64. Drew, *On the Edge*, 26–27; Starobin et al., "Clinton's A-Team," 2893; and Stephanopoulos, *All Too Human*, 346.

65. I. M. Destler, *National Economic Council: A Work in Progress* (Washington, DC: Institute for International Economics, 1996); Juster and Lazarus, *Making Economic Policy*; and Ben Wildavsky, "Under the Gun," *National Journal* (June 29, 1996).

66. Stephanopoulos, *All Too Human*, 135.

67. Rich Thomas and Keith Naughton, "Bush's Money Posse," *Newsweek* (January 15, 2001): 19–22.

68. Thomas and Naughton, "Bush's Money Posse" and Chris J. Dolan and Jerel A. Rosati, "U.S. Foreign Economic Policy and the Significance of the National Economic Council," *International Studies Perspectives* 7, no. 2 (2006): 22–37.

69. John B. Judis, "Bush League Economics," *American Prospect* (March 7, 2002): 14–17.

70. David E. Sanger, "Bush Plans to Stress Effects of Economics on Security," *New York Times*, January 6, 2001.

71. Sanger, "Bush Plans to Stress Effects of Economics on Security."

72. Sanger, "Bush Plans to Stress Effects of Economics on Security."

73. Sanger, "Bush Plans to Stress Effects of Economics on Security."

74. Richard W. Stevenson, "Bush Names Longtime Friend to Head Economic Council," *New York Times*, January 11, 2005.

75. Richard S. Dunham, "The Struggle to Sell the Economy's Sizzle," *Business Week* (January 23, 2006): 1.

76. Dunham, "The Struggle to Sell the Economy's Sizzle."

4

Presidential Budgeting and Fiscal Policy

The federal budget is an ordering of national priorities or, as author Aaron Wildavsky puts it, a "series of goals with price tags attached."[1] The budget is the focal point of debate over fiscal policy, because federal spending is an important determinant of aggregate demand in the economy. The interrelationships among budgets, deficit financing, and fiscal policy are among the important topics discussed in this chapter. To begin, however, we describe the roles of the executive and legislative branches in the budgetary process and how those roles have evolved historically. The development of the budgetary process is really a chronicle of the political battles for control over taxing and spending.

THE POLITICAL BUDGETARY PROCESS

Developing the federal budget can be conceptualized in three distinct phases: budget authority, obligations, and outlays. **Budget authority** is legislation that serves as the legal basis by which federal agencies make binding financial commitments. **Obligations** result when the federal government enters into contracts, employs personnel, or submits purchase orders for goods and services. **Outlays** are the actual checks, electronic fund transfers, or other payments made by the Treasury Department to departments and agencies.

The 1990 Budget Enforcement Act requires Congress to classify spending (outlays) based on these functional categories: defense, nondefense discretionary, and entitlements. **Discretionary programs** (for example, defense, K-12 education, research, housing, and infrastructure) are provided in annual appropriations acts and fall under the jurisdiction of the House and Senate Appropriations Committees. Altogether, nondefense discretionary programs comprise only 16% of total federal spending in 2007. **Entitlement programs** (Social Security, Medicare, Medicaid, and other programs like veterans' pensions) along with interest on the national debt total nearly two-thirds of federal spending in 2007. Interest is an entitlement because, unless the federal government chooses to declare bankruptcy and nullify its debts, the United States must make its interest payments, otherwise nobody would be willing to lend our government money in the future.

Revenues (receipts) are derived from several sources. Individual and corporate income taxes account for most receipts, whereas payroll and excise taxes, surcharges, and customs fees have become increasingly more important in recent years. A **budget deficit** occurs when the federal government spends more money than it collects in revenues, and a **budget surplus** occurs when revenues exceed spending. Also, the Treasury Department borrows money from creditors, including citizens, private banks, financiers abroad, and foreign governments to finance the current programs of the national government. The accumulation of yearly deficits over time is the **national debt**. Deviations from the tax code that reduce receipts, namely exemptions, deductions, and special rules, are known as **tax expenditures**, so-called because their net impact is to increase outlays just like spending increases would. Among the best-known tax expenditures are income tax deductions for mortgage and student loan interest, dependent child tax

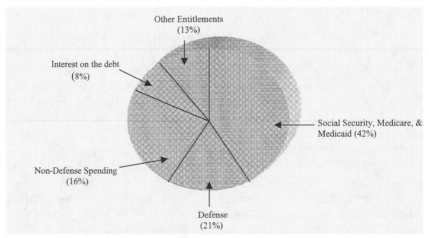

Figure 4.1.   Federal Spending, FY 2007

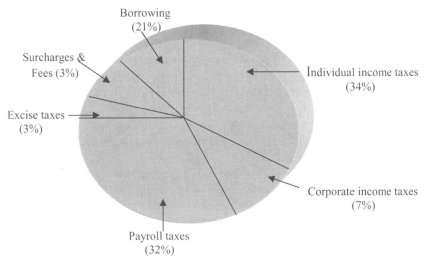

Figure 4.2.   Revenue Sources for the Budget, FY 2007

credits, child care, home improvements, professional travel, high medical costs, and charitable contributions.

Early Budgeting, 1789–1921

Federal spending can have a major countercyclical impact on the economy in addition to being a primary tool by which the federal government achieves its policy objectives. The Founding Fathers recognized the need for a budget but the Constitution includes fewer than forty words on the subject: "No money shall be drawn from the Treasury, but in Consequence of Appropriations made by Law; and a regular Statement and account of Receipts and Expenditures of all public Money shall be published from time to time." House and Senate procedures for receipts and expenditures are provided under a constitutional provision that permits each house to make its own rules. Article I of the Constitution specifies the "power To lay and collect Taxes, Duties, Imposts and Excises, to pay the Debts and provide for the common Defense and general Welfare of the United States. . . . To borrow Money on the credit of the United States. . . . To coin Money [and] regulate the Value thereof." Article I also stipulates that "no Money shall be drawn from the Treasury, but in Consequence of Appropriations made by Law." Collectively, these clauses define congressional control over both taxing and spending. It was James Madison who predicted that this "power of the purse" would be "the most complete and effectual weapon with which any constitution can arm the immediate representatives of the people, for obtaining a redress of every grievance, and for carrying into effect every just and salutary measure."[2]

The House of Representatives began reviewing appropriations bills through its Committee on Ways and Means, established in 1802 as the first House standing committee. In the Senate, appropriations bills continued to be under the jurisdiction of select committees until the Finance Committee was created in 1816. However, this unified control over finances was jeopardized by a new development: the use of separate funding bills for special purposes. Two appropriations bills were enacted as early as 1794, one funding administration and another for military spending. This practice escalated during the early 1800s, when separate appropriations were used for such purposes as the navy, post office, and military academy.

The Civil War fragmented budgetary authority even more, because no single committee was able to cope with the magnitude of wartime finances. In 1865 the House decided to limit the jurisdiction of Ways and Means to revenue bills and assigned spending bills to the newly created Appropriations and Banking Committees. Then Congress passed the Anti-Deficiency Act of 1870 to prohibit agencies and departments from spending more money than Congress had appropriated. It also forbade agencies from entering into contracts for future payments in excess of appropriations.

By 1876 the Appropriations Committee was allowed to reduce spending amounts, which undermined the authority of other standings committees. To curb the Appropriations Committee, the House authorized certain standing committees to report money bills directly to the floor. In 1877 the House moved against the Appropriations Committee to ensure funding for rivers and harbors, a classic example of "pork-barrel" legislation. According to author Louis Fisher, this assault occurred because legislators believed that it prevented them from delivering benefits to their districts.[3] The complete dismantling of the Appropriations Committee in the Senate came in 1899, when six other funding bills were assigned to those standing committees with legislative jurisdiction.

What began in the nineteenth century as a coherent procedure, had given way to a highly fragmented system by 1900. Tax bills were now under the control of the House Ways and Means Committee and the Senate Finance Committee. Annual spending was assigned to the House and Senate Appropriations Committees, while bills for specific projects were given to the standing committees charged with legislating in those areas. Although eventually the Appropriations Committees regained control over all regular annual spending bills, later in the twentieth century the House and Senate standing committees with jurisdiction over entitlement programs got the authority to oversee funding for those entitlements.[4]

Budgeting, 1921–1974

Although Congress passed many budgetary rules during the nineteenth and early twentieth centuries as it tried to effectively manage federal spending, few had any lasting effect. A movement toward budget reform was encouraged by deficits incurred during 1894–1899, 1904–1905, and 1910–1911. President William Howard Taft urged Congress to fund a five-member Commission on Economy and Efficiency to upgrade the budgetary process. Its final report in June 1912 recommended that the president review the estimated agency spending requests and coordinate them into one budget for Congress' approval. But Congress refused, so Taft directed his agency heads to prepare, in addition to the customary "Book of Estimates" for Congress, a national budget along the lines proposed by the Commission. In reaction, Congress ordered the agencies not to formulate any budget document, fearing that Taft might cut funding programs targeted to their districts.

Budgetary reform also interested President Woodrow Wilson since he was a former political science professor, but the issue was sidetracked by World War I. During the war, states and localities adopted a "unified executive budget" concept and bipartisan support for reform grew in Congress. An **executive budget** includes all spending requests combined into a single budget document, which is prepared by a central budgeting authority (usually the president). Its principal benefit is that an executive budget permits a clearer idea of total spending and how the individual components relate to the overall picture. In 1917 President Wilson asked Congress to move toward that goal by assigning all funding bills in each chamber to one committee. Although Wilson threw his support behind the concept of a unified executive budget, the federal government continued to operate without a comprehensive budget process.[5]

Real reform did not come until Congress passed the Budget and Accounting Act of 1921, which required the president to formulate a unified budget and formally submit it to Congress.[6] The act created the **Bureau of the Budget (BOB)** within the Department of the Treasury. The BOB was designed to "assemble, correlate, revise, reduce, or increase the estimates of the several departments or establishments" with the exceptions of Congress and the Supreme Court.[7] The basic requirement of the act is that the president should prepare and submit a unified budget to Congress.[8]

President Warren G. Harding appointed Charles G. Dawes as the first BOB director. Dawes's first major decision was to issue Budget Circular No. 40, which declared that all agencies must submit their budgets to the BOB so they could be forwarded by the president to Congress as a unified budget. Under Harding, Coolidge, and Hoover, the BOB was mainly concerned with efficiency. This narrow focus prompted FDR to rely on a "Brain

Trust" to develop budget strategy during the Depression. The BOB reached its zenith under presidents Harry Truman and Dwight Eisenhower, who both used the bureau to determine if program requests by the agencies fit into the president's legislative program.[9] The 1921 Act also created the **General Accounting Office (GAO)** (in 2004 the name was changed to the **Government Accountability Office**). The GAO serves as a nonpartisan, independent auditor and is the investigative arm of Congress charged with examining matters relating to the receipt and payment of public funds.

While the hope was that the Appropriations Committee would bring a unified budget to the floor, the House began the practice of reviewing subcommittee reports of the Appropriations Committee one by one. These relationships were facilitated by the norm of "reciprocity" whereby subcommittees would defer to each other, and the Appropriations Committee simply ratified their spending decisions.[10]

In subsequent years Congress made additional attempts to manage the budget. The Revenue Act of 1941 created the Joint Committee on the Reduction of Federal Expenditures, consisting of members of the House and Senate Appropriations Committees. The goal was to provide oversight of the president's annual budget request. The Legislative Reorganization Act of 1946 created the Joint Committee for the Legislative Budget, which was entrusted with preparing a budget for recommending estimated receipts and spending for the upcoming fiscal year. If estimated expenditures exceeded receipts, a concurrent resolution accompanying the committee's report would increase the public debt.[11]

Until the mid-1960s, preparation and enactment of the budget followed a predictable pattern, guided by acceptance of general principles. According to Wildavsky, these included a commitment to balanced (or nearly balanced) budgets, a belief that government spending was basically beneficial, and a preference for "hidden" taxes or selective tax changes rather than across-the-board changes in the tax code.[12] On the whole the BOB supervised the preparation of the executive budget and developed a reputation for nonpartisan mastery of budgetary details. The House Appropriations Committee trimmed presidential requests, while the Senate Appropriations Committee played the role of "court of appeals," restoring portions of the House cuts.[13] Although spending authority rested with the two Appropriations Committees and taxing authority rested with the House Ways and Means Committee and Senate Finance Committee, the tolerance for small federal deficits helped coordinate their disparate budgetary activities.

This consensus began to dissolve during the Johnson administration, which pushed for massive new spending in his Great Society program at the same time it made new defense spending requests to wage the Vietnam War. To implement his new spending programs, Johnson initiated a process of using the BOB to integrate policy proposals and economic task force operations into his annual legislative program.[14] The 1960s, however, was a period of significant prosperity and Keynesian economists were arguing that larger deficits were not detrimental as long as the economy was expanding. However, President Johnson's deficit financing occurred during an era of full employment (1965 to 1968), a departure from pure Keynesian theory, and it pushed aggregate demand beyond what was necessary to achieve full employment and, consequently, contributed to the inflationary cycle of the 1970s.[15]

Other changes also contributed to the collapse of the old budgeting system. Among the most significant was President Richard Nixon's acceleration of the trend toward politicizing the budget office, by utilizing it as a weapon in disputes with Congress. In 1970 Nixon reorganized the BOB into the **Office of Management and Budget (OMB)**.[16] Rather than rely on civil servants, Nixon made the OMB responsive to his political interests by moving it into the West Wing of the White House and by adding politically appointed associate-level directors to manage the OMB's examining divisions responsible for formulating the budget.[17] The emphasis on "management" in the new title highlighted Nixon's desire to extend administrative control over the bureaucracy. Such politicization blurred the line between the OMB's institutional authority and its political power as an extension of the White House staff.[18] The political backlash prompted Congress to pass legislation in 1974 requiring that the OMB director be subject to Senate confirmation, an indication that the OMB was viewed as a political tool of the White House.

Congress also passed the **Budget and Impoundment Control Act of 1974** over President Nixon's veto.[19] What instigated this fundamental change in budgeting procedures was Nixon's claim that the president possessed the power to **impound** funds, that is, to refuse to spend funds appropriated by Congress and to transfer impounded funds to other areas (specifically to prosecute the Vietnam War).[20] The Impoundment Control provision restricts presidential impoundment, and the Congressional Budget provision modifies the budgetary process. The Congressional Budget Act created Budget Committees in both the House and Senate entrusted with formulating a "congressional budget" and enforcing legally binding spending and revenue targets.[21] The **Congressional Budget Office (CBO)** was established to replace the Joint Committee on the Reduction of Federal Expenditures. The CBO provides Congress with annual economic forecasts, reviews the president's annual budget, and prepares various reports for Congress as a check on the OMB. The purpose of the CBO is to provide nonpartisan budget information and analyses to Congress and its committees. It is one of three government agencies (the others are the GAO and the Congressional Research Service) usually referred to as "legislative agencies" that report to the Congress rather than to the executive branch. The 1974 act requires the CBO to serve at the will of the budget, the appropriations, and the revenue committees in this order. The CBO produces five-year economic projections, baseline projections, spending and revenue options for reducing the deficit, and general fiscal analysis. The CBO director is asked to testify about the outlook for the budget and the economy as well as related issues. As author Howard Shuman puts it: "The Congress passed the 'Impoundment Control Act' to discipline the president. It passed the 'Congressional Budget Act' to discipline itself."[22]

Budgeting since 1974

The 1974 Act established a timetable that calls for the final adoption of a **congressional budget resolution**.[23] On or before the first Monday in February, the president and the OMB submit the executive budget, officially titled *The Budget of the United States*. It consists of detailed requests for the fiscal year, which runs from October 1 to September 30. The fiscal year is the federal government's twelve-month period for calculating annual financial reports for its array of agencies and departments. Prior to the 1974 Act, the fiscal year ran from July 1 to June 30. The change was made to prevent delays in appropriations bills and to make sure that funding for all departments and agencies could be completed before the start of the new fiscal year. The budget request developed by the OMB accomplishes three important objectives. First, it tells Congress what the administration believes fiscal policy should be, as indicated by three components: (1) how much money the government should spend, (2) how much revenue it should collect, and (3) how much a deficit or surplus the federal government should expect.[24]

Second, the budget request lays out the president's spending priorities by detailing how much money should be spent on defense, education, agriculture, transportation, and so on. It sketches fiscal policy and budget priorities, not only for the coming year but also for the next five years, and provides historical tables that review past budget figures. The executive budget is accompanied by various supplemental publications that give detailed specifics.

Third, the budget signals to Congress the president's recommended spending and taxation levels. However, much of the budget is automatically set.[25] Interest paid on the national debt is automatically established, although the ceiling on the national debt must be raised from time to time by legislation so the government is authorized to continue borrowing to finance programs. In March 2006 President Bush signed a bill that raises the debt ceiling by $781 billion to $8.9 trillion.[26] In addition, spending on entitlement programs is permanently set by legislation.

Since the passage of the 1974 Act, House and Senate Budget Committees have been responsible for "marking up" and reporting budget resolutions. Each Budget Committee holds hearings and receives "views and estimates" reports from other committees based on research provided by the CBO director. In their initial hearings each year, the Budget Committees receive testimony from the OMB director, the treasury secretary, and the chairman of the Council of Economic Advisers. The "views and estimates" reports of House and Senate committees provide the Budget Committees with information on the preferences and legislative plans of congressional committees regarding budgetary matters within their jurisdiction.

The CBO assists the Budget Committees in developing the budget resolution by issuing reports on the economic and budget outlook, the president's budgetary proposals, and spending and revenue options for reducing the deficit. The extent to which the Budget Committees consider particular programs when they act on the budget resolution varies from year to year. Specific program decisions are left to the Appropriations Committees and other committees with programmatic jurisdiction, but there is a strong likelihood that major issues will be discussed in markup, in the Budget Committees' reports, and during floor consideration of the budget resolution.[27]

Floor consideration of the budget resolution is guided by House and Senate rules and practices. The House Rules Committee usually reports a "special rule" that establishes the terms and conditions under which the budget resolution is considered. This "special rule" typically specifies which amendments may be considered and the sequence in which they are to be offered and voted on. It has been the practice in recent years to allow consideration of a few amendments (as substitutes for the entire resolution) that present broad policy choices. In the Senate the amending process is less structured, relying on agreements reached by the leadership through a broad consultative process, although the rules prohibit filibustering the budget resolution on the Senate floor.

The tools that Congress can use to enforce the budget resolution during the year are **spending floors** and **spending ceilings** as well as committee allocations and subdivisions of spending. A spending floor indicates that a minimum amount of funding must be spent on a designated activity or program. A spending ceiling stipulates that a specified activity or program can obligate no more funding than a maximum dollar amount. In order for these enforcement procedures to work, Congress must have access to budgetary information so that it can relate individual measures to overall budget policies and determine whether adoption of a particular measure would be consistent with those policies. Substantive and procedural "points of order" are designed to obtain congressional compliance with budget rules. A point of order may bar House or Senate consideration of

Table 4.1.   Contemporary Budget Timetable

Deadline	Action
First Monday in February	The president and the OMB submit the budget to congressional budget committees.
February 15	The Congressional Budget Office completes and submits a report on economic and budget forecasts for budget committees.
Six weeks after president's budget is submitted	Budget committees complete views and estimates.
April 1	House and Senate Budget Committee reports budget resolution.
April 15	Congress complete action on budget resolution.
June 10	House and Senate appropriations committees report the last annual appropriations spending bill.
June 30	House and Senate complete action on appropriations bills and any authorization and reconciliation bills.
July 15	The president and the OMB submit midsession review of the budget to Congress.
October 1	Fiscal year begins.

legislation that violates the spending ceilings and floors in the budget resolution, committee subdivisions of spending, or congressional budget procedures.[28] The budget timetable is described in table 4.1.

Once the budget resolution has established spending and revenue levels, the Appropriations Committees are given a **section 302(a)** spending allocation. This allocation serves as an internal control mechanism, enforceable through points of order and other procedural mechanisms in both the House and Senate Appropriations Committees. When the Appropriations committees receive the allocation, they divide it into **section 302(b)** suballocations for each subcommittee (a more specialized, smaller committee within the Appropriations Committee) to begin work on annual spending bills for its specific agency areas.[29]

BUDGETS AND FISCAL POLICY

The most important consequence of current budgetary trends is that fiscal policy has been weakened as a useful instrument for countercyclical policy. Recall that the basic purpose of fiscal policy is to use government taxing and spending to influence the level of aggregate demand, stimulating the economy during recessions and slowing it down during periods of inflation. Two separate but interrelated factors have rendered this difficult to do. First, large deficits have dominated nearly all the discussion of budgeting, crowding out most other considerations, including fiscal policies to address inflation and unemployment. With rising inflation and budget deficits in the range of $300 to $400 billion under President George W. Bush, it is difficult to contemplate moving expenditure levels in any direction other than toward smaller deficits. Of course, as demonstrated by the 1984 and 1992 presidential elections, the public will not likely support a candidate who wants to raise taxes in order to shrink the deficit. Second, enormous expenditures for entitlements and defense means that a smaller portion of the federal budget can be used for short-term manipulation in order to influence the economy. Nondefense discretionary spending covers virtually all government activities other than entitlement programs, such as space and technology, natural resources and the environment, community and economic development, education and student loans, job training, food safety and public health, housing, veterans benefits, hospitals, federal law enforcement, rural programs, general government operations, transportation, energy, agricultural and biomedical research, and international aid. At one time nondefense discretionary spending was a relatively constant share of the gross domestic product (GDP), but more recently, except for the years 1975–1983 when it rose to 5% of GDP, total federal spending for nondefense discretionary programs has been falling, from 3.4% in 2001 to 3.1% of GDP in 2007.[30]

During the Reagan, George H. W. Bush, and George W. Bush presidencies, policy makers denounced deficits but did little to reduce them. Changing levels of public support for defense spending in the wake of the collapse of the Soviet Union only moderately expanded the available policy options. But even those options narrowed further in the aftermath of the terrorist attacks of September 11, 2001, since the second Bush administration asked Congress to substantially increase defense spending for the War on Terrorism and the Iraq War.

Why Budgets Continue to Grow

By any standard the budget has grown by a staggering amount. Over the past six decades, total "real" spending—adjusted for inflation—increased nearly nine times as fast as the growth in the economy and over forty times faster than the increase in population. During recession years, spending usually increases, having been triggered mainly by **automatic stabilizers**, which are taxation and spending items already built into the budget that adjust without direct approval by Congress or the president. One example is unemployment insurance, for which the government spends more money during recessions when the jobless rate is higher. The tax code also acts as an automatic stabilizer insofar as the amount of tax revenue collected is higher during a boom than during a recession. But beyond these short-term, cyclical adjustments in federal spending since the New Deal of the 1930s and the Great Society of the 1960s, there have been structural increases in budgetary expenditures. Prior to 1956, in fact, there was no steady year-by-year increase in expenditures; the pattern was quite erratic. Since then, however, we have seen increasing federal expenditures every year except 1965. This upward trajectory continued long after the Vietnam War because programmatic expansions of various New Deal and Great Society initiatives obligated the federal government to fund a variety of increasingly costly programs. And since revenues have not kept pace with these spending commitments, deficits have resulted in forty-nine of the fifty-eight years during the period from 1948 through 2006.

But why do budgets continue to grow? One basic reason is bureaucratic endurance. Agencies provide jobs to thousands of government personnel, accumulate political power and status, and distribute benefits to interest groups and citizens. As a consequence, few programs are eliminated. One study found that 85% of the 175 agencies existing in 1923 still operated fifty years later.[31] Similarly, Common Cause, a citizen's advocacy group, reported in 1976 that, during the previous fifteen years, 236 new agencies were created but only twenty-one had been canceled.[32]

Another reason budgets continue to grow is **incrementalism**. Congress does not have enough time or staff to study the entire budget, and prior to 1974 no standing committee had this responsibility. Moreover, members of Congress are primarily concerned about whether pet programs for their states and districts will get more funding next year than the previous year. The presumption is that existing government programs should be continued; the only question is at what rate. It all adds up. As Senator Everett Dirksen (R-IL) is alleged to have said, "A billion dollars here and a billion dollars there and pretty soon you're talking real money."[33]

Clearly the expansion of expensive entitlement programs has contributed markedly to the growth of the federal budget. Entitlements are government programs that supply financial benefits to a large number of citizens who have a legal right to receive them if they meet certain eligibility conditions. The most important entitlement programs include Social Security, Medicare, Medicaid, veterans' benefits, federal employee and military retirement benefits, unemployment compensation, food stamps, and agricultural price supports for farmers.

From the standpoint of fiscal policy, entitlements create problems for the president and Congress in controlling the size of the budget. First, it is difficult to forecast how many individuals will meet the various criteria during any given year. As a result, the president is often unable to set policies to ensure full employment and lower inflation because these objectives require careful preplanning of the budget. Second, the number of people on entitlement programs depends on overall economic conditions. Social Security pensions and government retirement programs have been indexed to inflation (**COLAs** or cost of living adjustments), so the size of the benefit has to be adjusted according to a fixed formula based on unpredictable changes in the consumer price index. Third, the Senate and House Appropriations Committees cannot rewrite entitlement programs, which fall under the jurisdiction of the House and Senate standing committees with programmatic authority (so-called authorization committees), and the law that specifies who gets how much and under what conditions. Changing eligibility or benefits requires new legislation. The scope of entitlement programs means that the president and Congress can scrutinize no more than one-third of the annual budget for possible cutbacks if, for example, inflationary pressures loom on the horizon.

The inflexibility built into the federal budget reduces the practicality of trying to counteract the ups and downs of the overall economy with fiscal policy. The Appropriations Committees, therefore, are limited to adjusting annually appropriated defense and nondefense discretionary programs. But that is not easy either, because a significant portion of these programs tend to be **pork-barrel projects** that are targeted to a large number of states and districts. They are not easily cut because well-organized interests in the states and districts benefit from those pork-barrel projects. President Carter learned this lesson the hard way. He wanted to cut funding for eighteen public works projects in western states but was forced to retreat in the face of political pressure from senators on the Interior Committee, his own Interior Department, and agriculture interest groups that benefited from those projects.

The president has no weapon he can wield against pork-barrel projects. One attempt was the **Line-Item Veto Act of 1996**, which enabled President Clinton to veto specific line items in spending bills. The president then returned the lined-out items to Congress, which could either override those items or accept them. After Clinton issued line-item vetoes against provisions in the Balanced Budget Act of 1997 and the Taxpayer Relief Act of 1997, a group of Democratic and Republican senators challenged the constitutionality of the line-item veto in federal court. In a 6–3 decision the U.S. Supreme Court in *Clinton v. City of New York* (1998) declared the Line-Item Veto Act unconstitutional.

Pork-barrel spending dates back to the early nineteenth century, but a new variation on that old practice is the use of legislative **earmarks.** It has become a highly controversial practice. Earmarks are expenditures inserted into appropriations bills that directly fund specific projects in the districts or states of key legislators. Lobbyists and interest groups influence Appropriations Committee members to earmark funds for specific recipients. Since 2003, pork-barrel spending has increased by 29%, and an analysis by the Congressional Research Service identified over 15,000 earmarks in 2005 appropriations bills.[34] In 2006 Citizens Against Government Waste (CAGW) identified roughly 10,000 projects in eleven appropriations bills that cost taxpayers a record $29 billion.[35]

In late 2005 and early 2006 a legislative battle over whether to formally require the disclosure of earmarks was fueled by a series of corruption scandals and questionable fundraising tactics linked to the use of earmarks. In November 2005 Representative Randy "Duke" Cunningham (R-CA) resigned from Congress and pled guilty to conspiring to take $2.4 million in bribes from two defense contractors who received earmarks from his office. Likewise, Representative John T. Doolittle (R-CA) helped steer $37 million in defense funding to PerfectWave Technologies, which raised roughly $85,000 for Doolittle and his political action committee from 2002 to 2005. In December 2005 Representative Allan Mollohan (D-WV) received campaign contributions from companies that won contracts based on earmarks he helped secure. Mollohan resigned from his post on the House Ethics Committee following allegations he lied on financial disclosure forms. Representatives Katherine Harris (R-FL) and Virgil Goode (R-VA) both received illegal campaign funds from the Wade and MZM corporations. In February 2006 Senator Arlen Specter (R-PA) directed thirteen earmarks worth $48.7 million in defense contracts to clients of the husband of one of his top aides.

Two highly publicized earmarked projects occurred in Alaska and Iowa. In December 2003 Senate Appropriations Committee chairman Ted Stevens (R-AK) profited from investments with corporations who received government contracts and other favors through his efforts. Since 1999 Stevens, along with Senator Lisa Murkowski (R-AK), secured more than $3 billion in pork-barrel projects. The project that received the most media attention was the $223 million "Bridge to Nowhere," a project designed to connect Ketchikan to Gravina, an island with an airport and a population of fifty including members of Murkowski's family. Similarly, Senate Finance Committee chairman Charles Grassley (R-IA) inserted an earmark into the 2004 Energy and Water Appropriations bill providing $50 million for an indoor rainforest in Coralville. The project was the brainchild of Des Moines millionaire Ted Townsend (heir to the Townsend meatpacking fortune). To obtain federal funding for the project, Townsend's nonprofit group hired Grassley's former assistant John W. Conrad III. The indoor rainforest and the "Bridge to Nowhere" were two of the largest earmarked pork projects in recent history. The widespread use of earmarks affirms the reality that, for many legislators, the ability to secure funding for pet projects is the very reason why they are in Congress. Harvesting federal funding for voters and interest groups in their states and districts is a way of creating and protecting jobs.

Budgetary Pressures

Not only has federal spending increased but the composition of budgetary expenditures has also changed dramatically. Spending on entitlement programs has increased from less than one-third of spending in 1962 to roughly two-thirds in 2006. Most of that growth has been concentrated in Social Security, Medicare, and Medicaid. Together these programs now account for about 42% of all spending, compared with 25% in 1975 and 2% in 1950 (before Medicare and Medicaid).[36] Under President George W. Bush, entitlement spending as a share of GDP has ballooned.[37] If entitlement spending continues to escalate, deficits will expand and the national debt will rise unless taxes are increased or cutbacks are made elsewhere in the budget. Left unchecked, those outcomes could harm the economy, undermine public confidence in elected leaders, and prevent the government from meeting the future needs of its citizens.

One challenge that the second Bush administration tried to address, without success, is how to guarantee that entitlements can meet the retirement needs of the baby-boom generation (the large number of people born between 1946 and 1964). The aging of the population is likely to combine with rapidly rising health care costs to create ever-growing resource demands for Medicare, Medicaid, and Social Security. Spending for the Social Security program grows more slowly and is far more predictable. In the absence of legislative changes, it is estimated to increase by two-fifths as a share of GDP by 2030 and to rise slowly thereafter. The CBO projects that Social Security spending will increase from 4.2% of GDP in 2003 to 6.2% in 2050, an increase of 47%.[38] If the growth in initial benefits were to be reduced by 1% per year beginning with those individuals who became eligible for retirement benefits in 2029, costs would still grow to 5.4% of GDP, an increase of 29%.[39]

The retirement of the baby-boom generation portends a significant, long-lasting shift in the age of the population, which will dramatically alter the balance between the working-age and retirement-age components of that population. The share of people age sixty-five or older is projected to grow from 12% in 2000 to 19% by 2030, and the number of workers per Social Security beneficiary will decline significantly over the next three decades from about three to one in 2006 to two to one in 2030. Moreover, the CBO projects that Social Security benefits will rise from 4.2 % of GDP in 2006 to 5.9 % in 2030.[40]

The financial pressures on Social Security, however, pale in comparison to the likely spending increases on Medicare and Medicaid. Rising health care costs are boosting spending to a greater degree than can be explained by the growth of enrollment in those programs and general inflation alone.

Since 1970 those factors as well as policy changes have caused annual costs per Medicare recipient to rise 3% faster than GDP. With the passage in 2003 of the Medicare prescription drug benefit plan, the percentage of funding directed at entitlement spending is bound to increase in the immediate future. While it was estimated that the new drug plan would cost $534 billion over ten years, the actual cost of the program will be roughly between $720 billion and $1.2 trillion.[41]

Nor does the future hold much promise for cutting defense spending. Following the end of World War II, the Cold War and its accompanying arms race led to a period of relatively high defense spending. Defense spending slightly declined following the Vietnam War to a low of $266.4 billion in 1977 or 6.2% of GDP.[42] But President Reagan gave military preparedness a high priority, with defense spending reaching a post–Vietnam War high of $409.2 billion, or 7.2% of GDP, in 1987.[43] The end of the Cold War was marked by deep cuts in defense spending, which fell by $94.3 billion to 4.6% of GDP.[44] However, beginning in 2003, defense expenditures exceeded their twenty-year average and will likely remain higher for a number of years due to the ongoing wars in Iraq and Afghanistan and the global war on terrorism. To illustrate, defense spending rose from 3.8% in 2003 to 4.0% of GDP in 2004.[45] In FY 2007 the Bush administration plans to spend $448 billion, or 4.8% of GDP, on defense, which does not include any supplemental appropriations for Afghanistan and Iraq.[46]

It is clear that the expansion of entitlement programs have contributed to dramatic increases in annual deficits. To alleviate those pressures, the Republican-controlled Congress passed a reconciliation bill in 1995 that cut taxes by $245 billion but also reduced entitlement spending on Social Security, Medicare, and Medicaid as well as discretionary spending on education, agriculture, job training, and environmental programs. But President Clinton vetoed the legislation, and negotiations with Republican congressional leaders broke down over their attempt to enact six (of thirteen) regular appropriations bills.[47] Without adequate funding for government operations, two federal government shutdowns occurred in November and December. Although the Clinton White House waged a successful public relations campaign that painted the Republican Congress as insensitive to the elderly, the poor, and women, nonetheless, by mid-1996 the legislative-executive negotiators had fully restored the appropriations and agreed, in addition, to support legislation that would balance the budget by 2002.[48]

Forecasting Economic Conditions

One source of budgetary uncertainty is the difficulty in making accurate forecasts of economic activity. This task is important since changes in the level of unemployment or the rate of inflation can alter the projected revenues or outlays by billions of dollars. A **forecast** is the best guess today of the outcome of some future event. The difficulties of forecasting economic activity are reflected in the disparity between forecasts of future economic activity and actual economic conditions from 1981 to 2007 (see table 4.2). Not only is there wide variation between the OMB forecasts and actual economic conditions, but there also seems to be a partisan bias in OMB forecasting. Administrations may be inclined to exaggerate a particular economic problem that concerns their core constituents in order to pursue fiscal policies designed to address that problem. That is, OMB forecasting indicates that Republican administrations overemphasize the danger of inflation while Democratic administrations overestimate the degree of unemployment.[49] The fact that the OMB and the Congressional Budget Office are competitors in this process may also help to politicize economic forecasts.[50]

Table 4.2. OMB Budgetary Forecasts versus Actual Economic and Fiscal Conditions, 1981–2007

Fiscal Year	GDP	Inflation	Unemployment	Budget Surplus (+) or Deficit (–) as % of GDP
Reagan				
1981 Forecast	1.5%	5.9%	7.5%	–1.1%
1981 Actual	2.5%	6.7%	7.6%	–2.6%
1982 Forecast	2.5%	7.5%	8.3%	–1.4%
1982 Actual	–2.0%	8.5%	9.7%	–4.0%
1983 Forecast	2.7%	6.0%	9.7%	–3.1%
1983 Actual	4.3%	6.1%	9.6%	–6.0%
1984 Forecast	4.7%	5.1%	7.7%	–5.3%
1984 Actual	7.3%	3.2%	7.5%	–4.8%
1985 Forecast	3.5%	4.7%	7.3%	–4.7%
1985 Actual	3.8%	4.3%	7.2%	–5.1%
1986 Forecast	4.0%	2.9%	6.9%	–4.1%
1986 Actual	3.4%	3.6%	7.0%	–5.0%
1987 Forecast	1.5%	3.2%	6.7%	–3.1%
1987 Actual	3.4%	1.9%	6.2%	–3.2%
1988 Forecast	4.0%	5.5%	5.2%	–2.2%
1988 Actual	4.2%	3.7%	5.5%	–3.1%
G. H. W. Bush				
1989 Forecast	3.5%	5.5%	5.7%	–2.4%
1989 Actual	3.5%	4.0%	5.3%	–2.8%
1990 Forecast	2.5%	4.0%	5.7%	–1.6%
1990 Actual	1.9%	4.7%	5.5%	–3.8%

(continued)

Table 4.2. *(Continued)*

Fiscal Year	GDP	Inflation	Unemployment	Budget Surplus (+) or Deficit (–) as % of GDP
1991 Forecast	1.0%	5.5%	6.2%	–1.1%
1991 Actual	–0.2%	5.3%	6.7%	–4.5%
1992 Forecast	2.2%	3.3%	7.0%	–4.5%
1992 Actual	3.3%	4.1%	7.4%	–4.7%
Clinton				
1993 Forecast	3.5%	3.5%	6.2%	–5.3%
1993 Actual	2.7%	3.0%	6.8%	–3.9%
1994 Forecast	0.7%	3.0%	7.0%	–3.8%
1994 Actual	4.0%	2.6%	6.1%	–2.9%
1995 Forecast	2.6%	3.0%	6.0%	–2.3%
1995 Actual	2.5%	2.8%	5.6%	–2.2%
1996 Forecast	3.0%	3.0%	6.0%	–2.6%
1996 Actual	3.7%	2.8%	5.4%	–1.4%
1997 Forecast	2.5%	3.0%	5.5%	–1.7%
1997 Actual	4.5%	2.0%	5.0%	–0.3%
1998 Forecast	3.0%	2.5%	5.0%	–1.6%
1998 Actual	4.2%	1.6%	4.5%	–0.3%
1999 Forecast	3.9%	3.0%	5.0%	–1.3%
1999 Actual	4.5%	2.2%	4.2%	0.8%
2000 Forecast	4.0%	3.0%	4.0%	0.1%
2000 Actual	3.8%	2.5%	4.1%	1.3%
G. W. Bush				
2001 Forecast	3.0%	3.5%	4.5%	1.2%
2001 Actual	0.8%	2.8%	4.8%	2.4%
2002 Forecast	2.5%	1.5%	5.0%	2.2%
2002 Actual	1.6%	1.6%	5.8%	–1.5%
2003 Forecast	3.0%	2.0%	5.0%	–0.7%
2003 Actual	2.7%	2.3%	6.0%	–3.5%
2004 Forecast	3.5%	3.0%	5.5%	–1.2%
2004 Actual	3.6%	2.7%	5.5%	–3.9%
2005 Forecast	4.0%	3.5%	5.0%	–2.3%
2005 Actual	3.5%	3.4%	5.1%	–4.2%
2006 Forecast	3.5%	3.5%	5.0%	–2.6%
2006 Actual	3.9%	3.5%	4.8%	–2.9%
2007 Forecast	4.1%	3.6%	4.5%	–2.8%
2007 Actual				

Errors in forecasting can have substantial impact on budgeting for two reasons. First, they may seriously underestimate the future spending or overestimate expected revenues, which is the starting point for the preparation of the executive budget. Second, the estimates of macroeconomic conditions influence the policy priorities of the president and Congress. During the 1990–1991 recession, for example, both private and government economists predicted that the recession would be mild and that a recovery would occur without additional federal spending. These forecasts of future economic activity caused President George H. W. Bush to delay seeking any fiscal stimulus until his 1992 State of the Union address, which came too late and did little to allay the public perception that Bush was an ineffective economic manager.

Also during the 1990s, projections of future budgetary deficits were notoriously inaccurate. The actual budget deficit of $107 billion in 1996 was projected to grow to $124 billion in 1997, but the CBO projection for FY 1997 was wrong by over $100 billion. Its projected $124 billion deficit became an actual deficit of $22 billion. And the budgetary picture continued to improve despite the official forecasts. The $5 billion deficit projected for 1998 was wrong by $75 billion, because the federal budget actually showed a surplus of $70 billion that year, its first since 1969.[51]

The Balanced Budget Act of 1997 was estimated to cut the deficit by $127 billion between 1998 and 2002. The caps on discretionary spending were lowered, now requiring that the dollar value of discretionary spending remain constant between 1999 and 2002. Constant nominal expenditures, however, translate into a "real" (after controlling for inflation) decline in discretionary spending. Thus, for the period 1999–2007, these policy changes added over $600 billion to the surplus projections, but stronger than predicted economic growth had an even larger effect on future surpluses. For 1998 both the OMB and the CBO forecasted 3.0% GDP growth but actual growth was 4.2%. For 1999 they both forecasted 3.9% GDP growth but actual growth was 4.5%.[52] Simply changing economic assumptions added billions to the projected surplus. In the four months between October 1997 and January 1998, the surplus projected by the CBO increased by $22 billion for 1998 and an additional $28 billion for 1999. Updated economic assumptions between 1998 and 1999 similarly added $270 billion to the projected surpluses.[53]

THE POLITICS OF DEFICIT REDUCTION

Throughout most of American history, deficits were the result of either wars or recessions. Wars necessitated major increases in military spending while recessions both reduced federal tax revenues and (in modern times) increased expenditures for social welfare programs. Federal budgets showed deficits during the War of 1812, the recession of 1837, the Civil War, the depression of the 1890s, and World War I. Once wartime ended or prosperity returned, however, the federal budget yielded surpluses that helped to pay down the national debt.

The Great Depression and New Deal spending programs forced the federal government to rely on deficit spending, which lasted for the entire decade of the 1930s. Then World War II ballooned the federal deficit because the United States government had to spend unprecedented resources on national defense. Between 1948 and 2007 the federal government has balanced the budget only nine times. In other words, deficit financing has become the norm.

As noted before, one reason for the string of federal deficits is the decision-making process by which budgets are formulated. After World War II, the budget process settled into a routine called incrementalism. Annual budgets became the "baseline" from which to assess how much more money to give each agency for the next fiscal year. One study of thirty-seven agencies over twelve years found that their spending requests were within 5% of the previous year's budget in one-third of the cases, and a majority did not differ by more than 10%.[54] Each agency requested more funds than necessary on the assumption that cuts would be made by the BOB or also by the House Appropriations Committee. Just as routinely, those agencies would appeal any funding cuts to the Senate Appropriations Committee, which would often make some restorations. The recommendations of the two spending committees were very important, and this research found no difference between the funding level recommended by the Appropriations Committees and subsequent appropriations enacted by the House or Senate in almost 90% of the cases.[55]

When revenues grow at a slower rate than the rate of increase for federal spending, the resulting deficits make it more difficult for politicians to divide up the fiscal pie among competing programs, let alone promise the voters new benefits. This disparity caused small deficits in 1957 and 1958 and during the Kennedy/Johnson term. The four-year deficit of 1965–1968 was almost double the previous term, though still modest by today's standards, because over Johnson's term the increase in federal revenues nearly paralleled the increase in federal spending. The growing economy and modest inflation rate allowed LBJ to launch his War on Poverty, because middle-class Americans were enjoying a higher standard of living despite the fact that a larger share of federal funds was being diverted to helping the poor. The deficit grew slightly over Nixon's first term since the growth in federal revenues exceeded the growth in federal expenditures. The gap between revenues and expenditures widened, however, during the Nixon/Ford term due to the impact of entitlement programs. The budgetary record of

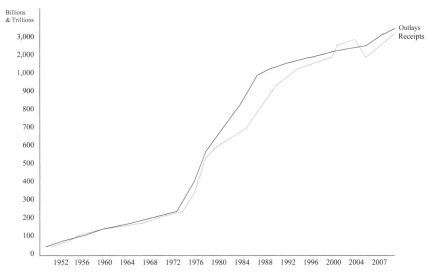

Figure 4.3. Total Federal Government Outlays and Receipts, 1952–2007. *Source:* Council of Economic Advisers, *Economic Report of the President* (Washington, DC: U.S. Government Printing Office, January 2006), table B-4.

1977–1980 shows, in fact, that Jimmy Carter managed to constrain the growth of federal spending since nominal expenditures grew at a rate almost equal to that of federal revenues.

Gramm-Rudman-Hollings Acts

In 1980 Republican presidential candidate Ronald Reagan promised to cut taxes, increase defense spending, cut domestic social spending, and balance the budget at the same time. In his first year in office, he fulfilled the first of these pledges with the Economic Recovery Tax Act of 1981 (ERTA), which cut marginal personal income tax rates by 23% over three years and indexed future income tax rates to inflation.[56] The result was a series of enormous deficits. While the Nixon/Ford deficits totaled $193.9 billion over eight years and the Carter years added $226.8 billion more, Reagan's deficits totaled $1.4 trillion from 1981 through 1988.[57]

The income tax cuts coupled with the 1981–1982 recession undercut revenues at the same time expenditures increased. From 1978 to 1981 federal revenues grew by about $200 billion, a 50% increase, whereas from 1981 to 1984 the increase was only $67 billion, or about 11%.[58] The FY 1983 budget showed a deficit of $208 billion—with roughly $100 billion being the cyclical deficit from the 1981–1982 recession and the rest representing "structural" deficit.[59] A **cyclical deficit** is an imbalance between revenues and outlays produced by contractions in the business cycle. When economic conditions improve, such deficits are either reduced or eliminated (so, in fact, budget surpluses could result). In contrast a **structural deficit** is a revenue-outlay gap that exists even under conditions of "full" employment. According to author Michael Levy, the 1983 budget was "the first in postwar history with a built-in 'structural deficit' that cannot be cured by successive years of economic expansion."[60]

To bring the runaway spending under control, Congress enacted the **Balanced Budget and Emergency Deficit Control Act of 1985** (better known as the **Gramm-Rudman-Hollings Act**, also called GRH-I). Gramm-Rudman-Hollings made important changes in the congressional rules in order to enforce maximum deficit amounts for each fiscal year and to strengthen congressional budget enforcement procedures.[61] If the thirteen regular appropriation bills provided for total spending in excess of the deficit target set by the congressional budget resolution and if Congress could not agree on how to make spending cuts or increase revenues to meet that deficit target, then an "automatic" form of spending cutback would take place. This automatic spending cut is called **sequestration**. If Congress failed to meet the deficit target, then the president was empowered to issue a "sequester order" designed to meet that goal by cutting categories of nonexempt spending.[62]

The sequestration process had the effect of strengthening the power of the CBO relative to the OMB in the budget process. And because of the heightened CBO role, the Supreme Court ruled in 1986 that the sequestration provision of the 1985 Act violated the separation of powers. The Court argued that the CBO's role in the calculation of how much spending to cut in order to meet deficit reduction targets was an unconstitutional assumption by the legislative branch of the executive branch's responsibility for executing law. In response, Congress passed the **Balanced Budget and Emergency Deficit Control Reaffirmation Act of 1987** (called GRH-II), which assigned the entire responsibility for calculating the sequestration cuts to the OMB.

Both the 1985 and 1987 acts mandated a five-year deficit-reduction process, with yearly deficit ceilings that would eventually fall to zero, or a balanced budget (by 1992 according to GRH-II).[63] Roughly 50% of the spending cuts were to come from national defense and the other 50% were to come from domestic discretionary programs. Cuts in Medicare were limited to 1% in 1987 and 2% each year thereafter, despite the fact that the increasing cost of entitlement programs is a major reason for the growth in federal spending. In political terms GRH-I and GRH-II gave our elected leaders political cover. "They can be social liberals and fiscal conservatives at the same time," observed economist Barry Bosworth. "It's not good public policy, but its good politics."[64]

Budget Enforcement Act of 1990

Congress soon realized the deficit would exceed the targeted limits because Gramm-Rudman-Hollings exempted entitlement programs from the sequestration process. The first Bush administration accumulated a staggering aggregate deficit of $933 billion, an amount greater than the total deficits incurred between 1789 and 1980, and the problem of deficit financing has been persistent and steadily worsening over the last twenty years. While the average yearly deficit for the eight Nixon/Ford years was $24 billion, it grew to $57 billion during the Carter years, $167 billion during the Reagan years, $233 billion during the G. H. W. Bush years, and $356 billion during the G. W. Bush years of 2002 to 2007. During the Clinton years, there was an average yearly surplus of $59 billion.[65]

A new budget crisis arose when it was reported that the OMB data on which President George H. W. Bush based his FY 1990 budget were far too optimistic. Furthermore, the OMB did not factor in the 1990 recession or the economic fallout from the collapse of savings and loan institutions. Bush was forced by the Democratic Congress to call a budget summit, which resulted in the **Budget Enforcement Act of 1990 (BEA)**. Its primary objective was to establish a five-year plan for reducing the deficit to $83 billion by 1995.[66] To do so, the legislation set up "fire walls" within the realm of discretionary spending. Three separate categories of discretionary spending were established: defense, domestic, and foreign aid. A deficit in any one of those budget categories could not be remedied by shifting funds from another category, but any savings incurred in any one category had to be put toward debt reduction. By signing the 1990 legislation, President Bush broke his "read my lips, no new taxes" pledge of the 1988 presidential campaign, which partly contributed to Bush's reelection defeat in 1992.[67]

The 1990 Act established new provisions that replaced the Gramm-Rudman-Hollings regime with two independent enforcement mechanisms. The first was a system of discretionary spending caps designed to limit the total amount of budget authority and outlays that Congress could provide. The second was the **pay-as-you-go (PAYGO)** sequestration procedure that would require legislation to increase the deficit or decrease the surplus.[68] PAYGO mandated that any increase in those expenditures that lie outside the purview of the annual appropriations process (like entitlements) be offset by either revenue increases or by spending cuts elsewhere so there is no net increase in the deficit. PAYGO would be enforced automatically if spending limits were breached. If the breach occurs during the last quarter of the fiscal year (from July 1 to September 30), the limits for discretionary spending in that category of expenditures would be reduced for the next fiscal year by the amount of the breach. In essence, the law substantially altered the sequestration process by eliminating deficit targets as a factor in budget enforcement and establishing adjustable limits in the discretionary spending that is funded through the annual appropriations process. But there was a loophole: Social Security benefits, emergency spending, and revenue legislation was exempted from the PAYGO process.

Omnibus Budget Reconciliation Act of 1993

In January 1993 the Bush administration predicted a $255.09 billion deficit.[69] Also, the national debt was projected to rise from $3.29 trillion in 1993 to $4.86 trillion in 1998 even though revenues were projected to grow more rapidly than outlays.[70] The persistence of deficit financing presented newly elected president Bill Clinton with the challenge of reconciling his promise to limit the size of the deficit as well as provide new spending. Although the deficit was not an issue that Clinton emphasized during his 1992 presidential campaign, President Clinton demonstrated a willingness to reduce the red ink. And unlike other recent presidents, President Clinton immersed himself in the details of budgeting.

Clinton proposed to trim expenditures, but he relied mainly on tax increases to reduce the deficit. Yet, he also urged a short-term economic stimulus package to boost job creation by pumping billions of dollars into new social spending programs. Clinton's deficit-reduction package proposed a cut of $493 billion over four years, with $247 billion coming from spending cuts, mostly on defense programs, and $246 billion from tax increases. The goal was to reduce annual deficits by $325 billion between 1994 and 1997.[71]

Clinton's call for tax increases was a direct repudiation of the economic philosophies of his two Republican predecessors, since Clinton believed that Reagan and Bush chose to stimulate economic growth through tax cuts at the expense of high deficits. Most of the new revenue in Clinton's plan came in the form of higher taxes on wealthy Americans and corporations, mainly through the creation of new upper-income tax brackets of 36% and 39.6%. Overall, more than 50% of the new taxes would fall on individuals making more than $200,000 a year.[72] According to one journalist, "Clinton's fiscal policy served as a laboratory for a change in economic thought" because he sought "balanced budgets—or better yet, surpluses—[which] are believed to hold down interest rates, free capital for the private sector and reassure investors about long-term economic stability."[73] Clinton's budget was enacted in the Omnibus Budget Reconciliation Act of 1993, which was approved 218–217 in the House and 51–50 in the Senate (with Vice President Gore breaking the tie) without a single Republican vote. But the legislation had something that offended almost everyone in Congress. Conservatives were uncomfortable with the $246 billion tax increases, and liberals were uneasy about the $247 billion in cuts in entitlement programs.

Between 1994 and 1997, however, annual deficits shrunk dramatically faster than anyone predicted. Every year during the Clinton administration, the federal government produced a budget with a lower deficit or higher surplus than forecast. The FY 1993 deficit of $255.09 billion fell to $203.23 in FY 1994, $166.99 in FY 1995, $107.47 in FY 1996, and to $21.94 billion in FY 1997.[74] While other factors, most notably the strong economic growth of the 1990s and the stable low inflation rates orchestrated by Fed chairman Alan Greenspan, helped reduce the deficit, the 1993 act was important as well.

The Balanced Budget Act of 1997

Although the 1993 plan exceeded all expectations in terms of reducing the deficit, the task of reaching a balanced budget required one more legislative push. That would come about with the historic **Balanced Budget Act of 1997 (BBA)**. Originally designed to balance the budget by 2002, the BBA provided for $247 billion in savings over five years.[75] It also extended the solvency of the Medicare trust fund for at least ten years, provided for the largest investment in higher education since the GI Bill of Rights in 1945, made the largest expansion in children's health care since the creation of Medicaid in 1965, and authorized a $500-per-child tax credit for families.

Clearly the deficit reduction efforts were paying off. In a development that was thought by many to be impossible, there were budget surpluses every year from 1998 to 2001, the first years since 1969 that the federal government has not run in the red. In 1998 the budget reported its first surplus of $69 billion. In 1999 the surplus nearly doubled to $124 billion and then increased to $236 billion in 2000 before declining to $128 billion in 2001.[76] As author Allen Schick states, "Liquidating the deficit ranks as one of the supreme budgetary accomplishments in American history."[77] Moreover, the national debt was reduced from $3.8 trillion in 1997 to $3.6 trillion in 2000.[78] Eliminating the budget deficit had completely changed the dynamics of the federal budget process, at least for a time.

Coping with Returning Deficits

Between 2001 and 2003, Congress approved three of President Bush's tax cuts, totaling roughly $1.5 trillion, and increased defense spending by over $100 billion.[79] And in May 2006, Congress approved yet a fourth tax cut of $70 billion and set December 31, 2010, as the expiration date for all four tax cuts.[80] As a consequence, government revenues were forecast to decline from 19.8% of GDP in 2001 to 17.3% in 2007 and, therefore, the $128 billion surplus recorded in FY 2001 was transformed into a deficit of $370 billion by FY 2007.[81]

To make some attempt to control the spiraling costs, President Bush signed the Omnibus Budget Reconciliation Act in 2005, which sought to halve the annual deficit by 2010 by freezing spending on nondefense discretionary programs.[82] Anticipated cuts in Medicare benefits, however, were effectively canceled by new spending for the prescription drug plan that was expected to cost between $800 billion and $1.2 trillion. Spending restraint is crucial to deficit reduction, but the five-year freeze in nondefense discretionary spending was unrealistic given the pace of spending growth. When Congress and President Clinton confronted the deficit problem in the 1990s, their efforts focused mainly on reducing the deficit with a combination of spending cuts and tax increases. But the Bush 2005 deficit reduction act does not prevent further tax cuts.

Nor does the 2005 deficit reduction act affect entitlements. In his 2005 State of the Union address to Congress, Bush acknowledged "unprecedented strains on the federal government" caused by entitlement programs that would force Congress to confront "impossible choices: staggering tax increases, immense deficits or deep cuts in every area of spending."[83] His answer was to create the President's Commission to Strengthen Social Security to examine the impact of baby-boom retirement on Social Security, Medicare, and Medicaid and develop alternatives on entitlement spending, issues that the Congress refused to take up.

In addition to declining revenues from tax cuts, the series of Bush deficits are also directly related to escalating outlays. The six-year pace of federal spending increased by over $800 billion to reach $2.66 trillion in 2007.[84] This represents the largest total spending increase by any president since the Johnson administration. President Bush and Congress markedly increased spending on national defense as well as domestic programs such as the No Child Left Behind Act of 2001 and the 2003 Medicare prescription drug benefit.

THE DANGERS OF DEFICITS AND DEBT

The ballooning deficits have renewed the debate over the economic consequences of a rising national debt. The federal government currently owes its public creditors about $8.5 trillion.[85] When President George W. Bush took office in 2001, the debt was $5.6 trillion.[86] To finance the national debt, the federal government must borrow funds from private sector banks, the general public through savings bonds, and foreign entities.[87] This results from the issuance of **U.S. treasury securities**. Treasury securities are government bonds issued by the Treasury Department that serve as debt financing instruments for the federal government. Because deficits require an infusion of billions of dollars from credit markets each year, the growing national debt would put upward pressure on interest rates. Rising interest rates, in turn, add to the cost of financing the debt. Moreover, businesses and households are less able to borrow money when interest rates increase.[88] The "crowding out" of private investment due to higher interests rates could have adverse effects on the economy if the United States government had to rely entirely on the domestic credit market to finance its national debt.

But economic globalization offers a strategy by which the United States can address its fiscal imbalance. There is a world credit market that is expanding as the globalization of trade and commerce attracts more financial participants. To provide some perspective, the total debt owed by the United States, European Union, United Kingdom, Japan, and Canada is roughly $50 trillion.[89] Therefore, the United States government does not

Table 4.3. Major Foreign Holders of U.S. Treasury Securities, February 2007 (billions)

Countries	Amount
Japan	617.8
China	416.2
United Kingdom	119.0
OPEC	110.8
Caribbean Banking Centers	66.4
Brazil	60.7
Luxembourg	59.7
Taiwan	57.5
Hong Kong	57.4
South Korea	57.0
Germany	47.9
Mexico	35.0
Switzerland	32.7
Singapore	31.2
Canada	28.9
Turkey	25.4
France	22.8
Netherlands	21.8
India	19.5
Thailand	16.8
Sweden	15.0
Italy	13.5
Israel	13.4
Ireland	12.8
Poland	12.7
Belgium	12.3
Norway	11.8
All others	145.4
Total	**2,141.3**

Source: U.S. Department of the Treasury/Federal Reserve Board, http://www.ustreas.gov/tic/mfh.txt.

have to rely on the domestic credit market, and an important change in
debt management is the holdings of U.S. debt by foreign governments and
international financiers. During the 1980s, foreign investors began purchasing U.S. government debt and helped finance that round of heavy borrowing by the federal government. Today, however, a much greater portion
of the national debt is owned by foreign investors. In 1985 roughly 15% of
the debt was owned by non-U.S. entities, and by 2000 that percentage rose
to 31%. The percentage today is about 46%.[90]

More important than the absolute size of deficits and the national debt
is a comparison of total public indebtedness to the size of the GDP. It is important to determine whether the national debt is growing or shrinking in
relative terms. After World War II, the debt was much higher relative to the
size of the economy, being 90% of GDP. During the Cold War era, the relative size of the debt fell, from a high of 121.7% of the GDP in 1946 to a
low of 32.5 % of the GDP in 1981.[91] The year 1981 marked a turning point
because the debt doubled over the next decade, reaching 70% of GDP in
1993. The deficit-cutting measures of the Clinton administration reduced
the national debt to roughly 58% of GDP by 2000, but under President
George W. Bush the debt rose again to roughly 70% of GDP by 2007.[92]

Sustained and rising deficits could harm the economy by diverting funds
from national savings and decreasing the capital available for private investment. Lowered investment might result in less production and falling
wages. If that scenario continued long enough and was fueled by rising

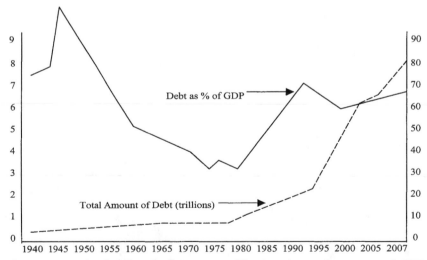

**Figure 4.4. National Debt: Total Amount (trillions) and as a Percentage of GDP,
1940–2007.** *Source:* Office of Management and Budget, *Budget of the United States*
2007, (Washington, DC: U.S. Government Printing Office, 2007), table 7.1.

deficits, the combination might lead to a severe contraction in the economy. And borrowing from abroad is not without economic consequences. Over time, private foreign investors and foreign governments would claim larger shares of American economic output, resulting in few resources available for America's insatiable demand for imported goods.[93] At some point foreign investors might stop investing in U.S. treasury securities, then the value of the dollar could plunge, interest rates could climb, and prices in the United States could shoot up. In other words, the interconnectedness of the global economy means that economic problems in the United States could spill over to the rest of the world and seriously weaken the economies of U.S. trading partners.[94]

Although higher inflation would reduce the national debt in "real" dollars, promoting inflation is not a feasible long-term strategy for dealing with persistent budget deficits. Due to the dramatic increases in energy prices, the rising inflation rate (3.4% in 2005 and 3.7% in 2006) under President George W. Bush enabled the federal government to repay its debts with cheaper dollars, but financial markets will not be fooled forever. Investors will eventually demand higher interest rates as a condition for purchasing U.S. government securities. If the government were to print money to finance its deficits, the situation would lead to hyperinflation. Interest rates could remain high for some time even after inflation was brought back under control. In the final analysis, deliberate inflationary financing is a bad solution to the fundamental problem of deficit financing.

Of course the nation could continue with Bush's argument that the U.S. economy can "grow" down the size of the deficit, but that seems problematic as a long-term solution. Economic growth per se is unlikely to solve budgetary problems because faster growth would not only increase revenues but also spending.[95] Social Security benefits, for example, depend on worker wage histories, so gains in wages would automatically translate into higher Social Security costs over the long-term.

Looking long-term, the most fundamental objection to deficits is that the national debt represents a transfer of economic resources from the current generation of Americans to future generations.[96] Today, roughly 8% of the budget is interest paid to finance the debt, which means that a sizable portion of spending is not being invested into public programs.[97] The impact of the national debt would be less negative if those interest payments reflected deficit spending on infrastructure, education, and research and development that had lasting impacts for years and, therefore, would benefit future generations. However, most deficit spending is devoted to current consumption in the form of entitlements, pensions, and health care benefits. So long-term, the next generation will have to find the money to not only pay for their current needs but also for the consumption of past generations, which means that higher taxes, possibly more inflation, and or

cutbacks in social programs would be the ultimate legacy from potentially unsustainable public indebtedness today. In sum, today's national
debt burden may lower the standard of living for the next generation of
Americans.

KEY TERMS

automatic stabilizers
Balanced Budget Act of 1997 (BBA)
Balanced Budget and Emergency Deficit Control Act of 1985
Balanced Budget and Emergency Deficit Control Reaffirmation Act of
    1987
Budget and Impoundment Control Act of 1974
budget authority
budget deficit
Budget Enforcement Act of 1990 (BEA)
budget surplus
Bureau of the Budget (BOB)
congressional budget resolution
Congressional Budget Office (CBO)
cost of living adjustments (COLAs)
cyclical deficit
discretionary programs
earmarks
entitlement programs
executive budget
forecast
General Accounting Office (GAO)
Government Accountability Office (GAO)
Gramm-Rudman-Hollings Act
impound
incrementalism
Line-Item Veto Act of 1996
national debt
obligations
Office of Management and Budget (OMB)
outlays
pay-as-you-go (PAYGO)
pork-barrel projects
section 302(a)
section 302(b)
sequestration
spending ceilings

spending floors
structural deficit
tax expenditures
U.S. treasury securities

ADDITIONAL READINGS

Berman, Larry. *The Office of Management and Budget.* Princeton, NJ: Princeton University Press, 1979. Case study of the OMB with historical treatment of its predecessor, the Bureau of the Budget.

Fisher, Louis. *Presidential Spending Power.* Princeton, NJ: Princeton University Press, 1975. This pioneering study traces the historical development of budget making in the executive branch.

Palazzolo, Daniel J. *Done Deal? The Politics of the 1997 Budget Agreement.* Chatham, NJ: Chatham House, 1999. Explores the 1997 budget agreement to understand how a Democratic president and a GOP-controlled Congress could reach a historic agreement to balance the budget.

Schick, Allen and Felix Lostracco. *The Federal Budget: Politics, Policy, Process.* Washington, DC: Brookings, 2000. Explains how the deficit was liquidated and provides insights on how to protect against future deficits. This book analyzes the changes in the appropriations process and other reforms of the budgetary process and contains vital statistics, important documents, and case studies.

Shuman, Howard E. *Politics and the Budget: The Struggle between the President and the Congress,* 3rd ed. Englewood Cliffs, NJ: Prentice-Hall, 1992. An overview of executive-legislative budgetary relationships.

Wildavsky, Aaron. *The New Politics of the Budgetary Process.* Glenview, IL: Scott Foresman, 1988. This updated version of a classic study of the budgetary process assesses the various strategies of the decision makers who shape the federal budget.

NOTES

1. Aaron Wildavsky, *The Politics of the Budgetary Process,* 4th ed. (Boston: Little, Brown, 1984), 2.

2. James Madison, "Federalist No. 58," in *The Federalist Papers,* eds. James Madison, Alexander Hamilton, and John Jay (New York: Penguin, 1987).

3. Louis Fisher, *Presidential Spending Power* (Princeton: Princeton University Press, 1975), 23.

4. In addition, the boundaries between authorizing and appropriating are often blurred. For example, floor amendments are sometimes attached to budget bills that have the effect of prohibiting certain activities, an activity that traditionally would be part of authorizing legislation. See Aaron Wildavsky, *The New Politics of the Budgetary Process* (Glenview, IL: Scott Foresman, 1988), 18–19.

5. Lester M. Salmon, "The Presidency and Domestic Policy Formulation," in *The Illusion of Presidential Government,* eds. Hugh Heclo and Lester M. Salmon (Boulder, CO: Westview Press, 1981), 179.

6. James L. Sundquist, *The Decline and Resurgence of Congress* (Washington, DC: Brookings, 1981), 199.

7. The Budget and Accounting Act of 1921, Public Law 67-14.

8. Fisher, *Presidential Spending Power*, 35.

9. Richard E. Neustadt, "President and Legislation: The Growth of Central Clearance," *American Political Science Review* (September 1954): 641–670 and Robert S. Gilmour, "Central Clearance, A Revised Perspective," *Public Administration Review* (March–April 1971): 150–158.

10. Richard F. Fenno Jr., *The Power of the Purse* (Boston: Little, Brown, 1966), 162–163.

11. Richard E. Neustadt, "The Presidency and Legislation: Planning the President's Program," *American Political Science Review* (December 1955): 980–1018; Larry Berman, *The Office of Management and Budget and the Presidency* (Princeton: Princeton University Press, 1979), 42–43; and Stephen J. Wayne, *The Legislative Presidency* (New York: Harper & Row, 1978), 103–105.

12. Wildavsky, *The New Politics of the Budgetary Process*, 136–138.

13. See Fenno, *The Power of the Purse.*

14. Lyndon B. Johnson, *The Vantage Point* (New York: Holt, Rinehart and Winston, 1971), 326.

15. Norman C. Thomas and Harold L. Wolman, "The Presidency and Policy Formulation: The Task Force Device," *Public Administration Review* (September–October 1969): 459–471.

16. Terry Moe, "The Politicized Presidency," in *The New Direction in American Politics*, eds. John E. Chubb and Paul E. Peterson (Washington, DC: Brookings, 1985).

17. James P. Pfiffner, "OMB: Professionalization, Politicization and the Presidency," in *Executive Leadership in Anglo-American Systems*, eds. Colin Campbell and Margaret Jane Wyszomirski (Pittsburgh, PA: University of Pittsburgh Press, 1991), 195–218; Shelley Lynne Tomkin, *Inside OMB* (Armonk, NY: Sharpe, 1998), 54.

18. Margaret Jane Wyszomirski, "The De-Institutionalization of Presidential Staff Agencies," *Public Administration Review* (September–October 1982): 455.

19. Allen Schick, *Congress and Money* (Washington, DC: Urban Institute, 1980), 17.

20. James P. Pfiffner, *The President, the Budget, and Congress* (Boulder, CO: Westview, 1979), 40–44.

21. Allen Schick, *The Federal Budget: Politics, Policy, Process* (Washington, DC: Brookings, 1995), chap. 5.

22. Howard Shuman, *Politics and the Budget: The Struggle between the President and the Congress* (New York: Prentice-Hall, 1992), 214.

23. Schick, *The Federal Budget*, chap. 5.

24. Shuman, *Politics and the Budget*, 230, 233.

25. R. Kent Weaver, *Automatic Government: The Politics of Indexation* (Washington, DC: Brookings, 1988).

26. Carl Hulse, "Senate Votes to Raise U.S. Debt Limit to Nearly $9 Trillion," *New York Times*, March 16, 2006.

27. Schick, *The Federal Budget*, chap. 5.

28. Schick, *The Federal Budget*, chap. 5.

29. Martha Coven and Richard Kogan, *Introduction to the Federal Budget Process* (Washington, DC: Center on Budget and Policy Priorities, August 2003).

30. Center on Budget and Policy Priorities, "The President's 2007 Budget."

31. Herbert Kaufman, *Are Government Organizations Immortal?* (Washington, DC: Brookings, 1976), 34.

32. David V. Edwards, *The American Political Experience* (Englewood Cliffs: Prentice-Hall, 1979), 223.

33. Dirksen quoted in David Broder, "A Lump of Coal from the President," *Washington Post*, December 4, 2002.

34. Congressional Research Service Appropriations Team, "Earmarks in Appropriations Acts: FY 1994, FY 1996, FY 1998, FY 2000, FY 2002, FY 2004, FY 2005," memorandum, January 26, 2006, http://www.fas.org/sgp/crs/misc/m012606.pdf.

35. Tom Finnigan, "All about Pork: The Abuse of Earmarks and the Needed Reforms," Citizens Against Government Waste, May 3, 2006, http://www.cagw.org/site/DocServer/PorkFinal.pdf?docID=1621.

36. Dennis S. Ippolito, "The United States: The Past and Future of the Entitlement State," (paper presented at the Woodrow Wilson International Center, Washington, DC: June 1–2, 2005), http://www.irpp.org/events/archive/jun05/ippolito.pdf.

37. U.S. Office of Management and Budget (OMB), *Historical Tables: Budget of the United States Government, 2006* (Washington, DC: Government Printing Office, 2005), table 8.1, 125, http://www.whitehouse.gov/omb/budget/fy2007/pdf/hist.pdf; Sheryl Gay Stolberg, "The Revolution That Wasn't," *New York Times*, February 13, 2005.

38. Social Security Administration, *The 2003 Annual Report of the Board of Trustees of the Federal Old-Age and Survivors Insurance and Disability Insurance Trust Funds* (March 17, 2003) and Congressional Budget Office, *Uncertainty in Social Security's Long-Term Finances: A Stochastic Analysis* (December 2001).

39. Social Security Administration, *The 2003 Annual Report of the Board of Trustees of the Federal Old-Age and Survivors Insurance and Disability Insurance Trust Funds* and Congressional Budget Office, *Uncertainty in Social Security's Long-Term Finances.*

40. Social Security Administration, *The 2003 Annual Report of the Board of Trustees of the Federal Old-Age and Survivors Insurance and Disability Insurance Trust Funds* and Congressional Budget Office, *Uncertainty in Social Security's Long-Term Finances.*

41. Dean Baker, "The Savings from an Efficient Medicare Prescription Drug Plan," Center for Economic and Policy Research, January 2006, http://www.cepr.net/publications/efficient_medicare_2006_01.pdf and Ceci Connolly and Mike Allen, "Medicare Drug Benefit May Cost $1.2 Trillion," *Washington Post*, February 9, 2005.

42. Allison Thomson, "Defense Related Employment and Spending, 1996–2006," *Monthly Labor Review* 121, no. 7 (July 1998), http://www.bls.gov/opub/mlr/1998/07/art2exc.htm#1a#1a.

43. Thomson, "Defense Related Employment and Spending."

44. Thomson, "Defense Related Employment and Spending."

45. Congressional Budget Office, *The Long-Term Budget Outlook* (December 2003), chap. 4, http://www.cbo.gov/showdoc.cfm?index=4916&sequence=5.

46. Judd Gregg, "President Bush's 2007 Budget: A Brief Overview," U.S. Senate Budget Committee (February 6, 2006), http://www.senate.gov/~budget/republican/pressarchive/Analysis.pdf.

47. Alissa J. Rubin, "Congress Readies Budget Bill for President's Veto Pen," *Congressional Quarterly Weekly Report* (November 18, 1995): 3512.

48. Alfred Hill, "The Shutdowns and the Constitution," *Political Science Quarterly* (Summer 2000): 274 and Peri Arnold, "Clinton and the Institutionalized Presidency," in *The Postmodern Presidency*, ed. Steven Schier (Pittsburgh: University of Pittsburgh Press, 2000), 28–31.

49. John Frendreis and Ray Tatalovich, "Accuracy and Bias in Macroeconomic Forecasting by the Administration, the CBO, and the Federal Reserve Board," *Polity* (Summer 2000): 623.

50. Allen Schick, "The Three-Ring Budgetary Process: The Appropriations, Tax, and Budget Committees in the Congress," in *The New Congress*, ed. T. Mann and Norman Ornstein (Washington, DC: American Enterprise Institute, 1981) and Mark S. Kamlet and David C. Mowery, "The First Decade of the Congressional Budget Act: Legislative Imitation and Adaptation in Budgeting," *Policy Sciences* 18 (December 1985): 313–334.

51. Congressional Budget Office, "The Budget Outlook," in *The Economic and Budget Outlook, Fiscal Years 1998–2007* (January 1997), chap. 2, xiii.

52. Congressional Budget Office, "The Economic Outlook," in *The Economic and Budget Outlook, Fiscal Years 1999–2007* (August 1998), chap. 1, 26 and Congressional Budget Office, "The Economic Outlook," in *The Economic and Budget Outlook, Fiscal Years 1999–2007* (January 1999), chap. 1, 37.

53. Congressional Budget Office, "The Economic Outlook," (August 1998); Congressional Budget Office, "The Economic Outlook," (January 1999); and Daniel J. Palazzolo, *Done Deal? The Politics of the 1997 Budget Agreement* (Chatham, NJ: Chatham House, 1999).

54. Wildavsky, *The Politics of the Budgetary Process*, 14.

55. Wildavsky, *The Politics of the Budgetary Process*, 14, 48–55.

56. Congressional Budget Office, "Effects of the 1981 Tax Act on the Distribution of Income and Taxes Paid," (August 1986), http://www.cbo.gov/showdoc.cfm?index=6173&sequence=0.

57. OMB, *Historical Tables*, table 1.1, 21–22.

58. Council of Economic Advisers, *Economic Report of the President* (Washington, DC: U.S. Government Printing Office, January 1993), 435, http://fraser.stlouisfed.org/publications/ERP/issue/1587/download/5996/ERP_1993.pdf.

59. Council of Economic Advisers, *Economic Report of the President* and OMB, *Historical Tables*, table 1.1, 21–22.

60. Michael E. Levy, "'Staying the Course' Won't Help the Budget," *Challenge* (May–June, 1983): 37. Also see Michael E. Levy "The Budget: You Can't Get from Here to There," *Challenge* (May–June 1982): 15–20.

61. Jonathan Fuerbringer, "Like It or Not, Deficit Plan Will Pass, Lawmakers Say," *New York Times*, November 21, 1985.

62. Gerald M. Boyd, "Reagan Aids Prod Congress on Debt," *New York Times*, October 31, 1985.

63. Francis X. Clines, "Budget-Balancing Bill Is Signed in Seclusion," *New York Times*, December 13, 1985 and Steven V. Roberts, "Lawmakers Challenge Scope of Budget Measure," *New York Times*, December 13, 1985.

64. Quoted in Peter T. Kilborn, "Future for Deficit-Reducing Law: A Political Balancing Act is Required," *New York Times*, December 13, 1985.

65. Jackie Calmes, "The Voracious National Debt," *Congressional Quarterly Weekly Report* (March 24, 1990): 896; George Hager, "Deficit Shows No Gain from Pain of Spending Rules," *Congressional Quarterly Weekly Report* (July 20, 1991): 1963; and OMB, *Historical Tables*, table 8.1, 125.

66. Shuman, *Politics and the Budget*, 326–335; Congressional Budget Office, *The Economic and Budget Outlook: Fiscal Years, 1992–1996* (Washington, DC: U.S. Government Printing Office, 1991), 43–57.

67. Paul Simon, "Discipline Is Overdue," *New York Times*, May 20, 1992.

68. Richard Doyle and Jerry McCaffery, "The Budget Enforcement Act of 1990: The Path to No Fault Budgeting," *Public Budgeting and Finance* 11 (Spring 1991): 25–40.

69. OMB, *Historical Tables*, table 1.1, 21–22.

70. OMB, *Historical Tables*, table 7.1, 126–127.

71. George Hager, "Time Is Ripe for Agreement but Gridlock Dies Hard," *Congressional Quarterly Weekly Report* (November 16, 1996): 3280–3281.

72. Congressional Budget Office, *Reducing the Deficit: Spending and Revenue Options* (Washington, DC: U.S. Government Printing Office, February 1993).

73. Richard W. Stevenson, "The Wisdom to Let the Good Times Roll," *New York Times*, December 25, 2000.

74. OMB, *Historical Tables*, table 1.1, 21–22.

75. Palazzolo, *Done Deal?*

76. OMB, *Historical Tables*, table 1.1, 21–22.

77. Allen Schick, "A Surplus if We Can Keep It: How the Federal Budget Surplus Happened," *Brookings Review* (Winter 2000): 36.

78. Office of Management and Budget, *A Citizen's Guide to the Federal Budget, Budget of the United States Government, Fiscal Year 2001*, chap. 4, 2, http://www.gpoaccess.gov/usbudget/fy01/pdf/guide.pdf.

79. OMB, *Historical Tables*, table 3.1, 52.

80. "Bush Tax Cut Extensions Signed Into Law," *USA Today*, May 17, 2006.

81. OMB, *Historical Tables*, tables 1.1, 3.1.

82. The specifics of the act can be reviewed in Congressional Budget Office, "Congressional Budget Office Cost Estimate" (January 27, 2006), http://www.cbo.gov/ftpdocs/70xx/doc7028/s1932conf.pdf.

83. George W. Bush, State of the Union address (January 31, 2006), http://www.whitehouse.gov/stateoftheunion/2006.

84. OMB, *Historical Tables*, table 1.1, 21–22.

85. See the website of the Bureau of the Public Debt in the U.S. Department of Treasury, http://www.publicdebt.treas.gov/opd/opdpdodt.htm.

86. OMB, *Historical Tables*, table 1.1, 21–22.

87. Robert Barro, "Are Government Bonds Net Wealth?" *Journal of Political Economy*, 82 (November–December 1974): 1095–1117; Paul Evans, "Consumers Are

Not Ricardian: Evidence from Nineteen Countries," *Economic Inquiry* 31, no. 4 (October 1993): 534–548; and T. D. Stanley, "New Wine in Old Bottles: A Meta-Analysis of Ricardian Equivalence," *Southern Economic Journal* 64, no. 3 (January 1998): 713–727.

88. Joseph E. Stiglitz, *Economics* (New York: Norton, 1993), 1034.

89. Stiglitz, *Economics*.

90. Office of Management and Budget, *Analytical Perspectives, Budget of the United States Government, Fiscal Year 2007* (Washington, DC: U.S. Government Printing Office, 2006), table 16–6, 233–234. See also the Treasury Department's Financial Management Service website which compiles data on foreign ownership of U.S. Treasury securities, http://www.fms.treas.gov.

91. OMB, *Historical Tables*, 5–6.

92. OMB, *Historical Tables*, table 7.1, 126–127.

93. Edwin M. Truman, "Policy Brief 01-7: The International Implications of Paying Down the Debt," Institute for International Economics (May 2001), http://www.iie.com/publications/pb/pb.cfm?ResearchID=75.

94. Stanley, "New Wine in Old Bottles," 713–727.

95. Congressional Budget Office, *Uncertainty in Social Security's Long-Term Finances.*

96. Stiglitz, *Economics*, 1032–1035.

97. OMB, *Historical Tables*, 7–9.

5

The Federal Reserve Board and Monetary Policy

In the preceding chapter we discussed how large budget deficits, depleted revenue, and entitlement spending pressures have reduced the ability of policy makers to employ fiscal policy to manage the economy. In this chapter we evaluate the control of the money supply (**monetary policy**) by the Federal Reserve System (the Fed). As with fiscal policy, the benefits of monetary stimulus depend on whether the economy is close to full employment. If the economy is below full employment, as during a recession, increases in the money supply may stimulate the economy with little effect on prices. However, if the economy is near full employment, a monetary stimulus may lead to inflationary pressures.

Monetarism has challenged the Keynesian orthodoxy by arguing that growth in the monetary supply is the primary determinant of economic performance, although for different reasons.[1] Monetarism was developed by economist **Milton Friedman**, long affiliated with the University of Chicago.[2] Monetarists contend that only the supply of money influences changes in prices and economic growth. Even here, attempts to "fine tune" the economy by manipulating the money supply will affect prices in the short run, leading to price instability.[3] Monetarists also believe that growth in the money supply should be constant (roughly 3% to 4% per year), which would accommodate economic growth but not lead to price instability.

THE FEDERAL RESERVE SYSTEM

The very first federal agency with the minimal responsibilities for overseeing the money supply was the First Bank of the United States, chartered in 1791, and the Second Bank of the United States, chartered in 1816. After President Andrew Jackson vetoed legislation to charter yet a Third Bank of the United States, there began an era of "free banking"—a period of virtually no federal government regulation of the economy that lasted until the Civil War. The number of state banks mushroomed from 329 in 1829 to 1,500 in 1860.[4] On the eve of the Civil War, there were more than nine thousand different types of banknotes in circulation.[5] As a consequence, there was no uniform currency across the entire nation and only gold and silver coinage held its value. This chaotic system ended with the passage of the 1863 National Banking Act. At the turn of the century, in the aftermath of the financial panic of 1907, private bankers petitioned the White House to pass legislation designed to stabilize the money supply. Over the objections of agrarian groups led by William Jennings Bryan, President Woodrow Wilson signed the **Federal Reserve Act of 1913** (also known as the Owen-Glass Act). The act created the Federal Reserve System, which was charged with supervising and regulating commercial banks and controlling the volume of currency issued by the U.S. Mint and the Bureau of Engraving and Printing in the Treasury Department. The organization of the Federal Reserve System includes a seven-member board of governors, twelve regional Federal Reserve banks, a twelve-member Federal Open Market Committee, and approximately fifty-four hundred commercial banks.[6]

Power over monetary policy is concentrated in the hands of the **board of governors**. The seven members on the board of governors are appointed by the president and confirmed by the U.S. Senate. Each member serves one nonrenewable term of fourteen years. One board member is designated by the president to be the Fed chairman and another is the vice-chairman, both of whom can serve renewable four-year terms. The board of governors is an elite policy group largely acceptable to the financial community and the economics profession. Over its history, three-fifths of board members had previous experience within the Federal Reserve System before they were appointed to the board of governors.[7] According to author John T. Woolley, the individual members of the board are a very homogeneous group: "The Federal Reserve continues a long history of administration by white, male, upper-middle-class technicians."[8] The obvious result is that Fed decision making tends to be consensual.[9]

The entire board of governors also sits on the **Federal Open Market Committee (FOMC)** along with five Federal Reserve bank presidents, one of whom must be the president of the Federal Reserve Bank of New York (other bank presidents serve one-year terms on a rotating basis). By tradi-

Board of Governors
7 members appointed by the president; Confirmed by the U.S. Senate
1. Sets reserve requirements and discount rates;
2. Supervises and regulates commercial banks;
3. Establishes and administers protective regulations in consumer finance;
4. Oversees Federal Reserve Banks

12 Federal Reserve Banks
Boston, New York, Philadelphia, Cleveland, Richmond, Atlanta, Chicago, St. Louis, Minneapolis, Kansas City, Dallas, San Francisco

Each bank has 9 directors that appoint the president of the Federal Reserve Bank
1. Proposes discount rates;
2. Holds reserve balances for banking institutions;
3. Furnishes currency;
4. Collects/clears checks & transfers funds for banks;
5. Manages the national debt & cash balances.

Federal Open Market Committee
Composed of the Board of Governors and 5 Presidents of each Federal Reserve Bank

Directs Open Market Operations (buying/selling government securities)

Commercial Banks
5,400 member banks belonging to the 12 Federal Reserve Banks

Figure 5.1. Structure of the Federal Reserve System. *Sources:* The Federal Reserve officially identifies districts by number and reserve bank city. In the twelfth district, the Seattle branch serves Alaska, and the San Francisco Bank serves Hawaii. The system serves commonwealths and territories as follows: the New York Bank serves the Commonwealth of Puerto Rico and the U.S. Virgin Islands; the San Francisco Bank serves American Samoa, Guam, and the Commonwealth of the Northern Mariana Islands. The board of governors revised the branch boundaries of the system in February 1996. See http://www.federalreserve.gov/otherfrb.htm and http://www.federalreserve.gov/pubs/frseries/frseri.htm.

Table 5.1. Chairmen of the Federal Reserve System, 1914–2006

President	Chairman	Tenure
Wilson	Charles S. Hamlin	1914–1916
	William Proctor Harding	1916–1921
Harding	William Proctor Harding	1921–1923
Coolidge	Daniel Crissinger	1923–1927
	Roy A. Young	1927–1929
Hoover	Roy A. Young	1929–1930
	Eugene Meyer	1930–1933
Roosevelt	Eugene R. Black	1933–1934
	Marriner S. Eccles	1934–1945
Truman	Marriner S. Eccles	1945–1948
	Thomas B. McCabe	1948–1951
	William McChesney Martin	1951–1952
Eisenhower	William McChesney Martin	1952–1961
Kennedy	William McChesney Martin	1961–1963
Johnson	William McChesney Martin	1963–1969
Nixon	William McChesney Martin	1969–1970
	Arthur F. Burns	1970–1974
Ford	Arthur F. Burns	1974–1977
Carter	Arthur F. Burns	1977–1978
	G. William Miller	1978–1979
	Paul Volcker	1979–1981
Reagan	Paul Volcker	1981–1987
	Alan Greenspan	1987–1989
G. H. W. Bush	Alan Greenspan	1989–1993
Clinton	Alan Greenspan	1993–2001
G. W. Bush	Alan Greenspan	2001–2006
	Ben S. Bernanke	2006–

tion the chairman of the board of governors acts as chairman of the FOMC, and the president of the Federal Reserve Bank of New York is the vice-chairman. The FOMC is responsible for managing "open market operations," by which the Fed tries to direct the level of interest rates by purchasing and selling U.S. government securities. Consensus in FOMC decision making is very high. During a sixteen-year period, 86% of the decisions made by the Federal Open Market Committee were unanimous, and three-fifths of the split decisions involved only one dissenting vote.[10]

The Money Supply

The total amount of money in circulation is known as the **money supply** and key measures of the money supply reflect different degrees of liquidity. **Liquidity** refers to the ease with which assets (for example, bonds or property) can be converted into cash. The narrowest measure, M1, is restricted to the most liquid forms of money. M1 consists of currency held by the public, namely traveler's checks, demand deposits in checking accounts, and other deposits against which checks can be written. M2 includes M1, plus savings accounts, certificates of deposits (CDs) under $100,000, and balances in retail money market mutual funds. M3 includes M2 plus CDs over $100,000, balances in institutional money funds, repurchase liabilities issued by banks, and euros held by Americans at U.S. banks around the world and at all banks in the United Kingdom and Canada.[11]

The Fed began reporting monthly data on the amount of money in circulation, demand deposits, and time deposits in the 1940s. In 1971 the Fed introduced aggregate statistics for the money supply categories of M1, M2, and M3. The original M1, for example, consisted of currency plus demand deposits in commercial banks. Over time, however, new bank laws and financial innovations blurred the distinctions between commercial banks and so-called thrift institutions, and the basis of the classification scheme for key money supply measures shifted to liquidity. The **Full Employment and Balanced Growth Act of 1978** (better known as the Humphrey-Hawkins Act) required the Fed to set one-year target ranges for money supply growth twice a year and to report them to Congress.[12]

In 1981 commercial banks were allowed to offer **Negotiable Order of Withdrawal (NOW) accounts**. NOW accounts allow customers to write checks from interest-bearing accounts. This caused the relationship between M1 growth and the gross domestic product (GDP) to break down because account holders were allowed to immediately move funds from standard savings accounts into NOW accounts. In 1982 the M1 growth exceeded the Fed's target range even though the economy experienced its worst recession in decades. This led the Fed to de-emphasize M1 as a guide for monetary policy and to stop announcing growth ranges for M1 in 1987.

By the early 1990s, the relationship between M2 growth and GDP also broke down. Interest rates were at the lowest levels in more than three decades, prompting some savers to move funds out of the savings and time deposits (which are part of M2) into stock and bond mutual funds, which are not included in any of the conventional money supply measures. After the economy had been growing for roughly two years, Fed chairman Alan Greenspan gave the following testimony in 1993: "The historical relationships between money and income, and between money and the price level have largely broken down, depriving the aggregates of much of their usefulness as guides to policy. At least for the time being, M2 has been downgraded as a reliable indicator of financial conditions in the economy, and no single variable has yet been identified to take its place."[13]

A variety of factors continue to complicate the relationship between the money supply and GDP. For example, the money in circulation rose rapidly in late 1999, caused by Y2K-related fears. **Y2K** (the year 2000 problem) resulted from a practice in computer programming design that caused some date-related processing to operate incorrectly on or after January 1, 2000. Fueled by extensive media coverage and media speculation, the fear was that financial institutions and government operations would cease to function at midnight on January 1, 2000. Since financial institutions and government agencies had upgraded their systems, no significant computer failure ever took place. But the fear prompted many people to increase their holdings of the most liquid types of money.[14]

The size of the M1 aggregate also has been depressed in recent years by "sweeps"—the practice that banks adopted of shifting funds out of checking accounts, which are subjected to Fed reserve requirements, into savings accounts that are not subjected to any Fed reserve requirements.[15] In 2000, therefore, the Fed announced that it was no longer setting target ranges for money supply growth. As of March 23, 2006, information regarding M3 was no longer published by the Fed, although M1 and M2 aggregates are still available.

The function of the Fed has evolved over time. Originally, the Fed was created to maintain liquidity in the banking system in order to prevent bank failures during financial panics. Since then, the major function of the Federal Reserve Board has been to stabilize the economy through monetary policy.[16] To achieve that objective, the Fed tries to control the money supply with four types of actions: (1) reserve requirements, (2) discount rate, (3) federal funds rate, and (4) open market operations.

Reserve Requirements

Since the Fed allows commercial banks to lend up to 90% of the money they have on deposit, **reserve requirements** become an optimal monetary policy instrument to influence the M1 money supply.[17] Reserve requirements are the minimum amount of funds banks must hold in order to meet customer withdrawals. The board of governors has authority over the total amount of reserve requirements. The **Depository Institutions Deregulation and Monetary Control Act of 1980** requires that all commercial banking institutions (private banks, savings and loan associations, savings banks, credit unions, branches of foreign banks, and U.S. agencies) must meet the reserve requirements of the Fed. Reserves are either cash on hand at those institutions (vault cash) or on deposit at a Federal Reserve bank (reserve balance), and they must equal specific fractions of the total amounts of their deposits.[18] The **required reserve ratio** is the minimum amount of cash reserves to deposits that the Fed requires banks to hold. Put simply, it is the percentage of the outstanding money supply (or loans) that banks need to keep in their vaults.

The dollar amount of a bank's reserve requirement is determined by applying the required reserve ratios specified by the Fed to a bank's so-called **reservable liabilities**. These liabilities are accounts, deposits, balances, loans, and assets held by customers at their banks.[19] The Garn-St. Germain Act of 1982 exempted the first $2 million of reservable liabilities from reserve requirements. This "exemption amount" is adjusted each year according to a formula specified by the act. The amount of net transaction accounts is subject to a reserve requirement ratio of 3% on the first $25 million and is adjusted on a yearly basis.[20] The required reserve ratio established in the 1980 act means, in effect, that a bank must have $1 on reserve for every $8.33 in deposits, adjusted for inflation. For example, if that reserve ratio is lowered to 10%, then eighty-three cents on reserve would support the same $8.33 in deposits.

Since excess reserves can be used to make loans to borrowers, when the Fed lowers the required reserve ratio, it provides banks with more excess reserves for expanding credit with the consequence that interest rates will fall.[21] When the Fed raises the required reserve ratio, it cuts the volume of deposits supported by a given level of reserves and curbs the supply of credit, thereby forcing up interest rates. However, required reserve ratios are not used to make short-term or day-to-day corrections in monetary policy, since severe fluctuations in the reserve ratios would disrupt financial planning.

Federal Funds Rate and Discount Rate

The board of governors also determines the level of money in circulation by managing two key interest rates: the **federal funds rate** and the **discount rate**.[22] The federal funds rate is the rate at which Federal Reserve banks lend percentages of their reserve funds to commercial banks. During the 1980s the philosophy underlying the management of interest rates gradually shifted toward achieving a specified level for the federal funds rate, a process that was largely completed by the end of the decade.[23] Beginning in 1994 the FOMC began to announce changes in its policy stance, and in 1995 it began to explicitly state its target level for the federal funds rate.[24]

Commercial banks can also borrow credit via a so-called **discount window**. The **discount rate** is the rate charged to commercial banks on several lines of credit that are available from their regional Federal Reserve banks. The Federal Reserve banks offer three discount window programs to commercial banks, each with its own interest rate: primary credit, secondary credit, and seasonal credit.[25] Under the primary credit program, loans are extended for a short term (usually overnight) to banks in sound financial condition. Depository institutions that are not eligible for primary credit may apply for secondary credit to meet short-term liquidity needs, resolve severe financial difficulties, or deal with recurring intrayear fluctuations in funding needs (like banks that serve small agricultural or seasonal resort communities).

Federal Reserve bank presidents propose adjustments in both the federal funds and discount rates to the Federal Reserve Board, which makes the final decision on whether to raise or lower the discount rate. Since January 2003 the Fed has set the discount rate higher than the federal funds rate in order to keep commercial banks from turning to reserve funds before they have exhausted other less expensive alternatives. Originally, the power to determine the discount rate was the most important monetary policy instrument of the board. As the "lender of last resort," the Fed provides credit to banks facing liquidity crises during, for example, seasonal shopping periods (Christmas) and heightened commercial activity.[26]

Lower federal funds and discount rates stimulate economic activity by lowering the cost of borrowing, making it easier for consumers and businesses to make purchases and to invest. Higher rates tighten economic activity and encourage borrowers to save by increasing the actual cost of borrowing money. The Federal Reserve Act of 1913 envisioned that the discount rate of each reserve bank would vary according to the credit conditions in each district. However, the development of an integrated national financial market has produced more uniform interest rates across the entire nation.

The management of the federal funds and discount rates determine the **prime rate** (see figure 5.2). The prime rate is the interest rate charged by banks to their most creditworthy individual and business customers. The prime rate is usually higher than the federal funds and discount rates. The prime rate is probably the most consequential rate offered by banks for their customers on a daily basis, because it is used in calculating mortgages, home improvement loans, lines of equity, and other fixed and adjustable loans. It is also used to calculate interest rates for subsidized and unsubsidized student loans and credit cards with variable interest.

Open Market Operations

The management of **open market operations** by the Federal Open Market Committee (FOMC) constitutes the most powerful and flexible monetary policy instrument.[27] The FOMC operates through the Federal Reserve Bank of New York by purchasing and selling **U.S. government securities** on the secondary market.[28] U.S. government securities are debt obligations is-

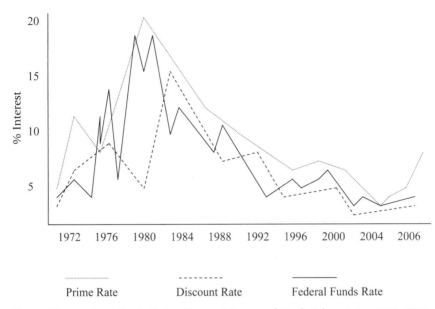

Prime Rate   Discount Rate   Federal Funds Rate

Figure 5.2. Federal Funds Rate, Discount Rate, and Bank Prime Rate, 1972–2006.
Source: Current and historical H.15 data are available on the Federal Reserve Board's websites at http://www.federalreserve.gov/RELEASES/h15/data/Annual/H15_FF_O.txt, http://www.federalreserve.gov/RELEASES/h15/data/Annual/H15_PRIME_NA.txt, http://www.federalreserve.gov/RELEASES/h15/data/Annual/discontinued_DWB_NA.txt, and http://www.federalreserve.gov/RELEASES/h15/data/Annual/H15_DWPC_NA.txt.

sued by the Treasury Department and various other federal agencies that want to borrow money from private individuals and financiers, also foreign investors, in order to finance current government programs. Securities are available in two basic forms: treasury securities and agency securities. U.S. treasury securities are direct obligations of the federal government and U.S. agency securities issued by the various government agencies, mainly the home-mortgage lending group Fannie Mae, the Federal Farm Credit Bank (FFCB), the Federal Home Loan Bank (FHLB), and the Tennessee Valley Authority (TVA).

The FOMC meets generally four times a year in Washington, D.C., to decide on whether to purchase or sell securities. If circumstances require consultation or consideration of an action between these regular meetings, members may be called on to participate in a special meeting. At each regularly scheduled meeting, the FOMC votes on the policy to be carried out during the interval between meetings. The Fed must regularly purchase and sell securities worth billions of dollars in order to have a measurable effect on the money supply.

The buying and selling of government securities are handled by specialized dealers located mainly in New York City. These transactions by the FOMC change the reserve base of the entire depository system. When the FOMC purchases securities from a primary dealer—a government securities dealer who has an established relationship with the Fed, such as Morgan Stanley, Smith Barney, Goldman Sachs, or American General—it pays for those securities by transferring funds to the primary dealer's account at its clearing bank, simultaneous with the delivery of the securities to the Fed. This injects reserve funds into the banking system, thereby increasing the money supply. When the Fed sells securities to a primary dealer, it drains reserves from the banking system, which decreases the amount of money in supply.

Economic Indicators

Changes in reserve requirements, the federal funds rate, the discount rate, and open market operations are intended to affect the overall supply of reserves in the banking system. Any shift in monetary policy, especially changes in the discount rate, is closely watched by the financial community and our political leaders as a signal to whether the Fed is going to tighten or loosen the money supply. To make that determination, the Fed monitors various economic indicators to judge future trends. The specific indicators watched most closely at any particular time depend on economic conditions and perceptions of what problems are most pressing. During the late 1980s, when neither unemployment nor inflation seemed severe but greater concern was expressed over the trade deficit, trade reports were more closely watched. A few years later, during the recession of 1990–1991, unemployment and GDP figures were much more closely monitored.

Each month the **Bureau of Economic Analysis (BEA)** in the Department of Commerce and the **Bureau of Labor Statistics (BLS)** in the Department of Labor publish leading economic indicators that are widely publicized by the mass media.[29] The BEA provides timely and closely watched economic statistics that influence the decisions made by government officials, business people, households, and individuals. BEA economic statistics are key ingredients in critical decisions affecting monetary policy, tax and budget projections, and business investment plans. The primary statistic published by the BEA is the national income and product accounts, which feature the GDP. Other indicators issued by the BEA include budget analysis (budget deficits and/or surpluses), industry economic accounts (business investment plans), regional economic accounts (federal funds to the states and local governments), and international financial transactions (imports, exports, trade deficit, trade debt, and foreign direct investment in the United States).

The BLS is the principal federal fact-finding agency for the field of labor economics and statistics. It tracks the inflation rate by publishing the consumer price index (CPI), which includes monthly data on changes in the retail price paid by consumers for a bundle of goods and services. It also issues the producer price index (PPI), which measures monthly data on changes in the prices charged by the producers of those goods and services. Another key indicator is the consumer expenditure survey, which is a compilation of data on the buying habits of American consumers according to socioeconomic factors.

The **leading indicators composite index**, compiled monthly by the Conference Board, a business membership and research organization, is the most important forecast of changes in economic performance.[30] The index is comprised of ten economic components that detail fluctuations in the economy: average weekly hours worked by manufacturing workers; average number of initial applications for unemployment insurance; amount of manufacturers' new orders for consumer goods and materials; delivery speed of new merchandise to vendors from suppliers; amount of new orders for capital goods unrelated to defense; amount of new building permits for residential buildings; S&P 500 stock index; inflation-adjusted monetary supply; long- and short-term interest rates; and consumer confidence. A decline in this index over several months usually signals a recession; a rise means that a new recovery is on the horizon. These forecasts are generally accurate. One study found that the leading indicators have forecasted every downturn and "growth recession" (when there is positive economic growth but nonetheless an increase in the unemployment rate) since 1948.[31]

POLITICS AT THE FED

The political leadership of the Federal Reserve System is exercised by the chairman of the Federal Reserve Board, and he is a very important decision maker in the economic policy making process.[32] The Fed chair is a powerful symbol of financial integrity and prudence for the American economy. The appointee must have the confidence of the business community. For example, this criteria weighed heavily in Kennedy's decision to reappoint the conservative William McChesney Martin: "In mid-1961 . . . until fairly late in 1961, Kennedy was still thinking of replacing Martin, but as the date for reappointment or new appointment came up, Martin's standing in the domestic and international financial community kept rising . . . and by the time the date arrived, Kennedy had decided to reappoint Martin."[33] Similarly, the increased concern among business executives and financiers that followed the departure of Fed chairman Arthur Burns in 1978 only ended with the choice of Paul Volcker in 1979. As *Business Week* observed: "Shattered confidence in the Carter Administration left the President no choice but to select a man who would be instantly hailed as the savior of the dollar, even though that meant bringing in a Fed chairman far more conservative than Carter would have preferred."[34]

The Fed chairman dominates the Federal Reserve System largely because of his far-reaching powers over monetary policy. He acts as the primary monetary spokesperson for the Fed, Wall Street, and the White House. In addition, members of Congress listen to the chairman's every utterance for an indication of future monetary policy. The chairman also networks with other federal agencies, and he can make decisions without formal review by the entire board of governors. In fact, the chairman possesses supervisory authority over the Fed staff and usually can sway votes at formal meetings of the board of governors and the FOMC.

Fed Chairs

With the exception of Thomas B. McCabe, who served only three years under Truman, and G. William Miller, who resigned to become President Carter's secretary of the treasury, Fed chairmen have enjoyed long tenures in office. Marriner S. Eccles chaired the Fed for fourteen years under Roosevelt and Truman. Eccles was an early defender of Keynesianism and an advocate for the New Deal who believed that monetary policy should complement fiscal policy. Yet Eccles also believed that the Fed should be independent of both the White House and the Treasury Department.

One issue that divided Eccles and the Roosevelt administration occurred when the Fed proposed to buy government bonds in order to lower interest rates and increase the money supply, but President Roosevelt and his Treasury Department acted to reduce government borrowing, thereby preventing the Fed from using monetary policy for broader countercyclical goals.[35] This policy disagreement was aggravated when the federal government had to borrow heavily to finance the Korean War. In 1951 President Truman organized an interagency committee, including Fed chairman Eccles, CEA chairman Leon Keyserling, and Assistant Treasury Secretary William McChesney Martin, to find a resolution to the different priorities in monetary policy between the Fed and the White House. The outcome of these meetings was the famous **Federal Reserve-Treasury Accord of 1951,** which stated: "The Treasury and the Federal Reserve System have reached full accord with respect to debt management and monetary policies to be pursued in furthering their common purpose to assure the successful financing of the Government's requirements and, at the same time, to minimize monetization of the public debt."[36] In other words, the Fed was no longer formally obliged to maintain stable interest rates to assist Treasury's debt management. Now the Fed could make independent decisions on monetary policy designed to achieve countercyclical objectives.

The nineteen-year tenure of William McChesney Martin spanned the Truman, Eisenhower, Kennedy, Johnson, and Nixon administrations. Among Martin's most notable monetary accomplishments was strong economic growth premised on controlling inflation by effectively managing interest rates. Under Martin, the Fed often served as the voice of reason in good times and bad: "The job of the Federal Reserve is to take away the punch bowl just when the party starts getting interesting."[37] Martin institutionalized his achievements within the FOMC by gathering the opinions of all governors within the system before making decisions. As a result, his decisions were often supported by unanimous votes on the FOMC.

Under Martin, the Fed became a strong independent political force. According to author John T. Woolley, "the basic factor producing conflict between the president and the Federal Reserve seems to be their differential responses to the economic conditions experienced in the late phases of economic upswings and downswings. That is, the Federal Reserve is typically faster to switch to a restrictive policy and slower to move to an expansionary policy than the president."[38] The Fed's autonomy under Martin was greatly facilitated by President Eisenhower, who preferred not to become embroiled in a policy debate with the Fed. Kennedy and Johnson, however, were quite frustrated by Martin's independent monetary policy actions, especially with what they believed was his overly strident view of any price increases. Kennedy's CEA chairman, Walter Heller, warned the president that Martin's "foot is poised nervously above the anti-inflationary brake pedal."[39] In response, Kennedy made more frequent use of the informal "**quadriad**" meetings of Fed chairman Martin, CEA chairman Walter Heller, the BOB director (first David Bell, then Kermit Gordon), and Treasury Secretary Douglas Dillon. These consultations helped to smooth Fed–White House relations. In the end, President Kennedy reappointed Martin as Fed chairman after he cooperated with the Kennedy administration in implementing a new policy, dubbed "Operation Twist," designed to improve the U.S. balance-of-payments problem.

After President Johnson succeeded to the White House and secured congressional enactment of the tax cut proposed by President Kennedy, the prospect of an economic boom worried Martin so much that on June 1, 1965, he warned the country about the threat of another depression. After Johnson escalated his military buildup in Southeast Asia, Martin began to signal his intentions to tighten the money supply. Although CEA chairman Gardner Ackley and Treasury Secretary Henry Fowler argued that monetary restraint was not necessary, the Fed voted to raise the discount rate from 4% to 4.5%, and its policy of tight control of the money supply continued.[40]

By 1967 President Johnson announced cuts in federal spending, a suspension of corporate tax incentives, and recommended a 10% tax surcharge to pay for the Vietnam War. Johnson's actions caused the Fed to ease off the monetary brake to allow Congress enough time to act on the tax increase proposal. However, when it became apparent that the surcharge would be too little and too late, the Fed again moved to tighten the money supply. Author Donald F. Kettl notes, "the Fed's tightening in 1966, ease in 1967 through 1968, and renewed tightening in 1969 were thus the product of an elaborate political minuet in which Martin struggled to accommodate the Fed to a turbulent environment."[41] The upshot was that President Johnson chose to reappoint Martin in 1967 to an unprecedented fifth term as Fed chairman.

During his long tenure, Martin vigorously defended the Fed's autonomy from the White House, pursued independent monetary policies, and regularly asserted that the Fed was solely responsible to Congress. In 1970 Martin was replaced by Arthur Burns, who had been Eisenhower's CEA chairman and was serving as President Nixon's economic counselor at the time of his appointment. Although Burns was a partisan who continued to work closely with Nixon, Burns did not allow the White House to dictate monetary policy. In fact, Nixon angrily viewed Burns's strong advocacy of controls on wages and prices to combat rising inflation as an act of disloyalty. Eventually, though, Nixon accepted wage-price controls, and he reappointed Burns as Fed chairman in 1974. Burns's reappointment, however, was widely viewed as a political payoff to Burns for reducing interest rates that helped get President Nixon reelected in 1972.[42] Under President Ford, the White House did not attempt to interfere with Chairman Burns's operations at the Fed.[43]

A more serious challenge to the Fed's independence and Burns's leadership erupted not from the executive branch but from the legislative branch. Rising prices, which threatened the U.S. economy during the early 1970s, prompted Congress to look into how the Fed set monetary targets, and its inquiries culminated in new oversight legislation. In 1975 Congress enacted Concurrent Resolution 133 in an attempt to influence Fed policy making and increase its accountability to both the House and Senate. Two years later the **Federal Reserve Reform Act of 1977** was signed into law by President Carter.[44] In addition to requiring Senate confirmation of the president's designations of the Fed chairman and vice-chairman, the act stated:

> The Board of Governors shall consult with Congress at semiannual hearings before the Committee on Banking, Housing and Urban Affairs of the Senate and the Committee on Banking, Finance and Urban Affairs of the House of Representatives about the Board of Governors' and the Federal Open Market Committee's objectives and plans with respect to the ranges of growth or diminution of monetary and credit aggregates for the upcoming twelve months, taking account of past and prospective developments in production, employment and prices. Nothing in this Act shall be interpreted to require that such ranges of growth or diminution be achieved if the Board of Governors and the Federal Open Market Committee determine that they cannot or should not be achieved because of changing conditions.[45]

According to author Robert Weintraub, "Congress, though willing to legislate monetary policy goals and basic long-run guidelines for its conduct, is not willing to pick the aggregate for carrying them out. The choice of the target M [whether M1, M2, or M3] of open market and other day-to-day monetary policy operations is viewed as a technical, not a legislative matter."[46]

The next year Congress enacted the Full Employment and Balanced Growth Act of 1978 (better known as the Humphrey-Hawkins Act), which added further oversight mechanisms. The act requires the Fed to give Congress its monetary policy goals within thirty days after its receipt of the CEA *Economic Report of the President* and explain their relationship to the president's short-term economic objectives.[47] In its semiannual reports to the Congress, the FOMC must also issue an economic projection of GDP, inflation, and unemployment for the upcoming year.

New tensions with the White House developed because President Carter became worried about Burns's independent streak and anti-inflation stridency. In 1978 Carter replaced Burns with G. William Miller, whose financial connections were supposed to establish confidence on Wall Street. However, when inflationary pressures roared back and Miller signaled a willingness to follow the White House lead by voting against a discount rate increase (which the Fed approved in late 1978), *Fortune* magazine labeled Miller "a fainthearted inflation fighter."[48] When inflation hit double-digits, Carter decided to fire Treasury Secretary Michael Blumenthal and persuaded Miller to step down from the Fed chairmanship and accept an appointment to treasury secretary.

The deteriorating financial and political situation had to be contained and, to repair the damage, President Carter appointed the president of the Federal Reserve Bank of New York, Paul Volcker, to succeed Miller as Fed chairman. Volcker had the reputation of being an ardent inflation fighter and his appointment was supported by the financial community. The Fed under Paul Volcker is widely credited with ending the inflation crisis of the 1970s, based on his actions that limited the growth of the money supply.[49] His policies allowed regional Federal Reserve banks to increase their discount rates; new reserve requirements were established to curb the growth of bank credit; and open-market operations with the purchasing and selling of U.S. government securities were now used to regulate the supply of bank reserves instead of influencing interest rates.[50] The latter represented a fundamental realignment in FOMC operations, one which echoed the long-standing criticisms of Fed policy by monetarist economists. Indeed, economists Paul A. Samuelson and William D. Nordhaus describe Fed policy from October 1979 through the fall of 1982 as "a monetarist experiment," in which the Fed attempted to keep monetary growth relatively constant, without regard to short-term fluctuations in economic activity or interest rates.[51]

These policy changes telegraphed to the business community and the American people that Volcker was determined to directly control inflation without concern for its impact on unemployment and economic growth. Ronald Reagan's administration initially encouraged the Fed to maintain stable growth in the money supply, but in mid-1981 some administration officials openly engaged in Fed bashing.[52] Despite interest rates at 20% in 1981, inflation fell only slightly, but the radical shift in monetary policy undoubtedly helped to plunge the economy into recession between July 1981 and September 1982, one which yielded the highest unemployment level since the Great Depression. Joblessness rose to nearly 10% at the height of the 1981–1982 recession.[53] However, by 1983 inflation was brought under control and has remained relatively low ever since. Unemployment also decreased, resulting in considerable economic growth during the 1980s.

Volcker's decisive role during this trying period, argues Kettl, meant that "for the first time in the Fed's history, its chairman controlled the agenda for macroeconomic policy. He had in 1979 pushed control of inflation to the keystone of economic policy making. He followed that by developing a strategy to break inflation, and he succeeded in winning political support for it."[54] A steadfast monetary policy was crucial for the success of Reagan's tax cuts, and Volcker generally enjoyed the good will of President Reagan. Although such powerful voices as House Majority Leader Jim Wright (D-TX) and Congressman Jack Kemp (R-NY) had called for his resignation, Volcker was reappointed Fed chairman by President Reagan with the resounding support of Wall Street.

After Volcker's departure in 1987, President Reagan named Alan Greenspan Fed chairman. Greenspan was subsequently reappointed by Presidents George H. W. Bush, Bill Clinton, and George W. Bush until he retired in January 2006. At first Greenspan was praised for his response to the 1987 "Black Monday" stock market crash, when the Dow-Jones industrial average dropped 508 points and for his leadership during the global financial crises and technology boom of the 1990s. Greenspan is largely credited with achieving record-low inflation, spawning the 1990s economic boom, and rescuing key foreign currencies from financial collapse.[55] During the 1990s, the United States experienced extraordinary prosperity. For example, between 1993 and 2000 the economy created over twenty million new jobs, unemployment remained between 4% and 5%, and GDP expanded by 3.8% a year. Fiscal discipline was reflected in the Clinton administration's ability to reduce the budget deficit every year between 1993 and 2000, with surpluses produced between 1998 and 2001. The United States had the best of both economic worlds: stable low inflation with sustained economic expansion.[56]

Greenspan's leadership at the Fed played an important role in fostering the conditions that allowed the U.S. economy to surge in the 1990s.[57]

Clearly, he helped attain long-term price stability. However, this was due in large measure to Greenspan's predecessor, Paul Volcker, who broke the back of inflation when he assumed the reins of the Fed. In 1979 inflation was at 12%; when Greenspan succeeded Volcker in 1987 inflation stood at 4%.[58] Although inflation slowed even further over the next fourteen years, 80% of the decrease in the inflation rate had occurred under Volcker. Greenspan's task was to continue implementing Volcker's anti-inflationary policies. This assessment is not meant to minimize Greenspan's overall impact, however, because in only one year (1990) in Greenspan's seventeen-year tenure at the Fed did inflation increase more than 5%, whereas for eleven years the inflation rate was 3%.[59]

Greenspan was willing to drive down interest rates to very low levels in order to promote long-term monetary stability and rapid economic growth.[60] While this contributed to prosperity, it also produced a destabilizing and speculative stock market "bubble" in the late 1990s that fueled the rapid expansion of the high-technology sector of the economy.[61] With interest rates low and the federal budget nearing a surplus, Internet-based companies (dot-coms) were founded between 1996 and 2000 in response to increasing stock prices, individual stock speculation, and widely available venture capital. This created an exuberant environment in which many of these businesses dismissed standard business models and emphasized increasing market share at the expense of the bottom line. In this new environment of soaring stocks and free spending, economic growth accelerated and extreme wealth was generated on the hope that such new **Internet** companies as eBay, Amazon.com, Priceline.com, and Google would be the vanguard for the "new economy" of the twenty-first century. However, the speculative frenzy officially burst the "dot.com bubble" on April 14, 2000, when both the Dow-Jones industrial average and the NASDAQ composite index logged their biggest single-day losses. The Dow declined 5.66% (617.78 points) and the NASDAQ lost 9.67% (355.49 points). Most dot-coms ran out of capital and were acquired or liquidated by "old economy" competitors or domain name investors.

In order to spur economic activity in the wake of the 9/11 terrorist attacks, the Fed cut interest rates by 0.50% in November 2001, which pushed the federal funds rate down to 1.25% and the discount rate down to 0.75%. The Fed cut interest rates a further 0.25% in June 2003, pushing the federal funds and discount rates to 1.00%, the lowest since 1958. This promoted bubbles in other key asset markets, especially in sales of single-family homes and in new home construction. As a consequence, residential property values soared in most urban and suburban areas, with overpricing concentrated in California, Florida, northern Virginia, and New England. By 2005, annual prices for single-family homes rose to record highs in many states, along with double-digit increases in property values. Shortly after

Hurricane Katrina in 2005 and in response to higher interest rates and energy prices, the residential property market cooled down and prices leveled off or fell in many areas. In the first quarter of 2006, bank foreclosures on homes were roughly 5% higher than in the first quarter of 2005. During the same time period, delinquencies, which foreshadow foreclosures, were up 7%.[62] However, even with these devaluations, the national real estate market can hardly be said to have crashed.[63]

Both the stock market and residential property bubbles have had some negative effects on the American economy. While rising home values have offset personal indebtedness by making people "feel" more affluent, that kind of rationalization assumes that property values will continue to increase over the long-term. Between 2001 and 2005 the accumulated personal debt of Americans was 60% larger than overall economic growth.[64] Many Americans now spend disproportionate shares of their monthly incomes on mortgage and credit card interest, leaving them in a highly uncertain financial position. The bind on those Americans with precarious financial balances began when the Fed decided to raise the federal funds rate for seventeen consecutive quarters between June 2004 and August 2006, making this the longest sustained campaign of interest rate hikes. The objective was to encourage more personal savings and less borrowing by making it more expensive to go into debt.

The high-consumption, savings-starved U.S. economy may be living beyond its means. This problem is compounded by America's huge annual trade deficit, which by 2006 rose to $768 billion. America is now the world's largest debtor nation. Under Greenspan, an enormous amount of U.S. dollars were accumulated by central banks in China and the EU.[65] These countries then recycle this cash back into the United States by buying U.S. government securities, which subsidize domestic U.S. interest rates and entice Americans into purchasing more foreign-made goods and services.

In January 2006 President Bush named Ben Bernanke to be Fed chairman, succeeding Alan Greenspan. Bernanke was confirmed by the U.S. Senate a month later. In his Senate confirmation hearings, Bernanke emphasized that monetary policy falls under the exclusive domain of the Federal Reserve and that taxation and spending were the responsibility of the elected branches of government. Under Bernanke the Fed has continued to be primarily concerned about the inflationary pressures associated with extremely high energy prices. Therefore, the Fed decided to resume raising the federal funds and discount rates, leading to interest rate increases on credit cards, auto loans, adjustable-rate home mortgages, home-equity lines of credit, and long-term, fixed-rate mortgages.

Bernanke is trying to guide monetary policy during a period of economic uncertainty. While credit remains relatively cheap, Americans have felt the squeeze as higher borrowing costs have slowed down the residential property market. Although Bernanke's Fed raised the federal funds rate an additional quarter point to 5.25% in June 2006, the highest it has been since 2004 (when it was at 1%), it decided to leave rates unchanged in August on the belief that a modest economic slowdown would subdue inflation.[66] While inflation was still modest, it has been stoked by surging oil prices that have led to rising costs for materials, labor, and transportation. At the same time, the GDP dropped from 5.6% in the first quarter to 2.5% in the second quarter of 2006, unemployment increased from 4.6% to 4.8%, and the budget deficit for 2006 was $248 billion.[67]

Politicization of the Fed

Despite a general pattern of cooperation between the Fed and the White House, presidents still try to exert influence over monetary policy. For example, the Reagan administration consistently wanted more assurances from the Fed that monetary policy would complement its supply-side policies. In October 1985 Reagan nominated Manuel H. Johnson and Wayne D. Angell to the Federal Reserve Board. Both Johnson (who had been assistant secretary of the treasury for economic policy) and Angell were very sympathetic to supply-side arguments. Alan Blinder of the Brookings Institution describes the Johnson appointment this way: "I'm very disappointed to see someone so personally associated with supply-side economics on the Federal Reserve Board."[68] After being confirmed by the Senate, Johnson and Angell joined two existing Reagan appointees (Preston Martin and Martha R. Seger) as the so-called gang of four who lobbied Fed chairman Volcker to allow two reductions in the discount rate in early 1986.

Few members of Congress have the requisite knowledge or the political incentives to give much attention to monetary policy. Usually Congress will threaten to intervene in Fed policy making in the wake of highly publicized hikes in interest rates or slumps in housing construction (since mortgages are interest sensitive). This scenario occurred in the mid-1970s so the opportunity was ripe for legislative sanctions against the Fed.[69] Recall that Congress in 1975 enacted House Concurrent Resolution 133 to oblige the Fed chairman to make regular appearances before congressional hearings to explain the Fed's monetary objectives.[70]

During the Clinton tenure, Alan Greenspan was accused of setting monetary policy too much in harmony with fiscal policy. Greenspan worked closely with the Clinton economic team to craft responses to international financial crises, measures to reduce the deficit and national debt, and lobbying efforts to oppose Republican tax cuts.[71] As a result, budget surpluses, low inflation and unemployment, and high economic growth occurred during the 1990s. However, in 2001 Greenspan sent a much different signal when his support for President Bush's tax cuts was instrumental to securing their passage in Congress. Greenspan told the Senate "that sufficient resources will be available to undertake both debt reduction" and tax cuts. He further suggested that tax cuts could be rescinded if surplus projections proved wrong, but the lawmakers ignored that idea. Interestingly, in 2003 Greenspan made it tougher for Bush to win Capitol Hill approval for his tax plans when he told the Senate Banking Committee that he favored ending the double taxation of corporate dividends but not at the expense of huge budget shortfalls. "Deficits must be maintained at minimal levels," Greenspan testified. He also argued that the economy is "being held back" by uncertainty over war with Iraq.[72]

Tensions between Greenspan and Congress intensified in 2005 after Senate Minority Leader Harry Reid (D-NV) referred to Greenspan as "one of the biggest political hacks we have here in Washington."[73] Reid and other Democrats tried to highlight the enormous deficits that resulted from three consecutive Bush tax cuts, which Greenspan seemingly had supported. Greenspan also was criticized for his support of Bush's plan for partial privatization of the Social Security program.[74] Charges that Greenspan was veering beyond the Fed's purview of monetary affairs into fiscal policy and other issues traditionally left to lawmakers became more prevalent.[75]

For his part, Ben Bernanke has been reluctant to offer advice on political issues and fiscal policy. This restraint, however, has not insulated Bernanke from legislative criticism. After Bernanke testified in April 2006 before the House of Representatives that he would recommend an additional quarter-percentage-point increase in the federal funds rate, both Republican and Democratic lawmakers urged the Fed to stop raising interest rates prior to the end of the election year. This came at a time when the Bush administration sought to reassure disgruntled voters that the economy was strong despite rising energy prices.[76]

MONETARY POLITICS AND GOALS

The original purposes of the Federal Reserve System were to create an elastic currency, supervise the banking system, and allow for "discounted" commercial credits. In effect, the Fed was created to prevent the waves of bank failures associated with previous financial panics and depressions by serving as the "lender of last resort" for banks, thereby maintaining the liquidity of the banking system. In the years since its inception, its purpose has evolved such that the Fed is now expected to take a leadership role in achieving broader economic goals.[77] Specifically, it is supposed to permit enough long-term growth in the money supply and credit to accommodate economic growth with relative price stability. In the short-term, the Fed utilizes monetary policy to avoid the deflationary and inflationary pressures associated with the business cycle.

Thus far our discussion seems to imply that the Fed is able to influence the economy through such tools as reserve requirements, the discount rate, and open market transactions. It may be worth considering this point more carefully. The operational problem is that it is much easier for the Fed to maintain liquidity in the banking system than to achieve the more ambitious goal of macroeconomic management.[78] The goal of Fed policy is to influence the total amount of bank reserves available in the banking system. Changes in the money supply are supposed to raise or lower the cost of borrowing and thereby stimulate or deflate economic activity. Changes in monetary policy, however, appear to influence prices in the long run but employment and production only in the short run. When the Fed slows down the growth rate of the money supply, the eventual result will be a lower rate of inflation. But the transition to lower inflation will likely involve some "lag" time during which unemployment will rise.[79] This illustrates the short-term trade-off between inflation and unemployment, which is popularly known as the Phillips Curve (see chapter 6).[80]

A recent policy dilemma has been the so-called monetary policy shocks, which are random and sudden movements in some measure of monetary policy (M1, M2, or M3) that cannot be predicted. Once these shocks are identified, scholars have been able to trace their effects on employment, production, inflation, and other economic variables of interest. In the late 1990s, for example, the U.S. economy experienced significantly low inflation and unemployment and high economic growth. In 1999 the inflation rate was 2.2% and unemployment was 4.2% with economic growth running at 4.5%.[81] To some casual observers these fortuitous events suggested that the short-run trade-off between inflation and unemployment no longer existed.[82] Why did the U.S. economy experience this rare combination of low unemployment and low inflation? This could be due to Volcker's and Greenspan's consistent and sustained anti-inflationary policies. Or, on the other hand, the more fundamental reason may be the acceleration in long-term U.S. economic growth that has occurred since World War II.

Monetary policy making is a complex and difficult process, although one truism, based on a huge body of research on optimal monetary policy, is that the Fed must raise interest rates in response to higher rates of inflation. This policy prescription is called the **Taylor principle**. According to the Taylor principle, the Fed should pursue an active monetary policy by adjusting nominal interest rates by more than a one-to-one ratio in response to changes in current inflation.[83] For most economists the Taylor principle establishes the minimum baseline that monetary policy must meet in order to have a stabilizing influence on the economy and to ensure that monetary shocks do not produce rapid and uncontrollable increases in inflation. The successes of monetary policy over the last twenty years are testimony to the efficacy of the Taylor principle.[84]

Is There a Political Monetary Cycle?

To what extent does monetary policy accommodate the political needs of the White House? The president can try to influence Fed decision making through his appointments, but the long and staggered terms of the board of governors assure that no president can make wholesale personnel changes during one four-year term. Having said that, it is noteworthy that all members of the Federal Reserve Board have been appointed by President George W. Bush. The current membership, therefore, offers an interesting test case of whether the Fed can maintain its independence from the White House. Or maybe presidential pressure on the Fed is more subtle insofar as the Fed chairman, a politically astute leader, may shape monetary policy to anticipate the political needs of the administration?

One specific research question is whether monetary policy shows a pattern that might be called a "**political monetary cycle**" to the degree that the Fed deliberately shapes policy in order to stimulate the economy immediately before national elections.[85] Since the Fed is likely more responsive to the president than Congress, this hypothesized effect should be tied more to presidential elections rather than congressional midterm elections. A study by Robert Weintraub tracked the growth in M1 from 1951 to 1977 and found that significant monetary policy "thrusts" occurred in 1953, 1961, 1969, 1971, 1974, and 1977, and each of those years with the exception of 1971 represented incumbency turnover in the White House.[86] Other statistical patterns were consistent with qualitative evidence about monetary policy making in each administration since the Fed-Treasury accord. As Weintraub concludes, "each administration monetary policy fitted harmoniously with the President's economic and financial objectives and plans."[87]

Do presidents actively pressure the Fed to set expansionary monetary policies to boost incomes and lower the unemployment rate before the election? Conventional wisdom argues that the independence of the Fed insulates monetary policy from political pressures, whereas fiscal policy would be the economic tool of choice for incumbents seeking to manipulate the economy for political advantage. While any president may have the electoral motivation for encouraging a political monetary cycle, there is little empirical evidence to support that claim.[88] Author Nathaniel Beck found no evidence that the Fed engages in this sort of behavior, which he attributes to the Fed's fear of risking its relative independence. While there have been surges in the M1 money supply associated with approaching presidential elections, this may be attributed to expansive fiscal policies rather than Fed policy tinkering.[89]

Yet there do appear to be important differences in monetary policy depending upon the presidential administration and turnover in the Fed chairmanship. Beck contends that, because Democratic presidents typically want lower unemployment even at the cost of higher inflation, it is hypothesized that they would prefer a relatively loose monetary policy (i.e., one with more growth in the money supply). In fact, the evidence suggests to Beck that Fed policy is generally tighter under Republicans than under Democrats.[90] Beck also examined the relationship between monetary and fiscal policy. He found that "by the 1970s easy fiscal policy was often associated with tight monetary policy."[91] While seemingly a contradictory countercyclical strategy, it may reflect a political logic which results from the inability of Congress and the president to contain inflationary pressures through the budget process. This bifurcated approach would allow the popular branches to focus their attention on the unemployment problem and let the Fed worry about inflation. If interest rates should go too high, then both Congress and the White House can resort to "bashing" the Fed as a political scapegoat.

The growing importance of monetary policy in economic stabilization addresses certain political realities. The difficulties experienced by presidential administrations since the 1970s suggest that fiscal policy may be an inappropriate tool to fight inflation. Combating rising prices requires elected officials to take unpopular actions like reducing spending or raising taxes, while traditional fiscal policy solutions to fighting unemployment tend to be more popular since they require increasing spending or cutting taxes.

Political realities seem to dictate that the unelected Fed chairman and board of governors may be more suited to making politically unpopular monetary policies during times of inflation. The Fed's more recent strategy of "inflation targeting" and adherence to the Taylor principle seems to validate this hypothesis.[92] Under Volcker and Greenspan, inflation was stabilized and, over the last two decades, the economy has experienced only two relatively mild recessions, in 1990 and 2001. The Fed did not explicitly articulate a strategy of "inflation targeting," though the Taylor principle seemingly was a powerful informal norm that guided monetary policy during Volcker's and Greenspan's tenures.

Given the time "lags" between the enactment of monetary policy and its impact on the economy, monetary policy should be anticipatory.[93] In other words, monetary policy must anticipate inflationary or deflationary pressures before they occur. Between 1994 and 1995 the Fed raised interest rates to head off increases in prices, and the inflation rate fell. In January 2001 the Fed then reversed course, cutting the rate by 1% and later proceeding with another rate cut at the end of the year.[94] This time the policy prevented a relatively mild recession from worsening, given the adverse shocks to the economy from the 9/11 terrorist attacks and the spate of corporate and financial scandals.

In conclusion, therefore, it should be stressed that monetary policy is primarily driven by the Fed's response to economic conditions such as the money supply, the unemployment rate, and the inflation rate. Studies that test for any political influences on Fed policy begin by correlating monetary policy decisions to those objective economic indicators, and then assessing whether political considerations seem to interfere with the fundamental economic relationships. To be sure, the Fed may alter its countercyclical target over time, sometimes being concerned with employment and other times focusing on price stability, and there are episodes—like during the monetarist experiment of 1979–1982—when the Fed adopts a radically new understanding of what it should be doing to stabilize the economy. But to a degree seldom seen in other economic policy arenas, the recent inflation-targeting activities suggest that the Fed is much less likely to shift monetary policy in response to shifts in public opinion and, instead, is much more likely to adopt policies based on its analytical assessments of what best promotes long-term price stability and steady growth in the money supply.

KEY TERMS

board of governors
Bureau of Economic Analysis (BEA)
Bureau of Labor Statistics (BLS)
Depository Institutions Deregulation and Monetary Control Act of 1980
discount rate
discount window
federal funds rate
Federal Open Market Committee (FOMC)
Federal Reserve Act of 1913
Federal Reserve Reform Act of 1977
Federal Reserve-Treasury Accord of 1951
Full Employment and Balanced Growth Act of 1978
Internet
leading indicators composite index
liquidity
Milton Friedman
monetarism
monetary policy
money supply
negotiable order of withdrawal (NOW) accounts
open market operations
political monetary cycle
prime rate
quadriad
required reserve ratio

reservable liabilities
reserve requirements
Taylor principle
U.S. government securities
Y2K

ADDITIONAL READINGS

Greider, William. *Secrets of the Temple: How the Federal Reserve Runs the Country*. New York: Simon & Schuster, 1988. A populist account of the Fed from its beginnings to 1987.

Jones, David M. *Unlocking the Secrets of the Fed: How Monetary Policy Affects the Economy and Your Wealth-Creation Potential*. New York: Wiley, 2002. This book goes inside the world of monetary and fiscal policy making to explain how understanding and anticipating the actions of the Federal Reserve is critical for investment success.

Kettl, Donald F. *Leadership at the Fed*. New Haven: Yale University Press, 1986. Excellent account of the leadership styles of four influential Fed Chairmen: Marriner Eccles, William McChesney Martin, Arthur Burns, and Paul Volcker.

Maisel, Sherman J. *Managing the Dollar*. New York: Norton, 1973. A member of the Fed's board of governors from 1965 to 1972 gives an insider's view of the workings of monetary policy.

Mayer, Martin. *Fed: The Inside Story of How the World's Most Powerful Financial Institution Drives the Markets*. New York: Penguin, 2002. This book explores the Federal Reserve System under the leadership of Chairman Alan Greenspan and its role in both the U.S. and world economies.

Timberlake, Richard H. Jr. *The Origins of Central Banking in the United States*. Cambridge, MA: Harvard University Press, 1978. An intellectual history of central banking and monetary policy before the Fed was established.

Woodward, Bob. *Maestro: Greenspan's Fed and the American Boom*. New York: Simon & Schuster, 2001. *Maestro* is not a biography of Greenspan so much as a history of the economy and markets during the period of his stewardship. Greenspan's forceful leadership of the Federal Open Market Committee profoundly influenced the path of monetary growth during the 1990s.

Woolley, John T. *Monetary Politics: The Federal Reserve and the Politics of Monetary Policy*. Cambridge, UK: Cambridge University Press, 1984. A study of how the Fed operates, the background of its members, and its relations with the executive and legislative branches.

NOTES

1. A clear exposition of the differences between conventional monetary theory and monetarism is found in Paul A. Samuelson and William D. Nordhaus, *Economics* (New York: McGraw-Hill, 1992), chap. 35.

2. Milton Friedman, "The Quantity Theory of Money: A Restatement," in *Studies in the Quantity Theory of Money*, ed. Milton Friedman (Chicago: University of Chicago Press, 1956) and Milton Friedman, "A Theoretical Framework for Monetary Analysis," *Journal of Political Economy* 78 (March–April): 193–238.

3. Thomas Mayer, *Monetarism and Macroeconomic Policy* (Aldershot, UK: Edward Elgar, 1990).

4. Paul Studenski and Herman E. Krooss, *Financial History of the United States* (New York: McGraw-Hill, 1963), 104.

5. Robert C. Puth, *American Economic History* (Chicago: Dryden Press, 1982), 175.

6. Martin Mayer, *Fed: The Inside Story of How the World's Most Powerful Financial Institution Drives the Markets* (New York: Penguin, 2002) and David M. Jones, *Unlocking the Secrets of the Fed: How Monetary Policy Affects the Economy and Your Wealth-Creation Potential* (New York: Wiley, 2002).

7. John T. Woolley, *Monetary Politics: The Federal Reserve and the Politics of Monetary Policy* (Cambridge: Cambridge University Press, 1984), 56–57.

8. Woolley, *Monetary Politics*, 67.

9. William Greider, *Secrets of the Temple: How the Federal Reserve Runs the Country* (New York: Simon & Schuster, 1987).

10. Woolley, *Monetary Politics*, 61.

11. Frederic Mishkin, *The Economics of Money, Banking and Financial Markets* (Boston: Pearson, 2005).

12. Benjamin M. Friedman, Kenneth N. Kuttner, Mark Gertler, James Tobin, "A Price Target for U.S. Monetary Policy? Lessons from the Experience with Money Growth Targets," *Brookings Papers on Economic Activity*, no. 1 (1996): 77–146.

13. Board of Governors of the Federal Reserve, "1993 Monetary Policy Objectives: Midyear Review of the Federal Reserve Board," (July 20, 1993): 9–10.

14. Federal Reserve Bank of St. Louis, "Meeting the Y2K Demand for Base Money," *Monetary Trends* (1999), http://www.stlouisfed.org/publications/mt/19991101/mtpub.pdf.

15. Richard G. Anderson, "Federal Reserve Board Data on OCD Sweep Account Programs," Federal Reserve Bank of St. Louis (May 30, 2002), http://research.stlouisfed.org/aggreg/swdata.html; Richard G. Anderson, "Retail Sweeps and Money Demand," *Monetary Trends* (November 2002); Barry E. Jones, Donald H. Dutkowsky, and Thomas Elger, "Sweep Programs and Optimal Monetary Aggregation," *Journal of Banking and Finance* (February 2005): 483–508; and Donald H. Dutkowsky and Barry Z. Cynamon, "Sweep Programs: The Fall of M1 and the Rebirth of the Medium of Exchange," *Journal of Money, Credit, and Banking* (April 2003): 263–280.

16. Michael D. Reagan, "The Political Structure of the Federal Reserve System," *American Political Science Review* 55 (1961): 64–76.

17. See John Kenneth Galbraith, *Money: Whence It Came, Where It Went* (New York: Houghton Mifflin, 1975).

18. Donald R. Wells, *The Federal Reserve System: A History* (McFarland, 2004).

19. Paul Bennett and Stavros Peristiani, "Are U.S. Reserve Requirements Still Binding?" (paper presented at a conference sponsored by the Federal Reserve Bank of New York, April 2001) and Joshua Feinman, "Reserve Requirements: History, Current Practice, and Potential Reform," *Federal Reserve Bulletin* (June 1993).

20. Thomas Lloyd, *Money, Banking and Financial Markets* (New York: McGraw-Hill, 1996), 253–263.

21. This assumes that the demand for loans stays the same. If demand increases, interest rates may actually stay the same or even rise. Whatever the specific effect on interest rates, the overall effect is stimulative, by making credit more available.

22. Wells, *The Federal Reserve System.*

23. Stavros Peristiani, "The Growing Reluctance to Borrow at the Discount Window: An Empirical Investigation," *Review of Economics and Statistics* 80, no. 4 (November 1998): 611–620.

24. Leonardo Bartolini, "Day-to-Day Monetary Policy and the Volatility of the Federal Funds Rate," *Journal of Money, Credit, and Banking* 34, no.1 (February 2002): 137–159.

25. James A. Clouse, "Recent Developments in Discount Window Policy," *Federal Reserve Bulletin* (November 1, 1994).

26. Steward C. Myers and Raghuram G. Rajan, "The Paradox of Liquidity," *Quarterly Journal of Economics* 113 (1998), 733–771 and Joseph Stiglitz and Andrew Weiss, "Credit Rationing in Markets with Imperfect Information" *American Economic Review* 71, no. 3 (1981): 393–410.

27. Wells, *The Federal Reserve System.*

28. William Poole and Robert Rasche, "Perfecting the Market's Knowledge of Monetary Policy," *Journal of Financial Services Research* 18, no. 2–3 (December 2000): 255–298.

29. For more information, see the websites for the BEA and the BLS at http://www.bea.gov and http://www.bls.gov.

30. See the website of the Conference Board at http://www.conference-board.org.

31. Ronald A. Ratti, "A Descriptive Analysis of Economic Indicators," *Federal Reserve Bank of St. Louis Review* 67–71 (January 1985): 328. This study has been reprinted by the Institute of Chartered Financial Analysts in *CFA Digest* (Fall 1985): 15.

32. See Sherman Maisel, *Managing the Dollar* (New York: Norton, 1973).

33. Quoted in Erwin C. Hargrove and Samuel A. Morely, *The President and the Council of Economic Advisers: Interviews with CEA Chairmen* (Boulder; Colorado: Westview, 1984), 191.

34. "The Dollar Chooses a Chairman," *Business Week* (August 6, 1979): 20.

35. Donald F. Kettl, *Leadership at the Fed* (New Haven, CT: Yale University Press, 1986), 66.

36. Cited in Kettl, *Leadership at the Fed*, 74.

37. Quoted in Heather Stewart, "Central Bankers Plot Path through the Minefields," *Observer* (June 4, 2006): 21.

38. John T. Woolley, *Monetary Politics: The Federal Reserve & the Politics of Monetary Policy* (London: Cambridge University Press, 1984), 119.

39. Quoted in Kettl, *Leadership at the Fed*, 93.

40. Allan H. Meltzer, "Origins of the Great Inflation," *Federal Reserve Bank of St. Louis Review* (March–April 2005): 145–175.

41. Kettl, *Leadership at the Fed*, 109.

42. Jeff Madrick, "Mr. Fix It," *New York Review of Books* (July 19, 2001), http://www.nybooks.com/articles/14394.

43. James E. Anderson, "The President and Economic Policy: A Comparative View of Advisory Arrangements" (paper presented at the annual meeting of the American Political Science Association, 1991), 11.

44. Bennett T. McCallum, "The United States Deserves a Monetary Standard," (unpublished manuscript, November 12, 2000), http://wpweb2.tepper.cmu.edu/faculty/mccallum/MonStandard1.pdf.

45. See HR 50 (Public Law 95-523), October 27, 1978. For more on the act, see J. Kevin Corder, "Evaluating Representative Control of Monetary Policy: Do Hearings Matter?" (paper presented at the annual meeting of the Midwest Political Science Association, Chicago, IL, April 1999).

46. Robert E. Weintraub, "Congressional Supervision of Monetary Policy," *Journal of Monetary Economics* (April 1978): 347.

47. John H. Makin, "The Fed Struggles to Balance Growth," *Ecomomic Outlook* (American Enterprise Institute for Public Policy Research online monthly newsletter, March 1, 2000), http://www.aei.org/include/pub_print.asp?pubID=11334.

48. Cited in Kettl, *Leadership at the Fed*, 170.

49. Joseph B. Treaster, *Paul Volcker: The Making of a Financial Legend* (New York: Wiley, 2005).

50. Treaster, *Paul Volcker*.

51. Samuelson and Nordhaus, *Economics*, 645.

52. Stephen S. Roach, "Think Again: Alan Greenspan," *Foreign Policy* (March–April 2005).

53. U.S. Department of Labor, Bureau of Labor Statistics, "Consumer Price Index," ftp://ftp.bls.gov/pub/special.requests/cpi/cpiai.txt.

54. Kettl, *Leadership at the Fed*, 185.

55. Justin Martin, *Greenspan: The Man behind the Money* (New York: Perseus, 2001).

56. Alice McGillivray, Richard Scammon, and Rhodes Cook, *America at the Polls 1920–2004* (Washington, DC: CQ Press, 2005); U.S. Department of Commerce, Bureau of Economic Analysis, "GDP and Other Major NIPA Series, 1929–2006"; U.S. Department of Labor, Bureau of Labor Statistics, "Consumer Price Index," ftp://ftp.bls.gov/pub/special.requests/cpi/cpiai.txt; U.S. Department of Labor, Bureau of Labor Statistics, "Employment Status of the Civilian Non-institutional Population, 1940 to 2006."

57. Bob Woodward, *Maestro: Greenspan's Fed and the American Boom* (New York: Simon & Schuster, 2001).

58. U.S. Department of Labor "Consumer Price Index."

59. Stephen K. Beckner, *Back from the Brink: The Greenspan Years* (New York: Wiley, 1996).

60. Woodward, *Maestro*.

61. Robert Shiller, *Irrational Exuberance* (Princeton, NJ: Princeton University Press, 2000) and Charles A. E. Goodhart, "Can Central Banking Survive the IT Revolution?" *International Finance* 3 (July 2000).

62. See Mortgage Bankers Association of America, "Residential Mortgage Foreclosures and Delinquencies Decrease since Last Quarter, according to MBA National Delinquency Survey," (June 19, 2006), http://www.mortgagebankers.org/NewsandMedia/PressCenter/42843.htm.

63. Daniela Deane, "In Real Estate Fever, More Signs of Sickness," *Washington Post*, April 17, 2005.

64. Roach, "Think Again: Alan Greenspan."

65. Ravi Batra and Raveendra N. Batra, *Greenspan's Fraud: How Two Decades of His Policies Have Undermined the Global Economy* (New York: Palgrave-Macmillan, 2005).

66. Nell Henderson, "Tighter, Tighter: When Will Fed Increases Start to Pinch?" *Washington Post*, June 29, 2006, and Paul Blustein, "Fed Leaves Interest Rates Unchanged," *Washington Post*, August 8, 2006.

67. U.S. Department of Commerce, Bureau of Economic Analysis, "Gross Domestic Product," news release, BEA-06-33, July 28, 2006, and Paul Blustein, "White House Lowers Deficit Estimate," *Washington Post*, July 12, 2006.

68. Quoted in Peter T. Kilborn, "New Fed Nominees: Manuel H. Johnson," *New York Times*, October 15, 1985.

69. See Woolley, *Monetary Politics*, 44–147.

70. Robert Weintraub, "Monetary Policy and Karl Brunner," *Journal of Money, Credit, and Banking* 9 (February 1977): 255–258.

71. Steven Greenhouse, "Clinton Goes Head to Head with the Fed," *New York Times*, January 18, 1993, and Steven Greenhouse, "Fed Chief Sways to Clinton's New Economic Tune," *New York Times*, February 27, 1993.

72. Dana Milbank and Nell Henderson, "Some Democrats Say Greenspan Has Gone from Maestro to Partisan," *Washington Post*, March 5, 2005.

73. Joyce Howard Price, "Reid Sticks by Greenspan Comments," *Washington Times*, May 5, 2005.

74. Paul Krugman, "Three-Card Maestro," *New York Times*, February 18, 2005.

75. Brian Knowlton, "Greenspan under Fire for Tax Cuts," *International Herald Tribune*, March 7, 2005.

76. Nell Henderson, "Bernanke: Fed Rate Hikes May Pause," *Washington Post*, April 28, 2006.

77. See Reagan, "The Political Structure of the Federal Reserve System," 64–76.

78. Samuelson and Nordhaus, *Economics*, chap. 29.

79. Christina D. Romer and David H. Romer. "Monetary Policy Matters," *Journal of Monetary Economics* 34, no. 1 (1994): 75–88.

80. The Phillips Curve has received considerable attention in academic literature. See Alban William Phillips, "The Relation between Unemployment and the Rate of Change of Money Wage Rates in the United Kingdom, 1861–1957," *Economica* 25 (1958): 283–289; A. Atkeson and L. E. Ohanian, "Are Phillips Curves Useful for Forecasting Inflation?" *FRB Minneapolis Quarterly Review* (Winter 2001): 2–11, http://www.mpls.frb.org/research/qr/qr2511.html; and E. S. Phelps, "Phillips Curves, Expectations of Inflation, and Optimal Unemployment over Time." *Economica* (34): 254–281.

81. U.S. Department of Commerce, Bureau of Economic Analysis, "GDP and Other Major NIPA Series, 1929–2006," tables 1–4.

82. James Stock and Mark W. Watson. "Forecasting Inflation," *Journal of Monetary Economics* 44 (October 1999): 293–335.

83. John B. Taylor, "Discretion versus Policy Rules in Practice" *Carnegie-Rochester Conference Series on Public Policy* 39 (1993): 195–214; John B. Taylor, "A Historical Analysis of Monetary Policy Rules," in *Monetary Policy Rules*, ed. John B. Taylor

(Chicago: University of Chicago Press, 1999), 319–341; and Michael Woodford, "The Taylor Rule and Optimal Monetary Policy," *American Economic Review* 91, no. 2 (2001): 232–237.

84. Richard Clarida, Jordi Gali, and Mark Gertler, "Monetary Policy Rules and Macroeconomic Stability: Evidence and Some Theory," *Quarterly Journal of Economics*, 115, no. 1 (2000): 147–180; John B. Taylor, "Applying Academic Research on Monetary Policy Rules: An Exercise in Translational Economics," *MSESS* 66 (supp., 1998); and Christina D. Romer and David H. Romer, "A Rehabilitation of Monetary Policy in the 1950s," *American Economic Review* 92 (May 2002): 121–127.

85. These arguments are more fully developed in William Nordhaus, "The Political Business Cycle," *Review of Economic Studies* 42 (1975): 69–190; Edward Tufte, *Political Control of the Economy* (Princeton: Princeton University Press, 1978); and Emery Trahan and Edward Renshaw, "Presidential Elections and the Federal Reserve's Interest Rate Reaction Function," *Journal of Policy Modeling* 12, no. 1 (1990): 29–34.

86. Weintraub, "Congressional Supervision of Monetary Policy," 349.

87. Weintraub, "Congressional Supervision of Monetary Policy," 350.

88. Stuart D. Allen and Donald L. McCrickard, "The Influence of Elections on Federal Reserve Behavior," *Economic Letters* 37, no. 1 (1991): 51–55; Reik Leertouwer and Philipp Maier, "Who Creates Political Business Cycles: Should Central Banks Be Blamed?" *European Journal of Political Economy* 17, no. 3 (2001): 445–463; and Simon Price, "Political Business Cycles and Macroeconomic Credibility: A Survey," *Public Choice* 92 (1997): 407–427.

89. Nathaniel Beck, "Elections and the Fed: Is there a Political Business Cycle," *American Journal of Political Science* 31, no. 1 (1987): 194–216.

90. Nathaniel Beck, "Domestic Political Sources of American Monetary Policy: 1955–1982," *Journal of Politics* 46 (1984): 786–817 and John T. Woolley, "Partisan Manipulations of the Economy: Another Look at Monetary Policy with Moving Regression," *Journal of Politics* 50 (1988): 335–360.

91. Nathaniel Beck, "Domestic Political Sources of American Monetary Policy," 810–812.

92. Athanasios Orphanides, "Historical Monetary Policy Analysis and the Taylor Rule," *Journal of Monetary Economics* 50 (2003): 983–1022.

93. Stephen McNees, "Modeling the Fed: A Forward-Looking Monetary Policy Reaction Function," *New England Economic Review* (November-December 1986): 3–8.

94. Jonathan Weisman, "The Tax Cut Pendulum and the Pit," *Washington Post*, October 8, 2004.

6

Presidential Economic Management, Approaches, and Policies

How a president makes fiscal policy, utilizes key policy makers, and shapes public sentiment depends to a great extent on his decision-making approach, management style, and political ideology. What emerges is a personalized, informal, and ad hoc style of economic management which, in most cases, is tilted toward reinforcing the president's political goals. Political scientist Michael Genovese classifies modern presidents according to their ideology (pro-business "enterprisers" or pro-government "statists") and strategy ("traditionalists" who pursue incremental goals and "innovators" who pursue bold new economic objectives). Genovese classified only Franklin Roosevelt and Ronald Reagan as innovators, but within the larger category of traditionalists Genovese found "the division is clearly along partisan lines, with the Democrats supporting a statist position, and the Republicans favoring an enterpriser approach."[1]

There is scholarly disagreement over whether macroeconomic policy is nonpolitical or partisan. Those in the first camp say that economic problems are publicized so much by the media that no president can systematically favor one group of voters over others when making economic policy.[2] The counterargument is that presidents are influenced by political ideology and party affiliation to shape economic policy in ways that benefit their supporters rather than the opposition.[3] The divergent styles of economic management adopted by various presidents, however, support the view that economic advice tends to reinforce the White House policy agenda.

THE POSTWAR ECONOMY

With the end of World War II it was feared that peacetime and the decline in military spending would reignite an economic contraction. However, unprecedented consumer demand for both durable and nondurable goods drove economic growth in the immediate postwar period. The automobile industry successfully converted to producing cars and new industries such as aviation and electronics arose in the late 1940s. A housing boom stimulated by affordable mortgages for returning members of the armed forces added to the economic growth. With the economies of Western Europe and Japan devastated by war, America's gross domestic product (GDP) increased from roughly 200 million in 1940 to 300 million in 1950.[4] In fact, our GDP was equal to roughly 50% of total world economic production.[5]

The need to spend many billions of dollars on a standing army and military armaments gave rise to what President Dwight D. Eisenhower in 1960 called the **"military-industrial complex,"** which grew even stronger during the Cold War.[6] As East-West tensions increased between the United States and the Soviet Union, our nation stationed large numbers of American troops throughout the Pacific and Western Europe and invested billions of dollars developing its nuclear weapons arsenal.[7] American economic aid was sent to the war-ravaged economies of Japan and Western Europe under President Harry Truman's Marshall Plan, which also helped maintain markets for U.S. goods.[8] America and its western allies also established the Bretton Woods System, an international monetary system of currency based on the value of the U.S. dollar, and created both the International Monetary Fund (IMF) and the World Bank to promote a capitalist international economy.[9]

Eisenhower and Economic Orthodoxy

By nominating Dwight D. Eisenhower in 1952, the Republican Party repudiated the darling of its conservative wing—Senator Robert Taft of Ohio—in favor of a World War II hero who could win. The literature plays down the stereotypes that Eisenhower was old-fashioned in his views and passive in his responsibilities. Author John W. Sloan concludes that Eisenhower "was the most significant player in determining his administration's macroeconomic policy" and was "constantly attentive and often assertive in this policy area."[10] However Eisenhower, being a career military man, also "recognized his lack of expertise and experience in economic policy making and attempted to learn from those he felt had greater knowledge."[11]

When Eisenhower assumed the presidency, the United States was by far the world's premier economic powerhouse. The United States produced almost one-half of the world's manufactured goods, automobiles, electricity, steel, and oil during the Eisenhower years.[12] By 1960 our GDP stood at $526.6 billion, the highest in the world.[13] Budget surpluses were produced in 1956, 1957, and 1960, and when deficits existed they were relatively small. Three minor recessions occurred in 1953–1954, 1957–1958, and 1960–1961, but they did not degenerate into major contractions because of New Deal–era **automatic stabilizers**.[14] Automatic stabilizers are tax and spending items already built into the budget that adjust according to economic conditions without direct approval by Congress or the president. For example, food stamps and unemployment compensation are designed to produce an upsurge in spending when joblessness increases but a decrease in spending when unemployment drops. The presence of such stabilizers is believed to be one reason why the magnitude of shifts between the peaks and troughs of the business cycle has narrowed since the Great Depression. Automatic stabilizers moderate the fluctuations in the business cycle.

The primary concern of the Eisenhower administration was inflation. According to Sloan: "As is true of most conservatives, Eisenhower feared inflation more than unemployment." Moreover, "he rejected the notion espoused by liberal Democrats and many Keynesian economists that more public intervention to manipulate aggregate demand would improve the economy and possibly eliminate the negative consequences of the business cycle."[15] Over Eisenhower's two terms the consumer price index stabilized at an incredibly low level; between 1952 and 1960 prices rose on average only 1.4% per year.[16]

Eisenhower did not openly repudiate the Keynesian theory behind the Employment Act of 1946 nor did he dismantle New Deal programs. Arthur Burns, Eisenhower's Council of Economic Advisers (CEA) chairman, acknowledged the importance of the New Deal and spent much of his energy trying to counter the conservative opinions of Treasury Secretary George M. Humphrey.[17] According to author Edward Flash: "The Burns Council . . . reconcile[d] Republican conservatism with the Administration's counter-cyclical responsibilities. Through its activities, the Council achieved a . . . liberalization of Administration views—not as much as a revision, but an updating to modern circumstances."[18] However, Eisenhower did recruit businessmen as senior advisers who collectively "shared an [economic] orthodoxy based on simple precepts which had filtered down out of the eighteenth and nineteenth centuries."[19]

Although Eisenhower believed that the role of government should be restricted, his administration increased spending on domestic programs to promote national security.[20] For example, the Interstate Highway Act of 1956 was justified as being necessary to transport troops and military during an emergency. Higher education enrollments increased from the expansion of subsidized loans to college students and the GI Bill of Rights. Following the Soviet launch of *Sputnik* in 1957, massive investments were made in mathematics and science programs in schools and colleges. The result was an enormous national security bureaucracy supporting a huge military-industrial complex. Throughout the 1950s, one-half or more of total federal spending was devoted to national defense. In 1960, Eisenhower's last year, spending on national defense and veterans programs totaled $48.1 billion in a $92.2 billion budget.[21]

Economic Ups and Downs

From the outset of his presidency Eisenhower's goal was to proceed slowly, consolidate the reforms of past decades, and assure domestic and world stability after the turmoil of warfare. He expressed support for the Employment Act of 1946 but did not aggressively utilize countercyclical fiscal or monetary policies.[22] Particularly in his first term, unemployment was much more a problem than inflation. The expansion that began in October 1949 peaked in July 1953, followed by a recession that lasted until May 1954.[23] Economic growth followed this trough in the business cycle until August 1957 (after Eisenhower's reelection campaign). During his first term, Eisenhower also could point to relative price stability, since the consumer price index (CPI) increased by an average annual percentage rate of 1.3% during 1953–1956.[24] The Eisenhower administration approach to the inflation threat was to curb federal spending and budget surpluses were recorded in three years. But GDP grew by an annual rate of 2.6%—less than half the rate during Truman's term—and real per capita disposal personal income increased by a meager 1.3%.[25]

The business cycle was not kind to Eisenhower in his second term. A second recession began in August 1957 and bottomed out in April 1958, and by June there was agreement that recovery was underway. But this economic upswing cannot be attributed to economic policies.[26] Moreover, the short-lived recovery did not prevent the federal government from recording a record peacetime deficit (at that time) of $12.8 billion in 1959.[27] Then a second contraction in April 1960 extended through February 1961 (into Kennedy's term). These back-to-back recessions led liberal economists to criticize the relaxed Eisenhower view of countercyclical policy. In 1958 John Kenneth Galbraith wrote his influential book, *The Affluent Society*, in which he pointedly observes: "Nothing in our economic policy is so deeply ingrained, and so little reckoned with by economists, as our tendency to wait and see if things do not improve by themselves."[28]

Both the 1957–1958 and 1960–1961 recessions were accompanied by a rise in inflation and unemployment, and this unique occurrence prompted much discussion among economists about new "**cost-push inflation**" (rather than "**demand-pull inflation**").[29] Cost-push inflation is caused by large increases in the cost of production such as wages or other raw materials like petroleum.[30] According to authors Robin Bade and Michael Parkin, "Rising wage rates or rising prices of raw materials . . . lead firms to decrease the quantity of labor employed and to cut production."[31] Demand-pull inflation, on the other hand, arises when aggregate demand (total spending in the economy) is greater than aggregate supply (the total supply of goods and services). Among the primary factors that expand aggregate demand are marked increases in government expenditures and deficit financing.[32]

THE HIGH POINT OF KEYNESIANISM

The work of prominent Keynesian economists—John Kenneth Galbraith, Seymour Harris, Paul Samuelson, and James Tobin—had significant influence during the early 1960s.[33] The policy views of these Keynesians, which became known as the **new economics**, may be summarized as follows: (1) investment is the unstable element in the economic system and leads to instability in national income; (2) of the twin problems of unemployment or inflation, unemployment is the more severe problem and must be given primacy even when inflation threatens; (3) fiscal policy is activist and should be oriented to spurring aggregate demand; (4) both fiscal policy and monetary policy are required to achieve full employment; but (5) fiscal policy is more effective in the short-run and perhaps in the long-run in changing the level of GDP.

The New Frontier

During the 1960 presidential campaign, Senator John Kennedy (D-MA) promised to move the country toward the New Frontier. At forty-three the youngest elected president, Kennedy recruited an energetic staff to achieve his domestic objectives, and he elevated the prestige and influence of the economics profession like no previous executive.[34] Kennedy's CEA chairman, Walter Heller, believed that fiscal policy could guide economic growth, and the CEA wasted no time confronting the 1960–1961 recession. Although the recession was the least severe of the four postwar recessions to date, it had followed the shortest period of economic expansion. In his 1961 State of the Union address, President Kennedy explained that the problem was not merely recession but "seven months of recession, three and one-half years of slack, seven years of diminished economic growth, and nine years of falling farm income."[35] To lay the foundation for economic growth, Kennedy endorsed more federal spending, extended jobless benefits, additional stimulus for housing construction, and urban renewal projects. Kennedy also recommended a monetary policy to the Fed which coupled low interest on long-term bonds with high interest on short-term bonds. This strategy was designed to encourage domestic investment and attract foreign capital while curbing the outflow of U.S. dollars abroad.[36]

But world events intervened to force changes in economic policy during Kennedy's first year. The ill-fated Bay of Pigs invasion of Cuba was in April 1961, and the Berlin crisis followed in June and July. To meet the Soviet challenge in Berlin, President Kennedy pondered an increase in defense spending, and his proposal renewed debate within his administration over whether deficits should be allowed to rise or taxes increased. Heller stood against any tax increase but Kennedy was unsure. Finally in July 1961, Kennedy requested $3.4 billion in new defense spending without a tax increase but, to placate the opposition, he stated he would submit a balanced budget for the next fiscal year.[37]

President Kennedy promised to "get the country moving again," and records show that he and President Johnson were able to take credit for a vastly improved economy. The recession inherited from the Eisenhower years bottomed out in February 1961, and a period of economic expansion unsurpassed in the postwar era lasted through December 1969. During 1961–1964 unemployment averaged 5.8% and the CPI grew at an average annual percentage rate of 1.2%.[38] Except for unemployment (which was lower during the 1950s), the economy accelerated and the economic outlook was upbeat.

Most important for economic policy, Kennedy departed from economic orthodoxy when he recommended tax cuts and deficit financing to anticipate, and thereby prevent, a future recession. Kennedy's 1963 State of the Union recommended cutting taxes by $13.5 billion. He recommended reducing personal income taxes from the existing 20%–91% rates to 14%–65% and dropping the corporate income tax rate from 52% to 47%.[39] However, Congress did not approve tax cuts in 1963, because the legislative debate got bogged down over issues of reforming versus cutting taxes, the size of the budget, and the deficit.[40]

On November 22, 1963, President Kennedy was assassinated and Vice President Lyndon B. Johnson succeeded to the presidency. Now Johnson had the task of prodding Congress to act. Johnson prevailed by promising to keep his 1965 budget under $100 billion. As a result, tax legislation was readied for his signature on February 26, 1964. The Revenue Act of 1964 coupled with the Excise Tax Reduction Act of 1965 cut taxes by an estimated $11 billion for individuals and $3 billion for business.[41] The tax cuts were designed to raise personal incomes, stimulate consumption, and encourage businesses to increase capital investment.[42]

Evidence shows that those effects were probably achieved by the Kennedy tax cut.[43] The gross national product (GNP) gap was narrowed from a peak $50 billion annually in the first quarter of 1961 to an annualized rate of $10 billion in the first quarter of 1965. Kennedy's economic advisers believed that the GNP gap represented the shortfall between the actual GNP and the potential GNP that could be achieved if the economy was operating at "full" employment. As the GNP gap narrowed, consequently, the unemployment rate dropped from 5.2% in 1964 to 4.5% in 1965 and even further in 1966. Real GNP growth of 4% in 1963 rose to 5.5% in both 1964 and 1965.[44] And despite the tax cuts, federal revenues actually increased from 1964 to 1965, and this experience was cited by the "supply-siders" who advised President Ronald Reagan to cut income taxes during the 1980s.[45]

"Guns and Butter"

Elected in a landslide in 1964, President Lyndon B. Johnson declined to run for reelection four years later in the face of strong opposition within his own party. His term was marked by an explosion of legislation to address social problems, yet his administration was ultimately undone by the unpopular Vietnam War. Johnson presided over an economy which showed its best overall performance since World War II. Good economic news coupled with his enormous popularity allowed President Johnson to promote his Great Society programs to extend social welfare, fight racial discrimination, and uplift the poor. The share of the federal budget devoted to human services for the poor grew from 4.7% in 1961 to 7.9% in 1969.[46]

Even more costly, though not realized at the time, was the passage of two new Great Society entitlement programs: **Medicare** and **Medicaid**. Medicare provides medical coverage to citizens sixty-five years of age and older, some disabled citizens under sixty-five, and people with End-Stage Renal Disease (permanent kidney failure treated with dialysis or a transplant). The original Medicare program contained two parts: Part A (hospital insurance), and Part B (medical insurance). However, neither Part A nor Part B provides full coverage for a qualified citizen's medical costs since each part contains premiums, deductibles and co-pays (payments due from the covered individual). Today, Medicare is America's largest health insurance program, covering roughly 43 million citizens. Medicaid is a joint federal-state program that provides health insurance coverage to low-income parents and children, senior citizens, and people with disabilities. Each state operates its own Medicaid system, but this system must conform to federal guidelines in order for the state to receive matching funds and grants. This federal funding only pays for about one-half of total Medicaid costs, with the states themselves funding the remainder.

These are called **entitlements** because the laws creating them require the federal government to spend as much money as is required to cover the costs of providing benefits to all people who qualify. Qualifying persons are "entitled" to benefits and cannot be denied them—regardless of whether

Congress wishes to fund them. Therefore spending for entitlement programs is considered "uncontrollable" by policy makers.[47]

Johnson also began a massive military buildup in Southeast Asia that would eventually lead to five hundred thousand U.S. troops in South Vietnam. The objective was to prevent a takeover of South Vietnam by Communist North Vietnam, but the war led to social unrest at home, the death of more than fifty-eight thousand Americans (and a far greater loss of life among Southeast Asians), and billions from the Treasury. Defense spending rose from $49.5 billion in 1965 to $81.2 billion in 1969 (Nixon's first year in office) before falling, and since no new taxes were levied, deficits were incurred and the national debt grew.[48]

The economy did grow substantially over Johnson's term and, as a consequence, personal income more than doubled as compared to Eisenhower's tenure. The 4% annual rate of increase in productivity also was an improvement over the 1950s.[49] The jobless rate was driven down from 4.5% in 1965 to an average of 3.9% over the next four years, a rate not achieved since the Korean War.[50] Due in large part to increased defense spending on the Vietnam War, however, budget surpluses were declining. The budgetary surplus over the period 1965–1968 was one-half the amount generated during the 1961–1964 period.[51]

The major impact of the emergence of deficit spending was upward pressure on consumer prices. The yearly change in the CPI grew steadily each year—reaching 4.2% in 1968—indicating that the serious inflationary pressures that materialized during the 1970s had already begun by the end of Johnson's term. Johnson was reluctant to ask Congress to enact an income tax surcharge. When he finally did so in August 1967 (which Congress did not approve until June 1968), his action was too little and came too late. This period was not characterized by tough-minded fiscal policy making. As one economist remarked: "It would be difficult to find a more perfect example of irresponsible government action that inevitably would have serious inflationary consequences."[52] The serious problem of dealing with inflation was left to Johnson's Republican successor.

MONETARISM

Richard Nixon's economic advisers believed that the fundamental economic problem they faced was demand-driven inflation caused by Great Society and Vietnam War spending and aggravated by the delayed enactment of the 1968 tax surcharge. They also felt that the impact of fiscal policy alone was "probably slower and smaller than commonly assumed and more difficult to predict."[53] The Nixon CEA thus discounted government's ability to fine-tune the economy by using spending and taxes and, for this reason, was sympathetic to the arguments being raised by a new breed of economist—the monetarists.

The **monetarist** school of thought had its origins in a 1950 study by economist Clark Warburton, which concluded that changes in the money supply preceded turning points (contraction or expansion) in the business cycle.[54] The implication was that economic policy can exacerbate or even cause business fluctuations. In 1956 Milton Friedman offered a new understanding of the role of money in the economy by arguing that the money supply affects both prices and output.[55] Friedman validated these relationships in an empirical study coauthored with Anna Schwartz in 1963. Looking at twenty business cycles, they confirmed that changes in the money supply preceded changes in national income during expansions and contractions. More importantly, they found that policy decisions by government usually led to these changes in the money supply.[56] Thus, unlike Keynesians, monetarists believe that price levels and production could be explained in terms of the quantity of money in circulation.[57] One key argument in the monetarist critique of Keynesianism, moreover, is that short-term monetary or fiscal policies that stimulate aggregate demand and seek to drive unemployment below a certain "natural" level will fuel inflationary pressures without actually cutting the jobless rate.[58]

Monetarism addressed the credibility of the so-called **Phillips Curve** (named after the late economist A. W. Phillips). It depicts a trade-off between employment and inflation; when unemployment rises, inflation falls and vice versa.[59] The Phillips Curve argues that fiscal policies designed to stimulate the economy in order to lower unemployment will only increase prices. The Phillips Curve—also called the Dilemma Model—had informed economic policy during the 1960s in hope of achieving an acceptable balance between unemployment and inflation. But the American economy during the 1970s did not conform to the trade-off assumed by the original Phillips Curve, suggesting that the curve shifted.[60] The initial formulation of the Phillips Curve assumed a fairly simple relationship between unemployment and inflation, but the contemporary scholarly view is that the trade-off is more complex.[61] Even with this qualification, however, the Phillips Curve poses a dilemma for economic policy makers, particularly when the inflation rate is higher than what the public finds tolerable.

In the short-term, there seems to be a trade-off between inflation and unemployment. Attempts to lower unemployment through stimulating the economy will lead to more price inflation to the degree that the economy approaches the "full" employment level. Conversely, price inflation can be reduced but only at the cost of higher unemployment.[62] In the long run, this relationship is more complex, because inflation has a strong inertial component. Inflation tends to stabilize at a certain level until it is jolted upward or downward by events—such as a sudden rise in oil prices or a large

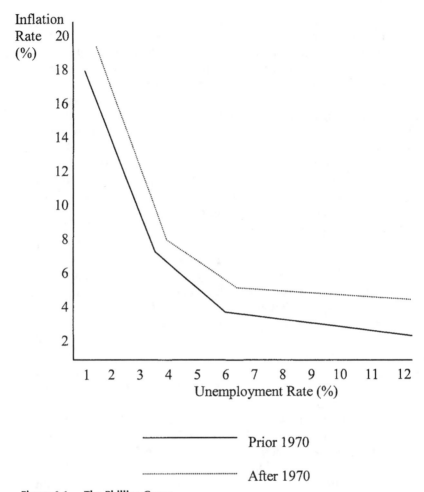

Figure 6.1.   The Phillips Curve

increase in unemployment. Thus, low unemployment is not necessarily associated with high inflation but with an increasing rate of inflation. Similarly, high unemployment may put downward pressure on the inflation rate but may not necessarily yield low inflation. Therefore, if the inertial level of inflation is high, then high unemployment may still be associated with high levels of inflation.

Gradualism and Nixon's New Economic Policy

The monetarist critique had a strong influence on the Nixon administration. When President Nixon entered office in 1969 most economists were

Keynesians who tended to be liberal Democrats. To ease the inflationary pressures of the late 1960s, however, the Nixon team adopted a "gradualist" economic game plan that used both fiscal and monetary policy. In March 1969 President Nixon asked Congress to extend the 1968 income tax surcharge, and he announced spending cuts in his 1970 budget. The next month Nixon followed with tax reforms, including the repeal of the investment tax credit, limits on tax shelters, and the removal of below-poverty households from the income tax rolls.

Unlike Kennedy, Nixon was not intrigued with economic policy, yet neither was he rigid when dealing with economic problems. As his CEA chairman observed: "Nixon was predisposed toward using the market to make most economic decisions, and toward maintaining a free-market economy. Mixed with this philosophy, he had a pragmatic turn of mind which tended to keep him free of being confined by any ideology."[63] The nearly decade-long economic expansion of the Kennedy/Johnson years ended in December 1969, and then a contraction held sway until November 1970. Unemployment averaged 5.0% over Nixon's first term but reached 5.9% in 1971, and the inflation rate increased during both 1969 and 1970.[64] During this same time, GDP increased at the very weak annual rate of 1.7%.[65] In 1970 some advisers expressed the view that cost-push inflation (from increased costs of production) was the fundamental problem, not excessive consumer demand. Such inflation was thought to be immune from countercyclical policy, thus implying that direct controls over prices might be needed.

Nixon made a fundamental shift in his economic game plan in 1971 when he announced a bold strategy called the **New Economic Policy (NEP)**. Ever since assuming office, Nixon was concerned with balancing domestic economics with foreign economics, and the NEP attempted to link the American economy more closely with the ever-changing global economy.[66] On the domestic economic side, the NEP sought to stabilize inflation by imposing government controls on wages and prices during 1971–1972. Initially the controls worked, but prices rose again after 1973, forcing the president to again impose price freezes. On the foreign economic side, Nixon "closed the gold window" by ceasing to refund claims by foreign creditors in gold, and he imposed a 10% surcharge on imports. The Bretton Woods System had established a fixed **exchange rate** where the value of all currencies was pegged to the value of the U.S. dollar, and the value of the U.S. dollar was pegged to the cost of gold (it cost $35 to purchase an ounce of gold). Thus, the NEP substituted a system of floating exchange rates to reflect the changing values of all the world's currencies. The immediate objective was to devalue (or cheapen) the U.S. dollar in world currency markets in order to discourage imports (it would cost Americans more to import goods) but encourage exports (it would be less expensive for Europeans to buy U.S. products). And this is what happened. During the period 1971–1973, the value of the U.S. dollar fell to the point where an ounce of gold would have cost $42 (of course, by closing the gold window the United States no longer paid its international debts in gold). In addition to aiding our balance of trade, Nixon's goal was to reduce speculative pressures against the U.S. dollar caused by decreases in the world's gold supply as well as increased economic competition from Western Europe and Japan.[67]

Nixon's gradualist game plan attempted to circumvent the policy dilemma of the short-term Phillips Curve. In his 1970 economic report the president stated: "After 5 years of sustained unemployment followed by 5 years of sustained inflation, some have concluded that the price of finding work for the unemployed must be the hardship of inflation for all."[68] Nixon could hardly admit to this dire scenario and instead offered hope that "if we apply the hard lessons learned from the sixties to the decade ahead, and add a new realism to the management of our economic policies, I believe we can attain the goal of plentiful jobs earning dollars of stable purchasing power."[69] Nixon hoped that restrictive fiscal and monetary policies would reduce aggregate demand gradually and thus allow only a modest rise in unemployment which, in turn, would slow down wage and price increases. This strategy, it was hoped, would also help to break the inflationary psychology, because once people realized that inflation was coming under control, they would expect greater price stability and soften their wage demands. But that economic game plan was clearly not successful in stabilizing inflation, because prices rose by an annual rate of 6.3% during the Nixon's tenure compared to 2.6% under Johnson.[70]

Other economic innovations by President Nixon involved social welfare. One was his proposal for a Family Assistance Plan (FAP) that would have replaced America's collection of welfare programs with a "negative income tax" (also advocated by Milton Friedman) and a guaranteed national income for families with incomes under the poverty level.[71] FAP would have covered more poor families than the existing Aid to Families with Dependent Children (AFDC), the major federal-state welfare program, and included incentives for employment and worker training.[72] But FAP was defeated in Congress. Another initiative was a vigorous affirmative-action program that targeted private firms which contracted with the federal government as well as unions whose employees worked on federally funded projects.[73] Also Nixon created the **Supplemental Security Income (SSI)** program, which provided monthly cash payments for food, clothing, and shelter to help senior citizens and blind and disabled people who have little or no income. SSI is funded by general tax revenues, and not the Social Security payroll tax.[74] Among his other policy triumphs were the creation of the Environmental Protection Agency (EPA) and the Occupational Safety and Health Administration (OSHA).[75] The EPA monitors environmental quality, establishes environmental guidelines, and mandates environmental regulations. Created within the Department of Labor, OSHA is entrusted with preventing work-related injuries, illnesses, and deaths by issuing and enforcing rules and standards for workplace safety and health.

Economic Decline

The economic expansion beginning in November 1970 peaked in November 1973, after which a new recession continued through March 1975. The March 1975 trough gave way to economic growth which continued through January 1980. However, the deep recession of 1973–1975 guaranteed poor economic performance. Unemployment averaged 6.7% during the Nixon/Ford years.[76] And prices did not fall. The average yearly rate of increase in the CPI was 8%.[77] Also during 1974 and 1975 there were declines in both real GDP and real per capita disposal personal income.

This economic unease led President Nixon to experiment with an **"incomes policy,"** a series of anti-inflation measures designed to preserve the purchasing power of personal income by restricting the annual growth of prices and wages. That is, an incomes policy is an attempt to ensure that a fair "share" of national income is apportioned between labor and capitalists. The most drastic method to achieve that objective is mandatory **wage and price controls**. These are economic policy measures in which the federal government places a ceiling on wages and prices to prevent incomes and goods and services from exceeding their levels of the previous year. Controls may take the form of voluntary wage and price guidelines (used also during the Johnson administration) or mandatory price and wage controls (as used during World War II). A third variant is "tax-based incomes policies" (TIPs), where a government fee is imposed on those firms that raise prices and/or wages more than the controls allow.[78]

Nixon's wage and price controls were imposed in several phases in response to rising gasoline prices that were exacerbated by the 1973 energy crisis and the OPEC oil embargo. But this experiment in wage and price controls was largely unable to contain inflation and was generally viewed as a failure. In 1972 the CPI rose 3.3%, but then jumped by 6.2% in 1973, 11% in 1974, and 9% in 1975 before falling to 5.8% as a recession took hold.[79] In the end Congress agreed to a phased termination of Nixon's incomes policy.

The recession of 1975 continued to plague Nixon's successor, President Gerald Ford, who refused to abandon the Nixon-style economic game plan as the 1976 presidential campaign approached. Ford's major concern was inflation, which he believed was caused by too much spending and the mounting costs of entitlement programs enacted during the 1960s and early 1970s. In late 1974 President Ford held an economic summit conference to obtain advice from a diverse group of economists, after which he announced a variety of strategies to hold down prices. One strategy was to personally wear a button that said "WIN" to symbolize his "Whip Inflation Now" campaign, which was widely ridiculed by his critics.

In response to the worsening recession, Ford proposed a $16 billion tax cut, a moratorium on new programs except energy, and a ceiling on domestic spending. But Congress approved a larger tax cut and more spending than Ford wanted, which led to an executive-legislative confrontation. To hold down federal spending, Ford wielded his veto frequently against bills passed by the Democratic-controlled Congress. Relative to his time in office, Ford vetoed more bills than any president except Grover Cleveland, Franklin Roosevelt, and Harry Truman.[80] As election day approached, unemployment rose to almost 8% and Ford's gamble with fiscal austerity failed. However, his immediate legacy was a much stronger economy. In 1976 the CPI rose at a slower rate; both real GDP and real per capita disposal personal income scored impressive gains; and even the jobless rate fell slightly.

Stagflation

In 1976 Jimmy Carter campaigned as an outsider with no ties to the Washington establishment. He cultivated the anti-Watergate feelings of the time and an image which stressed his personal integrity, moral and religious values, and centrist politics. To reassure liberal groups that he was a real Democrat, Carter detailed a far-reaching domestic agenda during the campaign. He pledged to "achieve an unemployment level of 4 percent or less by the end of [his] first term."[81] To attain this specific goal, Carter signed the **Humphrey-Hawkins Act of 1978** (also called the Full Employment and Balanced Growth Act), which makes the president responsible for achieving three specific objectives. First, it establishes numerical goals for the economy for the upcoming fiscal year. Second, it required the Federal Reserve Board to establish a monetary policy that maintains long-run growth, minimizes inflation, and promotes price stability. The objective was to connect the Fed's monetary policy with the president's fiscal policy. It also required the Fed to transmit a monetary policy report to Congress twice a year, outlining its monetary goals. Third, it made the president and Congress responsible for balancing the budget and fostering a balance of trade.[82]

According to Humphrey-Hawkins, by 1983 unemployment should be not more than 3% for persons aged twenty or over and not more than 4% for persons aged sixteen or over. The inflation rate should not be over 4%, dropping to 0% by 1988. However, the act allowed Congress to revise these goals as time progressed. If private enterprise lacks the resources to achieve these economic goals, then the federal government was authorized to create a "reservoir of public employment."[83]

During the Carter administration economists were concerned about **stagflation**, which is a period of high inflation, rising unemployment, sluggish economic growth, and diminished productivity. The major economic problem to beset Jimmy Carter was inflation caused primarily by a rapid escalation in oil prices and a short-term supply shortage of oil . The average rate of increase in the CPI over Carter's term was 9.8%, but it moved into the double-digits in 1979 (13.3%) and 1980 (12.5%).[84] The recession which bottomed out in March 1975 yielded an expansion that lasted through January 1980, but the timing of this business cycle was not fortuitous for Carter. The peak was followed by a quick contraction that lasted until July 1980, only four months before the presidential election.

Nor was Carter able to bring down the jobless rate, although a large number of new jobs were created during his administration.[85] Unemployment averaged 6.5% but was increased by the lackluster economy to 7.1% in 1977 and 1980.[86] The budget showed deficits in all four years of Carter's tenure, although the GDP managed to grow at an annual average rate of 3.1%. But apparently the voters who cast ballots in the 1980 presidential election focused on inflation and unemployment, and they were reminded of Carter's responsibility for the economy by his Republican opponent, Ronald Reagan, who asked: "Are you better off than you were four years ago?" The majority answered "no" in November 1980. Reagan was elected president, and he brought to Washington a new approach called supply-side economics.

THE SUPPLY-SIDE REVOLUTION

During the 1980 presidential campaign, the fundamental problem according to Reagan was "big government."[87] The game plan he offered voters was based on **supply-side economics**, a theory which alleged that increased spending has no direct effect on employment.[88] Instead the supply-siders proposed deep cuts in the marginal income tax rates on individuals and corporations.[89] The long-term risk, however, was that tax cuts could lead to additional borrowing, produce potentially unsustainable deficits by siphoning money away from private borrowers, and force greater reliance on foreign governments to fund the national debt.[90] What became known as **Reaganomics** was a hybrid economic program aimed at stimulating economic growth with a combination of tax cuts, less social welfare spending coupled with higher defense expenditures, a restrained monetary policy, and less government regulation.[91] These measures, Reagan promised, were designed to eliminate stagflation but, according to author F. Thomas Juster: "Seldom has an economic experiment been put in place with less conventional credentialing by professional economists."[92]

Supply-side theory was compatible with Reagan's political agenda, because the tax cuts prescribed by the theory were politically appealing to the electorate. Supply-side theory allowed Reagan and his Republican allies to promote an economic alternative to the Keynesian policies embraced by Democratic presidents since FDR.[93] The most famous supply-side economist was Professor Arthur Laffer of the University of Southern California. He promoted his famous **Laffer Curve**, which provided the economic rationale for President Reagan's income tax cuts. The goal was to set income taxes at the optimum rate. Lowering rates too much will obviously undermine revenue and produce too high deficits, but supply-siders argued that setting rates too high also can decrease revenue. At either extreme (0% or 100% rate of taxation) the federal government is unable to collect revenue. A rate of 0% simply means that the government collects no taxes. A rate of 100% results in zero revenue because taxpayers will radically change their behavior since they either have no incentive to work or will avoid paying taxes.[94]

To maximize its revenue, therefore, the federal government must find an optimal point (Point T on figure 6.2) somewhere between 0% and 100%.

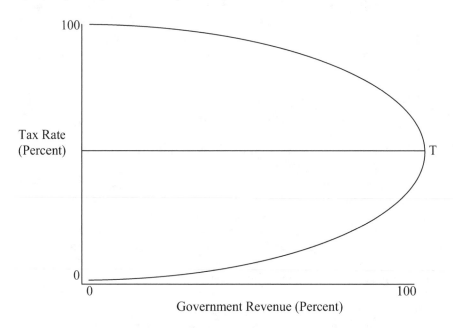

Point T: government collects maximum tax revenue and
            workers pay an optimal (not maximum) tax rate.

Figure 6.2.   The Laffer Curve

Point T is where government collects the maximum tax revenue because workers pay the optimal (not the maximum) tax rate. In theory, tax revenues should increase along with tax increases until a turning point is reached.[95] That turning point is the point at which marginal tax rates are so high that they create a strong disincentive against working. In addition to revenue raising, the optimal tax rate would theoretically affect the savings rate, which determines how much money will be available for capital investment. And capital investment should bring about increased productivity.[96]

Supply-side theory gave conservatives and the Republicans a coherent economic program. Tax cuts had immediate political appeal for the public and the business community. Supply-side economics also reinforced Reagan's conservatism and the Republican anti–big government philosophy. Most important, it offered a less painful solution to inflation. Where Keynesian "demand-side" theory dictates that inflation be curbed through tax increases and spending cuts designed to reduce aggregate demand, supply-side theory argues that inflationary pressures could be reduced by simply increasing the supply of goods and services on the market.

Cutting Taxes

This wishful supply-side thinking was reflected in the Kemp-Roth Bill, which Reagan endorsed, to cut individual and corporate income taxes by 30%.[97] In 1980 Jimmy Carter called that legislation irresponsible and even George H. W. Bush, who was Reagan's opponent for the Republican nomination, called supply-side tax cuts "voodoo economics."

The economic expansion that started in July 1980 came to a halt in July 1981, and a new recession began which did not bottom out until November 1982. This recession was a sixteen-month contraction that, at its trough, posted the highest unemployment rate since the Great Depression. That rise in unemployment, however, was the price the nation paid for achieving the greatest economic triumph of the Reagan administration: a significant lowering of inflation. The CPI jumped by 39% over Carter's term compared to a 24% rise during 1981–1984, and relative price stability continued into the twenty-first century.[98] What broke the back of inflation in the short-term was the 1981–1982 recession. Unlike his predecessors, President Reagan was willing to drive down inflation by exploiting the trade-off in the short-term Phillips Curve.[99] Fed chair Paul Volcker also took a determined stand to keep monetary policy tight despite the downturn. But the administration seemed to have underestimated the adverse political and economic impact of this "cold turkey" approach. White House staffers and Treasury Secretary Donald Regan began a "Fed bashing" campaign, fearing that the continuation of a deep recession might endanger President Reagan's reelection in 1984.[100]

The trough of the recession came in November 1982 when unemployment hit 10%, after which the nation began a period of sustained economic
growth. The reasons for this expansion are in dispute. Keynesians would argue that the 1980s recovery was a classic demand-led expansion, affected
little by supply-side calculations. Reducing personal income taxes by 23%
coupled with enormous budget deficits was bound to increase demand.[101]
Supply-side economists countered that long-term economic growth results
from greater incentives to work, save, and invest. Regardless of the merits or
demerits of this debate over supply-side economics, the unprecedented
deficits under Reagan destroyed the credibility of supply-side theory as a viable public policy.[102]

Economic Expansion amid Rising Deficits

From November 1982 to July 1990 there were ninety-two months of economic growth. Since 1854, this expansionary period was exceeded only by
the Kennedy/Johnson era, which spanned 106 months from February 1961
until December 1969. One point of similarity with the 1980s is that the
prosperity of the 1960s was also an economic byproduct of deficit spending by the federal government. Interestingly, economic growth in both the
1960s and the 1980s were partly fueled by massive increases in defense
spending.

The unemployment rate during 1985–1988 declined steadily, resulting in
a term average that approximated the jobless rate experienced during
Carter's term. The economy also showed real growth, with the four-year average exceeding 3%. Most important, the inflationary cycle was broken. Between 1985 and 1988 the inflation rate was 3.3%.[103] Potentially the most
serious problem was the series of triple-digit budget deficits. The four-year
budget deficit recorded during Reagan's first term, which was a postwar
record, more than tripled from 1985 to 1988.

Read My Lips: No New Taxes

In the midst of this economic expansion and with America at peace, Vice
President George H. W. Bush became the first sitting vice president to be
elected to the highest office in over 150 years. For the first eighteen months
of the Bush presidency, it seemed like the economic expansion would continue forever. But this was not the case. During 1990 the long expansion began to slow, finally reaching its turning point (peak) in July 1990 just as
Iraqi leader Saddam Hussein prepared to invade Kuwait. The juxtaposition
of the end of the long Reagan recovery and the invasion of Kuwait nicely
summarizes Bush's presidency.

The economy under President Bush was mixed. Inflation rose to 6.1% at the end of 1990, its highest level in eight years.[104] The downturn that began in July 1990 led to poor economic growth, which resulted in the GDP growth rate dropping from 1.9% in 1990 to -0.2% in 1991, technically qualifying this economic decline as a recession.[105] Moreover, the budget deficit dramatically expanded from $152 billion in 1989 to $290 billion in 1992.[106] As the election approached in November 1992, the public had yet to feel the effects of the slow recovery that began in the second quarter of 1991. The unemployment rate averaged 6.7% in 1991 and 7.4% in 1992, more than 2% higher than when Bush took office.[107] Poor economic performance converted the 1992 election into a referendum on the economy. A June 1992 *New York Times*/CBS News poll found that only 16% approved of how President Bush was handling the economy, lower than even the worst rating given to President Carter.[108]

The only economic initiative which Bush advocated during his term was a proposal to reduce the capital-gains tax. It was never enacted because Democrats charged that it was a windfall for wealthy Americans. Congressional Democrats wanted to raise corporate and individual income taxes for the highest income earners, a proposal Bush ardently opposed. In what conservatives believe was his biggest blunder, Bush reneged on his 1988 pledge to the Republican National Convention: "Read my lips: no new taxes."[109] In June 1990 Bush intimated that he would accept tax increases as part of a deficit reduction package to break the deadlock with Congress. The 1990 Budget Enforcement Act raised the tax rate from 28% to 31% on incomes over $80,000, phased out personal exemptions for incomes over $100,000, extended payroll taxes for Medicare from the first $54,000 of earnings to over $125,000, raised the gas tax by five cents, and added taxes on alcohol, tobacco, and luxury items.[110]

Conservatives blamed the budget deal on Treasury Secretary Nicholas Brady and OMB director Richard Darman.[111] Brady and Darman persuaded President Bush to compromise with the congressional Democrats in order to obtain strict spending limits in exchange for Bush's acceptance of higher taxes. Brady and Darman also believed that the recession was not as serious as people believed, and therefore they discouraged Bush from advocating more aggressive countercyclical policies. Bush pegged his reelection on an immediate recovery, but Democrats compared his passive leadership to Herbert Hoover's oft-quoted comment that prosperity is "just around the corner."[112] Although the Fed cut interest rates twenty-three times from mid-1989 through mid-1992 (bringing the discount rate to 3.25%), monetary policy seemed unable to rekindle the economy.[113] Pressure due to growing federal deficits kept long-term interest rates higher, which discouraged homebuyers from assuming mortgages. Households already burdened with consumer debt and little savings were afraid to make big-ticket purchases like automobiles. And businesses were downsizing while states and local governments were streamlining their operations to cut costs.[114]

THE RETURN TO ECONOMIC ORTHODOXY

The pursuit of supply-side policies during the Reagan administration was a significant break with the past, and the impact of Reaganomics on American politics was far-reaching. When Bill Clinton assumed the presidency in 1993, he was confronted with the challenge of chronic deficits and a growing national debt. To address the deficit problem, however, might jeopardize Clinton's promises of a middle-class tax cut and national health insurance, and additional social spending would be at risk. In the end President Clinton chose to be a deficit hawk, and his legacy is a "post-Keynesian" economic strategy that combined budget surpluses with free trade.

Post-Keynesianism

The Clinton 1992 presidential campaign can be summed up in the now-popular phrase: "It's the Economy, Stupid!"[115] In reflecting upon the end of the Cold War, Clinton declared that "the currency of strength in this era will be denominated not only in ships, tanks and planes, but also in diplomas, patents and paychecks."[116] Whereas George H. W. Bush promised a "new world order" abroad and the preservation of traditional family values at home, Clinton promised to reinvigorate the economy. The day after his election, president-elect Clinton declared on ABC's *Nightline* that he would focus "like a laser beam" on the national economy and strengthen America's leadership position throughout the world.[117]

President Clinton did not inherit a robust economy from Bush, though the seeds of recovery were there. In 1992 unemployment was 7.4% and the budget deficit was over $290 billion, which at the time was an all-time high. In early December 1992 Fed chairman Alan Greenspan met with Clinton to explain the relationship between the federal deficit and high long-term interest rates, arguing that a credible plan to reduce future deficits would persuade Wall Street and, eventually, yield lower interest rates. But during the presidential transition, Clinton promised to reduce the federal deficit and to enact an economic stimulus package, featuring a $4 billion tax credit to spur business investment and roughly $20 billion on public infrastructure.[118] The Clinton administration believed that both goals could be attained by raising taxes on the wealthy and by cutting defense spending.

Clinton's first national economic adviser, Robert Rubin, sought to reduce the deficit by roughly $145 billion.[119] A long-time Wall Street financier, Rubin persuaded Clinton to focus on deficit reduction and avoid proposing additional government spending. Rubin aligned himself with other moderately conservative policy makers—OMB director Leon Panetta, OMB deputy director Alice Rivlin, and Treasury Secretary Lloyd Bentsen—who frowned upon the red ink under Reagan and Bush.[120] This group utilized the newly created National Economic Council to resist new spending programs advocated by Clinton's liberal economic advisers, including CEA chairwoman Laura D'Andrea Tyson, Labor Secretary Robert Reich, and U.S. Trade Representative Mickey Kantor.[121] Rubin echoed the arguments made by Fed chairman Alan Greenspan that any decrease in aggregate demand from tax hikes and spending cuts would be offset by falling interest rates, once Wall Street bond traders became convinced that the White House was serious about deficit reduction.[122]

To jump-start the economy, in February 1993 Clinton proposed an economic package to Congress that reflected the disparate viewpoints of his economic team. The first element was $30 billion in stimulus spending on transportation, unemployment benefits, community block grants plus another $230 billion in spending and tax breaks for infrastructure improvements.[123] The second element included a $704 billion deficit reduction plan that required $375 billion in spending cuts and $328 billion in new taxes.[124] Although Clinton had promised to enact a middle-class tax cut, he reneged on that campaign pledge. But the economic stimulus plan was attacked not only by Republicans, who called it "pork-barrel" spending and who opposed the tax increases, but also by some deficit hawks among congressional Democrats who demanded that the leadership finalize a deficit-reduction plan before considering any economic stimulus package.[125] The House of Representatives approved both measures but a Republican filibuster in the Senate killed the stimulus legislation.

In March 1993 Clinton signed the 1993 Omnibus Budget Reconciliation Act, which would achieve $504.8 billion in deficit reduction over the period 1994–1998 based on $250.1 billion in new taxes, $71 billion in entitlement cuts, $108 billion in nondefense discretionary cuts, and $60 billion in interest savings.[126] The deficit reduction plan made the federal tax system more progressive by creating two additional tax brackets of 36% and 39.6% for high-income individuals.[127] While some of Clinton's political advisers, namely Paul Begala, James Carville, and George Stephanopoulos, urged using "soak-the-rich" rhetoric to frame the tax increases, Robert Rubin opposed that tactic.[128] Because the 1993 deficit-reduction law relied heavily on tax increases, it barely passed the House (218–217) and Senate (51–50)—necessitating a tie-breaking vote by Vice President Gore. Every Republican in both chambers voted against the measure.

In the 1994 midterm elections, the Republicans, led by Speaker-designate Newt Gingrich (R-GA), won control of both houses of Congress. One centerpiece of the Republican "Contract with America" was a constitutional amendment requiring a balanced federal budget. Although the amendment never passed, Republican pressure to balance the budget shaped the political agenda in 1995 when Clinton sent Congress a budget with little deficit reduction but no new programs. In response, congressional Republicans drafted their own budget that sought to balance the budget by 2002 with deep cuts in nondefense discretionary and entitlement programs plus tax relief.

As the economy improved, Clinton decided to engage the Republicans. The new OMB director, Alice Rivlin, argued at National Economic Council (NEC) meetings that a ten-year balanced budget was achievable without program cuts or tax hikes. Dick Morris, who was Clinton's political guru, backed Rivlin but George Stephanopoulos and Leon Panetta, the newly appointed White House chief of staff, both resisted. In Congress, Senate Minority Leader Tom Daschle (D-SD) and House Minority Leader Richard A. Gephardt (D-MO) also opposed Clinton, and by late April President Clinton acknowledged that he needed to develop his own balanced budget plan. His decision pushed Panetta's leadership to the forefront. "Senior NEC people were clearly engaged because of their individual talents and because it was something Panetta could provide them as an offset for taking away their process role."[129] But the National Economic Council as an institution was sidelined in this process of developing a deficit reduction plan.

Congressional Republicans pretty much ignored Clinton and proceeded to fashion their own tax and spending plans in order to achieve a balanced budget in seven years. Clinton vetoed continuing resolutions that would allow the government to continue operating, thereby precipitating the first government shutdown in November 1995 that furloughed eight hundred thousand federal employees.[130] Talks further broke down when Clinton refused to capitulate to Republican demands for a seven-year timetable to balance the budget. The collapse in talks led to a second government shutdown on December 16, idling 260,000 federal employees.[131]

It was not until April 1996—seven months after the start of the new fiscal year—that Congress and the White House finally passed a FY 1996 budget. However, before the FY 1996 budget was finalized, Clinton changed course and proposed a balanced budget over a seven-year timetable based on Republican forecasts. While the budget battle was extremely nasty and Republicans eventually forced Clinton to accept their demands, the president successfully placed the blame for the federal government shutdown on Congress. That contributed to Clinton's 1996 reelection over Senate Majority Leader Robert Dole (R-KS). Although Clinton deserves political credit for endorsing a balanced budget at a time when the economy was primed for exceptional growth, Fed chairman Alan Greenspan also exhibited economic leadership. His decision to lower interest rates complemented Clinton's fiscal policies and helped bring about the first balanced budget in nearly three decades.[132]

The **Balanced Budget Act of 1997 (BBA)** that President Clinton signed provided for $247 billion in additional savings by 2002.[133] The act established annual fixed dollar caps on both defense and nondefense discretionary spending. These caps were designed to yield substantial savings, with most savings concentrated in 2000–2002.[134] By 2002 total budgetary expenditures for all discretionary programs would have to be reduced by 10% to fit within the caps.[135] As a result of the 1993 and 1997 deficit-reduction legislation, the federal budget achieved a surplus of $69.2 billion in 1998 and another $125.54 billion surplus in 1999.[136] In 1999 Clinton reaffirmed his commitment to fiscal frugality by announcing that he wanted to reduce the national debt by ordering the Treasury Department to refinance government bonds. He also vetoed a sweeping $792 billion tax cut passed by Congress, arguing that there was enough money to pay down the debt and shore up Social Security and Medicare.[137] By vetoing the legislation and sticking to deficit reduction, Clinton's policies represented a significant break with supply-side economics. However, absolutely essential for deficit reduction was the unprecedented economic growth of the 1990s coupled with the loose monetary policies set by the Fed.

While deficit reduction was his primary concern, Clinton's economic program included other proposals that attempted to reverse twelve years of Reagan-Bush policies. Early in his tenure President Clinton signed the **Family and Medical Leave Act of 1993 (FMLA)**, a very popular program that allows employees to take up to twelve weeks of job-protected leave period for any illness that prevents the employee from working or requires the employee to care for an immediate family member. It also provides the same twelve-week protected leave for the birth and care of a newborn or the placement and care of an adopted child or a foster care child.[138] Clinton also expanded the Earned Income Tax Credit (EITC) as a way of cutting taxes for lower-income individuals and families. Furthermore, the Clinton administration's National Performance Review (NPR) achieved cuts in the federal bureaucracy by roughly one hundred thousand positions, reducing the number of federal personnel by 272,000.[139]

President Clinton also transformed key entitlement programs. The most important enactment was the **Personal Responsibility and Work Opportunity Reconciliation Act of 1996**, which provided for comprehensive welfare reform. Largely motivated by the congressional Republicans under Speaker Gingrich, the 1996 Act created the **Temporary Assistance for Needy Families (TANF)** program within the Department of Health and Human Services.[140] TANF replaced the Aid to Families with Dependent Children (AFDC) and the Job Opportunities and Basic Skills Training (JOBS) programs. AFDC, the more widely known program, was established by the

1935 Social Security Act to provide modest income support for widows and their children. By the 1980s, however, AFDC had evolved into a program of guaranteed payments for single, often never-married parents, and critics argued that AFDC bred dependence on the federal government, weakened self-reliance, and rewarded out-of-wedlock births.[141] The newly created TANF program allowed the president to grant waivers to states to require recipients of public assistance to work and attend job training programs within two years of receiving assistance, to cap such assistance at a maximum of five years, and to let states establish "family caps" denying additional benefits to mothers for children born while they are already on public assistance.[142] Prior to the act, the federal government set guidelines on a national basis and then parceled out money to the states to fund specific programs at certain levels. With the 1996 reform measure, federal money allocated for public assistance is sent to the states in the form of limited block grants and is limited to setting goals, penalties, and rewards.[143]

Surely the most ambitious effort by the Clinton administration to transform social policy was national health care reform. The Health Security Bill was Clinton's defining piece of health care reform legislation and also his most spectacular legislative failure.[144] The most notable element of the plan was universal medical coverage in which employers would be mandated to supply health insurance supported by government subsidies. Prior to Clinton's election in 1992, private medical coverage was poised to be a major issue as health care costs were rising at a rapid rate and had been doing so for well over a decade.[145] The number of uninsured was steadily rising, and the 1990 recession had brought new fears of insurance losses to the middle class.

With Clinton's election to the presidency, there was every expectation that health care reform would follow. When Clinton began designing the Health Security Bill in mid-1993, public support for the plan was relatively strong, but by the end of 1994 most Americans disapproved of the plan.[146] For their part, congressional Republicans believed that defeating the reform measure was key to Republicans winning control of the House and Senate in the 1994 midterm elections. The grassroots advertising campaign and legislative lobbying were spearheaded by important interest groups, namely the National Federation of Independent Businesses (NFIB), the American Medical Association (AMA), and the Health Insurance Association of American (HIAA).[147] The Health Security Bill was defeated in Congress and, though Clinton will be remembered for that legislative failure, he was able to obtain passage of other health care policies: expanded coverage for children and others with preexisting conditions, changes in long-term care and care for the disabled, and insurance portability.[148]

Rise of Global Trade

Although President George H. W. Bush had negotiated the North American Free Trade Agreement (NAFTA) with Canada and Mexico, the task of obtaining congressional approval was left to Clinton. Clinton was favorable toward free trade but also sympathetic to the concerns of labor unions and environmental groups which opposed NAFTA.[149] While the Clinton administration planned to negotiate "side agreements" with Mexico on labor conditions, environmentalism, and imports, timing forced them to deal with NAFTA early in the term.[150]

By late fall of 1993, NAFTA was scheduled for the legislative calendar under fast-track negotiating or **trade promotion authority**.[151] This allows the president to place bilateral or multilateral trade agreements and treaties on a "fast-track" legislative process that restricts Congress to either approving or rejecting such measures within ninety days and which disallows any amendments. To attain passage, Clinton and his congressional allies undertook an extensive public and legislative campaign to build support for NAFTA.[152] Congress enacted NAFTA on November 17, 1993, thanks to lopsided Republican and Southern Democratic support. The majority of (Northern) House and Senate Democrats voted no.[153]

All presidents since Gerald Ford in 1974 have gotten "fast-track" trade authority, but it lapsed in 1994 and Congress has not reauthorized it. Although bills that would have denied any extension of fast-track authority did not pass Congress in 1991, nonetheless they were early warning signs that congressional Democrats were uneasy about supporting trading policies against their union allies. In June 1993 Congress enacted an extension through April 16, 1994. It easily passed the Senate (76–16) but had more Democratic (145–102) than Republican (150–23) opposition in the House of Representatives. Seeing the political risks involved, President Clinton chose to forgo any request for fast-track authority. Later, when labor opposition seemed to soften, President Clinton made another attempt to resurrect fast-track legislation in 1997 but eventually backed off rather than face defeat in the House of Representatives.

Another trade initiative was the **General Agreement on Tariffs and Trade (GATT)**, which was the precursor to the **World Trade Organization (WTO)**. Originally created by the Bretton Woods Conference in 1944, GATT members committed themselves to reducing tariffs and other trade barriers. The Uruguay round of GATT negotiations began under President Reagan and, although President George H. W. Bush wanted to secure congressional approval for GATT before he left office, ratifying U.S. membership in GATT fell to Clinton. The 103rd Congress did not act due to strong antitrade sentiments among Democrats and, in addition, there was pressure to postpone any vote on GATT until after the 1994 midterm elections. Although the Republicans won control of Congress and House Speaker Newt Gingrich

(R-GA) supported GATT, key to its passage was the prospective 1996 Republican presidential candidate, Senate Majority Leader Robert Dole (R-KS). Dole favored a "trigger mechanism" that would allow Congress to vote to withdraw from GATT if the United States was subjected to unfair rulings by the Court of International Trade. However, the actual vote was anticlimatic as both House and Senate voted for GATT by huge bipartisan majorities.

Given his fierce criticism of President George H. W. Bush's handling of Chinese human rights abuses in the wake of the Tiananmen Square massacre in 1989, it was assumed that President Clinton would demand that China guarantee human rights before the United States would grant it trade privileges. Yet it was Robert Rubin who favored de-linking human rights from trade policy with China.[154] However, granting "most favored nation" trade status to China had to be reaffirmed each year pursuant to legislation requiring human rights reports to Congress. On seven previous occasions Congress acquiesced to President Clinton's favorable decision, despite memories of Tiananmen Square, but the issue became further complicated by allegations that the Chinese government had funneled funds to the 2000 Clinton-Gore campaign and that Chinese agents stole nuclear secrets from American research installations. It was thought that Congress might not be sympathetic to Clinton's pleas should he request legislation to permanently authorize **normal trade relations (NTR)** with China.[155] Ending the legislative deadlock over China trade eluded the administration until President Clinton and President Jiang Zemin personally met in 1999 for discussions on how to gain the admission of China into the WTO, which is the successor organization to GATT.

On November 15, 1999, U.S. and Chinese negotiators agreed on a pact for China to slash its protective tariffs and to open its markets in exchange for China's admission to the WTO. Approval of permanent normal trade relations with China along with other major trade legislation (pending also was the Africa Trade and Development Act of 1999) had to await approval by Congress in 2000, during the presidential primary season when Vice President Gore and former senator Bill Bradley would be competing for union support in their fight for the Democratic Party nomination. Surely Clinton has been the most committed free trader of any Democrat since Franklin D. Roosevelt signed the Reciprocal Trade Agreements Act of 1934, beginning the process of lowering barriers to international trade.

GEORGE W. BUSH: SUPPLY-SIDE, TAKE TWO

The fact that George W. Bush lost the popular vote to Albert Gore but won the Electoral College, thanks to the timely intervention of the U.S. Supreme Court, preordained nothing about Bush's stewardship of the economy. The most pressing issue confronting Bush was the slowing U.S. economy. While America had not yet experienced two consecutive quarters of economic shrinkage that technically constitute a recession, the plummeting stock markets of 2000, rising oil prices, and declining consumer confidence left most citizens in an economic quandary. Economic growth under Clinton made the downturn feel more painful. Christmas shopping in 2001 was depressed as buyers tightened their belts in the wake of the September 11th terrorist attacks. The recession did not begin under Clinton, but the projected economic growth of 4.0% rate for 2000 had to be revised downward to 3.8%, indicating a slowing of the economy in the last six months of 2000. In 2001, however, GDP grew by only 0.8%, down from the preliminary 1.2% projection.[156] Unemployment also increased to 6.0% by 2003.[157]

Tax Cuts, Corporate Scandals, and Policy Tinkering

President Bush's talk of a looming recession supplied him with the political firepower he needed to obtain passage of his proposed $1.6 trillion income tax cut. The tax cut was the brainchild of OMB director Mitch Daniels and Lawrence Lindsey, who served as Bush's economics adviser on the 2000 campaign.[158] However, by pushing for tax cuts, Bush was revisiting the Reagan supply-side formula that produced tremendous deficits. Bush advocated a "marginal rate reduction to serve as an insurance policy against a potential economic downturn" and to a "tax relief plan [that] is an integral part of economic recovery."[159]

Pressure on Bush to deal with the recession was intensified by the fact that his father's presidency was undone by Clinton's relentless focus on the recession of 1990–1991. Bush's convening of an economic summit in Austin paralleled a similar event held by Clinton during the 1992–1993 transition, but the styles of the summits could not have been more different. Clinton held an open forum of three hundred economists and business and labor leaders where he presided and took notes in front of a televised audience, whereas Bush met mostly with corporate leaders who preferred discussing his tax cuts behind closed doors.[160] Bush contended: "A lot of folks in this room have brought some pretty bad news—that their sales are slowing, that they're having to trim back their work force."[161] Despite the economic pessimism, what gave Bush and Lindsey some pleasure was word that the Federal Reserve Board would lower interest rates, a surprise move that delighted everyone in the room but left most participants calling for additional rate reductions. However, Bush added that rate cuts alone could not address the economic downturn and that tax cuts were an "integral part of economic recovery."[162]

Clearly the U.S. economy was devastated by the September 11th attacks. In response, the Fed cut the federal funds rate to the lowest point in four decades. At the White House, Bush, O'Neill, Lindsey, Daniels, Hubbard, and Greenspan met to shape a $100 billion package of tax cuts and spending initiatives (mostly financial bailouts of the airlines and businesses with ties to the World Trade Center), forming what Bush called an "economic security package."[163] At the time, Bush's famous rhetorical line was "the best way to stimulate demand is to give people money so they can spend it."[164] The problem was that it was likely to consume the projected $128 billion budget surplus.

By late October 2001, it seemed apparent that the bipartisan unity in the War on Terrorism would not spark a love fest on economic policy. By the time President Bush delivered his State of the Union address in early 2002, the economic stimulus measure was stalled in Congress, with the White House and Senate only agreeing to extend unemployment benefits to workers for an additional thirteen weeks. The president used his weekly radio address to put pressure on the Senate's one-vote Democratic majority. On December 15, he declared that "the Senate has failed to act. And while the Senate has failed to do its work, more and more Americans have been thrown out of work."[165]

Shortly after the failure of the economic stimulus measure, President Bush signed the **No Child Left Behind Act of 2001 (NCLB)**. The NCLB represents one of the most significant changes in American education policy since the passage of the Elementary and Secondary Education Act (ESEA) in 1965. The NCLB creates standards for what a child should know and learn in math, reading, and science.[166]

But overshadowing the president's legislative success with the NCLB was a series of corporate scandals that threatened to undermine the Bush economic program. Executives of the Houston-based Enron Corporation revealed that the company used partnerships to hide losses and to sell millions in company stock while prohibiting its own employees from unloading their 401(k) shares. Although Enron made campaign donations to both Republicans and Democrats in Congress, it funneled millions to Bush's 2000 presidential campaign. Questions were raised over Bush's knowledge of the company's schemes, including Oval Office meetings between the president and Enron CEO Kenneth Lay.[167]

After the Enron scandal came a rash of other corporate misdeeds. Arthur Andersen, the well-known accounting firm, which made millions for auditing Enron's books and serving as its consultant, was found guilty of obstructing justice after it revealed its accountants had shredded documents related to Enron's accounting misdeeds. (Later the Supreme Court reversed most of the judgment against Arthur Andersen, but by that time the company had laid off most employees and faced bankruptcy.) WorldCom/MCI announced the largest bankruptcy in U.S. history after CEO Bernard Ebbers "borrowed" millions of dollars in company stock to finance his lavish lifestyle. Adelphia Communications founder John Rigas was incarcerated on federal charges that he and his sons defrauded investors by using the company as a "personal piggy bank."[168] Then Enron's chief financial officer pled guilty to conspiracy to commit wire fraud and money laundering, keeping the Enron scandal fresh in people's minds. The political fallout led to the enactment of the Corporate Responsibility Act of 2002, which passed Congress with huge bipartisan majorities. It established an Accounting Oversight Board to register accounting firms and set accounting standards and also authorized the Securities and Exchange Commission to establish conflict-of-interest regulations for accountants and corporations.

Despite all this bad economic news, the Democrats were unable to gain any political traction in the 2002 midterm elections. In fact, between the presidential inauguration and the midterm elections, the value of the Standard & Poor's 500 stock index suffered a steeper decline under Bush than any president except Herbert Hoover.[169] Nonetheless, the Republicans actually made history by gaining seats in Congress, which demonstrated how national security concerns overwhelmed public apprehension over the economy.

Despite the lackluster performance of the overall economy, President Bush did win some important battles in foreign economic policy. During the summer of 2002, he signed legislation restoring presidential trade promotion authority over global trade negotiations. As mentioned before, this "fast-track" trade authority was first delegated to President Ford in 1974 but lapsed in 1994 because President Clinton was unable to persuade Congress to restore this legislation. Bush won a major legislative victory when Congress decided to reauthorize this presidential power in 2002. It allows the president to make trade deals through 2007, which Congress can approve or reject but not change, and Bush promised to use his newly won power to aid the ailing economy. Bush said his administration would move quickly to negotiate trade agreements with Chile, Singapore, and Morocco in addition to forging a Free Trade Area of the Americas. The Free Trade Area of the Americas, an agreement between thirty-four nations, would integrate most North and South American economies into one free-trade bloc analogous to the NAFTA pact agreed to by the United States, Canada, and Mexico. As a result of the passage of presidential trade promotion authority, the president and Congress accepted Jordan, Chile, and Singapore as free-trading partners in 2003. However, Bush's free-trade principles gave way to political calculations as his reelection campaign approached. The Bush administration made an appeal to steelworkers and steel companies in the electorally significant states of West Virginia, Ohio, and Pennsylvania by imposing tariffs on steel imported from Europe, Asia, and South America.[170]

Between 2003 and 2006 President Bush signed three additional tax cuts for individuals and investors, which were extended to 2010. In sticking to a straightforward supply-side script, the Bush administration's argument was that the tax cuts would "pay for themselves."[171] In effect, the administration believed the cuts would increase business and worker productivity to the point where increased individual and corporate incomes would replace and exceed the depleted revenue. According to a Treasury Department analysis, national income could increase by 0.7% by making the cuts permanent and paying for them with future spending reductions. However, the effect of this assumed additional economic growth would offset only a tiny fraction of the cost of the tax cuts.[172] According to the Congressional Budget Office, a 0.7% increase in national income would represent only an additional $146 billion in revenue between 2006 and 2016. Even if the Treasury's most optimistic assumptions are accepted, the cost of the tax cuts in 2016 would still be more than 90% of the cost of the tax cuts under the standard cost estimates.[173]

Along with the tax cuts, the president increased spending on such non-defense discretionary programs as education and homeland security. But the most significant increase in spending was the enactment of a massive new entitlement program, the **Medicare Prescription Drug Program of 2003** (Medicare Part D). The original ten-year cost estimate of the plan was $400 billion, which was boosted to $534 billion by 2004 and was expected to eventually cost between $720 billion and $1.2 trillion.[174] The new entitlement program allows Medicare recipients to obtain prescription drug coverage through two types of private plans. Either the beneficiaries can join a prescription drug plan (PDP) to obtain only drug coverage, or they can join a Medicare advantage plan (MA) that also covers prescription drugs (MA-PD).[175] These programs were designed to control drug costs through a system of tiered formulas in which lower cost drugs were assigned to lower tiers that would be easier to prescribe. By embracing tax cuts and new entitlement spending despite the burgeoning red ink, President George W. Bush has not been distracted by deficits the way his father, President George H. W. Bush, was.

Attempts at Reform

Although his economic policy agenda was dominated by tax cuts and additional spending, President Bush did propose several initiatives that were designed to transform the American economy. One of the most far-reaching was the presidential initiative to transform Social Security with the creation of a system of **personal retirement accounts**. It was introduced to the public and Congress by the president in a series of campaign speeches throughout 2004.[176] Following his reelection, the president argued that the "political capital" he earned should be used to push the plan through Congress.[177]

President Bush's personal accounts system would allow (not require) workers to invest up to 50% of their Social Security payroll taxes (roughly 3.5% of their weekly salary) into a government-managed portfolio that includes traditional stocks and bonds, global equities, real estate, and guaranteed, fixed-income, money-market, inflation-indexed, growth, and social-choice funds. However, at retirement, workers who have chosen to invest in the accounts would be subjected to automatic reductions in their Social Security benefits equivalent to the amount that would be in their personal account if the payroll taxes diverted to the account had earned interest at the same rate as the rate paid on Treasury bonds.[178] According to the White House, the accounts have advantages, especially for less well-off workers who do not already own stocks. In other words, the president argued that accounts offer a good chance for enhancing retirement by capturing healthy returns from the stock market.[179]

But the president failed to convince Congress and the American people, in large measure because of the general economic uncertainty, the risks associated with allowing federally guaranteed benefits to float in the stock market, and the determined opposition of AARP, a nonprofit membership organization for persons age fifty and over.[180] While Democrats were still disaffected from the results of the 2004 election, legislative support for the plan quickly deteriorated as the general feeling grew that the personal accounts could hasten Social Security's insolvency or require massive entitlement spending to create and establish the personal accounts. Similar to the failure of President Clinton's national health care plan in 1994, Bush's reforms of Social Security were politically dead on arrival in Congress. That could have been predicted, because congressional Democrats had virtually no input with the White House commission that was handpicked by Bush to reach the predetermined conclusion that personal accounts were necessary for reform.[181] Thus, Democrats were unified in their opposition to the Bush political calculus of building an electoral "investor" majority around Social Security reform.[182]

Nonetheless, the potential insolvency of Social Security remains one of the fundamental economic problems facing the United States. Although his political strategy was flawed, President Bush deserves credit for addressing the underlying problem that, in the absence of serious reform, Social Security is projected to run annual deficits beginning in 2017 and will be unable to meet its obligations in 2047. The only reason Social Security is not bankrupt yet is due to the massive baby-boom generation, which is still working and creating temporary surpluses. When baby boomers begin retiring in large numbers, massive deficits will result. Other short-term reforms, like raising the retirement age from sixty-five to sixty-seven, would probably not address the long-term issue concerning potential Social Security insolvency and excessive entitlement spending.

Another big issue that President Bush confronted was comprehensive immigration reform. How to deal with the millions of undocumented immigrants and their impact on the American economy is not new, though Bush's comprehensive approach to the problem was. In an attempt to improve relations with Mexico and appeal to Hispanic voters, Bush proposed a guest-worker program that would allow about 12 million illegal immigrants to temporarily work in the United States without having to apply for U.S. citizenship.[183] Workers in the program would be issued "tamperproof" identification cards.[184] Bush claimed that temporary or guest-worker programs would recognize a massive workforce that is completely unregulated by the federal government. While illegal immigrants work and pay taxes, they have no workplace protection and are vulnerable to exploitation or abuse. Proponents of guest-worker programs, including many business associations, say that illegal immigrants meet the labor needs of the U.S. economy.

The president submitted his proposal for a guest-worker program in November 2005, but he was immediately confronted with opposition in both the House and Senate, especially from conservatives within the Republican Party who believed his approach was a general grant of amnesty for illegal immigrants.[185] By mid-2006 Congress produced two sharply different proposals for reforming the U.S. immigration system. The House bill emphasized law enforcement efforts, including penalizing undocumented workers and employers who hire them; construction of a seven-hundred-mile fence along the U.S.-Mexican border and hiring more Border Patrol agents; and penalizing humanitarian groups that provide services to illegal immigrants. The Senate bill, by contrast, provided a path to citizenship for a majority of the estimated twelve million illegal immigrants in the country. A growing number of states have already introduced measures to cut off government support for illegal immigrants. The House and Senate deadlocked and were unable to reconcile their fundamentally different approaches to immigration reform. As the 2006 midterm election loomed and polls showed that the Republicans might lose control of the House and of seats in the Senate, there was political pressure to do something. In the end, the Senate yielded to the House demands, the seven-hundred-mile fence was authorized, and President Bush signed the bill without much public fanfare. But it was not enough to save the Republicans, who lost control of both the House and Senate in the 2006 elections. Whether the 110th Congress will actually provide funding to build the fence remains to be seen.

On the whole, then, the American economy has produced mixed results under President George W. Bush. Since the 2001 recession, the economy has created over 2 million new jobs, including new manufacturing jobs, and the gross domestic product has risen each year. While the unemployment rate has been relatively low, wages and salaries have been stagnant.

For three years, pay raises did not keep pace with the rising cost of living, although in 2006 the 4% average increase in salaries reflected "real" wage gains for American workers.[186]

FUTURE ECONOMIC CHALLENGES

The American economy is undergoing a fundamental transformation, one with significant economic challenges that presidents will be forced to contend with in the twenty-first century. Over the last several decades the labor force has shifted from the manufacturing sector to a service-oriented and knowledge-based economy. And because the economy is becoming more globally interconnected, technologically advanced, and dependent on foreign trade, the greater volatility in the labor market may have contributed to the stagnant wage growth in recent years.

The manufacturing sector has experienced a significant downturn in recent years, a trend that cannot be understated. Job losses during the 2001 recession were much worse compared to previous recessions in 1980, 1981–1982, and 1990–1991. In fact, all twenty-one manufacturing industries declined between 2001 and 2004.[187] The drop in manufacturing employment since the beginning of the 2001 recession is one reflection of the globalization of mass production. Beyond that, the share of consumer spending devoted to manufactured goods within the United States, the European Union, and Japan has declined. Today, China is the global center of manufacturing. One consequence is that the slowed rate of growth in the demand for U.S. manufactured goods has brought about a decline in the share of employment attributed to the manufacturing sector. As of 2005, 13.6 million Americans worked in manufacturing, a 17% decline from the 17.6 million of March 1998. On the other hand, and luckily for the American economy, the productivity of the U.S. workforce in the manufacturing sector has grown by an average annual rate of 3.3% since 1979.[188] There may be fewer manufacturing employees in the United States today, but they are much more efficient than employees were in the past.

The erosion of the U.S. manufacturing base has been accompanied by a rise in the service-sector economy. But the service sector is more integrated within the global economy than the manufacturing sector had been. With the rise in personal income, consumers have spent more of their disposable income on purchasing services, including financial services, education, health care, and telecommunications. Purchases of services, in fact, are growing at a faster pace than the consumption of goods. In 2000, 42% of U.S. consumer spending was devoted to goods, down from 53% in 1979 and 67% in 1950, whereas much of the increased spending on services has been tied to the rising costs of medical care and child care services.[189]

The trend away from manufacturing toward services signals the arrival of a "postmaterialist" or "knowledge" economy that may yield a bifurcated workforce: highly educated versus the unskilled. In the past, large numbers of unskilled or semiskilled workers found employment in the manufacturing sector, but those jobs may not be available for the next generation who lack sophisticated skills or a college education. Real wages for the lowest quintile of American workers have stagnated over the past three decades. From 1979 to 2004 average annual incomes increased by 27%; however, the rise in wages was narrowly concentrated at the top and offset by losses for the bottom three-fifths of Americans (those making less than $38,761 in 2004). On average, the bottom 60% of Americans made less than ninety-five cents in 2004 for each dollar they reported in 1979.[190] In 2004, total income declined by 1.4%.[191]

One cause of the stagnating wages has been the emergence of a new and rapidly expanding "underclass" which bears the brunt of rising income inequality.[192] In 2004 the poverty cutoff for a family of four was $19,157. As of 2003, 13% of the workforce earned under $8 per hour (or $16,500 annually), and these low-wage workers were employed primarily in service-sector jobs. In addition, 12% of Americans now live below the poverty line. The picture is one of growing inequality. Since 1996 annual income for those households in the top quarter has grown dramatically; for median income earners, the growth rate has been 35%; but those workers in the bottom 25% experienced an earnings decline of 41%.[193]

With wages stagnating in the lower-level service sector, on the one hand, and welfare reform promoting work as the primary strategy for alleviating poverty, on the other, the obstacles for facilitating upward earnings mobility for low-wage workers are apparent. The first noteworthy feature of low-wage work is the sheer number of individuals who are employed part-time or full time with wages at or near their state's minimum wage. To date, eighteen states and Washington, D.C., have established a minimum wage above the federally mandated level. With the Democratic takeover of both houses of Congress in November 2006, there is a strong likelihood that President Bush will be forced to sign legislation that raises the federal minimum wage.

Another mammoth economic problem on the horizon involves America's system of funding health care. Roughly forty years since Medicare and Medicaid and more than a decade after the Clinton administration failed in its bid to extend coverage to all Americans, employers, consumers, and federal and state governments have been strained by health care costs that have been growing at a pace five or six times the rate of inflation. Businesses have been passing an increasing share of the price tag to their workers, forcing them to dig deep into their pockets. The public health care system is overwhelmed by the country's 47 million uninsured Americans and 12 to 15 million undocumented immigrants who use hospital emergency rooms for routine care. Medicare is even projected to run out of funds by 2019 at the current rate of growth.

Consider the financial strain. Currently, total health care spending represents roughly 16% of GDP and is expected to reach 20% of GDP by 2015.[194] Health insurance expenses are the fastest growing cost component for employers. Unless something changes dramatically, health insurance costs will overtake profits by 2008.[195] In 2006 employer health insurance premiums increased by 7.7%, or twice the rate of inflation. The annual premium for an employer health plan covering a family of four averaged nearly $11,500; the annual premium for single coverage averaged over $4,200.[196] In 2006 workers contributed 10% more than they did in 2005. The annual premiums for family coverage significantly eclipsed the gross earnings for a full-time, minimum-wage worker ($10,712).

Even though roughly 47 million Americans are without medical coverage, the United States spends more on health care than other industrialized nations that provide universal health care (or insurance) for all their citizens.[197] It is generally believed that new medical technologies, litigation, excessive administrative expenses, inflated prices, poor management, inappropriate care, waste and fraud, and rising numbers of uninsured people have driven up health care costs for both employers and employees.[198]

A third daunting economic problem is America's insatiable demand for energy, particularly oil products. Since the oil crisis of the early 1970s, America has become painfully conscious of its dependence on foreign oil as a major source of its energy, a lesson made obvious by the over $3 per gallon gas prices of 2007. But a new political development may be an increased recognition by the public and policy makers that America cannot achieve energy independence while, at the same time, neglecting the need for increased environmental protection. In order to achieve sustainability on such environmental issues as climate change, which many scientists believe result from greenhouse gas emissions and pollution, policy makers have taken steps to limit emissions that will not jeopardize economic growth.[199]

Is there a trade-off between environmental protection and economic growth? Although historically, economic growth has proceeded at the expense of the environment, hope lies in technological progress. Through technological progress and the resultant rise in economic productivity, it may be possible to have a higher standard of living and a clean environment for everyone. The concept of "sustainability" aims to balance three targets with equal weight: "ecologically sound" and "economically viable" as well as "socially just."[200] Although progress on sustainability has been achieved almost exclusively in advanced industrialized nations, no major economy has been able to attain complete sustainability. For instance, global carbon dioxide emissions have increased by roughly 8% since the 1992 United Nations Conference on Environment and Development (UNCED) in Rio de Janeiro. And this increase in pollution occurred despite higher energy efficiency and despite a 1997 agreement made in Kyoto, Japan, by most industrial countries (though not the United States) to further reduce emissions.[201]

The desire to preserve economic growth while addressing the global ecosystem has caused environmentalists and policy makers to shift their focus to finding ways of obtaining energy from renewable sources. Oil and automobile companies have stepped up research and production of alternative energies and hybrid drive technologies. The objective is to lower dependence on fossil fuels and to reduce emissions of greenhouse gases through advances in residential and commercial solar energy, wind power, and fuel cells using renewable sources. Despite government incentives, technological improvements, greater use of alternative energies, and increased public awareness of environmental change, these positive developments may not be strong enough to satisfy—in the immediate future—the global hunger for energy, especially in developing countries and emerging markets.[202] In addition to improving our own domestic environment, the United States must be prepared to assist developing nations in reducing their dependence on natural resources and in building up new sectors of their economies while, at the same time, not adding to global environmental degradation.

KEY TERMS

automatic stabilizers
Balanced Budget Act of 1997 (BBA)
cost-push inflation
demand-pull inflation
entitlements
exchange rate
Family and Medical Leave Act of 1993 (FMLA)
General Agreement on Tariffs and Trade (GATT)
Humphrey-Hawkins Act of 1978
incomes policy
Laffer Curve
Medicaid
Medicare
Medicare Prescription Drug Program of 2003
military-industrial complex
monetarist
New Economic Policy (NEP)

new economics
No Child Left Behind Act of 2001 (NCLB)
normal trade relations (NTR)
Personal Responsibility and Work Opportunity Reconciliation Act of 1996
personal retirement accounts
Phillips Curve
Reaganomics
stagflation
supplemental security income (SSI)
supply-side economics
Temporary Assistance for Needy Families (TANF)
trade promotion authority
wage and price controls
World Trade Organization (WTO)

ADDITIONAL READINGS

Baumer, Donald C. and Carl E. Van Horn. *The Politics of Unemployment*. Washington, DC: CQ Press, 1985. An overview of federal jobs programs with special attention to CETA under both Jimmy Carter and Ronald Reagan.

Friedman, Milton and Walter W. Heller. *Monetary vs. Fiscal Policy*. New York: Norton, 1969. A celebrated debate between the foremost exponent of monetarism and the Keynesian CEA chairman under President Kennedy.

Hoff, Joan. *Nixon Reconsidered*. New York: Basic, 1994. This eye-opening reassessment of Richard Nixon argues, contrary to prevailing wisdom, that Nixon's most lasting achievements were in economic and domestic policy and not in foreign affairs.

Meyer, Jack A. *Wage-Price Standards and Economic Policy*. Washington, DC: American Enterprise Institute for Public Policy Research, 1982. Studies the U.S. Council on Wage and Price Stability from 1974 to 1980, giving primary attention to its implementation of wage-price standards under President Carter.

Pierce, Lawrence. *The Politics of Fiscal Policy Formation*. Pacific Palisades, CA: Goodyear, 1971. A solid examination of the political process underlying fiscal policy making, with special attention to President Johnson's decision to levy the 1968 income tax surcharge.

Silk, Leonard. *Nixonomics*. New York: Praeger, 1973. A well-written, popularized account of macroeconomic policy making during President Nixon's first term.

Sloan, John W. *Eisenhower and the Management of Prosperity*. Lawrence: University Press of Kansas, 1991. Definitive study of economic policy making during the Eisenhower administration.

Stockman, David A. *The Triumph of Politics: Why the Reagan Revolution Failed*. New York: Harper & Row, 1986. As the first OMB director under President Reagan,

David A. Stockman was the architect of Reaganomics but eventually became troubled about the mounting deficits and left the administration.

NOTES

1. Michael Genovese, "The Presidency and Styles of Economic Management" (paper presented at the annual meeting of the American Political Science Association, Washington, DC, August 1986).

2. Samuel Kernell, *Going Public: New Strategies of Presidential Leadership* (Washington, DC: Congressional Quarterly, 1997), 233–242.

3. Douglas A. Hibbs Jr., "The Mass Public and Macroeconomic Performance: The Dynamics of Public Opinion Toward Unemployment and Inflation," *American Journal of Political Science* 23 (November 1979): 543–563; Douglas A. Hibbs Jr., "The Dynamics of Political Support for American Presidents among Occupational and Partisan Groups," *American Journal of Political Science* 26 (1982): 312–332; and Paul P. Eretz, "The Politics of Fiscal and Monetary Policy," in *The Politics of American Economic Policy Making*, ed. Paul Peretz (New York: Sharpe, 1996), 101–114.

4. U.S. Department of Commerce, Bureau of Economic Analysis, "GDP and Other Major NIPA Series, 1929–2006."

5. Robert S. Walters and David H. Blake, *The Politics of Global Economic Relations* (Englewood Cliffs, NJ: Prentice-Hall, 1992).

6. Dwight D. Eisenhower, Farewell Address, January 17, 1961; see also Godfrey Hodgson, *America in Our Time: From World War II to Nixon—What Happened and Why* (New York: Vintage, 1976), 129; Godfrey Hodgson, "The Establishment," *Foreign Policy* 10 (Spring 1973): 3–40; and David Halberstam, *The Best and the Brightest* (New York: Random House, 1969).

7. Stephen E. Ambrose and Douglas Brinkley, *Rise to Globalism* (Middlesex, UK: Penguin, 1997); John Lewis Gaddis, *The United States and the Origins of the Cold War, 1941–1947* (New York: Columbia University Press, 1972); Walter LaFeber, *The American Age: United States Foreign Policy at Home and Abroad Since 1750* (New York: Norton, 1989); and Daniel Yergin, *Shattered Peace: The Origins of the Cold War and the National Security State* (Boston: Houghton-Mifflin, 1983).

8. Walter LaFeber, *America, Russia, and the Cold War* (New York: McGraw-Hill, 1997), 59.

9. Stephen D. Cohen, *The Making of U.S. International Economic Policy* (Westport, CT: Praeger, 2000).

10. John W. Sloan, *Eisenhower and the Management of Prosperity* (Lawrence: University Press of Kansas, 1991), 13.

11. Sloan, *Eisenhower and the Management of Prosperity*.

12. Hodgson, *America in Our Time*, 19.

13. U.S. Department of Commerce, Bureau of Economic Analysis, *National Income and Product Accounts of the United States, 1929–1994*, vol. 1; U.S. Department of Commerce, Bureau of Economic Analysis, *Survey of Current Business*, May 1999. Sources located in U.S. Census Bureau, *Statistical Abstract of the United States*.

14. U.S. Bureau of Labor Statistics, Bulletin 2307; *Employment and Earnings*, monthly; and, U.S. Department of Commerce, Bureau of Economic Analysis, *Survey*

of Current Business, September 1986. Sources located in U.S. Census Bureau, *Statistical Abstract of the United States*, 1999; Wallace C. Peterson, *Income, Employment, and Economic Growth* (New York: Norton, 1996).

15. Sloan, *Eisenhower and the Management of Prosperity*, 18–19.

16. U.S. Department of Labor, Bureau of Labor Statistics, "Consumer Price Index," ftp://ftp.bls.gov/pub/special.requests/cpi/cpiai.txt.

17. Thomas Parthenakis, "George M. Humphrey, Secretary of the Treasury: Eisenhower's Strongman or Svengali?" (paper presented at the Eisenhower Symposium, Gettysburg College, Gettysburg, PA, October 10–13, 1990).

18. Edward S. Flash, *Economic Advice and Presidential Leadership* (New York: Columbia University Press, 1965), 158.

19. Marquis Childs, *Eisenhower: Captive Hero* (New York: Harcourt Brace, 1958), 163.

20. Raymond J. Saulnier, *Constructive Years: The U.S. Economy under Eisenhower* (Washington, DC: University Press, 1991).

21. Source: U.S. Office of Management and Budget, *Historical Tables: Budget of the United States Government, 2006* (Washington, DC: Government Printing Office, 2005), annual, http://www.whitehouse.gov/omb/budget/fy2007/budget.html. Source located in the U.S. Census Bureau, *Statistical Abstract of the United States*, 1999.

22. Saulnier, *Constructive Years*.

23. U.S. Department of Commerce, Bureau of Economic Analysis, "GDP and Other Major NIPA Series, 1929–2006," tables 1–4.

24. U.S. Department of Labor, Bureau of Labor Statistics, "Consumer Price Index," ftp://ftp.bls.gov/pub/special.requests/cpi/cpiai.txt.

25. U.S. Department of Commerce, Bureau of Economic Analysis, "GDP and Other Major NIPA Series, 1929–2006," tables 1–4.

26. Wilfred Lewis, *Federal Fiscal Policy in the Postwar Recessions* (New York: Greenwood, 1980), 233.

27. U.S. Office of Management and Budget, *Historical Tables, Budget of the United States Government, Fiscal Year 2006* (Washington, DC: U.S. Government Printing Office, 2005), table 8.1, 124.

28. John Kenneth Galbraith, *The Affluent Society* (Boston: Houghton Mifflin, 1958), 207.

29. See Gardner Ackley, *Macroeconomics: Theory and Policy* (New York: Macmillan, 1978), 434–437.

30. Robin Bade and Michael Parkin, *Foundations of Economics* (Boston: Addison Wesley, 2003), 865.

31. Bade and Parkin, *Foundations of Economics*.

32. Bade and Parkin, *Foundations of Economics*, 862.

33. Herbert A. Stein, *The Fiscal Revolution in America: Policy in Pursuit of Reality* (New York: American Enterprise Institute, 1996).

34. See John W. Sloan, "The Management and Decision-Making Style of President Eisenhower," *Presidential Studies Quarterly* 20 (Spring 1990): 297.

35. John F. Kennedy, State of the Union address, January 30, 1961.

36. George L. Perry and James Tobin, *Economic Events, Ideas and Policies: The 1960s and After* (Washington, DC: Brookings, 2000).

37. Quoted in Flash, *Economic Advice and Presidential Leadership*, 204.

38. U.S. Department of Labor, Bureau of Labor Statistics, "Employment Status of the Civilian Non-institutional Population, 1940 to 2006"; U.S. Office of Management and Budget, White House, *Historical Tables*, annual, http://www.whitehouse.gov/omb/budget/fy2007/budget.html; and U.S. Department of Labor, Bureau of Labor Statistics, "Consumer Price Index," ftp://ftp.bls.gov/pub/special.requests/cpi/cpiai.txt.

39. Herbert Stein, *Presidential Economics: The Making of Economic Policy from Roosevelt to Reagan and Beyond* (New York: Simon & Schuster, 1984), 110.

40. Stein, *The Fiscal Revolution in America*, 448.

41. Peterson, *Income, Employment, and Economic Growth*.

42. Council of Economic Advisers, *Annual Report of the Council of Economic Advisers, 1963* (Washington, DC: U.S. Government Printing Office, 1963), 47–48.

43. Arthur M. Okun, "Measuring the Impact of the 1964 Tax Reductions," in *Perspectives on Economic Growth*, ed. Walter Heller (New York: Random House, 1968), 27 and James Tobin, "The Tax Cut Harvest," in *The Battle against Unemployment*, ed. Arthur M. Okun (New York: Norton, 1965), 157.

44. U.S. Department of Labor, Bureau of Labor Statistics, "Employment Status of the Civilian Non-institutional Population, 1940 to 2006" and U.S. Department of Commerce, Bureau of Economic Analysis, "GDP and Other Major NIPA Series, 1929–2006."

45. U.S. Office of Management and Budget, *Budget of the United States Government*, http://www.whitehouse.gov/omb/budget/fy2007/budget.html and U.S. Council of Economic Advisers, *Economic Report of the President*, http://a257.g.akamaitech.net/7/257/2422/13feb20061330/www.gpoaccess.gov/eop/2006/2006_erp.pdf.

46. See Henry J. Aaron, *Politics and the Professors: The Great Society in Perspective* (Washington, DC: Brookings, 1978), 11–12, tables 1-A1, 1-A3.

47. See the 2006 Annual Report of the Board of Trustees of the Federal Hospital Insurance and Federal Supplementary Medical Insurance Trust Funds, May 2006, Centers for Medicare and Medicaid Services, http://www.cms.hhs.gov/apps/media/press/release.asp?Counter=1846.

48. U.S. Office of Management and Budget, *Budget of the United States Government*.

49. U.S. Department of Commerce, Bureau of Economic Analysis, "GDP and Other Major NIPA Series, 1929–2006."

50. U.S. Department of Labor, Bureau of Labor Statistics, "Employment Status of the Civilian Non-institutional Population, 1940 to 2006."

51. U.S. Office of Management and Budget, *Budget of the United States Government*.

52. Peterson, *Income, Employment, and Economic Growth*.

53. Quoted in Neil de Marchi, "The First Nixon Administration: Prelude to Controls," in *Exhortation and Controls: The Search for a Wage-Price Policy 1945–1971*, ed. Craufurd D. Goodwin (Washington, DC: Brookings, 1975), 298.

54. Clark Warburton, "The Theory of Turning Points in Business Fluctuations," *Quarterly Journal of Economics* (1950): 46.

55. Milton Friedman, *Studies in the Quantity Theory of Money* (Chicago: University of Chicago Press, 1992).

56. Milton Friedman and Anna Schwartz, *A Monetary History of the United States, 1867–1960* (New York: Institute of Economic Affairs, 1992).

57. G. R. Steele, *Monetarism and the Demise of Keynesianism* (New York: St. Martin's, 1989).

58. K. Alec Chrystal, *Monetarism* (New York: Edward Elgar, 1990) and Gianni Vaggi and Peter D. Groenewegen, *A Concise History of Economic Thought: From Mercantilism to Monetarism* (New York: Palgrave-Macmillan, 2006).

59. Bruno Jossa and Marco Musella, *Inflation, Unemployment, and Money: Interpretations of the Phillips* Curve (New York: Edward Elgar, 1998); A. W. Phillips and Robert Leeson, *A.W.H.: Collective Works in Contemporary Perspective* (Cambridge, UK: Cambridge University Press, 2000); and A. W. Phillips, "The Relation between Unemployment and the Rate of Change of Money Wages in the United Kingdom, 1861–1957," *Economica* 25 (1958): 283–299.

60. Malcolm C. Sawyer, *Political Economy of the Phillips Curve* (New York: Edward Elgar, 2000).

61. Edmund Phelps, "Phillips Curves, Expectations of Inflation, and Optimal Unemployment Policy over Time," *Economica* 34 (1967): 254–281.

62. Anthony Santomero and John J. Seater, "The Inflation-Unemployment Trade-off: A Critique of the Literature," *Journal of Economic Literature* 16 (June 1978): 499–544 and Jonathan Temple, "Openness, Inflation, and the Phillips Curve: A Puzzle," *Journal of Money, Credit, and Banking* (May 2002).

63. Quoted in A. James Reichley, *Conservatives in an Age of Change: The Nixon and Ford Administrations* (Washington, DC: Brookings, 1981), 206.

64. U.S. Department of Labor, Bureau of Labor Statistics, "Employment Status of the Civilian Non-institutional Population, 1940 to 2006"; U.S. Department of Labor, Bureau of Labor Statistics, "Consumer Price Index," ftp://ftp.bls.gov/pub/special.requests/cpi/cpiai.txt.

65. U.S. Department of Commerce, Bureau of Economic Analysis, "GDP and Other Major NIPA Series, 1929–2006," tables 1–4.

66. Joan Hoff, *Nixon Reconsidered* (New York: Basic, 1994), 138.

67. Jonathan Kirshner, *Currency and Coercion: The Political Economy of International Monetary Power* (Princeton: Princeton University Press, 1997).

68. *Economic Report of the President* (Washington, DC: U.S. Government Printing Office, 1970), 3.

69. *Economic Report of the President.*

70. U.S. Department of Labor, Bureau of Labor Statistics, "Consumer Price Index," ftp://ftp.bls.gov/pub/special.requests/cpi/cpiai.txt.

71. Kenneth Bowler, *The Nixon Guaranteed Income Proposal* (Cambridge, MA: Ballinger, 1974); Vincent Burke and Vee Burke, *Nixon's Good Deed: Welfare Reform* (New York: Columbia University Press, 1974); William W. Lammers and Michael A. Genovese, *The Presidency and Domestic Policy* (Washington, DC: CQ Press, 2000), 237–240; and Daniel Patrick Moynihan, *The Politics of a Guaranteed Income: The Nixon Administration and the Family Assistance Plan* (New York: Random House, 1973).

72. Aid to Families with Dependent Children (AFDC) was the name of a welfare program in effect between August 14, 1935, and June 30, 1997, administered by the United States Department of Health and Human Services.

73. Lammers and Genovese, *The Presidency and Domestic Policy*, 240–241.

74. Burke and Burke, *Nixon's Good Deed*.

75. Lammers and Genovese, *The Presidency and Domestic Policy*, 240–241 and Hoff, *Nixon Reconsidered*, 22–27.

76. U.S. Department of Labor, Bureau of Labor Statistics, "Employment Status of the Civilian Non-institutional Population, 1940 to 2006."

77. U.S. Department of Labor, Bureau of Labor Statistics, "Consumer Price Index," ftp://ftp.bls.gov/pub/special.requests/cpi/cpiai.txt.

78. Hugh Rockoff, Louis Galambos, and Robert Gallmam, *Drastic Measures: A History of Wage and Price Controls in the United States* (Cambridge, UK: Cambridge University Press, 2003).

79. U.S. Department of Labor, Bureau of Labor Statistics, "Consumer Price Index," ftp://ftp.bls.gov/pub/special.requests/cpi/cpiai.txt.

80. A. James Reichley, *Conservatives in an Age of Change: The Nixon and Ford Administrations* (Washington, DC: Brookings, 1981), 323–325. Only Cleveland, FDR, and Truman cast more vetoes relative to their tenure in office. Of the sixty-six vetoes cast by Ford, thirty-nine affected the federal budget.

81. Quoted in Jeff Fishel, *Presidents and Promises: From Campaign Pledge to Presidential Performance* (Washington, DC: CQ Press, 1985), 100.

82. For an excellent historical analysis of the Humphrey-Hawkins Act, especially in comparison to the 1946 Employment Act, see J. Bradford De Long, "Keynesianism, Pennsylvania Avenue Style: Some Economic Consequences of the Employment Act of 1946," *Journal of Economic Perspectives* 10 (Summer 1996): 41–53.

83. See the *Full Employment and Balanced Growth Act of 1978*, Public Law 95-523, 95th Cong., 2d sess. (October 27, 1978).

84. U.S. Department of Labor, Bureau of Labor Statistics, "Consumer Price Index," ftp://ftp.bls.gov/pub/special.requests/cpi/cpiai.txt.

85. This seeming paradox is because the overall job pool grew rapidly during Carter's four years in office, due to the entry into the labor force of large numbers of "baby boomers" and women (who had not previously entered the labor force to the same degree). As a result, while the number of employed persons increased substantially—with average yearly increases greater than during the four-year expansion of the second Reagan term (1985–1988)—the percentage of those seeking jobs who were employed did not change to the same degree.

86. U.S. Department of Labor, Bureau of Labor Statistics, "Employment Status of the Civilian Non-institutional Population, 1940 to 2006."

87. Reagan's policies were also influenced by the rational expectations school, also known as the new classical economics, whose prominent proponents include Robert Lucas and Robert Barro of the University of Chicago. The major propositions of the rational expectations school include the following: money markets adjust very rapidly following a shock to the economy; if left alone, all markets will tend toward equilibrium at full employment; and fiscal policy is largely irrelevant.

88. Paul Craig Roberts, *The Supply-Side Revolution: An Insider's Account of Policymaking in Washington* (Cambridge, MA: Harvard University Press, 1984) and John W.

Sloan, *Reagan Effect: Economics and Presidential Leadership* (Lawrence: University Press of Kansas, 1999).

89. Thomas W. Hoekstra, Joseph A. Tainter, and T. W. Hoekstra, *Supply-Side Sustainability* (New York: Columbia University Press, 2003).

90. Frank Ackerman, *Reaganomics: Rhetoric vs. Reality* (Boston: South End, 1982).

91. Charles Hulten and Isabel Sawhill, *Legacy of Reaganomics: Prospects for Long-term Growth* (New York: Urban Institute, 1984).

92. F. Thomas Juster, "The Economics and Politics of the Supply-Side View," *Economic Outlook USA* (Autumn 1981): 81.

93. Michael Boskin, *Reagan and the Economy: The Successes, Failures, and Unfinished Agenda* (New York: ICS, 1998) and Howard Winant, *Stalemate: Political Economic Origins of Supply-Side Policy* (New York: Greenwood, 1988).

94. Arthur Laffer and Charles Kadlac, *The Jarvis-Gann Tax Cut Proposal: An Application of the Laffer Curve* (Boston: C.H. Wainright, 1978); Arthur Laffer and Jan Seymour, *The Economics of the Tax Revolt* (New York: Harcourt Brace Jovanovich, 1979); and Jude Wanniski, "Taxes, Revenues, and the 'Laffer Curve,'" *Public Interest* (Winter 1978): 1–13.

95. M. J. Malcolmson, "Some Analytics of the Laffer Curve," *Journal of Public Economics* 29 (1986): 263–279.

96. D. Fullerton, "On the Possibility of an Inverse Relationship between Tax Rates and Government Revenues," *Journal of Public Economics* 19 (1982): 3–22.

97. Donald W. Kiefer, "An Economic Analysis of the Kemp-Roth Tax Cut Bill HR 8333," *Congressional Record* (August 2, 1978).

98. Alan Blinder, "The Anatomy of Double-Digit Inflation," in *Inflation: Causes and Effects*, ed. Robert E. Hall (Chicago: University of Chicago Press, 1982) and U.S. Department of Labor, Bureau of Labor Statistics, "Consumer Price Index," ftp://ftp.bls.gov/pub/special.requests/cpi/cpiai.txt.

99. Robert Gordon, "Why Stopping Inflation May Be Costly: Evidence from Fourteen Historical Episodes," in *Inflation: Causes and Effects*, ed. Robert E. Hall (Chicago: University of Chicago Press, 1982).

100. A theoretical discussion of "cold turkey" verses "gradualism" is found in Rudiger Dornbusch and Stanley Fischer, *Macro-Economics*, 3rd ed. (New York: McGraw-Hill, 1984), 446–451.

101. Robert L. Bartley, *The Seven Fat Years: And How to Do It Again* (New York: Free Press, 1992), 26, 163, 167; Lawrence Lindsey, *The Growth Experiment: How the New Tax Policy Is Transforming the U.S. Economy* (New York: Basic, 1991); and David Stockman, *The Triumph of Politics: The Inside Story of the Reagan Revolution* (New York: Avon, 1987).

102. William A. Niskanen and Stephen Moore, "Cato Policy Analysis No. 261: Supply Side Tax Cuts and the Truth about the Reagan Economic Record," (Washington, DC: Cato Institute, 1996), http://www.cato.org/pubs/pas/pa-261.html and Bruce Bartlett, "Trickle-Down Economics," *National Review* (September 2, 1996): 63.

103. U.S. Department of Labor, Bureau of Labor Statistics, "Consumer Price Index," ftp://ftp.bls.gov/pub/special.requests/cpi/cpiai.txt.

104. U.S. Department of Labor, Bureau of Labor Statistics, "Employment Status of the Civilian Non-institutional Population, 1940 to 2006" and U.S. Department

of Labor, Bureau of Labor Statistics, "Consumer Price Index," ftp://ftp.bls.gov/pub/special.requests/cpi/cpiai.txt.

105. U.S. Department of Commerce, Bureau of Economic Analysis, "GDP and Other Major NIPA Series, 1929–2006."

106. Office of Management and Budget (OMB), *Historical Tables, Budget of the United States Government, Fiscal Year 2006* (Washington, DC: U.S. Government Printing Office, 2005), table 8.1.

107. U.S. Department of Labor, Bureau of Labor Statistics, "Employment Status of the Civilian Non-institutional Population, 1940 to 2006."

108. Quoted in David E. Rosenbaum, "On the Economy, Bush Followed Reagan's Lead, Not His Success," *New York Times*, June 29, 1992. See also Brit Hume, "The Bush Crack-Up," *The American Spectator* (January 1993): 23–24.

109. John Woolley and Gerhard Peters, eds., "George H. W. Bush Acceptance Speech: August 18th, 1988—New Orleans, LA," The American Presidency Project website, http://www.presidency.ucsb.edu/shownomination.php?convid=4.

110. Richard Doyle and Jerry McCaffery, "The Budget Enforcement Act of 1990: The Path to No-Fault Budgeting," *Public Budgeting and Finance* (11): 25–40; George Hager, "Deficit Shows No Gain from Pain of Spending Rules," *Congressional Quarterly Weekly Report* (July 20, 1991): 1963; and Paul Simon, "Discipline Is Overdue," *New York Times*, May 20, 1992.

111. John O'Sullivan, "Why Bush Lost," *National Review* (November 30, 1992): 7–10.

112. See Davis W. Houck, "Rhetoric as Currency: Herbert Hoover and the 1929 Stock Market Crash" *Rhetoric & Public Affairs* 3, no. 2 (2000): 155–181.

113. Robert E. Scott and Christian Weller, "Fed Up," *Economic Policy Institute Issue Brief #148* (January 29, 2001), http://www.epinet.org/content.cfm/issue briefs_ib148.

114. National Bureau of Economic Research, "U.S. Business Cycle Expansions and Contractions," (Cambridge, MA: National Bureau of Economic Research, 2001).

115. See Bob Woodward, *The Agenda: Inside the Clinton White House* (New York: Simon & Schuster, 1994), 54.

116. David Wessel, "Economic Security Council Stirs Debate." *Wall Street Journal* November 10, 1992.

117. Clinton is quoted in Jim Impoco, Nick Cumming-Bruce, Hannah Moore, "Where Growth Is Job One," *U.S. News & World Report* (December 21, 1992): 70.

118. Susan Dentzer, "What's Cooking, Mr. Clinton?" *U.S. News & World Report* (December 7, 1992): 63.

119. I. M. Destler, *The National Economic Council: A Work in Progress* (Washington, DC: Institute for International Economics, 1996), 14.

120. Elizabeth Drew, *On the Edge: The Clinton Presidency* (New York: Simon & Schuster, 1995), 25, 26–27; George Stephanopoulos, *All Too Human: A Political Education* (Boston: Little, Brown, 1999), 346; and Bob Woodward, *The Agenda* (New York: Simon & Schuster, 1994), 60–63, 75–76.

121. Stephanopoulos, *All Too Human*, 135 and Woodward, *The Agenda*, 75–76.

122. David Hage and Robert F. Black "Pain Today, Gain Tomorrow," *U.S. News & World Report* (January 25, 1993): 36–28; Howard Fineman, "The Clinton Revolution," *Newsweek* (March 1, 1993): 24–28; and Stephanopoulos, *All Too Human*, 126.

123. Ruth Marcus and Ann Devroy, "Asking Americans to 'Face Facts,' Clinton Presents Plan to Raise Taxes, Cut Deficit," *Washington Post*, February 18, 1993.

124. Douglas W. Elmendorf, Jeffrey B. Liebman, and David W. Wilcox, "Fiscal Policy and Social Security Policy during the 1990s" (paper presented at a conference, John F. Kennedy School of Government, Harvard University, June 27–30, 2001), 9–12.

125. Tom Morgenthau, Rich Thomas, and Eleanor Clift, "One for the Hawks," *Newsweek* (December 21, 1992): 34.

126. "Deficit-Reduction Bill Narrowly Passes," *Congressional Quarterly Almanac 1993* 49:108.

127. Congressional Budget Office, *Reducing the Deficit: Spending and Revenue Options* (Washington, DC: U.S. Government Printing Office, February 1993).

128. John B. Judis, "The Old Master: Robert Rubin's Artful Role." *The New Republic* (December 13, 1993): 21.

129. Destler, *The National Economic Council*, 53.

130. John F. Harris and John E. Yang, "Clinton Says He Won't Be 'Blackmailed' by Gingrich on Budget," *Washington Post*, September 26, 1995, and Allison Mitchell, "With First Veto, Clinton Rejects Budget-Cut Bill," *New York Times*, June 19, 1995.

131. David S. Cloud and Jackie Koszczuk, "GOP's All-or-Nothing Approach Hangs on a Balanced Budget," *Congressional Quarterly Weekly Report* (December 9, 1995); Ann Devroy and Eric Pianin, "Clinton Vetoes GOP's 7-Year Balanced Budget Plan," *Washington Post*, December 7, 1995; and Jerry Gray, "Battle over the Budget: The Legislation: House Fails to Override Veto of Spending Bills," *New York Times*, January 4, 1996.

132. Rudi Dornbusch, "Say Goodbye to Easy Money," *Business Week* (April 21, 1997): 26 and Alicia H. Munnell, Dean Baker, and Robert Eisner, "The Great Surplus Debate," *American Prospect* (May 1998): 80.

133. Daniel J. Palazzolo, *Done Deal? The Politics of the 1997 Budget Agreement* (Chatham, NJ: Chatham House, 1999).

134. Center on Budget and Policy Priorities, "Without Reductions in Discretionary Programs, There Would be Little Budget Surplus outside Social Security," (March 23, 1999), http://www.cbpp.org/3-23-99bud.htm.

135. Center on Budget and Policy Priorities, "Without Reductions in Discretionary Programs."

136. U.S. Office of Management and Budget, *Historical Tables, Budget of the United States Government, Fiscal Year 2006* (Washington, DC: U.S. Government Printing Office, 2005), table 8.1, 124.

137. Eric Pianin and Charles Babington, "Clinton Vetoes GOP Tax Cut Bill," *Washington Post*, September 24, 1999.

138. Lammers and Genovese, *The Presidency and Domestic Policy*, 317–318, 324–325.

139. Colin Campbell and Bert A. Rockman, introduction to *The Clinton Presidency: First Appraisals*, by eds. Colin Campbell and Bert A. Rockman (Chatham, NJ: Chatham House, 1996), 7–8.

140. For more on the politics of the welfare reform measure, see Peri Arnold, "Bill Clinton and the Institutionalized Presidency: Executive Autonomy and Presidential Leadership," in *The Postmodern Presidency: Bill Clinton's Legacy in U.S. Politics*, ed. Steven E. Schier (Pittsburgh: University of Pittsburgh Press, 2000).

141. Steven M. Teles, *Whose Welfare: AFDC and Elite Politics* (Lawrence: University Press of Kansas, 1996).

142. Ron Haskins, *Work over Welfare: The Inside Story of the 1996 Welfare Reform Law* (Washington, DC: Brookings, 2006); Isabel V. Sawhill, Andrea Kane, Kent Weaver, and Ron Haskins, *Welfare Reform and Beyond* (Washington, DC: Brookings, 2003); and Alvin L. Schorr, *Welfare Reform: Failures and Remedies* (New York: Greenwood, 2001).

143. "Social Policy," *Congressional Quarterly Weekly Report* (November 2, 1996): 3148–3149 and Jack W. Germond and Jules Witcover, "On Welfare Reform, It's Politics as Usual," *National Journal* (August 5, 1995): 2021.

144. George C. Edwards III, "Frustration and Folly: Bill Clinton and the Public Presidency," in *The Clinton Presidency: First Appraisals*, ed. Colin Campbell and Bert A. Rockman (Chatham, NJ: Chatham House, 1996), 246–247, 251–252.

145. Graham K. Wilson, "The Clinton Administration and Interest Groups," in *The Clinton Presidency: First Appraisals*, ed. Colin Campbell and Bert A. Rockman (Chatham, NJ: Chatham House, 1996), 226–229 and Lammers and Genovese, *The Presidency and Domestic Policy*, 319–321.

146. Lammers and Genovese, *The Presidency and Domestic Policy*, 320–321.

147. William Lammers, "Presidential Leadership and Policy," in *Health Politics and Policy*, 3rd ed., eds. Theodore J. Litman and Leonard Robins, chap. 5 (Albany, NY: Delmar, 1997).

148. See James R. Tallon Jr., "New Conundrums: Public Policy and the Emerging Health Care Marketplace," *Syracuse University Maxwell School of Citizenship and Public Affairs/Center for Policy Research: Policy Brief No. 11/1998* (November 1998): 10, 13, http://www-cpr.maxwell.syr.edu/pbriefs/pb11.pdf.

149. Woodward, *The Agenda*, 49.

150. Chris J. Dolan and Jerel A. Rosati, "U.S. Foreign Economic Policy and the Significance of the National Economic Council," *International Studies Perspectives* 7, no. 2 (May 2006): 114–115.

151. Fast track negotiating authority was renamed to trade promotion authority with the passage of the Trade Act of 2002.

152. Linda Feldman, "Wheeling and Dealing Led to NAFTA Victory," *Christian Science Monitor* (November 19, 1993): 2–3; Paul Krugman, "The Uncomfortable Truth about NAFTA: It's Foreign Policy, Stupid," *Foreign Affairs* 72 (November–December): 13–19; and David Cloud, "Clinton Turns up the Volume on NAFTA Sales Pitch," *Congressional Quarterly Weekly Report* (October 23, 1993): 2863–2864.

153. Paul R. Krugman, "NAFTA: An Empty Victory?" *U.S. News & World Report* (November 29, 1993): 30.

154. Destler, *The National Economic Council*, 39.

155. John T. Rourke and Richard Clarke, "Making U.S. Foreign Policy toward China," in *After the End: Making U.S. Foreign Policy in Post-Cold War*, ed. James M. Scott (Durham: Duke University Press, 1998); Gerald Segal, "Does China Matter?" *Foreign Affairs* (September–October 1999): 24–36; and James Mann, "Our China Illusion," *American Prospect* (June 5, 2000): 21–25.

156. U.S. Department of Commerce, Bureau of Economic Analysis, "GDP and Other Major NIPA Series, 1929–2006."

157. U.S. Department of Labor, Bureau of Labor Statistics, "Employment Status of the Civilian Non-institutional Population, 1940 to 2006."

158. Rich Thomas and Keith Naughton, "Bush's Money Posse," *Newsweek* (January 5, 2001): 19–22.

159. John Woolley and Gerhard Peters, eds., "Bush Meets with Congressional Leadership: Monday, December 18, 2000," American Presidency Project website, http://www.presidency.ucsb.edu/showtransition2001.php?fileid=bush_congress 12-18; David E. Sanger, "The Rate Cut," *New York Times*, January 4, 2001.

160. Gary Susswein, "President-Elect Renews Call for Tax Cut after Meeting with CEOs," *Atlanta Journal-Constitution*, January 4, 2001, 1.

161. Sanger, "The Rate Cut," *New York Times*.

162. Rich Miller, Laura Cohn, and Lee Walczak, "The Kindest Cut of All," *Business Week* (January 15, 2001): 32.

163. Ann Kornblut, "Bush Plans to Aid the Economy," *Boston Globe*, October 5, 2001.

164. Jeff Toedtman, "America's Ordeal, Healing the Economy," *Newsday*, October 3, 2001.

165. Timothy J. Burger, "Bush Blames Senate for Stalled Economic Plan," *New York Daily News*, December 16, 2001.

166. For more on the NCLB, see Patrick J. McGuinn, *No Child Left Behind and the Transformation of Federal Education Policy, 1965 to 2005* (Lawrence: University Press of Kansas, 2005) and Paul E. Peterson and Martin R. West, *No Child Left Behind? The Politics and Practice of School Accountability* (Washington, DC: Brookings, 2004).

167. Robert Scheer, "Enron, Symbolic of Bush Blunders," *Newsday*, December 27, 2001.

168. Howard Fineman and Michael Isikoff, "Laying Down the Law," *Newsweek* (August 5, 2002): 20–25.

169. Harold Meyerson, "Squandering Prosperity," *American Prospect* (June 2003): 26.

170. Jeffery Frankel, "The Crusade for Free Trade," *Foreign Affairs* (March–April 2001): 155 and Paul Magnusson, "Bush's Steely Pragmatism," *Business Week* (March 18, 2002): 44.

171. Matthew Benjamin, "A Believer in Tax Cuts," *U.S. News & World Report* (June 25, 2005), 36 and Thomas E. Nugent, "Do Tax Cuts Pay for Themselves?" *National Review Online* (June 29, 2006), http://article.nationalreview.com/?q=Mzg0M2 QwZDFhODRmZDllMjEwODc2N2M1MWQzYzRiYzc=.

172. "A Dynamic Analysis of Permanent Extension of the President's Tax Relief," *Mid-Session Review of the Budget for Fiscal Year 2007*, 3–4.

173. Richard Kogan and Aviva Aron-Dine, "Claim That Tax Cuts 'Pay for Themselves' Is Too Good to be True: Data Show No 'Free Lunch' Here" (Center on Budget and Policy Priorities, June 14, 2006).

174. Dean Baker, "The Savings from an Efficient Medicare Prescription Drug Plan," (Center for Economic and Policy Research, January 2006), http://www.cepr.net/publications/efficient_medicare_2006_01.pdf and Ceci Connolly and Mike Allen, "Medicare Drug Benefit May Cost $1.2 Trillion," *Washington Post*, February 9, 2005.

175. For more on the details of the new Medicare Part D drug coverage plan, see the U.S. Department of Health and Human Services at http://www.cms.hhs.gov/PrescriptionDrugCovGenIn.

176. Melissa Favreault et al., "Reform Model Two of the President's Commission to Strengthen Social Security: Distributional Outcomes under Different Economic

and Behavioral Assumptions," (working paper, Center for Retirement Research, 2004), 19.

177. Gloria Borger, "A Really Not-So-Capital Idea," *U.S. News & World Report* (December 20, 1994): 34.

178. White House website, "Strengthening Social Security for the 21st Century," February 2005, http://www.whitehouse.gov/infocus/social-security/200501/strengthening-socialsecurity.html.

179. U.S. Congressional Budget Office, *Long-Term Analysis of the President's Commission to Strengthen Social Security Plan 2* (Washington, DC: Congressional Budget Office, 2004).

180. Rich Lowry, "AARP in the Hot Seat," *National Review Online* (February 16, 2005), http://www.nationalreview.com/lowry/lowry200502160736.asp and Bret Schulte, "The Democrats Get Set to Rumble," *U.S. News & World Report* (March 14, 2005): 34.

181. Ramesh Ponnuru, "Doomed Like Clinton Health Care?" *National Review* (February 17, 2005): 29.

182. Richard Wolffe and Holly Bailey, "The Oval: Heavy Going" *Newsweek* (March 2, 2005): 40.

183. Michael Barone, "Be Our Guest," *U.S. News & World Report* (May 7, 2001): 27 and Mark Krikorian, "A Stern Face and a Warm Welcome," *National Review* (October 27, 2003): 20.

184. Michael Crowley, "Border War," *New Republic* (March 28, 2005): 12 and Reed Karaim, "Getting Real on the Border," *U.S. News & World Report* (June 5, 2006): 28.

185. Michael A. Fletcher and Darryl Fears, "Bush Pushes Guest-Worker Program," *Washington Post*, November 29, 2005.

186. See Mark Trumbull, "A Brisk Rise in American Wages" *Christian Science Monitor* (November 20, 2006), http://www.csmonitor.com/2006/1120/p01s03-usec.htm.

187. U.S. Congressional Budget Office, "What Accounts for the Decline in Manufacturing Employment?" Economic and Budget Issue Brief, February 18, 2004.

188. U.S. Congressional Budget Office, "What Accounts for the Decline in Manufacturing Employment?" The Bureau of Labor Statistics' data on productivity in manufacturing is available from 1987. For earlier years, the Congressional Budget Office used figures from the recently discontinued SIC system. The two series of data show virtually identical growth in productivity, on average, between 1987 and 2002.

189. U.S. Department of Labor, Bureau of Labor Statistics, "Consumer Expenditure Surveys," Washington, DC.

190. Brett Theodos and Robert Bednarzik, "Earnings Mobility and Low-Wage Workers in the United States," *Monthly Labor Review* (July 2006): 34–36.

191. David Cay Johnston, "2004 Income Was Below 2000 Level," *New York Times*, November 28, 2006.

192. Eduardo Porter, "After Years of Growth, What about Workers' Share?" *New York Times*, October 15, 2006.

193. Theodos and Bednarzik, "Earnings Mobility and Low-Wage Workers," 35.

194. Christine Borger et al., "Health Spending Projections through 2015: Changes on the Horizon," *Health Affairs* 25, no. 2 (February 22, 2006).

195. Borger et al., "Health Spending Projections."

196. The Henry J. Kaiser Family Foundation, *Employee Health Benefits: 2006 Annual Survey* (September 26, 2006), http://www.kff.org/insurance/7315/index.cfm.

197. R. Pear, "U.S. Health Care Spending Reaches All-Time High: 15% of GDP," *New York Times*, January 9, 2004.

198. Victoria Colliver, "In Critical Condition: Health Care in America," *San Francisco Chronicle*, October 14, 2004.

199. James A. Barnes, "Is Bush Poisoning His Well?" *National Journal* (April 14, 2001): 1120–1121.

200. William C. Clark and R. E. Munn, *Sustainable Development in the Biosphere* (New York: Cambridge University Press, 1986).

201. Stanley P. Johnson, The Earth Summit (London: Graham and Trotman/Martinus Nijhoff, 1993); Robert Repetto and Jonathan Lash, "Planetary Roulette: Gambling with the Climate," *Foreign Policy* 108 (Fall 1997): 84-98; and Intergovernmental Panel on Climate Change, *IPCC Third Assessment Report-Climate Change 2001*, http://www.ipcc.ch/pub/un/syreng/spm.pdf.

202. Calvin Sims, "Poor Nations Resist Role in Warming," *New York Times*, December 13, 1997.

7

The International Economy and U.S. Foreign Economic Policy

In late August 2006 Fed chairman Ben Bernanke convened a conference of the Fed Board of Governors in Jackson Hole, Wyoming, along with all the Federal Reserve bank presidents and some leading economists and financiers. The discussions centered on how to devise a monetary policy designed to reduce inflation and assess how it would be impacted by international economic trends. In recent years global economic integration made it easier for the Fed to manage price levels. Dramatic increases in low-cost imports from China and other countries kept prices relatively low even though American consumers spent heavily and built up unprecedented amounts of personal debt. However, the conference attendees warned that these global trends could slow down or even reverse in the very near future. China's tremendous economic growth and its status as a low-cost manufacturer of consumer goods may not guarantee that prices will remain low forever. Moreover, China's increased demand for oil and other raw materials will likely drive up energy prices by diverting more oil away from the U.S. market. By 2006 the inflation rate was already above Bernanke's unofficial target of 2% per year, excluding energy and food prices.

Regardless of what the Fed does to interest rates, economists at the conference concluded that the forces of economic globalization coupled with America's huge foreign debt could limit its monetary policy options and constrain its ability to manage the money supply. According to Raghuram Rajan of the International Monetary Fund (IMF), developing nations have relied less on foreign capital than many advanced nations, which has allowed them to save more than they invest. For example, due in large part to soaring copper prices, Chile paid off its foreign debt and had a budget surplus equal to 7% of its gross domestic product (GDP) in 2006.[1] Chilean leaders are putting the budgetary surplus into a long-term stability fund, part of which is invested in foreign securities to maintain government operations if copper prices plummet. Even though capital is flowing to the developed nations, Rajan concluded "it doesn't mean these flows are optimal, safe or permanent."[2]

As the Fed acknowledges, **globalism** and **economic globalization** can profoundly shape domestic economic stability and prosperity. Globalism describes a world characterized by networks of all kinds—political, economic, and financial—that span multicontinental distances. It attempts to understand the interconnections of the modern world. In contrast, globalization refers to the increase or decline in the degree of globalism by highlighting the dynamism of these changes. In particular, economic globalization involves the increasing integration of international markets brought about by rapidly expanding worldwide flows of goods, services, capital, information and technology, and people. Economic globalization has given rise to a new global economy that is powerful enough to transform our traditional conceptions of employment, prices, and prosperity. As Bernanke maintains: "One of the defining characteristics of the world in which we now live is that, by most economically relevant measures, distances are shrinking rapidly."[3] This shrinking has led author Thomas Friedman to famously observe that economic globalization has contributed to the "flattening" of the world on a broad scale.[4]

The growing importance of the international economic arena presents new challenges for economic policy making. Today, America finds itself engaged in intense competition with an array of economic rivals, including the advanced economies of Japan and the European Union as well as the developing economies of China, India, South Korea, Singapore, and Malaysia. Another "power shift" in the global arena has taken place insofar as nongovernmental organizations (NGOs), such as citizen groups, organized interests, foreign investment firms, and transnational corporations, as well as supranational organizations (the United Nations, World Trade Organization, World Bank, and International Monetary Fund) have become as powerful as governments in shaping the global economy.[5] The forces of globalization have implanted a strong sense of economic internationalism in the minds of most policy actors and segments of the public.[6] Presidential management of the economy, therefore, is constrained by the forces of economic globalization and the interdependence of the United States on the global economy.[7]

This chapter assesses the impact of economic globalization on the U.S. economy and on the ability of the president to manage economic policy. We begin with a historical perspective by tracing the ebb and flow of the global economy and its impact on the United States. Then we detail the most significant policies and issues affecting U.S. foreign economic policy.

ECONOMIC GLOBALIZATION

Two of the most significant and transformative global changes in this generation was the end of the Cold War and the disintegration of the Soviet Union. The Cold War, characterized by East-West tensions and regional and international alliance structures, provided the global framework within which the world economy functioned. The United States and its allies generally subordinated economic issues to national security demands and the need to maintain political cooperation. National security policy in support of the Western alliance provided the political glue that held the world economy together and that facilitated compromises between nations over economic issues.[8]

The Genesis of the Global Economy

The organization of the global economy during the Cold War began when the United Nations Monetary and Financial Conference (commonly known as the Bretton Woods Conference) was convened by the United States and its World War II allies in Bretton Woods, New Hampshire, between July 1 and July 22, 1944.[9] The meeting established the **Bretton Woods System**. The objective was for America to lead the international economic order since the United States had escaped much of the economic devastation that plagued the economies of Europe and Asia during World War II. Bretton Woods became an international economic regime of stable monetary exchange based on the U.S. dollar backed by gold. The U.S. dollar was given a fixed value of 1/35 an ounce of gold ($35 per ounce of gold), and the U.S. government guaranteed to purchase dollars held by other countries for gold at this rate. All other national currencies also were set at "**fixed**" **exchange rates** relative to the U.S. dollar. Global currency markets, which mainly included the United States and its Western allies, would operate within a narrow range around the fixed rate. Should any nation's currency fall more than 1% from the fixed rate, then its government was obligated to use its hard currency reserves to buy back its own currency in order to shore up the price.[10]

The Bretton Woods Conference also established the **International Monetary Fund (IMF)** and the **International Bank for Reconstruction and Development (IBRD)**—better known as the **World Bank**. Initially the IMF was designed to assist Western governments in managing their imports and exports and to stabilize their currencies based on gold and the fixed rates of exchange.[11] In the postwar era, the World Bank supplied loans to governments for economic recovery and to facilitate capital investment. Both the IMF and the World Bank were financed by cash donations by member states, which had "weighted" voting privileges determined by the size of their donations. Since the United States had the most financial resources for subsidizing both organizations, it controlled most of the votes (roughly one-third).

The IMF and the World Bank were dominated by the United States, and from the outset they both received bipartisan support in the U.S. Congress. For example, the House voted 345–18 and the Senate voted 61–16 to authorize U.S. membership in each organization, and the headquarters of both organizations are located in Washington, D.C. Furthermore, the director of the World Bank has always been an American (at the time of this book's publication in 2007, Paul Wolfowitz is president of the World Bank), and it is quite common for Americans to dominate the senior positions in the IMF.

By the late 1960s, however, the U.S. dollar rapidly declined in global financial markets. There was an overabundance of U.S. dollars held by other nations, who became less willing to maintain U.S. dollars as their reserve currency. Moreover, the amount of gold held by U.S. Federal Reserve banks in proportion to the number of U.S. dollars held by foreign nations dropped.[12] At the same time, the United States was competing with the Europeans and Japanese over its role in sustaining global financial markets. As authors Charles Kegley and Eugene Wittkopf observe: "The Europeans and Japanese came especially to resent the prerogatives the United States derived from its position as the world's banker and from its ability to determine the level of international liquidity."[13] And later, Western Europe and Japan protested the international economic consequences that resulted from U.S. military involvement in the Vietnam War.

Upon taking office, President Richard Nixon believed that the global economic system should be transformed from one that was unilaterally sustained by the U.S. dollar to a system based on multilateral cooperation. On August 15, 1971, the Nixon administration formally abandoned the Bretton Woods System. In 1971 Nixon's **"New Economic Policy"** proposed to remove the U.S. dollar from the gold standard and to impose a 10% surcharge on imports. Once the convertibility of the U.S. dollar into gold at $35 an ounce was discarded, a new system of **"floating" exchange rates** was created for major world currencies. Currency rates would be determined by supply and demand in the global currency markets, where private investors, banks, and governments buy and sell currencies. Supply and demand allowed each nation's currency to constantly adjust to market conditions, although governments could periodically intervene in financial markets by buying and selling currencies in order to influence their value and "manage the float."[14]

America had legitimate concerns about the increased financial competition that would result with other nations. One important consideration involves the **current account balance**, which consists of the merchandise trade balance (exports and imports), income from services and investments, and transfers such as the exchange of U.S. government grants, pensions, foreign aid, military transactions, and travel and service receipts. During the Bretton Woods System, the United States consistently produced surpluses in trade (where exports exceed imports), services, and investment income. The merchandise trade balance has varied over time, with both surpluses and deficits (where imports exceed exports). From 1960 to 1970 the United States averaged annual trade surpluses of $3.1 billion, but in 1971 the United States ran a trade deficit of $1.3 billion—the first time since the end of World War II.[15] After President Nixon abandoned Bretton Woods, U.S. exports began to decline as demand for U.S.-made goods and services waned. This situation led to demands by labor unions, farmers, and businesses for higher tariffs on imports in order to protect the American economy from foreign competition. Even though America's share of world trade had declined, the value of that trade as a percentage of GDP rose, indicating not only the degree of global economic integration but also the increased U.S. economic vulnerability to the international economy.[16] During the 1990s the United States enjoyed the second-longest period of sustained economic growth since records began in 1854, but the irony is that this prosperity aggravated the U.S. trade imbalance.

Evolution of the Global Economy

The United States and much of the developed world have certainly benefited from the rapid expansion of economic globalization. Economic globalization has increased America's standard of living by roughly $1 trillion per year. Since 1945 the average American household is about $9,000 per year richer and, since 1991, U.S. income has increased by a further $500 billion per year as a result of greater integration with the global economy.[17] A recent study by the Institute for International Economics concluded that American living standards are 10% higher as a result of economic globalization's benefits (cheap imports, greater competition, new technologies). In 2004 the global economy grew almost 5%, with Asia leading the way at 8%, Latin America at 5.6%, and the United States at 3.1%.[18]

A primary objective of presidential leadership in today's global economy is to promote American access to foreign markets.[19] And key to the expansion of global trade has been the dramatic decline in trade barriers resulting from successive rounds of international trade negotiations. Since World War II the combined tariff levels of advanced countries dropped from roughly 40% to 6%, and barriers to trading in services have also been lowered. A defining feature of the postwar international economic system has been sustained growth of global trade. Global trade's share of world GDP rose from 13% in 1970 to 21% in 1995.[20] The composition of trade also

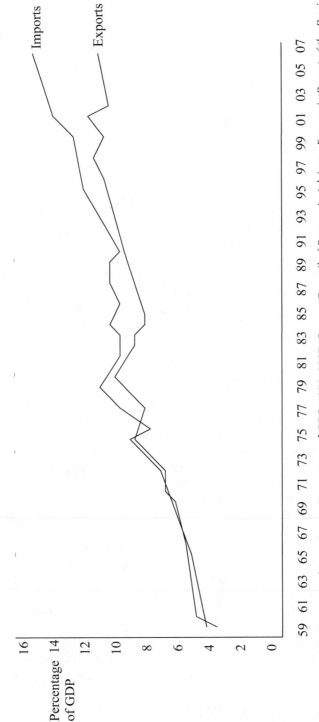

Figure 7.1. U.S. Exports and Imports as a Percentage of GDP, 1959–2007. *Source:* Council of Economic Advisers, *Economic Report of the President,* table B-4, http://a257.g.akamaitech.net/7/257/2422/15feb20061000/www.gpoaccess.gov/eop/2006/B4.xls.

has changed in two ways: (1) the expansion of trade in services and (2) the growth of manufacturing exports from developing countries.

Since the mid-1970s, financial deregulation coupled with technological advances in the communications industry also have contributed to the development of a highly integrated international financial system. The volume of foreign exchange trading (buying and selling national currencies) in the late 1990s reached approximately $1.5 trillion per day, an eightfold increase since 1986. By contrast, the global volume of exports (goods and services) for all of 1997 was only $6.6 trillion, or $25 billion per day. The amount of investment capital seeking higher returns also has grown enormously. By the mid-1990s mutual funds, pension funds, and the like totaled $20 trillion.[21]

The United States and other Western economies still control a preponderant share of global wealth, but that share has declined in relative terms because newly industrializing economies, especially China, have gained economic importance. Before the 1997 East Asian financial crisis, Asia's economic success had been extremely impressive. Many of the Asian economies achieved average annual growth rates of 6% to 8%.[22] Despite the financial crisis, such economic "fundamentals" as high savings rates and excellent workforces give credence to the argument that these emerging Asian markets will continue to be important actors in the global economy.

Driven by the activities of transnational corporations, various stages of the production process can now be located in different countries. The resulting globalization of production activities has opened new opportunities for developing countries. One recent innovation is the practice of **outsourcing**, which involves the delegation of certain workplace operations from inside a corporation to an external entity, usually overseas. More precisely, outsourcing is the "the process of transferring an existing business function, including the relevant physical and/or human assets, to an external provider in order to strategically use outside resources to perform activities previously handled in-house."[23] Outsourcing should not be confused with **offshoring**, which entails transferring essential and nonessential operations entirely from the United States to another country. The term "outsourcing" became well known due to the growth in small high-tech companies in the early 1990s that could not maintain large customer service departments. The business units that are typically outsourced include information technology, human resources, and accounting.[24] A number of companies also outsource customer support and telemarketing services, manufacturing, and engineering. An outsourcing business often takes advantage of certain expertise that is not available inside the client organization.

Outsourcing was heavily criticized by U.S. senator John Kerry (D-MA), the 2004 Democratic presidential candidate, who argued that it hurt American jobs. Kerry highlighted comments by President Bush's CEA chairman

N. Gregory Mankiw that the outsourcing of American jobs is "probably a plus for the economy in the long run."[25] Between 2000 and 2003 the vast majority of American jobs lost to outsourcing were in manufacturing, in particular high-paying managerial positions.[26] Still outsourcing has not undermined the fundamentals of the U.S. economy. Every quarter the economy generates more jobs than are lost to outsourcing. Also most of the U.S. jobs lost through outsourcing pay less than the average U.S. wage, which suggests that many of these jobs may face medium-term elimination through technological change regardless of whether or not they are outsourced to offshore locations. Without doubt some occupations have declined, with losses concentrated in low-skilled information technology positions.[27]

As a consequence, the makeup of exports from developing countries has changed, from once being once almost entirely raw materials (such as iron ore, grain, or natural gas) to being increasingly composed of manufactured goods and services. Between 1985 and 1995 the share of manufactured goods in the exports of developing countries rose from 47% to 83%. In 1995 developing countries made up 20% of the global manufacturing market for that year.[28] Since then, developing countries saw their share of the world merchandise trade rise to 31% in 2004, the highest since 1950.[29] Especially important is the growing export trade from the East Asian economies, whose share of world manufacturing output grew from 6.8% in 1980 to 11% in 1995.[30] Overall, the five nations of China, South Korea, Mexico, Brazil, and South Africa account for more than 60% of the exports of manufactured goods from the developing nations.[31]

Oil and Global Economics

The rapidly increasing trade deficit has focused attention on other pressing economic concerns. One is the rising dependence of the United States on foreign energy sources, mainly petroleum. Even if the United States could end dependence on imports for 64% of its crude oil demand, the European Union would still import roughly 80% and Japan almost 100%.[32] Any shutdown of Persian Gulf or central Asian oil exports due to terrorism or war could have severe repercussions on the preeminent economies of the world.

In recent years the most significant international event at the nexus of oil and global economics has been the Iraq War. In 2002 the price per barrel of crude oil averaged roughly $24 but rose to $32 per barrel when the U.S. invasion was launched in March 2003. The price increase was mainly attributed to an increase in stockpiling in response to worries about supply interruptions. While the price did drop to approximately $27.1 in 2003, it increased to almost $36 in 2004 and shot up to $48 by 2005.[33] The dam-

Table 7.1.   Impact of Oil Prices

Year	Total Oil Imports (thousands of barrels per day)	Total Imports per Year (billions of barrels)	Refiner Acquisition Cost of Imported Oil (billions $/barrel)	Total Cost of Imported Oil (billions $)
2000	11459.3	4.19	27.7	116.2
2001	11871.3	4.34	22.0	95.3
2002	11530.2	4.22	24.1	99.8
2003	12264.4	4.49	27.1	124.0
2004	13145.1	4.81	35.9	172.7
2005	13415.5	4.91	47.9	234.7
2006	13952.1	5.11	72.0	292.3

Sources: "Oil Price History and Analysis," *WTRG Economics,* http://www.wtrg.com/prices.htm; *A Primer on Gasoline Prices,* Energy Information Administration, May 2006, http://www.eia.doe.gov/bookshelf/ brochures/gasolinepricesprimer/eia1_2005primerM.html.

age to key oil refineries on the Gulf Coast inflicted by Hurricane Katrina in August 2005 forced further hikes in oil prices and gasoline at the pumps, with the average price for a barrel of imported crude oil hitting an all-time high of $72 in August 2006.[34]

Political instability in the Middle East also poses increased risks to multinational corporate investments. Although Iraq is not an oil producer on the scale of Saudi Arabia or Russia, crude oil production in Iraq plummeted after the war began in 2003. Under Saddam Hussein, Iraq produced roughly 2.6 million barrels a day in 2002 (the same level as Kuwait, Nigeria and the UK), but by 2006 Iraqi oil production dropped to 1.1 million barrels a day.[35]

America is especially sensitive to the decisions made by the leaders of the **Organization of Petroleum Exporting Countries (OPEC)**. OPEC membership includes Iran, Iraq, Kuwait, Saudi Arabia, Venezuela, Algeria, Indonesia, Libya, Nigeria, Qatar, and the United Arab Emirates. OPEC's objective is to achieve unified decisions on petroleum policies in order to regulate the supply of petroleum on the market and, therefore, to manipulate the prices received by petroleum producers. In recent years OPEC has held petroleum prices at 50% to 75% above market levels and, as a result, the cost of energy in the United States as a share of our GDP tripled since 1997. Since the oil crisis of the 1970s, when OPEC was established, prices have fluctuated from 15% to 300% of competitive levels. As noted by former Fed chairman Alan Greenspan, the recessions of 1973–1975, 1980, 1981–1982, 1990–1992, and 2001 "have all been preceded by spikes in the price of oil."[36] Higher corporate energy costs and gasoline prices have depressed the GDP of the United States and other oil-importing countries by roughly 15% to 30%. It has been estimated that U.S. economic growth could be boosted by at least 1% a year if OPEC allowed energy prices to be determined purely by market forces.[37]

Financial Crises in the Global Economy

Another issue related to the huge trade imbalances among nations is the stability of global financial markets. After the Bretton Woods System ended in 1971, exchange rates for most currencies were allowed to float, but central banks still intervened to prevent sharp fluctuations. Governments with large trade surpluses began selling their currencies to prevent them from "appreciating" (gaining value) whereas governments with large deficits started purchasing their own currencies in order to prevent "depreciation" (losing value).

Since many financial flows are short-term, highly volatile, and speculative, international finance has become an unstable component of the global economy. The immense scale, velocity, and speculative nature of financial movements across national borders have made governments more vulnerable to sudden shifts in these movements. Therefore governments, even in highly developed economies, can easily fall prey to currency speculators. This happened in the 1992 European financial crisis when the United Kingdom was forced to withdraw from the European Exchange Rate Mechanism. Similar monetary crises caused the punishing collapse of the Mexican peso in 1995, the East Asian financial crisis in 1997–1998, and several currency collapses in South America in 2001.

The growing international financial interdependence has exacerbated American vulnerability to fluctuations in global financial markets. The primary goal of the International Monetary Fund is to extend short-term credit to nations who are unable to meet their foreign debts through their own efforts to increase exports, secure long-term loans, or draw down their own currency reserves. While standard IMF policy requires stringent fiscal and monetary measures in order to obtain short-term credits, in the mid-1990s some countries faced severe problems paying their foreign debts. This problem resulted from abrupt shifts in flows of private investment dollars as well as "structural" deficiencies in their economies.

Mexican Peso Crisis

In late 1994 the Mexican peso went into a free fall for one week, shedding roughly 40% of its value. The general feeling was that if the United States did not intervene in the peso crisis, the impact on the dollar would be catastrophic.[38] Moreover, it was believed that U.S. exports to Latin America under NAFTA would be drastically impacted, which could explode America's overall trade debt. Although Mexican president Carlos Salinas had linked the exchange rate of the peso to the U.S. dollar in order to hold down prices at home, the peso still rose because the Mexican inflation rate was much higher than the American rate.[39] In early January 1995, newly installed Mexican president Ernesto Zedillo responded with an emergency recovery program that instituted wage and price controls, spending cuts, and privatized state-owned industries in an effort to stabilize Mexican financial markets and restore investor confidence.[40]

In mid-January President Clinton asked Congress for $40 billion in U.S. loan guarantees, credits, and other assistance to Mexico, and he directed his National Economic Council (NEC) and the Treasury Department to lead the U.S. response to the peso crisis.[41] Clinton designated Treasury Secretary Robert Rubin as the White House's point man. To garner the necessary votes in Congress, Clinton and Rubin worked with House Speaker Newt Gingrich and Senate Majority Leader Bob Dole, who both endorsed the White House loan package and agreed to mobilize the needed legislative support to bolster the peso and restore investor confidence in Mexico.[42] The goal was to assure Congress that the loan guarantee package would not require any U.S. taxpayer funds but, instead, would be backed by a pledge of revenue from Mexican oil exports.[43]

In addition, after two days of lobbying by Undersecretary of the Treasury Lawrence Summers, on January 28 the IMF notified the Clinton administration that it would supply the Mexican government with $7 billion in loan guarantees. Although the White House had hoped that IMF assistance would help to garner votes in Congress, legislative support quickly diminished as House members called on President Clinton to tie the level of U.S. financial assistance to Mexico's efforts to stem the tide of illicit drugs crossing into the United States. On January 31 Clinton withdrew his initial $40 billion plan from consideration and, instead, transferred $20 billion from the Treasury Department's Exchange Stabilization Fund (ESF) as loan guarantees to the Bank of Mexico. Clinton cited a federal statute that the ESF is "under the exclusive control of the secretary [and] . . . decisions of the secretary are final and may not be reviewed by another officer or employee of the government."[44] Revenue from oil exports from PemEx, Mexico's state-run oil corporation would be used to repay the U.S. Treasury.

Ultimately, Lawrence Summers was able to persuade the IMF to provide an additional $10 billion in assistance for Mexico on the condition that the Mexican government produce a domestic budget surplus and privatize state-owned businesses. This brought the IMF total contribution to $17.8 billion. Of this amount, $7.8 billion was to be disbursed immediately and additional conditional assistance would become available beginning in July 1995. Summers also influenced the Bank for International Settlements (BIS) to provide $10 billion in short-term assistance to the Bank of Mexico. Including the ESF funds, the total package amounted to $52.8 billion.[45]

Asian Financial Crisis

Then in 1997, economic and political turmoil swept through several key East Asian countries following the collapse of currencies and stock markets in Thailand, Hong Kong, South Korea, Indonesia, and Malaysia. The crisis posed a threat to our trade policy with key East Asian nations aimed at securing the value of the dollar and also maintaining political stability in the region.[46] The Clinton administration feared that if East Asia destabilized, then the United States would be forced to contend with an array of economic and security issues that could upset the entire international system and unravel U.S. global leadership.[47]

President Clinton responded with an aggressive policy of pressuring Japan to assume the lead in promoting financial reforms. In November 1997 Robert Rubin and Lawrence Summers devised a strategy to obtain congressional approval for funds to reinforce the IMF. Clinton also extended $10 billion in loans and credits to South Korea. In Indonesia, after the rupiah lost 24% of its value against the dollar, Clinton withheld $3 billion in U.S. assistance until dictator Suharto was forced from power in 1999 and violence in East Timor subsided.[48]

Congressional criticism of Clinton intensified after he requested an additional $18 billion in January 1998 to help replenish the IMF. To gain approval, National Economic Adviser Gene Sperling set three objectives: promote structural reforms at the IMF, pressure Japan to promote the economic recovery of East Asia, and assert U.S. leadership to prevent a global financial contagion. Rubin and Greenspan testified several times before Congress in support of regional stability, military cooperation, and free trade between the United States and East Asia.[49] Sperling and Rubin also appealed to key constituency groups. In a speech at Georgetown University on January 21, 1998, Rubin declared: "The United States has enormously important economic and national security interests at stake in promoting restoration of financial stability in Asia."[50]

More Crises in Latin America

The spate of monetary crises continued soon after President George W. Bush entered the White House. Several South American countries were embroiled in financial turmoil in 2001 and 2002. In 2001 a financial crisis hit Argentina but Lawrence Lindsey, who was Bush's National Economic Adviser, said it was not serious and favored letting markets work out the instability. Lindsey also doubted that the United States or the IMF could do anything about it, arguing that any response would make matters worse. Treasury Secretary Paul O'Neill even blamed Argentina for its dire predicament, arguing that its financial problems could not be rectified by the IMF or the World Bank. O'Neill noted: "Nobody forced them to be what they are."[51] Later O'Neill stated that if Argentina's economy did implode, it would not affect other nations, even though leaders in Buenos Aires threatened to default on Argentina's foreign loans.[52]

Instead of advising its leadership to abandon the outmoded currency arrangement that U.S.-educated economists had implemented, the Bush administration demanded that Argentina slash spending in order to receive aid. Argentina complied, but significant job losses resulted, leading to riots and massive protests. Moreover, by December 2001 the financial crisis had spread to Uruguay and Brazil. But now the Bush administration shifted course and announced a temporary loan of $1.5 billion from the Treasury Department's ESF to Uruguay. Two problems remained, however. First, since Bush's new policy was so late, it appeared the Argentine crisis already had spread. Second, Bush put O'Neill in charge of enforcing the new policy, despite his previous harsh rhetoric about the problem.[53]

TRADE LIBERALIZATION

A defining feature of the postwar international economic system has been the sustained growth of global trade. In 1990 the total value of international trade was less than 40% of global GDP. Even though the world economy grew 50% between 1990 and 2004, trade exceeded 55% of global GDP by 2004. Trading in goods, which increased an average 7% per year during that period, now represents 81% of total trade transactions. The value of global trade in services also nearly tripled over that period, with its share of GDP rising from less than 8% to roughly 10%.[54]

While the impact of economic globalization on the United States has been transformative, unknown economic perils may lie in the huge global trade imbalances and the financial pressures they create. The basic dilemma is that the world needs American trade deficits as an engine of economic growth in order to sustain the European and Asian economies. But trade deficits could eventually destabilize the American economy because Americans' insatiable demand for cheap foreign goods and services sends large amounts of dollars abroad. In 2004 the U.S. trade deficit reached $650 billion or 5.6% of GDP, the highest ever. In the same year, Japan's trade surplus was 3.7% of GDP, Germany's was 2.9%, and China's was 2.3%. In 2006 America's trade deficit approached $768 billion or 6.4% of GDP.[55]

In order to promote economic stability and prosperity at home, the hope is that economic growth will occur not only in the United States but also in our trading partners. Fundamental changes in the structure of the global economy, however, have made the conduct of U.S. trade policy much more difficult. As of 2005, for example, the economic output of the European

Union surpassed the United States. The European Union is now the largest global trading bloc and the euro has become a key currency alongside the U.S. dollar. The so-called emerging market economies in China, India, and East Asia have forced American workers to improve their technological skills and U.S. corporations to become more flexible in their business approach.[56] China has become a regional economic superpower, while South Korea, Singapore, Malaysia, Thailand, and Indonesia have created an economic bloc that comprises roughly 20% of the global economy.[57]

Reducing Trade Barriers

If presidents are able to integrate the domestic economy with international economics, they will be able to magnify the benefits from economic globalization.[58] Since World War II, U.S. foreign economic policy has been devoted to eliminating artificial barriers to trade—tariffs, quotas, and subsidies—that countries use to protect their domestic industries from foreign competition.

America's first free-trade agreement, with Israel, went into effect in 1985. The second was with Canada in 1989.[59] In 1993 the **North American Free Trade Agreement (NAFTA)** was signed to create a free trade zone between the United States, Canada, and Mexico. Between 1994 and 2003 bilateral trade between the United States and Mexico roughly tripled, from $81 billion to $232 billion.[60] As a result, the U.S. economy created millions of new jobs, and the unemployment rate was lower than it was the year before NAFTA took effect. Roughly four hundred thousand Americans have qualified for trade adjustment assistance under a special program for workers displaced by imports from Mexico, not a huge number over a period of ten years when compared to the millions of jobs that have been created. America's manufacturing output rose 41% over the past ten years, compared to 34% in the preceding ten years. By allowing some manufacturers to reallocate their production facilities from the United States to Mexico, one NAFTA effect was to aid U.S. worker productivity since the mid-1990s.[61]

However, there have been some significant negative impacts associated with NAFTA as well, according to the Congressional Budget Office, which analyzed NAFTA impacts from 1993 to 2002.[62] NAFTA had a comparatively small yet expansive impact on U.S.-Mexican trade. Exports to Mexico ranged from a low of 2.2% in 1994 to a high of 11.3% in 2001, while U.S. imports from Mexico ranged from a low of 1.9% in 1994 to a high 7.7% in 2001.[63] Beginning in 1995, the United States watched its annual trade surplus with Mexico become a staggering trade deficit. In 1994 the U.S. trade surplus with Mexico was $1.4 billion, but one year later the rapid rise in Mexican imports created a $15.8 billion deficit.[64] The United States had average yearly trade deficits of $27.5 billion between 1995 and 2006.[65]

Moreover, NAFTA increased America's GDP only marginally. In 1994 the U.S. GDP increased by 0.003%; in 2001, GDP increased by 0.03%.[66] The deteriorating U.S. trade deficit with Mexico and the paltry impact of NAFTA on U.S. GDP has been attributable to the 1995 crash of the peso, the prolonged U.S. economic boom of the mid to late 1990s, and the Mexican recession in late 2000 and 2001.[67] Mexico has benefited more from NAFTA than the United States largely because Mexico's economy is smaller than the American economy. The NAFTA-induced increase in exports from the United States during 1993–2002 equaled roughly 2% of Mexican GDP, while the NAFTA-induced increase in imports from Mexico equaled 1.7% of Mexican GDP by 2002.[68]

Following NAFTA, the number of free trade agreements negotiated by the United States markedly increased. In 2001 an agreement was signed with Jordan and subsequent agreements were negotiated with Singapore and Chile. One year later the Bush administration negotiated free-trade agreements with Australia as well as the Southern African Customs Union, which includes Botswana, Lesotho, Namibia, South Africa, and Swaziland. President George W. Bush also announced an Enterprise for ASEAN Initiative, the goal being to negotiate numerous bilateral free trade agreements with other members of the Association of Southeast Asian Nations (ASEAN) patterned after the agreement with Singapore. In addition, the United States in late 2003 established free trade agreements with Morocco and Bahrain, the eventual goal to establish a Middle East Free Trade Area.[69] In 2005 the Congress narrowly approved the **Central American Free Trade Agreement (CAFTA)**, which included the United States, Costa Rica, El Salvador, Guatemala, Honduras, and Nicaragua. Also in 2005 the United States completed negotiations for a **Free Trade Area of the Americas (FTAA)**, which includes the United States and thirty-four countries in the Western Hemisphere. President Bush intends to complete negotiations with the Philippines, Thailand, Indonesia, and Malaysia by the end of his term.

One nation that has frustrated U.S. trade policy is Japan. Beginning in the mid-1980s the Reagan administration and Congress sought to address America's tremendous trade deficit with Japan. From 1984 to 1986, while U.S. exports to Japan rose by roughly $3 billion, U.S. imports of Japanese goods and services grew by $20 billion. Many observers argued that Japan was unfairly discriminating against U.S. products in its markets, particularly through the use of government-sponsored trade barriers and collusion between major Japanese firms and the Japanese government. In April 1987 President Reagan imposed a 100% tariff on certain Japanese-made computers, televisions, and power tools. However, these items accounted for only $300 million of the export trade in Japanese electronics products (which totaled $23 billion in 1986).[70] Later that month the House of Representatives narrowly passed (218–214) a measure calling for retaliatory actions against Japan's unfair trading practices. Partly to prevent this trade problem from becoming a political issue, the first Bush administration began Structural Impediments Initiative (SII) talks with Japan in 1989 to remove trade barriers. However, the SII yielded only an agreement to continue the talks for a fourth year even as the U.S. trade deficit continued to rise between 1990 and 1992.[71]

The Clinton administration promised to "get tough" with Japan. Leading the charge were U.S. Trade Representative (USTR) Mickey Kantor, Deputy USTR Charlene Barshefsky, and CEA chairwoman Laura D'Andrea Tyson. They urged President Clinton to adopt a "results-oriented" trade policy, to include import quotas and sanctions against Japanese goods and businesses operating in the United States. As Deputy USTR Charlene Barshefsky argued: "The political climate between the United States and Japan will be determined by economics. If the economics aren't right, the political climate isn't going to be right. To the extent that the Japanese are concerned about the political climate, they have it in their power, to ensure that the political climate is positive."[72] To back up her tough talk, Tyson sought congressional approval for the Fair Trade in Financial Services Act of 1993, which would slap sanctions on foreign governments that discriminate against private lending institutions.

The World Trade Organization

President Truman desired to lower bilateral and multilateral trade tariffs and quotas and thereby build upon the provisions of the landmark **Reciprocal Trade Agreements Act of 1934 (RTAA)**. Passed to remedy the extraordinarily high trade protections that were enacted by the Smoot-Hawley Tariff Act of 1930 (which analysts thought had worsened the Great Depression), the RTAA allowed the president to reduce bilateral import barriers by up to 50% but only if trade reductions were reciprocal. While the RTAA did not unilaterally eliminate U.S. trade barriers, it was a modest first step by President Truman to promote the multilateral principles of the **General Agreement on Tariffs and Trade (GATT)**.[73] First commenced in 1947, the GATT was not a formal organization but a series of multilateral negotiating sessions (that became known as "rounds") among sovereign governments. But since the GATT lacked any authority to enforce its rules or to settle disputes among nation-states, the Truman administration proposed the creation of an International Trade Organization (ITO) in 1947. But the ITO was withdrawn from legislative consideration after trade protectionists in the Senate threatened to reject it on the grounds that the ITO could overturn U.S. trade laws.

Decades later the persistent international calls for a global organization authorized to rule on trade disputes got results. The 1993 Uruguay round

member
member: European Communities
observer: ongoing accessions
observer
non-member: negotiations pending
non-member

Formal W.T.O. Structure

1. **Ministerial Conference**: Brings together all members of the WTO, including foreign minister and customs unions. The Ministerial Conference can make decisions on all matters under any of the multilateral trade agreements.
2. **General Conference**: The daily work of the ministerial conference is handled by three groups the General Council, the Dispute Settlement Body, and the Trade Policy Review Body.
3. **Trade Councils**: The Councils for Trade work under the General Council. There are three councils - Council for Trade in Goods, Council for Trade-Related Aspects of Intellectual Property Rights, and Council for Trade in Services - each council works in different fields. Apart from these three councils, six other bodies report to the General Council reporting on issues such as trade and development, the environment, regional trading arrangements and administrative issues.
4. **Subsidiary Bodies**: Goods Council (agriculture, market access, subsidies, and anti-dumping measures); Services Council (financial services and domestic regulations); and Dispute Settlement panels and Appellate Body.
5. **Committees**: Trade and Environment; Trade and Development; Regional Trade Agreements; Balance of Payments Restrictions; and Budget, Finance and Administration.

Figure 7.2. The World Trade Organization. *Source:* http://www.wto.org/english/thewto_e/whatis_e/whatis_e.htm.

of the GATT created the organizational foundations of the **World Trade Organization (WTO)**. Located in Geneva, Switzerland, the WTO is an international organization that formulates and implements standards for the global trading system and resolves disputes among its 149 member states. The U.S. Senate approved U.S. membership in the WTO on January 1, 1995. Arguably its most important function is to oversee thirty multilateral legal agreements that deal with global trade on agriculture, intellectual property, antidumping, textiles and clothing, customs valuation, pre-shipment inspections, manufacturing, medical equipment, and electronic goods.

The increasingly large membership of the WTO means that more countries must reach agreements in each subsequent round of negotiations. Most new members are developing countries whose economic interests are different from the United States and other advanced economies, which had dominated the earlier rounds. One might expect that the first agreements (in early negotiating rounds) were easier since countries likely chose to eliminate their least politically sensitive trade barriers, thus leaving the more difficult issues for later rounds.

One of the most significant trade developments during the 1990s was the Clinton administration's ability to secure China's membership in the WTO.[74] Clinton delegated to his new national economic adviser, Gene Sperling, the responsibility for developing a plan to gain admission for China in the WTO. Sperling worked in close association with White House chief of staff John Podesta, who was responsible for making sure the China initiative did not appear too soft for Congress or too tough for American business groups. Other major players were Treasury Secretary Robert Rubin, USTR Charlene Barshefsky, Commerce Secretary William Daley, National Security Advisor Sandy Berger, and Secretary of State Madeleine Albright. To appease anti-China forces in Congress, Sperling and Podesta persuaded President Clinton to take action against China under the 1974 Trade Act, which empowers the president to slap import quotas on nations engaging in "unfair trading" practices.[75] Since China was not a WTO member at the time, sanctions would not violate global trading rules. The tactic was popular in Congress, where some members had complained that the administration had not adequately responded against China for its piracy of U.S. intellectual property. Sperling and Podesta believed that, once Congress had Beijing's attention, Clinton would support permanent normal trade relations and fashion a larger framework for dealing with China's WTO membership.

But the Clinton administration struggled to mollify both Chinese officials and U.S. business leaders angry over the damage that they believed may have been inflicted on U.S.-Chinese relations. To demonstrate their commitment to WTO membership for China, Sperling and Barshefsky convened a meeting with the business community on April 12. One industry official in attendance observed, "Business people were concerned about this whole deal [China's WTO entry] unraveling."[76] On November 15, after six days of meetings, U.S. and Chinese negotiators agreed on terms for China's entry into the WTO. The agreement lowered agricultural tariffs, eliminated state subsidies on exports, established a special court to review violations of intellectual property rights, and increased competition in the automobile and electronics industries.[77]

President Clinton believed that, by admitting China to the WTO, America's enormous trade deficit would drop. Over 33% of our trade deficit was with China. Tying Beijing's benefits in the global free trade system to WTO rules that lower or eliminate export subsidies and import quotas was seen as the best way to improve the U.S. trade deficit. However, other issues, notably campaign allegations that Chinese leaders sought influence in the 1996 presidential election, increased conflict between China and Taiwan. Also widely alleged human rights abuses in China threatened to undermine U.S.-China economic relations.[78]

In January 2000 Clinton convened a press conference at the White House to announce an "all-out" effort to win support from key interest groups and to persuade Congress to grant China permanent normal trade relations (PNTR). National Economic Adviser Gene Sperling argued that "the congressional vote on PNTR for China is the most important foreign policy and economic issue our country will face this year—and perhaps the most profound foreign policy issue this country will face over a ten-year period."[79] The 1974 Trade Act requires the president to issue a yearly waiver to allow the granting of **normal trade relations (NTR)**. NTR does not necessarily imply unrestricted trade since it applies only to tariffs, and many other highly restrictive nontariff trade barriers or embargos can be employed. Since 1980 China was required to obtain an annual waiver to maintain its NTR status, and between 1989 and 1999 legislation had been introduced in Congress to disapprove the president's waiver. The legislation sought to tie China's NTR renewal to meeting certain human rights conditions that go beyond freedom of emigration. All attempts failed. However, the requirement of an annual waiver was inconsistent with WTO rules, and in order for China to join the WTO, the Congress had to grant China permanent NTR.

Clinton's support for PNTR was also a touchy subject for Democrats. Since his victory on NAFTA in 1993 (due mainly to Republican congressional support), Clinton had been relatively successful in making the Democratic Party more supportive of free trade and, therefore, closer to big business. With the November 2000 elections approaching, environmentalists and labor unions could withhold or delay their support for Democratic candidates, particularly for Vice President Al Gore. To overcome congressional opposition and defeat those constituencies within his party, Clinton assembled a special NEC-coordinated cabinet committee on PNTR for

China.[80] In the end, the House passed permanent NTR with China on May 24, 237–197, and on September 19, the Senate voted 83–15.

However, China's elevation to the WTO and its PNTR status has not reduced the U.S. trade deficit with China.[81] In 2006 the deficit with China increased by 11.9% in June to $19.7 billion as U.S. exports to China fell by 4.3%, while imports of Chinese products into the United States rose by 8.1%.[82] The import gains were led by increases in clothing and computers. In 2006 the Commerce Department revealed that, for the first time in ninety-one years, the United States paid more money to its foreign creditors than what it received from its overseas investments (a $2.5 billion gap). Contrast this with China. In September 2006 China's foreign-exchange reserves topped $1 trillion, due in large part to foreign investment in China and its huge trade surplus. China's reserves have grown so quickly that the country has replaced Japan in first place, with reserves of $880 billion at the end of August 2006.

The second Bush administration sought to expand U.S. foreign economic interests under the banner of "competitive trade liberalization."[83] The slogan meant that the United States was committed to trade negotiations with individual nations, groups of nations, and whole regions on the theory that through the utilization of U.S. markets, such negotiations would fuel a competitive process toward global free trade. However, the same free trade principles that drove U.S. foreign economic policy have given way to important strategic political calculations, namely having to appeal to steelworkers and steel companies in politically important states like West Virginia, Ohio, and Pennsylvania. American steel companies based in those key states complained that high import fees and tariffs levied on U.S. steel by the European Union have undercut domestic production. In an attempt to win these important states in 2000, then-candidate Bush promised to retaliate and, once in office, it was difficult for him to distance himself from his campaign promises. In response to a report from the International Trade Commission that U.S. steel companies, in fact, had been injured by European tariffs, Bush imposed three years of quotas ranging from 8% to 30% on a variety of imported steel.[84]

The U.S. trade policy based on free trade principles under the WTO framework has not been without opposition. In 1999 protesters demonstrated on the streets of Seattle to disrupt WTO meetings. Rowdy protests also occurred at other multilateral trade proceedings, like meetings of the Group of Eight (G-8) countries in Ottawa and Genoa, meetings convened by the Asia-Pacific Economic Cooperation (APEC), and meetings to expand the Free Trade Agreement of the Americas (FTAA) in Washington, D.C. Some of the most significant opposition occurred in 2005 when protesters descended on Mar Del Plata, Argentina, to oppose President Bush and to disrupt FTAA meetings.

Other Mechanisms of Trade Liberalization

Created to advance the process of institutionalizing trade liberalization and economic globalization is the multilateral **Group of Eight (G-8)**. The G-8 is not a formal organization but a series of meetings and negotiations among the world's largest and wealthiest economies, namely the United States, United Kingdom, France, Germany, Italy, Canada, Japan, and Russia (an honorary member). The G-8 began in the late 1970s as the G-7 (excluding the USSR) at a secret meeting in New York City and quickly developed into a high-profile, twice a year meeting of heads of state and foreign ministers. While G-8 meetings mainly provide photo opportunities for the leaders of the most powerful economies, the forum attempts to formulate and implement global economic policy on a range of topics.

In our global economy the United States must contend with regionally based economic institutions that hold considerable influence. The most powerful is the **European Union (EU)**, which evolved from the 1957 Treaty of Rome and the original six-member European Common Market—France, Italy, West Germany, Belgium, Netherlands, and Luxembourg. Today, the EU includes twenty-five member states united into one economic and monetary union based on its common currency, the euro.[85] Further evolution into a political union was temporarily abandoned in 2005 after popular elections in Denmark and France rejected a charter that would merge national political systems.

Another regional economic organization is the **Free Trade Agreement of the Americas (FTAA)**. The FTAA is a proposed agreement designed to reduce trade barriers among thirty-four countries in North, Central, and South America (except for Cuba and Bolivia).[86] Put simply, the FTAA is an extension of NAFTA. The goal of the FTAA is to achieve substantial progress toward accelerated reductions in tariffs by creating a free trade zone for all member states in the Western hemisphere. FTAA negotiations began in Miami in December 1994, but more high-profile talks were held during the Quebec City Summit of the Americas in 2001, which resulted in massive antiglobalization protests. Another summit held in January 2006 at Mar Del Plata in Argentina also was racked by protests. Unlike the European Union, the FTAA is much less formalized and structured.

Another regional entity is the **Asia-Pacific Economic Cooperation (APEC)**, which was established in 1989 to enhance economic growth and prosperity for Pacific economies. Since its inception, APEC states have sought to reduce tariffs across the Asia-Pacific region, creating efficient domestic economies and dramatically increasing exports. APEC has twenty-one member states including the United States that account for about 40% of the world population, approximately 56% of world GDP, and 50% of world trade.[87] Key to achieving APEC's free trade objectives are the "Bogor

Goals," which promises free and open trade and investment in the Asia-Pacific for all member states by 2020. APEC is the only intergovernmental grouping that operates on the basis of nonbinding commitments and open dialogue among its participants. Unlike the WTO or other multilateral trade bodies, APEC imposes no treaty obligations on its participants, and decisions are reached by consensus and commitments are undertaken on a voluntary basis.

ECONOMIC STATECRAFT:
FOREIGN ASSISTANCE AND ECONOMIC SANCTIONS

Foreign Assistance

Foreign assistance programs are important levers in American foreign economic statecraft. They include all funds that would be classified as official development assistance, such as military aid, political development programs, export promotion, debt forgiveness, and lending by bilateral and multilateral organizations. The dispensation of U.S. foreign assistance is managed by the **U.S. Agency for International Development (USAID)**, which was created with the passage of the Foreign Assistance Act of 1961 (FAA). Aid programs under the supervision of USAID have different purposes. Assistance designed to foster economic reforms or improve production methods is likely to have a greater impact on development than military assistance. However, military aid may enable a country to devote a greater percentage of its own resources to developmental programs, since military assistance enables a country to build stronger armed forces than would have been otherwise possible.[88]

To understand the role of foreign aid, one must understand the various objectives of supplying bilateral and multilateral assistance. Bilateral assistance, in which USAID provides foreign assistance directly from the United States to a recipient nation, is largely driven by the strategic foreign policy goals of the United States, not those of the countries that have the greatest need. The multibillion dollar Marshall Plan was very effective in not only rebuilding Europe after World War II but also in promoting America's strategic objective of containing the spread of Communism in Western Europe.

Multilateral assistance sends U.S. funds along with the funds of other donor nations to an international organization like the United Nations or the World Bank, which in turn allocates the aid to needy nations. The United States also contributes funding to various multilateral institutions that provide economic assistance to developing countries. The most prominent are the World Bank, the IMF, and some UN agencies, such as the

United Nations Children's Fund and the United Nations Development Programme. Currently, the United States allocates roughly $1.3 billion to multilateral assistance.[89] Such assistance has helped eradicate polio, reduced the incidence of small pox, increased life expectancy, and reduced fertility rates around the world. The United States often is called upon to assume a leadership role in amassing multilateral assistance, especially in the aftermath of humanitarian disasters. Recent aid programs have been targeted to the 2004 Indian Ocean tsunami, Operation Provide Comfort in Iraq in 1991, and food programs in East Africa.[90] While foreign aid can do little to prevent natural disasters and refugee crises, it can lessen the severity of humanitarian tragedies. Promoting economic development and human welfare, however, generally have been secondary objectives of U.S. foreign aid.

With the onset of the Cold War in the late 1940s, a critical priority of Washington was to rebuild the war-torn economies of Western Europe. With the **Marshall Plan**, named after Secretary of State George Marshall, the United States provided billions of dollars in aid to Western European countries. The Marshall Plan supplied them with food, clothing, and medicine in order to prevent starvation and disease. The Marshall Plan helped to rebuild their economies, thereby restoring and ultimately elevating their standard of living.[91] Politically, the program was intended to reduce or eliminate the wretched economic and social conditions that some U.S. policy makers believed might cause Western Europeans to turn to Communism for a solution.[92] The Italian and French Communist parties, in particular, were quite strong in the late 1940s. Restoring the prosperity of Western European countries also would make them better able to contribute to their own military defense against what appeared to be an increasingly menacing Soviet Union. Driven by the Truman Doctrine to contain the spread of the Soviet Union and Communism, the Marshall Plan, coupled with the military and economic aid programs to Greece and Turkey, constituted the bulk of U.S. bilateral aid between 1946 and 1952. Europe received 82% of U.S. bilateral assistance, or $267 billion during that period.[93]

In the 1950s the United States also inaugurated development and food assistance programs for developing countries. The original political and functional objective of those programs, as outlined by President Truman in the Point IV program of 1949, was to give other countries access to the skills and expertise that produce economic affluence. That approach differed from the Marshall Plan insofar as Western Europe only needed help to reconstruct a fully developed industrial economy; the technical skill and high levels of human capital already existed there. Those conditions, however, were not likely to be found in the third world countries receiving aid under Point IV.[94]

President Kennedy equated developmental assistance with security assistance, and he believed that threats to the United States were fueled by social injustice and economic chaos. Therefore, Kennedy signed the Foreign Assistance Act of 1961, which set up the Agency for International Development. The mission of that agency was to supervise and administer the U.S. developmental assistance program. The legislation ensured that most of that assistance would go to countries that were politically important to the United States.

After the Marshall Plan, the focus of foreign assistance programs shifted from Europe to Asia, namely South Korea, Taiwan, and Vietnam. Between 1953 and 1975, Southeast and East Asia received about 50% of all U.S. bilateral foreign assistance.[95] Such assistance was driven by America's Cold War political commitment. The objective was to help those recipient countries build stronger military forces in order to fight Soviet-backed forces or to prevent the spread of Communism. Following the collapse of the U.S.-backed government in South Vietnam in 1975, U.S. foreign assistance programs shifted away from Southeast and East Asia and toward the Middle East and Central Asia. With President Jimmy Carter's sponsorship of the 1979 Camp David Accords that established peace between Israel and Egypt, the United States began sending large amounts of bilateral military funds and economic assistance to those two countries. Other, newer recipients of U.S. aid in the Middle East included Iraq, Jordan, Tunisia, and Morocco as well as resistance groups in Afghanistan, Iran, and Pakistan. Since 1979 the Middle East has received about half of U.S. bilateral assistance.[96]

With the exception of the early 1960s and the mid-1980s, Latin America has not been the recipient of much bilateral assistance. Latin America never received more than 25% of the aid budget. President Kennedy's **Alliance for Progress** briefly boosted aid to the region, and the Reagan administration's effort to thwart the spread of Communism in Central America benefited El Salvador, Honduras, Costa Rica, and the Contra (anti-Marxist) rebels in Nicaragua.[97] Since 1979 Latin American countries received approximately 13% of U.S. assistance. Africa has historically received the least amount of U.S. assistance—at 10%.

With the breakup of the Soviet Union, new assistance programs have been created to help countries formerly under Soviet domination in their transition to free-market economies. Aid to Eastern European countries is funded through the Support for East European Democracy Act and the Freedom Support Act. A separate project funded through the Department of Defense, the Cooperative Threat Reduction program, provides funds and technical expertise to assist the states of the former Soviet Union in dismantling nuclear weapons.[98]

The end of the Cold War brought other changes in U.S. foreign aid. Egypt and Israel remain the largest recipients of U.S. bilateral assistance. However, other countries that had received hundreds of millions of dollars in U.S. assistance, mainly because they were allies during the Cold War (including

Pakistan and some Central American states), have found their funding cut. In 1997 the United States allocated about $2.5 billion for bilateral development assistance to agricultural, health, business, education, family planning, environmental, and economic reform projects. Roughly $600 million is spent on humanitarian assistance programs, mostly emergency food programs in developing countries suffering from war, natural disasters, or drought.[99]

In 2001 in the first major address concerning foreign assistance since the Kennedy administration, President George W. Bush announced his support for a "Millennium Challenge Account." Bush announced that the United States would increase its core development assistance by 50% over the next three years, resulting in a $5 billion annual increase over current levels.[100] These additional funds will go to a new Millennium Challenge fund to help developing nations improve their economies and standards of living.[101] The most significant component is the allocation of $15 billion in AIDS prevention programs to sub-Saharan Africa.[102]

While U.S. budgetary allocations for all forms of foreign assistance have fluctuated from year to year, it has steadily declined since the 1960s. Foreign assistance peaked during 1947, but by 2006 spending on both bilateral and multilateral foreign aid programs fell to roughly around $12 billion out of a $2.66 trillion federal budget. As a percentage of spending, foreign assistance is currently 0.5% of the budget, which is the lowest level since World War II.[103] The amount of spending on foreign assistance pales in comparison to interest on the national debt (8%), defense spending (21%), and Social Security, Medicare, and Medicaid (42%).[104] Although overall federal spending has increased by roughly an annual average of 19.5% between 1986 and 2006, spending on foreign assistance has fallen by 40% during this same period.[105]

Economic Sanctions

Economic sanctions are economic policies employed to limit business activity across borders. While sanctions are issued for an array of reasons, many are issued due to a desire to promote democratic and free market principles.[106] Some presidents have issued sanctions in retaliation against certain bad behaviors, such as state-sponsored terrorism, pursuing weapons of mass destruction programs, ethnic violence, human rights violations, and anti-U.S. business policies. By understanding the nexus between America's strategic foreign policy interests and the domestic political environment, one can understand the rationale for economic sanctions.[107]

Specifically, bilateral sanctions are strategic tools used to influence other governments and/or firms and citizens in other nations. Bilateral sanctions are issued either by the president unilaterally in the form of an executive agreement or as a law passed by Congress and signed by the president. These sanctions are designed to restrict commercial relations between American citizens and companies and the citizens and companies in a targeted country. Multilateral sanctions occur when the United States issues sanctions in cooperation with other countries or through a global organization such as the United Nations.[108] Bilateral and multilateral sanctions can include a trade embargo that prohibits the importing and exporting of all goods and services, limits trade prohibitions on certain goods or services, restricts investment, limits travel, and limits the transfer of nonfinancial assets, especially those involving military and technology transfers.[109]

Sanctions are classified according to their specific political objectives. One study differentiates among four different, though not mutually exclusive sanctions: purposeful, palliative, punitive, and partisan.[110] **Purposeful sanctions** are intended to inflict economic hardship and coerce the target country into changing its policies. **Palliative sanctions** are imposed to publicly register displeasure with the actions or policies of the target country. **Punitive sanctions** are intended to inflict harm on the target country without any expectation that the target nation will change its policies. **Partisan sanctions** are designed to promote commercial interests in order to aid or harm specific groups within the target country.

In recent years China, Cuba, Iran, and Iraq have been among the most frequent targets of U.S. sanctions. Beginning in the early 1950s, the United States imposed purposeful and punitive sanctions against China in order to prevent the spread of Communism in the region.[111] However, in 1971 the United States lifted most of its trade sanctions, signaling a willingness to resume a "normalization" of political relations with China under President Nixon's "Open Door Policy." It paved the way for the Carter administration's formal recognition of the Chinese Communist government in 1978. However, partisan sanctions remained on U.S. exports to China of high technology and commercial goods with military applications. The George H. W. Bush administration imposed an entire range of punitive sanctions against China in response to the Tiananmen Square massacre of prodemocracy demonstrators. It also issued palliative sanctions in retaliation for China's repression of Christian minority groups and other smaller religious denominations. It was not until the Clinton administration's push for approval of China's membership to the WTO and the granting of permanent normal trade status that most of the remaining sanctions on Chinese commercial activities were removed.[112]

In the case of Cuba, an almost total economic embargo has been in place since the Cuban Revolution of 1959. Until the collapse of the Soviet Union, which was the economic and political patron of Cuban leader Fidel Castro, U.S. sanctions were purposeful and palliative. Since 1990, U.S. policy toward Cuba has been somewhat relaxed, with sanctions now intended to bring about a democratically elected government and to improve Cuba's human rights practices. Both the Clinton and the second Bush administrations have allowed limited travel between Miami and Havana as well as restricted financial transactions between families. Although purposeful and palliative rationales remain, partisan sanctions have always been in place, since every president since Eisenhower has encouraged Cuban exiles, most of whom reside in south Florida, to resist Castro.[113]

The United States also imposed purposeful and palliative sanctions against Iran in response to the taking of American hostages during the Iranian Revolution in 1979. Those sanctions were largely purposeful and palliative until 1995, because they contained a loophole that permitted the United States to continue importing Iranian crude oil. This loophole was closed by Congress in 1995 and punitive sanctions against Iran were imposed by the Clinton administration, based on the Iran-Libya Sanctions Act, in retaliation against Iran's sponsorship of terrorist groups, namely Hezbollah in Lebanon.[114] Beginning in 2003 the George W. Bush administration sought multilateral sanctions at the UN Security Council against Iran for its alleged uranium enrichment programs.[115]

The story of the nearly thirteen years of unilateral and multilateral sanctions against Iraq is well known. On August 6, 1990, four days after Iraq's invasion of Kuwait, the UN Security Council passed Resolution 661, imposing comprehensive sanctions on Iraq that sought to stop trade with Iraq and shut down its oil exports.[116] Those sanctions devastated Iraq's economy and helped spur a prolonged humanitarian crisis that resulted in hundreds of thousands of preventable deaths and led to enhanced Iraqi support for dictator Saddam Hussein. Presidents George H. W. Bush and Bill Clinton viewed those unilateral sanctions as punitive instruments, and both administrations blocked all UN attempts to lift multilateral sanctions. America's position was contradicted by UN Security Council Resolution 687, which stated that sanctions should be lifted once Iraq lived up to UN disarmament obligations.[117]

One of the most controversial elements was the UN oil-for-food program, which was designed to alleviate civilian suffering. UN resolutions 706, 712, and 986 allowed Iraq to sell $1.6 billion of oil every six months and devote the profits to purchasing food and medicine for civilian use.[118] In May 1996 the United Nations expanded the oil-for-food program by agreeing to permit the sale of an additional $1 billion in oil revenue over a renewable ninety-day period to pay for food and medicine, war reparations, UN peacekeeping operations, and maintenance of oil pipelines.[119] The problem was that the oil-for-food program never effectively addressed hunger, disease, or malnutrition, and child mortality dramatically increased.[120] Moreover, corruption greatly undermined the oil-for-food program as Saddam Hussein evaded sanctions and mounted elaborate smuggling and kickback schemes to siphon cash from the program.[121]

Still, the sanctions worked since only a fraction of oil profits from the oil-for-food program reached the Iraqi government. The funds that Saddam illegally obtained were grossly insufficient to finance large-scale military development programs or weapons of mass destruction programs. U.S. government statistics show a drop in Iraqi military spending and arms imports after 1990. Iraqi defense expenditures plummeted from over $15 billion in 1989 to less than $1.4 billion a year through the 1990s.[122] The cumulative decline in arms imports from 1991 to 1998 was more than $47 billion, a deficit that Iraq's illicit schemes could not address. As a result, almost no money was available for the development of nuclear, chemical, or biological weapons systems, however much Saddam might have wished to rebuild his arsenal.[123]

KEY TERMS

Alliance for Progress
Asia-Pacific Economic Cooperation (APEC)
Bretton Woods System
Central American Free Trade Agreement (CAFTA)
current account balance
economic globalization
European Union (EU)
"fixed" exchange rates
Free Trade Agreement of the Americas (FTAA)
General Agreement on Tariffs and Trade (GATT)
globalism
Group of Eight (G-8)
International Bank for Reconstruction and Development (IBRD)
International Monetary Fund (IMF)
Marshall Plan
New Economic Policy
normal trade relations (NTR)
North American Free Trade Agreement (NAFTA)
offshoring
Organization of Petroleum Exporting Countries (OPEC)
outsourcing
palliative sanctions
partisan sanctions
punitive sanctions
purposeful sanctions

Reciprocal Trade Agreements Act of 1934 (RTAA)
U.S. Agency for International Development (USAID)
World Bank
World Trade Organization (WTO)

ADDITIONAL READINGS

Bergsten, C. Fred *The United States and the World Economy*. Washington, DC: Institute of International Economics, 2005. Thirteen contributors discuss global integration and such topics as the emergence of China in the global economy and the U.S. relationship to emerging-market economies.

England, Christopher M. *Outsourcing the American Dream: Pain and Pleasure in the Era of Downsizing*. New York: Writer's Club Press, 2001. Explores the consequences of corporate mismanagement and downsizing; offers innovative solutions for leaders in business and government; and candidly discusses the individual's own responsibility for job security and career satisfaction.

Friedman, Thomas L. *The World Is Flat: A Brief History of the Twenty-First Century*. New York: Farrar, Straus and Giroux, 2006. The lightning-swift advances in technology and communications have brought together people from all over the globe as never before and created an explosion of wealth in India and China.

Gilpin, Robert. *The Challenge of Global Capitalism: The World Economy in the 21st Century*. Princeton, NJ: Princeton University Press, 2001. Focuses on globalization and technological change since the end of the Cold War in an overview of broad economic developments.

Gowa, Joanne. *Closing the Gold Window*. Ithaca: Cornell University Press, 1983. Case study of Nixon's decision to stop converting U.S. dollars into gold, thus ending the international monetary system based on the Bretton Woods Agreement.

Kennedy, Paul. *The Rise and Fall of the Great Powers: Economic Change and Military Conflict from 1500 to 2000*. New York: Random House, 1987. Popularized the thesis that the United States is now in a period of decline.

Mayer, Martin. *The Fate of the Dollar*. New York: Times Books, 1980. Journalistic account of international monetary policy from Eisenhower through Carter.

Mishkin, Frederic S. *The Next Great Globalization: How Disadvantaged Nations Can Harness Their Financial Systems to Get Rich*. Princeton, NJ: Princeton University Press, 2006. Argues that financial globalization is essential in order for poor nations to become rich.

Nye, Joseph S. Jr. *Bound to Lead: The Changing Nature of American Power*. New York: Basic, 1990. Takes issue with the Paul Kennedy "decline" thesis by arguing that in the post–Cold War, the United States can direct more resources into the economy.

Solomon, Robert. *The International Monetary System, 1945–1981*. New York: Harper & Row, 1982. An insider account of the Bretton Woods System and international monetary relations between the United States and European nations.

NOTES

1. Heather Walsh, "Bachelet Resists Calls to Spend Chile's Copper Profits on Poor," Bloomberg.com (June 28, 2006), http://www.bloomberg.com/apps/news?pid=20601103&sid=aX9ELYngdg68&refer=news.

2. Edmund L. Andrews, "Global Trends May Hinder Effort to Curb Inflation," *New York Times*, August 28, 2006.

3. Nell Henderson, "Fed Chief Backs Global Wealth Sharing," *Washington Post*, August 26, 2006.

4. Thomas L. Friedman, *The World Is Flat: A Brief History of the Twenty-first Century* (New York: Farrar, Straus and Giroux, 2006), 50–200.

5. Jessica Matthews, "Power Shift," *Foreign Affairs* (January–February 1997): 50.

6. Robert O. Keohane and Joseph S. Nye, *Power and Interdependence*, 3rd ed. (Boston: Harper, 2001); C. Fred Bergsten, *The United States and the World Economy* (Washington, DC: Institute of International Economics, 2005); and Joseph Stiglitz, *Globalization and Its Discontents* (New York and London: Norton, 2002).

7. C. Fred Bergsten, "Foreign Economic Policy for the Next President," *Foreign Affairs* 83 (March–April 2004): 88–101 and Richard Rose, *The Post-modern President* (Washington, DC: CQ Press, 1991).

8. Walter LaFeber, *The American Age: U.S. Foreign Policy at Home and Abroad* (New York: Norton, 1989); Robert Gilpin, *The Political Economy of International Relations* (Princeton: Princeton University Press, 1987); and Joanne Gowa, *Allies, Adversaries, and International Trade* (Princeton: Princeton University Press, 1994).

9. Alfred E. Eckes, *Opening America's Market: U.S. Foreign Trade since 1776* (Chapel Hill: University of North Carolina Press, 1994).

10. Harold James, *International Monetary Cooperation since Bretton Woods* (New York: Oxford University Press, 1996) and Godfrey Hodgson, *America in Our Time* (New York: Vintage, 1976), 19.

11. The IMF manages the monetary position of member states. Since the 1960s, it has grown into a financial source for developing countries. A state's "balance-of-payments" summarizes the flow of money in and out of the country, including its trade balance, state remittances and transactions, foreign investments, and changes in foreign exchange reserves of gold or hard currency. "Fixed rates of exchange" are established official exchange rates that do not fluctuate with global currency markets.

12. David H. Blake and Robert S. Walters, *The Politics of Global Economic Relations*, 3rd ed. (Englewood Cliffs, NJ: Prentice Hall, 1987).

13. Charles W. Kegley Jr. and Eugene R. Wittkopf. *American Foreign Policy: Pattern and Process* (New York: St. Martin's, 1991), 191.

14. Jonathan Kirshner, *Currency and Coercion: The Political Economy of International Monetary Power* (Princeton: Princeton University Press, 1997); Kathryn Dominguez and Jeffrey Frankel, *Does Foreign Exchange Intervention Work?* (Washington, DC: Institute for International Economics, 1993); and George P. Shultz and Kenneth W. Dam, *Economic Policy beyond the Headlines* (Chicago: University of Chicago Press, 1998).

15. See the Department of Commerce, Bureau of Economic Analysis, *Survey of Current Business* (June 20, 2000).

16. In *Power and Interdependence*, Keohane and Nye discuss the concepts of sensitivity and vulnerability, which they see as dimensions of global interdependence. Degrees of sensitivity refer to how fast changes in one actor bring about changes in another and vulnerability is measured by the costs imposed on an actor by outside events, even if the actor tries to avoid those costs.

17. Bergsten, "Foreign Economic Policy for the Next President," 88–101.

18. Robert J. Samuelson, "Is the Global Economy Unstable?" *Washington Post*, March 16, 2005.

19. Chris J. Dolan and Jerel A. Rosati, "U.S. Foreign Economic Policy and the Significance of the National Economic Council," *International Studies Perspectives* 7, no. 2 (2006): 102–123.

20. World Bank, *Global Economic Prospects 2005: Trade, Regionalism and Development* (Washington DC: World Bank, 2004).

21. Robert Gilpin, *The Challenge of Global Capitalism: The World Economy in the 21st Century* (Princeton, NJ: Princeton University Press, 2001), chap. 2.

22. Gilpin, *The Challenge of Global Capitalism*.

23. This definition of outsourcing was found on the OutsourcingCenter website at http://www.outsourcing-faq.com/1.html.

24. Catherine Mann, *Accelerating the Globalization of America: The Role for Information Technology* (Washington, DC: Institute for International Economics, June 2006).

25. Quoted in Paul Blustein, "Survey Finds Little 'Off-shoring' Impact," *Washington Post*, June 11, 2004, and N. Gregory Mankiw and Phillip Swagel, "The Politics and Economics of Offshore Outsourcing," (November 9, 2005), http://post.economics.harvard.edu/faculty/mankiw/papers/Outsourcing%20-%20Mankiw-Swagel%20for%20C-R%20conference%20Nov%2010%202005.pdf.

26. Lou Dobbs, *Exporting America: Why Corporate Greed Is Shipping American Jobs Overseas* (New York: Warner, 2004); Daniel W. Drezner, "The Outsourcing Bogeyman," *Foreign Affairs* (May–June 2004): 22–35; and Christopher M. England, *Outsourcing the American Dream: Pain and Pleasure in the Era of Downsizing* (New York: Writer's Club Press, 2001).

27. Friedman, *The World Is Flat*, chap. 1.

28. Gary Clyde Hufbauer and Barbara Kotschwar, "The Future Course of Trade Liberalization," (paper for the World Bank, "Challenges for the Twenty-First Century," (Washington, DC: Peter G. Peterson Institute for International Economics, October 1998), http://www.iie.com/publications/papers/paper.cfm?ResearchID=320.

29. World Trade Organization, "World Trade, 2004, Prospects for 2005, Developing Countries' Goods Trade Share Surges to 50-year Peak" (April 15, 2005), http://www.wto.org/English/news_e/pres05_e/pr401_e.htm.

30. UN Conference on Trade and Development, *Trade and Development Report, 1997* (New York: United Nations, 1997).

31. World Trade Organization, "Supachai: Disappointing Trade Figures Underscore Importance of Accelerating Trade Talks," (October 7, 2002), http://www.wto.org/English/news_e/pres02_e/pr316_e.htm.

32. Alan P. Larson, Undersecretary of State for Economic, Business, and Agricultural Affairs, "Oil Diplomacy: Facts and Myths Behind Foreign Oil Dependency,"

House Committee on International Relations, 107th Congress, 2d sess. (June 20, 2002).

33. Scott Wallsten and Katrina Kosec, "The Economic Costs of the War in Iraq," (working paper 05-19, AEI/Brookings Joint Center for Regulatory Studies, September 2005) and Amy Belasco, "The Cost of Iraq, Afghanistan and Enhanced Base Security since 9/11," Congressional Research Service, Report for Congress (October 7, 2005).

34. Brad Foss, "Oil Prices Hold Steady at $72 a Barrel," *Boston Globe*, August 22, 2006, and Energy Informational Administration, "A Primer on Gasoline Prices," (May 1, 2006), http://www.eia.doe.gov/bookshelf/brochures/gasolinepricesprimer/eia1_2005primerM.html.

35. Rowan Scarborough, "Report: Iraq Oil Production Remains below Prewar Level," *Washington Times*, May 2, 2006.

36. Bergsten, "Foreign Economic Policy for the Next President," 97.

37. Bergsten, "Foreign Economic Policy for the Next President," 97.

38. Richard Lacayo, "The Plunger: The Peso Heads South," *Time* (January 9, 1995): 45–48.

39. Tod Robberson, "Mexican Financial Markets, Politicians Cheered by Clinton Initiative," *Washington Post*, February 1, 1995.

40. Tim Zimmerman and Lucy Conger "A Rough Welcome in Mexico," *U.S. News & World Report* (January 8, 1995): 38.

41. Tod Robberson, "Mexican Financial Markets."

42. Clay Chandler, "U.S. Leaders Agree on Help for Mexico," *Washington Post*, January 13, 1995.

43. Ann Devroy and Kevin Merida, "President Makes Final Push for Support of Financial Rescue Package for Mexico," *Washington Post*, January 19, 1995.

44. Chandler, "U.S. Leaders Agree on Help for Mexico."

45. Jorge G. Castaneda, "Mexico: The Price of Denial," *Atlantic Monthly* (July 1995): 21–25 and Susan Dentzer, Linda Robinson, Steven D. Kaye, and Jack Egan, "The Rescue of Mexico," *U.S. News & World Report* (January 23, 1995): 48–49.

46. William H. Cooper, "U.S.–East Asian Economic Ties: Impact of the Asian Financial Crisis," *Congressional Research Service Report* (March 20, 1998): 98–284.

47. Richard P. Cronin, "Asian Financial Crisis: An Analysis of U.S. Foreign Policy Interests and Policy Interests," *Congressional Research Service Report* (April 23, 1998): 98–74.

48. Terry McCarthy, "Indonesia Burning." *Time* (May 25, 1998): 44–45.

49. Alan Greenspan, House Banking and Financial Services Committee, "The Asian Financial Crisis," 105th Cong., 2d sess. (Washington, DC: Federal News Service, January 30, 1998) and Robert E. Rubin, House Banking and Financial Services Committee, "The Asian Financial Crisis," 106th Cong., 2d sess. (Washington, DC: Federal News Service, January 30, 1998).

50. Robert Rubin, "Treasury Secretary Robert E. Rubin Address on the Asian Financial Situation," (Washington, DC: U.S. Department of the Treasury, January 21, 1998).

51. T. Catan, M. Mulligan, and G. Robinson, "Bush Pledges to Work with Argentina's Government?" *Financial Times*, December 11, 2001.

52. Anthony Faiola, "Despair in Once Proud Argentina," *Washington Post*, August 6, 2002.

53. Richard A. Oppel, "Easing Its Stance, U.S. Offers Loans to Uruguay," *New York Times*, August 4, 2002.

54. For a compilation of all the trade data cited in this paragraph, see the World Bank Group, "World Development Indicators," (2006), http://devdata.worldbank.org/wdi2006/contents/Section6_1.htm.

55. For a compilation of all the trade data cited in this paragraph, see the World Bank Group, "World Development Indicators," (2006), http://devdata.worldbank.org/wdi2006/contents/Section6_1.htm.

56. Frederic S. Mishkin, *The Next Great Globalization: How Disadvantaged Nations Can Harness Their Financial Systems to Get Rich* (Princeton, NJ: Princeton University Press, 2006), chap. 1.

57. Dorothy Guerrero, "Regionalisms and Alternative Regionalisms in Asia and the Pacific Basin," (project discussion paper no. 5/2001, January 2001), http://www.wun.ac.uk/cks/teaching/horizons/documents/robertson/Guerrero.pdf.

58. Dolan and Rosati, "U.S. Foreign Economic Policy," 103.

59. Daniel W. Drezner, *U.S. Trade Strategy: Free versus Fair* (Washington, DC: Council on Foreign Relations, 2006).

60. David Armstrong, "Building Bridges: U.S., Mexico Look for Ways to Expand Trade," *San Francisco Chronicle*, June 10, 2003.

61. Daniel T. Griswold, "After 10 Years, NAFTA Continues to Pay Dividends," (Washington, DC: Center for Trade Policy Studies, CATO Institute, January 8, 2004), http://www.cato.org/dailys/01-08-04.html.

62. Congressional Budget Office, *The Effects of NAFTA on U.S.-Mexican Trade and GDP* (May 2003), http://www.cbo.gov/showdoc.cfm?index=4247&sequence=0.

63. Congressional Budget Office, *The Effects of NAFTA on U.S.-Mexican Trade and GDP*.

64. David M. Gould, "Has NAFTA Changed North American Trade?" *Federal Reserve Bank of Dallas Economic Review* (First quarter 1998): 12–23; International Trade Commission, *The Impact of the North American Free-Trade Agreement on the U.S. Economy and Industries: A Three-Year Review*, no. 3045 (July 1997); and International Trade Commission, *Potential Impact on the U.S. Economy and Selected Industries of the North American Free-Trade Agreement*, no. 2596 (January 1993): 2–7.

65. For annual data on the U.S. trade balance with Mexico, see the website of the Foreign Trade Statistics office of the U.S. Census Bureau at http://www.census.gov/foreign-trade/balance/c2010.html and Congressional Research Service, "U.S.-Mexico Economic Relations: Trends, Issues, and Implications," (July 11, 2005), http://www.fas.org/sgp/crs/row/RL32934.pdf#search=%22U.S.-Mexico%20%2B%20trade%20deficit%22.

66. Congressional Research Service, "U.S.-Mexico Economic Relations"; David M. Gould, "Has NAFTA Changed North American Trade?" 12–23; and U.S. International Trade Commission, *The Impact of the North American Free-Trade Agreement on the U.S. Economy and Industries: A Three-Year Review*.

67. Jorge Casteneda, *The Mexican Shock: Its Meaning for the U.S.* (New York: New Press, 1995); Francisco Gil-Diaz and Agustin Carstens, "One Year of Solitude: Some

Pilgrim Tales about Mexico's 1994–1995 Crisis," *American Economic Review* (May 1996): 164–169; International Monetary Fund, "Evolution of the Mexican Crisis," in *International Capital Markets: Developments, Prospects, and Key Policy Issues* (Washington, DC: IMF, 1995), 53–69; Robert Gilpin, *The Challenge of Global Capitalism*, 3–14; and M. Ayhan Kose, Guy M. Meredith, and Christopher M. Towe, "How Has NAFTA Affected the Mexican Economy? Review and Evidence," (working paper WP/04/59, International Monetary Fund, April 2004), http://www.imf.org/external/pubs/ft/wp/2004/wp0459.pdf#search=%22NAFTA%20and%20Mexican%20recession%20%2B%202001%22.

68. Congressional Research Service, "U.S.-Mexico Economic Relations."

69. Office of the U.S. Trade Representative, "U.S. and Bahrain Announce Intention to Seek to Negotiate a Free Trade Agreement: First Step in Implementing President Bush's Vision of a Middle East Free Trade Area," press release, May 21, 2003.

70. Gerald M. Boyd, "President Imposes Tariff on Imports against Japanese," *New York Times*, April 18, 1987.

71. Bruce Stokes, "Losing Steam," *National Journal* (June 27, 1992): 1518–1520.

72. Bruce Stokes, "A Get-Tough U.S. Trade Negotiator," *National Journal* (January 22, 1994): 286.

73. Richard Gardner, *Sterling Dollar Diplomacy in Current Perspective: The Origins and the Prospects of Our International Economic Order* (New York: Columbia University Press, 1987) and G. John Ikenberry, "A World Economy Restored: Expert Consensus and the Anglo-American Postwar Settlement," *International Organization* 46 (Winter 1992): 289–321.

74. Thomas Omstead, "Jiang, Clinton and Abe Lincoln," *U.S. News & World Report* (November 10, 1997): 66–67.

75. Bruce Stokes, "Almost Now-or-Never Time," *National Journal* (December 12, 1998): 2948–2949.

76. Paul Blustein, "U.S. Tries to Placate China on WTO Talks," *Washington Post*, April 13, 1999.

77. Steven Mufson, "In WTO Deal, Hard Part Starts Now," *Washington Post*, November 16, 1999.

78. Carl M. Canon, "What We Did in China," *National Journal* (July 18, 1998): 1668–1675 and Peter Baker, "Clinton, Defends China Approach," *Washington Post*, June 12, 1998.

79. Gene Sperling, "Remarks to the Committee for Economic Development," (Washington, DC: Office of the National Economic Council, May 18, 2000).

80. Charles Babington and Matthew Vita, "President Begins China Trade Push," *Washington Post*, March 9, 2000.

81. K. C. Fung and Lawrence J. Lau, "Adjusted Estimates of the United States–China Trade Balances: 1995–2002," *Journal of Asian Economics* 13, no. 2 (May 2002): 489–496.

82. For annual data on the U.S. trade balance with China, see the website of the Foreign Trade Statistics office of the U.S. Census Bureau at http://www.census.gov/foreign-trade/balance/c5700.html.

83. Bergsten, "Foreign Economic Policy for the Next President," 88–101.

84. Paul Magnusson, "Bush's Steely Pragmatism," *Business Week* (March 18, 2002): 44.

85. Member states of the EU include Belgium, France, Germany, Italy, Netherlands, Luxembourg, Denmark, Ireland, the UK, Greece, Portugal, Spain, Austria, Finland, Sweden, Cyprus, Czech Republic, Estonia, Hungary, Latvia, Lithuania, Malta, Poland, Slovakia, and Slovenia.

86. FTAA members states include Antigua and Barbuda, Argentina, the Bahamas, Barbados, Belize, Bolivia, Brazil, Canada, Chile, Colombia, Costa Rica, Dominica, the Dominican Republic, Ecuador, El Salvador, Grenada, Guatemala, Guyana, Haiti, Honduras, Jamaica, Mexico, Nicaragua, Panama, Paraguay, Peru, Saint Kitts and Nevis, Saint Lucia, Saint Vincent and the Grenadines, Suriname, Trinidad and Tobago, the United States, Uruguay, and Venezuela.

87. APEC's twenty-one member economies are Australia; Brunei Darussalam; Canada; Chile; People's Republic of China; Hong Kong, China; Indonesia; Japan; Republic of Korea; Malaysia; Mexico; New Zealand; Papua New Guinea; Peru; the Republic of the Philippines; the Russian Federation; Singapore; Chinese Taipei; Thailand; the United States; and Vietnam.

88. Carol Graham and Michael O'Hanlon, "Making Foreign Aid Work," *Foreign Affairs* (July–August 1997): 96–104.

89. Kathryn McConnell, "House Passes $21.3 Billion Fiscal 2007 Foreign Aid Spending Bill," (Washington, DC: U.S. Department of State, June 9, 2006), http://usinfo.state.gov/utils/printpage.html.

90. Alynna J. Lyon and Chris J. Dolan, "American Humanitarian Intervention: Toward a Theory of Co-Evolution," *Foreign Policy Analysis* 3 (2007): 46–79.

91. John Lewis Gaddis, *We Now Know: Rethinking Cold War History* (New York: Oxford University Press, 1997); Charles L. Mee, *The Marshall Plan: The Launching of the Pax Americana* (New York: Simon & Schuster, 1984); Alan S. Milward *The Reconstruction of Western Europe, 1945–51* (London: Methuen, 1984); and Martin Schain, *The Marshall Plan: Fifty Years After* (New York: Palgrave, 2001).

92. Vernon W. Ruttan, *United States Development Assistance Policy: The Domestic Politics of Foreign Economic Aid* (Baltimore: Johns Hopkins University Press, 1996), 38–41, 50.

93. Congressional Budget Office, "The Flow of Foreign Aid and Private Capital to Developing Countries," (May 1997), http://www.cbo.gov/showdoc.cfm?index=8&sequence=3.

94. Nicholas Eberstadt, *Foreign Aid and American Purpose* (Washington, DC: American Enterprise Institute, 1988), 25–31.

95. Congressional Budget Office, "The Flow of Foreign Aid and Private Capital to Developing Countries."

96. Congressional Budget Office, "Appendix: U.S. Spending on Foreign Aid," (May 1997), http://www.cbo.gov/showdoc.cfm?index=8&sequence=6.

97. Michael D. Gambone, *Capturing the Revolution: The United States, Central America, and Nicaragua, 1961–1972* (New York: Greenwood, 2001), 21–69 and Michael E. Lathem, *Modernization as Ideology: American Social Science and "Nation Building" in the Kennedy Era* (Chapel Hill: University of North Carolina Press), 2000.

98. Congressional Budget Office, "The Flow of Foreign Aid and Private Capital to Developing Countries."

99. Curt Tarnoff and Larry Nowels, "Foreign Aid: An Introductory Overview of U.S. Programs and Policy," *Congressional Research Service* (January 19, 2005),

http://fpc.state.gov/documents/organization/31987.pdf#search=%22CRS%20%2B
%20Foreign%20Aid%3A%20An%20Introductory%20Overview%20of%22.

100. Paul Blustein, "Bush Seeks Foreign Aid Boost," *Washington Post*, March 15, 2002, and James Dao, "With Rise in Foreign Aid, Plans for a New Way to Give It," *New York Times*, February 3, 2003.

101. Gene B. Sperling and Tom Hart, "A Better Way to Fight Global Poverty: Broadening the Millennium Challenge Account," *Foreign Affairs* 82 (March–April 2003): 9–14 and Lael Brainard, "The Millennium Challenge Account and Foreign Assistance: Transformation or More Confusion?" *The Brookings Review* 21 (Spring 2003): 41–44, http://www.brookings.edu/press/review/spring2003/brainard.htm.

102. Sheryl Gay Stolberg, "$15 Billion AIDS Plan Wins Final Approval in Congress," *New York Times*, May 22, 2003.

103. See the home page of the U.S. Agency for International Development at http://www.usaid.gov; Citizens for Global Solutions, "Analysis of the FY 2007 International Affairs Budget Proposal," (February 9, 2006), http://www.globalsolutions .org/hill/in_the_beltway/2006a/in_the_beltwayFY07.html; and Kathy Kiely, "Importance of Foreign Aid is Hitting Home," *USA Today*, December 2, 2001.

104. U.S. Office of Management and Budget, *Budget of the United States Government*, http://www.whitehouse.gov/omb/budget/fy2007/budget.html and U.S. Council of Economic Advisers, *Economic Report of the President*, http://a257.g .akamaitech.net/7/257/2422/13feb20061330/www.gpoaccess.gov/eop/2006/ 2006_erp.pdf.

105. U.S. Office of Management and Budget (OMB), *Historical Tables: Budget of the United States Government, 2006* (Washington, DC: Government Printing Office, 2005), table 1.1, 21–22 and Citizens for Global Solutions, "Analysis of the FY 2007 International Affairs Budget Proposal."

106. Robin Renwick, *Economic Sanctions* (Cambridge, MA: Center for International Affairs, Harvard University, 1981).

107. Richard N. Haass, *Economic Sanctions and American Diplomacy* (New York: Council on Foreign Relations, 1998).

108. Eileen M. Crumm, "The Value of Economic Incentives in International Politics," *Journal of Conflict Resolution* 32, no. 3 (1995): 313–330 and Margaret P. Doxey, *Economic Sanctions and International Enforcement* (New York: Oxford University Press, 1980).

109. Lisa L. Martin, *Coercive Cooperation: Explaining Multilateral Economic Sanctions* (Princeton: Princeton University Press, 1992).

110. H. G. Askari, J. Forrer, H. Teegen, and J. Yang, *Case Studies of U.S. Economic Sanctions: The Chinese, Cuban and Iranian Experience* (Westport, CT: Praeger, 2003).

111. Shu Guang Zhang, *Economic Cold War: America's Embargo against China and the Sino-Soviet Alliance, 1949–1963* (Palo Alto, CA: Stanford University Press, 2001).

112. Jean A. Garrison, *Making China Policy* (New York: Lynn Rienner, 2005) and James H. Mann, *About Face: A History of America's Curious Relationship with China* (New York: Knopf, 1998).

113. Patrick J. Haney, *The Cuban Embargo: The Domestic Politics of an American Foreign Policy* (Pittsburgh: University of Pittsburgh Press, 2005) and Patrick Schwab, *Cuba: Confronting the U.S. Embargo* (New York: Palgrave-Macmillan, 1998).

114. John Amuzegar, "Iran's Economy and the U.S. Sanctions," *Middle East Journal* 51, no. 2 (1997): 185–199.

115. Sasan Fayazmanesh, "The Politics of the U.S. Economic Sanctions against Iran," *Review of Radical Political Economics* 35, no. 3 (2003): 221–240.

116. See UN Security Council Resolution 661 at http://daccessdds.un.org/doc/RESOLUTION/GEN/NR0/575/11/IMG/NR057511.pdf?OpenElement.

117. See UN Security Council Resolution 687 at http://daccessdds.un.org/doc/RESOLUTION/GEN/NR0/596/23/IMG/NR059623.pdf?OpenElement.

118. See UN Security Council Resolution 706 and Resolution 712 at http://odsddsny.un.org/doc/RESOLUTION/GEN/NR0/596/42/IMG/NR059642.pdf?Open Element and http://ods-ddsny.un.org/doc/RESOLUTION/GEN/NR0/596/48/IMG/NR059648.pdf?OpenElement.

119. Food and Agriculture Organization of the United Nations, *Technical Cooperation Programme: Evaluation of Food and Nutrition Situation in Iraq* (New York: United Nations, September 1996).

120. Food and Agriculture Organization of the United Nations, *Technical Cooperation Programme: Evaluation of Food and Nutrition Situation in Iraq.*

121. George A. Lopez and David Cortright, "Containing Iraq: Sanctions Worked," *Foreign Affairs* (July-August 2004), and Bob Davis and Hugh Hope, "Once an Economic Dynamo, Iraq Is Now Financial Riddle," *Wall Street Journal*, April 9, 2003.

122. Lopez and Cortright, "Containing Iraq," 12.

123. Anthony H. Cordesman, "If We Fight Iraq: Iraq and the Military Balance," (Washington, DC: Center for Strategic and International Studies, June 28, 2002), http://www.csis.org/burke/mb/fightiraq_mb.pdf.

8

The Presidential
Economic Scorecard

During his campaign for the presidency in 1980, Ronald Reagan famously asked the electorate, "Are you better off today than you were four years ago?" The voter's response was "no," and challenger Reagan defeated President Carter. The same question might have been posed four years later, when President Reagan sought a second term. With inflation running at only half the double-digit rates recorded during 1979–1980, the obvious answer for most people was "yes," and President Reagan was reelected.

Improvements in the 1984 inflation rate compared to 1980 led people to believe that they, in fact, were better off, but a more precise assessment is how much better the overall economy under Reagan was as compared to Carter. In other words, what was the magnitude of economic improvement? This question can be asked about any president's performance. As a tentative answer, we have compiled indicators on the performance of the U.S. economy over the postwar era—a presidential economic scorecard.

REALITY CHECK: A PRESIDENTIAL ECONOMIC SCORECARD

The purpose of this book is to examine how the many complex domestic and international facets of presidential economic policy making shape and characterize national economic performance. As was noted before, presidents are often credited with strong and effective policies in times of prosperity and blamed for failed policies in periods of recession. While economic reality is more dynamic and complex, it is interesting to assess how well the economy has performed during each presidential administration in the postwar era. President Reagan's supply-side policies seemingly reversed the economic slide that began in the early 1970s, just as President Clinton has been praised for his stewardship of prosperity during the 1990s. On the other hand, President George H. W. Bush was blamed for the shallow recession of 1990–1991, while Presidents Nixon, Ford, and Carter were held accountable for the stagflation that gripped the economy during most of the 1970s. Today, President George W. Bush experiences polarized partisanship insofar as Republicans applaud his economic leadership whereas Democrats give Bush low marks for economic performance. Those divergent perceptions of presidential economic stewardship did not surface under President Clinton and may well be a new political development. Whether partisan assessments of the economy are unique to G. W. Bush or are a manifestation of the growing partisan polarization that characterizes American politics today awaits the arrival of the next president in 2009.

To what degree are these assessments of Reagan or Clinton or George W. Bush based on solid economic evidence or simply interpretations made through a political lens? One way to tentatively answer this question is to compare each president on the salient macroeconomic indicators. Since 1948 there have been fourteen four-year presidential terms, with eight Re-

Table 8.1.   Presidential Economic Scorecard

	Unemployment	Inflation	Economic Growth	Productivity	Current Account Balance	Overall Rank
Truman	4.4% (4)	2.5% (6)	5.7% (1)	4.3% (1)	0.6 (6)	2
Eisenhower I	4.2% (2)	0.6% (1)	2.6% (8)	2.3% (7)	2.0 (5)	4
Eisenhower II	5.5% (6)	2.2% (4)	2.3% (11)	2.7% (6)	7.1 (4)	6
Kennedy/ Johnson	5.8% (8)	1.2% (2)	4.3% (3.5)	3.9% (2)	18.4 (2)	1
Johnson	3.9% (1)	2.9% (8)	4.6% (2)	2.8% (5)	11.6 (3)	3
Nixon	5.0% (5)	4.7% (11)	2.5% (9)	1.8% (8)	−4.5 (7)	7
Nixon/Ford	6.7% (13)	8.0% (13)	2.1% (13)	1.1% (11.5)	31.4 (1)	11
Carter	6.5% (11.5)	9.8% (14)	3.1% (7)	0.3% (14)	−29.8 (8)	13
Reagan I	8.6% (13)	6.0% (12)	2.4% (10)	1.5% (9)	−138.1 (9)	12
Reagan II	6.5% (11.5)	3.3% (9)	3.3% (5)	1.3% (10)	−554.1 (12)	10
G. H. W. Bush	6.2% (10)	4.4% (10)	1.0% (14)	0.6% (13)	−257.6 (10)	14
Clinton I	6.0% (9)	2.8% (7)	3.3% (6)	1.3% (11.5)	−444.8 (11)	9
Clinton II	4.3% (3)	2.1% (3)	4.3% (3.5)	2.9% (4)	−1,068.9 (13)	5
G. W. Bush I	5.6% (7)	2.4% (5)	2.2% (12)	3.8% (3)	−1,939.2 (14)	8
Average	5.7%	3.9%	3.1%	2.2%	−4,108.3 (total)	
Republicans	6.0%	4.0%	2.1%	1.9%	−2,893.5 (total)	
Democrats	5.3%	3.8%	4.1%	2.4%	−1,214.8 (total)	

publicans and six Democrats. Our objective is to assess patterns over time by political party and by incumbent based on these five indicators of economic performance: (1) unemployment, (2) inflation, (3) economic growth, (4) productivity, and (5) the current account balance.[1] The indicators are summarized as averages for each four-year presidential term.

We report figures for all postwar terms, beginning with Truman's second term, since he was the first president elected to a full term after World War II, and ending with George W. Bush's first term, since his second term at the time of this writing is not yet over. We rank the fourteen terms on each indicator from one (best) to fourteen (worst) and then average the five individual rankings to derive one overall rank order. We do not assume that the five indicators are equally significant in political terms. At any time the relative importance of unemployment, inflation, economic growth, productivity, or the current account balance is subjected to popular perceptions and political judgments. Although this ranking simplifies economic reality, our purpose is to summarize the economic conditions during each presidential term toward offering a guide for assessing the effectiveness of each administration in dealing with the macroeconomy.

In general, our five economic indicators have performed better under Democratic presidents. First, four of the five top-ranked terms had Democratic incumbents, as follows: Truman, Eisenhower I, Kennedy/Johnson, Johnson, and Clinton II. This suggests that Democrats are more successful in managing the economy, with the notable exception of President Jimmy Carter. Or it may suggest that Democrats simply were lucky to govern during expansionary periods in the business cycle. In fact, Republican presidents did experience recessions more often than Democrats. Since 1948 there have been ten recessions, eight under Republicans (Eisenhower, three; Nixon, one; Nixon/Ford, one; Reagan, one; George H. W. Bush, one; and George W. Bush, one) and only two under Democrats (Truman and

Table 8.2. Recessions, 1948–2006

Start (peak)	President (Party)	Duration (months to trough)
November 1948	Truman (D)	11
July 1953	Eisenhower (R)	10
August 1957	Eisenhower (R)	8
April 1960	Eisenhower (R)	10
December 1969	Nixon (R)	11
November 1973	Nixon/Ford (R)	16
January 1980	Carter (D)	6
July 1981	Reagan (R)	16
July 1990	G. H. W. Bush (R)	8
March 2001	G. W. Bush (R)	10

Carter).[2] Only five presidential terms have avoided recession: four Democratic terms (Kennedy/Johnson, Johnson, Clinton I, and Clinton II) and one Republican term (Reagan II). On average, recessions have been longer under Republican presidents (11.1 months) compared to Democratic presidents (8.5 months).

Second, the impact of wartime has had an uneven impact on economic performance. Despite the Korean and Vietnam wars, Presidents Truman and Johnson presided over strong economies. Yet recession accompanied the Persian Gulf War of 1991 under President George H. W. Bush, who presided over the worst economy overall than any postwar president. With the global War on Terrorism and the Iraq War still raging, the mixed economic conditions led to President George W. Bush being ranked eighth among the fourteen presidencies.

Third, economic conditions seem to wreak more havoc on recent presidents. Since the end of the Bretton Woods System, the worsening current account deficit has hurt the overall ranking of Carter, Reagan, George H. W. Bush, Clinton, and George W. Bush. A recalculation of the overall ranks without the current account data would raise the Clinton II term to the second best postwar presidential term. In terms of public opinion, it is likely that the current account balance and productivity have less political impact than more widely recognized (and reported) indicators like economic growth, unemployment, or inflation.

Prior to the termination of the Bretton Woods System, the current account balance for the United States regularly produced surpluses, since the United States dominated the global economy. At the same time, unemployment and inflation were low while gross domestic product (GDP) and productivity were relatively strong. As a consequence, Truman, Eisenhower I, Eisenhower II, Kennedy/Johnson, and Johnson received high marks for their economic stewardship. Since the early 1970s, the imbalance in the current account balance has soared both in nominal dollar terms and in relative terms, as a percentage of GDP. Prior to the late 1990s the current account deficit only exceeded 3% of GDP in the late 1980s; in the new millennium the current account deficit has regularly approached and now exceeds 5% of GDP.

Unemployment and inflation were higher while productivity and economic growth were lower during the 1970s and 1980s as compared to the twenty years from 1948 to 1968. Although the economy expanded during Clinton's second term and again in the last two years of George W. Bush's first term, with both unemployment and inflation falling and productivity dramatically increasing, nonetheless, the current account balance got worse. Today, economic problems seem to be more complicated and less amenable to simple policy solutions. Moreover, policy corrections are subjected to global fluctuations that constrain the ability of the White House to achieve economic stability and prosperity.

Recall how President Reagan asked voters to compare economic conditions in 1980 with 1976. How well did the economy perform during the Carter and Reagan administrations? While prices fell during Reagan's first term, unemployment rose, GDP slowed, and the current account balance markedly deteriorated, suggesting that some aspects of economic performance during Reagan's first term were inferior to Carter's term. In fact, both of these presidential terms rate relatively poorly on many economic dimensions compared to the entire postwar period. But the political reality is that President Carter ranked fourteenth with regard to the inflation rate, which was the most salient economic issue facing the voters at the time. Despite Reagan's relatively low overall rankings for his first (rank of twelve) and second (rank of ten) terms, history will judge Reagan as the more effective steward of the economy, because the inflationary spiral was broken during his first term, after which the economy entered a seven-year period of economic expansion.

Another curiosity is the difference between public perceptions of the economy and economic performance under President George W. Bush. Bush consistently received poor marks from most Americans with regard to his handling of the economy. Indeed, the public perceived that the economy had worsened during his presidency and, furthermore, believed that the country was heading in the wrong direction. According to our scorecard, however, the record was not nearly so negative. Bush's first term ranks third on productivity, fifth on inflation, and seventh on unemployment. Overall, economic performance during 2001–2004 was superior to what President Clinton experienced during his first term. It seems likely that President George W. Bush had been unfairly compared to the robust economic prosperity that occurred during Clinton's second term, which ranks fifth overall. However, the first George W. Bush term was marked by the first recession in three presidential terms and was followed by a long economic expansion. In addition, on the two most politically salient economic indicators, inflation and unemployment, the first Bush term represented a clear downturn from the preceding Clinton II term—though here, too, George W. Bush's first term showed better numbers than Clinton's first term. With the second-best economic record since the early 1970s, the 2004 presidential election should have found strong support for a Bush reelection, rather than the close election that actually occurred. Perhaps the public anxiety caused by the 9/11 attacks, the War on Terrorism, and the Iraq War overshadowed Bush's economic record.

CAN ANYONE MANAGE PROSPERITY?

The presidential economic scorecard poses an interesting question. Can any president really manage the economy? Does economic stewardship depend upon who is president or is economic performance largely a function of forces beyond presidential control? The correct answer is probably "yes and no." "No" in the sense that much economic performance is due to structural features of the U.S. economy and the market forces of supply and demand. The structural features that affect the economy include the quality of the workforce, the managerial styles of corporate America, labor-management relations, and advances in technology and equipment. Some of these factors can be subjected to government policy—investment decisions concerning plant modernization may be influenced by tax incentives, for example—but investment decisions, like most structural features, are under the control of private decision makers.

Similarly market forces may be influenced by policy makers, especially domestic markets, but increasingly the U.S. economy operates within global markets. Two significant examples are the global markets for capital (finances) and oil. After World War II, the U. S. capital market was far more autonomous, but today the cost and availability of capital is tied to world markets. In the oil market the United States is at the mercy of global prices. When major producers, like the Organization of Petroleum Exporting Countries (OPEC), banded together into a pricing cartel, oil prices rose and higher oil prices can contribute to rising inflation. When the OPEC cartel collapsed in the early 1980s, inflationary pressures moderated. In both these cases, however, oil prices in the United States were influenced more by global supply and demand rather than the decisions of U.S. policy makers. Richard Rose is one prominent scholar who argues that increasing global interdependence has made it more difficult for presidents to govern.[3] Rose believes that the "modern" presidency that began with Franklin D. Roosevelt has evolved into a "postmodern" phase. The postwar global economic hegemony of the United States has eroded so much, says Rose, that presidents can only govern effectively with the cooperation of foreign leaders. Presidents cannot issue commands but must cultivate influence with foreign leaders.

Nonetheless, the question of presidential stewardship of the economy cannot be answered entirely in the negative. The president and other policy makers do play important roles in shaping and directing the macroeconomy. The primary role is establishing targets for fiscal and monetary policy. These targets normally involve an assessment of whether inflation or unemployment should be reduced. Forty years of experience indicate that both fiscal policy and monetary policy can affect inflation and unemployment. But each president makes choices about which policy option(s) will most likely achieve the targeted goal for inflation or unemployment. Thus, President Lyndon Johnson chose to risk a higher inflation rather than sacrifice economic growth in 1967, whereas Fed chairman Paul Volcker (supported by Reagan) chose to pursue an anti-inflationary monetary policy that exacerbated the recession and caused higher unemployment. In both these cases the performance of the economy was a direct consequence of the policies adopted.

A better example of presidential influence is the federal budget. The persistent problem of budgetary deficits may be partly due to underlying social trends, like the aging of the population, but basically the fiscal problem is a political problem. The historically high deficits recorded since 1981 were and continue to be a direct consequence of the decisions of two presidents—Reagan and George W. Bush—to support large tax cuts without achieving deep spending cuts. Described in 1981 as an "experiment," supply-side economics clearly failed to balance the federal budget, as Reagan promised. With few exceptions (such as the deficit-reduction deal between congressional Democrats and President George H. W. Bush in 1990 and the 1993 Clinton budget reduction program), the leadership of both political parties has not summoned the political will to address the problem of chronic deficit financing.

THE FUTURE

The prospects for maintaining relatively strong economic growth appeared rather good as the end of 2006 approached. GDP continued to grow, unemployment remained low, and the continued growth of the global economy will send low cost goods into the American markets. However, increases in energy prices and greater U.S. dependency on foreign oil will exert upward pressure on the "core" inflation rate. Inflation fighting by the Fed is an essential component of monetary policy. Thus, the Fed's sequence of interest rate hikes during 2005–2006, which helped cool the real estate market, was generally accepted as necessary.

Looking ahead, one bleak statistic is the national debt (the accumulation of yearly budget deficits). The U.S. government has posted three-digit budget deficits most years since 1981 and, since 2001, has had to borrow $1.3 trillion to pay for tax cuts, a new Medicare drug benefit, growing numbers of Social Security recipients, and the War in Iraq. So far, luckily, financial institutions abroad and foreign governments have subsidized the national debt by purchasing U.S. Treasury securities. How long they will continue to do so remains to be seen. If foreign banks and financiers lose faith in America's financial outlook and stop investing in U.S. government securities, then the U.S. government will be forced to finance its deficits from domestic sources. In that scenario, the mounting national debt would eventually force interest rates up, thereby leading to more inflation.

The challenge for future presidents is to position the federal budget on a trajectory that will be sustainable as Americans grow older. Currently federal spending on entitlements like Social Security and Medicare, as a share of total expenditures, will continue to expand well into the twenty-first century. Slower growth in the workforce, unless accompanied by increasing productivity, may reduce economic growth and thereby cut tax revenues, further exacerbating budget deficits. Politicians believe that it would be political suicide to advocate cutbacks in Social Security and Medicare. Another option might be for policy makers to scale back expenditures for defense and nondefense discretionary programs in order to offset spending increases for entitlements. Or, future presidents may choose not only to reverse some of President George W. Bush's tax cuts but also to raise federal taxes above their historic averages. Without some kind of fiscal budgetary adjustment, continuing deficit financial, especially if deficits grow as a percentage of GDP, may become unsustainable. In that case, the ballooning national debt would hinder public investments in education, transportation, research, and science; impede capital accumulation by private enterprise; slow economic growth; and threaten our financial stability. Beyond all that, ultimately the national debt will place a tremendous financial burden on future generations and their standard of living.

Sooner or later the executive and legislative branches will be confronted with a very difficult choice. How large a share of the nation's economic resources should be devoted to federal programs, especially entitlement programs? The public must deal with paying higher taxes, receiving fewer government benefits, or both. Ultimately, tax rates will have to be set at a level sufficient to achieve a reasonable balance of spending and revenues over the long run. Lower tax rates will only be sustainable if entitlement spending is dramatically cut and held down to avoid large deficits. Those who support a more expansive role of the government must balance the benefits of government programs with the burden imposed by the additional taxes needed to pay for them.

Another statistic that shows consistent signs of deterioration is the string of annual trade deficits since the end of the Bretton Woods System. The enormous trade deficit increased from slightly more than $100 billion in 1995 to roughly $800 billion in 2006. In 2005 the United States imported $717 billion more in goods and services than it sold abroad, and in 2006 the United States posted a roughly $800 billion trade deficit. Since the end of the Cold War, U.S. dollars have been sent abroad to pay for an array of goods and services, namely energy, electronics, textiles, children's toys, and automobiles as well as to pay the costs of stationing U.S. military forces abroad. Foreign banks and governments, mainly China and India, have invested their (trade) surpluses in various financial instruments in the United States (government bonds, corporate bonds, and other securities like home mortgages). By the end of 2005, overseas investors held $13.6 trillion in U.S. stocks, bonds, real estate, businesses, and other assets. From that $13.6 trillion, subtract the $11.1 trillion in foreign assets owned by U.S. residents and companies, and the United States had a net negative balance of $2.5 trillion.

America's insatiable demand for imported goods and services is a concern. Huge deficits in the current account balance may eventually have a significant impact on our domestic economy. To continue sending U.S. dollars abroad may erode the value of the U.S. dollar in global financial markets. If a glut of foreign holdings of U.S. assets occurs, then presumably international creditors will become less willing to lend to Americans, except at higher rates of interest. If policy makers could encourage Americans to save more money, then more capital could be reallocated to investment rather than for consumption. If we save more, then perhaps we could reduce the volume of imports purchased in the United States. An increased savings rate also would ease upward pressures on interest rates. But changing the consumption patterns of Americans or their savings habits is not an easy task to accomplish. Nor is raising trade and financial barriers a viable economic strategy in an era of globalization, or is it compatible with the U.S. commitment to free trade.

A final, basic problem facing the U.S. economy deals not with reversing a single economic trend, but with deciding to what extent, if any, the nation will identify desirable structural changes and take steps to implement them. Contrary to the myth that the U.S. economy developed primarily through the actions of a myriad of individual actors, the national government—from Alexander Hamilton, through Abraham Lincoln, and on to Dwight Eisenhower (in whose administration the Interstate Highway System was begun)—has always played a role in national economic development. This has traditionally occurred in development of the national transportation infrastructure, but at this time the basic question concerns whether development efforts should extend beyond steel and concrete toward a restructuring of the economy itself. In areas as diverse as globalization, environmental change, energy use and independence, and the human capital of the American workforce (including its reliance upon illegal immigrants), significant discussion and action—or inaction—by the national government will have an important impact on the future course of the U.S. economy.

In a few years, the second George W. Bush term will be added to the presidential economic scorecard. Where will it rate? As we have seen from the discussions in this book, the answer will depend only partly upon the actions of President Bush. The economy will also respond to actions by other actors: the Fed, Congress, foreign governments, and private actors. Overshadowing them all will be the basic rhythms of the business cycle, both in the United States and around the world. One thing, however, is certain. Regardless of what the key causal agents will have been, the public will assign blame or credit to President Bush, holding him accountable as the manager of our national prosperity.

NOTES

1. The current account balance includes exports of goods and services and income receipts, imports of goods and services and income payments, and unilateral current transfers, such as the exchange of U.S. government grants, pensions, and private remittances.

2. National Bureau of Economic Research "Business Cycle Expansions and Contractions" (March 22, 2006), http://www.nber.org/cycles.

3. Richard Rose, *The Postmodern President: George Bush Meets the World*, 2nd ed. (Chatham, NJ: Chatham House, 1991).

Index

Note: Page numbers in *italics* indicate figures or tables.

About the Authors

Chris J. Dolan is assistant professor of political science at Lebanon Valley College in Pennsylvania. His research on the American presidency, U.S. foreign policy, and economic policy appears in a number of political science and international relations journals and in numerous edited volumes. He is the author of *In War We Trust* and coeditor of *Striking First*. He previously held positions at the University of Central Florida and Presbyterian College.

John Frendreis is professor of political science at Loyola University Chicago. His areas of scholarly expertise include American politics, with special emphasis on political parties and elections, and his publications include two books and numerous articles in journals, including *American Political Science Review, American Journal of Politics, Journal of Politics, Political Research Quarterly*, and *Polity*. His current research includes a multiyear, multistate study of the role of local political parties in state legislative elections.

Raymond Tatalovich is professor of political science at Loyola University Chicago. His areas of specialization are the presidency, the executive branch, and public policy analysis, with particular emphasis on moral conflicts in policy making. He has published over fifty scholarly articles, chapters, and monographs and authored or edited twelve books, including *Moral Controversies in American Politics, The Presidency and Political Science, Cultures at War: Moral Conflicts in Western Democracies*, and *Nativism Reborn? The Official English Language Movement and the American States*.